The Fronde

REVOLUTIONS IN THE MODERN WORLD
General Editor: Jack P. Greene

ROBERT ASHTON • *The English Civil War: Conservatism and Revolution,*
1603—1649

J. R. JONES • *The Revolution of 1688 in England*

JOHN L. H. KEEP • *The Russian Revolution*

JOHN LYNCH • *The Spanish American Revolutions 1808—1826, Second Edition*

STANLEY G. PAYNE • *The Spanish Revolution*

RAMÓN EDUARDO RUIZ • *The Great Rebellion: Mexico 1905—1924*

PETER N. STEARNS • *1848: The Revolutionary Tide in Europe*

OREST RANUM

The Fronde
A French Revolution 1648–1652

W · W · Norton & Company   NEW YORK · LONDON

The text of this book is composed in Baskerville with the display set in Gara-
mond #3. Composition and manufacturing by The Maple-Vail Book Manufacturing Group. Maps by Jacques Chazaud.

Library of Congress Cataloging-in-Publication Data
Ranum, Orest A.
   The Fronde : a French revolution, 1648–1652 / Orest Ranum.
      p. cm.
   Includes bibliographical references and index.
   1. Fronde. 2. France—History—Louis XIV, 1643–1715.
3. Taxation—France—History—17th century. 4. Bordeaux (France)—History—Uprising, 1652–1653. I. Title.
DC124.4.R36 1993
944'.033—dc20   93-6816

ISBN 0-393-03550-6

W. W. Norton & Company, Inc., 500 Fifth Avenue, New York, N.Y. 10110
W. W. Norton & Company Ltd., 10 Coptic Street, London WC1A 1PU

1 2 3 4 5 6 7 8 9 0

Au
Comte d'Adhémar de Panat
Gentilhomme érudit, Rouergat et Parisien
Frondeur dans l'âme

Contents

ACKNOWLEDGMENTS   ix

PART ONE: INTRODUCTION
1. France in 1648   25
2. The Parisians and the Parlement before 1648   51
3. Constructing Solidarities against Council
   Authority   82
4. The King's Council: From Absolute Power to
   Brittle Authoritarianism   115
5. The Joy of Revolution   147

PART TWO: GENERAL PERSPECTIVES
6. The Winter Wars of 1649   179
7. The Fronde in Bordeaux   215
8. The Year of the Ormée: Bordeaux, 1652–53   248
9. The Princely Fronde   271
10. The End of the Fronde   303

CONCLUSION   343

BIBLIOGRAPHIC ESSAY   349
INDEX   365

Acknowledgments

The general editor of the Norton series on revolutions, Jack P. Greene, must be thanked for the psychological acumen he displayed by never once asking me if I was progressing on this work. Robert Descimon, Pierre Goubert, Lloyd Moote, Sylvia Vance, and George Woodbridge gave me valuable criticism on the whole manuscript. John Kresge and Jotham Parsons spared me from error on specific points. The errors of fact and interpretation are my responsibility alone. The History Seminar of The Johns Hopkins University has for many years been my intellectual home, and I am thankful for its historical vitality and collegiality. Georges Dethan's work looms all over this book; our discussions while walking on the *causse* at Panat have always been helpful. Patricia M. Ranum became a collaborator many years ago; her help has been unstinting despite the demands of her own research and writing.

OR
BALTIMORE
February 1, 1993

The Fronde

Part One

France in 1648

Introduction

T HE years 1648–52 in France were years of instability, violence, war, and revolution. Contemporaries summed up this general crisis in one word, the *Fronde*.

The word *fronde* is translated "sling" or "slingshot," the leather thong with a pocket shaped into it that was used to project pebbles, in play or in violence. Picked up by street singers and writers of doggerel, the word *fronde* became a shorthand way to evoke a congeries of disorderly, illegal, and violent activities. Allusions to the *fronde* often center on the idea of a collective prank or an adolescent game that could turn sour, become violent, and even take the lives of some of the participants.

I. Breaking the Law

Is revolution breaking the law? The immediate response to this question is that revolution is much more complex and large-scale than mere lawbreaking. Many instances of petty crimes and felonies come quickly to mind, crimes that certainly must have occurred in seventeenth-century France, though there was nothing revolutionary about them.

But what obtains when individuals or groups of individuals willfully break the law? Or fail to comply with it? An inability, and a refusal, to pay taxes marked the beginnings of the Fronde.

And what happens when a complicity develops between lawbreakers and the residents of the neighborhood, city, or countryside where lawbreaking occurs? Law enforcement officers and individuals who were refusing to comply with the laws of the land alike felt surrounded by the eyes of a hostile crowd or population. Weapons brandished by the police and judges'

black robes suddenly failed to convey authority, as a silent complicity with the lawbreakers developed. Now, for all but a tiny
minority of the population, the French state was little more than
a law-enforcement agency and a tax collector. It offered nothing in the way of social services and could not always assure
order and respect for property. For seventeenth-century
Frenchmen the Fronde was an ever-widening and deepening
support for an increasingly radical and willful violation of the
king's laws.

Even if defended on some higher moral ground, lawbreaking and adamant refusals to comply with orders (for example,
an order to turn one's hay or crops over to the army) break the
tissue of respect and obedience that binds state and society. If
illegal action causes property damage, physical injury, or death,
those entrusted with maintaining order are compelled to prosecute offenders and bring them to justice.

What occurs when the people charged with keeping the
peace begin to break the law? In the France of the Fronde,
royal officials began showing a massive "lack of zeal" in prosecuting lawbreakers as early as 1645, and this complicity turned
into outright strikes and disregard for the law in the spring of
1648.

Tax officials reported to Paris that peasants simply would
not pay taxes, and that in many instances they could not do so.
Occasional reports of peasants breaking into tax offices and
destroying records, setting fire to houses in which tax officials
lived, or physically intimidating or accosting those officials were
all part of the routine of seventeenth-century government.
Without a company or two of soldiers to support his efforts to
raise taxes by confiscating property for non-payment, the tax
collector could do little but wring his hands and inform Paris
that tax revenues in his district had dried up.

The line between enforcing the law and complicity with
those who could not or would not pay was often very thin. After
all, while the recalcitrant peasant might be socially inferior, he
was a neighbor and on occasion even a relative. At the local
level the highest percentage of tax revenue did indeed come
from those who were the most well-off. While it is impossible to
discern just how able to pay were the *coqs du village*—that is, the
more propertied villagers or the owners of tiny plots who survived by selling their labor to others—it is nonetheless possible

to infer the existence of a complicity about non-payment among both the better off and the truly marginal laborer in a peasant community. And also the existence of a complicity with the tax collector, or to be more accurate simply a "lack of zeal" about carrying out his duties.

The Fronde in Paris began when the Parlement of Paris, the principal law court charged with prosecuting violators of the law, stopped hearing cases. In contemporary terms we would say that the judges went on strike. Though the judges broke no statutes when they suspended their work, they ignored a royal edict ordering them to resume trying cases. At precisely that moment the judges became lawbreakers, and the state's powers to enforce law and order virtually ceased.

The judges in the Parlement of Paris—and those in the Great Council, the Chamber of Accounts, and the Court of Excises who followed their lead—wanted the boy king, his mother the regent, and above all the Council of State to be aware that they were breaking the law. At this point, during the spring of 1648, they had not yet worked out lofty moral grounds for ceasing their duties. These would be articulated in the months ahead.

Carrying their illegal actions a step further, these judges from various courts joined together and solemnly decided to sit as a collective deliberative body—not in order to enforce the king's laws but to discuss the issues "troubling" the state. In short, by breaking the law, judges were making a bid for power, were striving to assume an exclusive right claimed by the Council of State, namely the right to rule France. The image of sober, black-robed judges meeting together to discuss tax cuts scarcely conforms to our contemporary image of a revolutionary council. These same judges were, however, lawbreakers; and as royal decrees from the Council of State thundered across the Seine from the Palais Royal ordering the judges to cease and desist their deliberations about matters on which only the Council could make decisions, it became evident that a general breakdown of law enforcement had occurred and that the state, as defined by contemporaries, was tottering and threatened with collapse.

The great lesson that early-modern European revolutions can teach the contemporary world is that revolutions may also be made by individuals who already hold power. One does not have to be excluded from power, or be a guerrilla warrior, to be a revolutionary. When law enforcement officers—tax collectors, police commissioners, and judges—stop enforcing the law, they in fact break the law and challenge the stability of society. Thus they tear away the power of the state.

In the early round of illegal activities, when the provincial tax officials in the provinces (the *élus* and treasurers) and the judges in Paris went on strike, the rest of the population looked on. It was, perhaps, bemused; but save for the general question of tax increases, it scarcely engaged in the issues that had prompted royal officials to strike. Some royal officials had broken the law over technical issues that touched only the well-to-do elite. The economic conditions and the protests of merchants, artisans, and peasants played no part in the immediate issues that provoked the strike; but the views of these social groups soon came up for consideration, as local officials and striking judges *claimed* to represent them. Some judges spoke out openly against high taxes and accused officials charged with tax collection of corruption.

An order of the Council of State to arrest prominent and respected judges who were involved in the strike galvanized lower-class Parisians into a temporary solidarity with the striking judges. By using special police and military power in an attempt to reestablish obedience to the law, the Council of State attracted attention to an otherwise obscure contest of wills—the wills of the striking judges and the will of the crown, as expressed by the Council of State. The Parisians' everyday routines of working and shopping were dramatically interrupted as special police and troops patrolled the city streets.

A regency government that had enjoyed an enormous amount of good will, simply as a result of hopes that a change would follow the deaths of the highly authoritarian Richelieu and Louis XIII, found itself in severe trouble when striking judges began to debate what could be done to restore law and order in the realm. As we shall see in Chapter 3, miscalculations had occurred in the scenarios about bargaining over taxes, but these miscalculations would not in themselves have prompted the breaking of the law had not a deeper and more fundamental impasse existed between royal officials and the French people.

Though the French did not at the time refer to these events as a revolution, a Venetian named Count Gualdo Priorato published a book in 1655 entitled *The History of the Revolution in France* that begins with a discussion of the lawbreaking that has just been briefly described. As early as the fourteenth century, the Italians had developed a special acuteness for describing and analyzing politics, and they pioneered in borrowing terms from physics, astronomy, and meteorology to further the analysis of power and politics. The French could only characterize the events of 1648 by using meteorological metaphors. The Fronde was a "storm," a "whirlwind," a "tornado."

II. The Actors, Both Individual and Collective, in the Fronde

When we hear of an arrest for breaking the law, we immediately wonder whether the person or persons charged with the crime are rich or poor, and what their occupations or professions are. This curiosity about the status and economic well-being of someone charged with a crime provides an important clue to understanding how the actors involved in the revolution of the Fronde differed from one another and how they were perceived as different by contemporaries.

In a fundamental way, our curiosity about social rank and wealth prompts the historian–social scientist to provide a social understanding or dimension to the study of criminality *and* revolution. The documents that survive from the period of the Fronde are laden with terms such as "bourgeois," *"curé,"* "peasant," "the Robe," "the boatsmen," "the merchants," "the lawyers," and so forth. Rarely is a name given in a document without the addition of what we would call rank or occupation.

In the analysis of the Fronde that follows, five groups will stand out: the peasants, whose potential for action prompted fear; the Parisians, who likewise aroused fear and raised the specter of pillage; the Parlement; the Council; and the princes headed by Condé. Each actor possessed its unique power; each group helped determine the challenges to the established political structures and the responses that would be made to those challenges by the queen and Mazarin.

Was seventeenth-century society increasingly rank- and wealth-conscious? The study of the Fronde reveals that anger, insecurities about status, and radical political activity were prompted by the large numbers of persons who changed their status as a result of a rapid increase in wealth. The rapid rise in the status of royal officials in the tax administration and the *partisans'* (tax farmers') palatial new residences and estates, their finery, their expenditures for artworks, and their marriages into the high aristocracy created fundamental divisions within the ranks of the elite and put severe stress on the correspondences between status and power that were the fabric of French society.

A more complete comprehension of how the hated tax officials and tax farmers threatened the very fabric of French society, as it was perceived by contemporaries, requires a description of the actors during the decade prior to the Fronde. Ranks and powers would be the actors in the days of revolution in Paris in 1648 and again in 1651, in Toulouse in 1645, in Aix and in Rouen in 1649, and in Bordeaux in 1652. By briefly noting the major theaters of revolutionary activity in the cities, I do not mean to suggest that the great force of the peasantry was absent. Their participation in the Fronde was not collectively direct, but the direct participants' calculations of what this great force might do require a description of its powers here. Let us begin with these shadow powers, certainly a living economic and political presence, but one which only played a role in the Fronde as a result of the *fears* experienced by the active participants about the effects of pillage, riot, and murder in the countryside upon their own families and incomes.

The great majority of the 14 to 16 million people called "peasants" by their contemporaries lived in villages of between 30 and 70 families, set amid fields, forests, and vineyards, in an incredibly complex and variegated land. Owning and tilling small plots for their own food, and giving up some of their modest harvests to their seigneurs, their priests, and the royal tax collectors, the peasant farmers of the mid-seventeenth century experienced such widely different living standards that it is impossible to generalize about their economic condition.

Still, it is possible to discern trends. From the 1620s on, diminished harvests occurred and put increasing stress on the food supply. This downturn was certainly less marked in the South than in the North, where the effects of long heavy rains and periods of unusually cold weather were always worse. In addition, the economic effects of smaller harvests were particularly marked after some decades of relative prosperity. The rural population had increased in the previous century; and despite occasional bad years and the dislocation caused by the civil wars at the end of the sixteenth century, the French rural communities generally sustained some growth until the decline that began in the 1620s.

From the letters that royal officials in the provinces sent to the central government it is possible to locate the pockets of desperate hardship. These royal officials were inclined to be suspicious when peasants cried poverty and hardship, but their on-site inspections of villages revealed the harsh economic conditions in rural areas, particularly in southwestern France during the 1620s, 1630s, and 1640s. The provinces of Périgord, Limousin, Guienne, and Normandy were theaters of dire hardship caused by several consecutive years of crop failures. The revolts of the armed peasants and seigneurs that took place there arose from a subtle and explosive combination of factors. Peasant communities and seigneurs did not respond mechanically to years of crop failure or to increased tax assessments. In some areas the lack of money and the rising assessments led to a sullen and silent refusal to pay, once a certain threshold of payment had been reached. In other communities, particularly in regions where peasants and seigneurs protested together, a massive refusal to comply with the new assessments was followed by an attack on the tax collectors and their property. The revolts of the Southwest were occasionally accompanied by strikes by royal officials in the region, and at that point officials in Paris perceived a province as "lost" or out of control.

The powers of the peasantry in the Fronde were founded on the very accurate perception that further crop failures and increased taxes might unleash a conflagration in the countryside. The "fire" metaphor recurs in speeches by judges in the Parlement and in letters sent to Paris by royal officials. What did the term mean? The pillaging of tax records, the burning of tax farmers' houses, and the murders of seigneurs known for their harsh and arbitrary justice and revenue collection fostered an image of fire as a potential power to be wielded by the peasants. The evidence for this image of power will be explored more carefully during this analysis of the Fronde at precisely those points where this sense of peasant power was expressed.

The power wielded by seigneurs in rural communities, and

the increasing cohesiveness of those communities when faced by the impossible demands of the tax collectors, were particularly evident in the so-called "revolt of the *croquants*," a series of aristocrat-led peasant revolts that took place in the Southwest. An aristocratic hunting party could end in the nobles' planning to join with the peasants in an armed attack on royal troops. A tradition of rebellion linked some great southwestern families such as the La Trémouille and the La Rochefoucauld to court factionalism and to plots to overthrow Richelieu. Seigneurs did not hesitate to take up arms for a cause they considered consistent with their notions of trust, friendship, honor, and provincial well-being. In Provence, seigneurs were often competitors in the political infighting over offices, patronage, and wine taxes: they did not hesitate to summon all the males who worked on their estates, arm them, and come to town, looking for a showdown with a royally appointed official or with the leader of another faction and his men. In the revolts at Aix, just as in the Southwest, their powers were expressed through fundamentally local hierarchies of patronage control and client networks. Almost always deeply divided as a result of competition for offices, honors, and pensions, nobles could and did respond to factional struggles briefly, and on the local level, with protests and military force; and they did not hesitate to call out their inferiors and create "armies" that would accomplish their purpose.

In these protests and wars involving seigneurial factions, the issues were, however, almost always so particular and the divisions so deep that revolution on a broader scale proved impossible. Provincial seigneurs could not focus on issues that would join them across entire regions, from North to South and from East to West. When the structure of powers within the monarchy was most deeply threatened, the nobles did not discuss joining ranks, to either rescue the king or overthrow him. Though a high-ranking aristocrat might pull together an army of 1,200 of his "vassals" and clients for a few days, instead of acting or becoming a persuasive force that could alter the direction of events in Paris these armies melted away without accomplishing anything.

In one sense, because the nobles were so deeply associated with the monarchy—and were indeed part of it—the movement was characterized by divisions rather than by collective actions. While royal servants were breaking the law, the nobles were, literally in some cases, riding off in all directions at once. In the terrible repression of the "Barefoot Revolt" in Normandy of 1639, it was the Parlement of Rouen and other royal officials, not the nobility, that suffered humiliation, divestiture of office, and execution. To put it succinctly, and to anticipate a more complete picture of the Fronde, it is evident that there was a Fronde of the royal officials (particularly the judges), a Fronde of the princes (supported by their clients), and even a Fronde of the Jansenist priests of Paris; but there was never a *noble* Fronde. No collective entity with that name played a part in the Parisian Fronde or in the various provincial Frondes.

Perhaps the most pitiful sight in the Fronde was the collection of some 450 nobles who met in Paris after an aborted call for an Estates-General. Well-intentioned and eager to play a part in restoring stability to the monarchy, this group of nobles quickly ended up as powerless supporters of Gaston d'Orléans, an enigmatic if not obscure position to occupy during a moment of intense factionalism within the elite structure. Their grievances, as revealed in the *Act of Union,* were almost entirely specific to persons of noble rank, not unlike the early stage of the Robe protest, when the judges protested the sale of new offices.

While individual clergymen acted powerfully to influence the course of events during the Fronde, the First Estate, or church, never acted collectively to hinder or to hasten reform, revolution, or stabilization within the political arena that was the Fronde. From the absence of both the nobles and clergy as forces in the Fronde, it is evident that enormous prestige and wealth alone did not permit a group to intervene in the political dynamics that threatened to undermine the state and to alter the course taken by the distribution of wealth and power as a result of Richelieu's policies and the war with Spain.

By contrast, the Parisians, and to a lesser extent the Rouennais, Bordelais, Toulousains, and Aixois, were collective actors in the Fronde. The power of urban populations who assembled by the thousands along the streets or who marched in militia columns, talked in the marketplace, and shouted *"Vive le roi!"*—or remained silent—was calculated and taken into account by all the forces acting in the Fronde. Rebellious princes such as Beaufort and, later, Condé courted popular support, while plotting prelates such as Retz personally distributed alms in order to enhance their popularity in the capital. Like many others, Retz dashed off pamphlets aimed at altering opinions about one or another crucial turn of events. Thus, though the Parisians were at once a varied mass of artisans, merchants, clergy, religious orders, boatmen, and "poor," their power nonetheless was a factor in every calculation, as other powers intervened in the revolution. During the Fronde in Bordeaux, the Bordelais (like the Parisians) reached toward a deeper division over political alternatives and a redistribution of powers within society than that sought by any other segment of French society.

And yet not all diverse urban populations participated in the Fronde. Lyon, the second-largest French city and boasting the largest salaried urban population of any city in France, sat on the sidelines during the Fronde. The serene stability of this great banking, luxury-cloth, and printing center at a time when the countryside and Paris were in turmoil provides an important counter-argument to social interpretations of urban revolt. Nor did the inhabitants of the smaller city of Dijon become actors in the Fronde.

Turning to the more elite participants in the Fronde, we first encounter the *élus* and the treasurers of France. Crucially important in the early moments of challenge to the crown, royal officials set the Fronde in motion by their increasing sympathy with those who could not or would not pay taxes and, finally, by their strike in the spring of 1648. By refusing to receive payments, to audit accounts, or to press subordinate assessors and collectors to do their work, the treasurers brought the administrative machinery of the state to a near halt. Without funds, the regency government could do nothing. Payments to the royal household, pensions to great nobles and foreign "friends," charitable donations, and above all payment for the infantry and its guns, powder, and shot would quickly cease if the treasurers could not be convinced to resume their duties. Moreover, the treasurers stood united in demanding changes in royal policy. Their corporate solidarity was at once a protection for protesting colleagues who pressed for a strike and rebellion and, in the end, an impediment against a deeper and more radical revolution that would have challenged the hierarchy of status and the private wealth of royal officials. As the Fronde raised deeper and deeper issues, the treasurers maintained their solidarity. Just how many stayed away from meetings to show their lack of sympathy for the aims of their more radical members is not known, but divisions clearly appeared early on, triggered by complex rounds of compromise and by the intransigence of the royal ministers.

Like the treasurers, the masters of requests decided to cease fulfilling their duties and in so doing deliberately joined forces with the treasurers. A physically more cohesive group because they all lived in Paris, the masters of requests undertook to bring the judicial system to a halt. These prominent and well-to-do judges were charged with general inquiry into almost every type of litigation: litigation between the crown and private parties and litigation between private parties. They not only judged cases themselves, they also reported cases to high courts and to the Council of State. Among their ranks sat sons of the very wealthy judicial families whose scions sat in the sovereign law courts, parlements, the Chamber of Accounts, the Great Council, the Court of Excises, and the Council of State. When the judges known as masters of requests struck and adressed protests to the crown, their decision sent an electric shock through the other superior courts.

The treasurers' decision to stop working had provided a stimulus to the masters of requests to do likewise. A sense of solidarity between the two groups of royal officers developed quickly during the spring of 1648. For while the duties of the masters of requests and those of the treasurers were quite different, and while the masters were more prestigious than the treasurers, the crown had forced both groups to admit new members beginning in the 1630s. With each of these all-too-frequent creations of offices, men already on duty felt ever more strongly that their ranks in the hierarchy of officials and the prices of the offices they held had diminished.

What must be called Robe solidarity in the Fronde thus began to spread from corps to corps among the officials, each corps a power in its own right and all the corps together constituting a very large, crucially important, and powerful segment of the royal administration. The Fronde began as a strike and protest by a small group of so-called "short-robed" royal officials, thus named because the gowns worn by masters of requests were shorter than those of their senior colleagues in the superior courts. While collegiality among the officials of the short and the long Robe existed more in rhetoric than in fact, these otherwise diverse and hierarchically organized professional groups were cemented into a united front of protest and strike as a result of the bold frontal attack of the Council of State, which created numerous new offices throughout the ranks.

The Parlement of Paris was the most prestigious court of law in the realm, composed of some 140 judges of various ages and ranks. How did its members respond to their junior colleagues' lawbreaking? The Parlement resolved to hear delegates sent by their striking colleagues. This important step toward Robe solidarity will be explored in Chapter 2, but at this point it is important to note that the royal officials, with their legal education, their wealth, their intermarriages, and their family tradition of service to the state in a royal office, had more potential for creating a large, cohesive force than did any other social or occupational group in the realm. An integral part of the government that controlled most municipal and local offices, the Robe was also influential in the church through its sizable donations and its management of church lands and finances. Were it to unite into a single, cohesive group, the Robe would wield enormous power.

Headed by the Parlement and other superior courts, the Robe was literally the government of the realm. Only a tiny minority of its members serving on the council seemed to be initiating, or at least approving, the odious decrees and raising taxes that created still more unwanted royal officials. Increased Robe solidarity would inevitably threaten the fragile hierarchies and boundaries determining duties and jurisdictions that kept royal officials from formulating common aims and common instruments to stamp out what they perceived as threats to their status and wealth.

At the summit of these professional government officials sat the Parlement and the other great superior courts, whose powers rested firmly on three fundamental features that determined the nature and distribution of powers in the monarchy. These courts could either increase royal authority and power by enforcing the laws, look the other way when the laws were broken, or themselves break the law. The last option was, however, inconceivable to the judges in the high courts, for *they were the law.* By definition they could not therefore break the law. Members of the Council of State would eventually accuse the Parlement of lawbreaking, because the Council—with the king as its head and the king's uncle, the chancellor, and the Prince de Condé as its dominant members—claimed to be a higher source of law than the Parlement. Claims and counterclaims about the source of law and about the superiority of the Council over the Parlement would be hotly contested during the Fronde. Interlocking bodies of royal officials who usually were mildly competitive but friendly suddenly began to square off and fire salvo after salvo at each other, in the form of decrees and *arrêts* duly signed by the king and sealed with his seal.

For very important matters of state, the Parlement sat as a special court presided over by the king himself. On these occasions its decrees were clearly superior to any proclamations of the Council of State. Sitting as a special court called a *lit de justice*, the king in "*his*" parlement established regencies and determined other major actions affecting the arrangement of powers in the state. But prior to the Fronde these special sessions had been called to drive through quite tawdry measures, chiefly revenue-producing schemes such as the creation of new masters of requests.

The crown's use of these solemn occasions for legislating fiscal matters deeply offended the court's dignity. After all, the Parlement had been the legitimator of the great power now exercised by the regent and her Council. Accustomed to trying treason cases and voting the death sentence without a twinge of remorse, the Robe now found itself compromised: the Council was taking initiatives to force the Robe to act in ways it believed inconsistent with its dignity and its financial interests. Important decisions of the Council affecting justice, officeholding, and taxes had to be approved not only by the Parlement of Paris but by the other superior courts in the capital and across the realm. Thus the judges by custom held the power to delay, to remonstrate, and to modify legislation sent them from the Council of State.

If the nobility lacked a sense of unity and of realm-wide solidarity, just the opposite was true for the Robe. Many of the judges had come to the capital from the provinces and had been itinerant judges or royal administrators prior to their service in the highest courts. If any group possessed a unified outlook on the affairs of state, and on the arrangement of powers in that state, it was this professionalized and all-important layer of officials spread across the land as treasurers, masters of requests, and judges in the various parlements and other superior courts.

Some of the thousands of lawyers, clerks, porters, scriveners, wax-warmers, sealers, recorders, notaries, professors, students, prosecutors, and other state servants perhaps did not consider themselves and their families as belonging to the Robe, but they all certainly had profound affinities with it and looked to the Parlement as the court that most completely expressed their idea of the state, justice, and political stability. And not the least important, the judges of the Parlement of Paris and of the other superior courts were very rich. Over the generations, dynasties of these legal professionals had accumulated capital and had invested these sums in offices, bonds, townhouses, rental properties, fine furnishings, coaches, farms, and country estates.

The power of the Robe certainly rested partly on their wealth, and not solely on their prestige as men of the law. While the judges in the lesser provincial parlements, Chamber of Accounts, and Court of Excises were less wealthy than their Parisian colleagues, they were rich compared with provincial elites. None other than Cardinal Richelieu had advocated (and practiced) amassing wealth in order to sustain the dignity and power of officeholding in the French church and state.

Only one authority stood above that of the parlements: the king and the regent in Council. More authority by custom, perhaps, but not necessarily more power. The Fronde challenged this hierarchy of authorities; and on several occasions the authority of the king in Parlement was almost established as being continuously, not just temporarily, superior to the authority of the king in Council.

In theory, the king could invite whomever he pleased to serve on his Council. In practice, the office of royal councillor was held by dozens of quite obscure officials who reported appeals and disputes on a quarterly basis in return for enhanced status and quite a good salary. Capping these administrators were small groups of prominent advisers who actually discussed foreign-policy questions, finances, justice, appointments, and military matters at a regularly scheduled weekly meeting. The Council received public and private appeals and could act as a court of law in its own right on cases reported to it by masters of requests and other officials. Use of the king's signature, and of the regent's, in Council, was the source of authority for *every* other echelon of the government administration. Thus, although every judge in the Parlement possessed enormous esteem, each held his office thanks to a royal letter emanating from the Council and validated by the chancery and other certification agencies. The power to affix the royal signature sustained the Council's claim to be the highest authority in the realm. Thanks to this authority, cases being tried by a parlement could, for example, be taken from that court and tried in Council. In short, the competence of the king in Council included all the competences of the French state, including the power to arrest both the mighty and the humble or to suppress a parlement, transfer it, or order it to cease functioning. The Council's decrees were *the* law of the land, although on some questions (for example, the creation of new offices and taxes) the decrees had to be presented to and approved by the parlements and/or the other superior courts.

Whenever the king of France personally exercised his power, the Council would find itself reduced to an executionary function. It then managed the paperwork in the monarch's name but exerted only minimal influence on the actual decisions about foreign policy, appointments, and taxes. Louis XIII had relied heavily on Richelieu and a handful of faithful minister-councillors to carry on the business of government. But these arrangements came to an abrupt end when Louis XIV became king in May 1643 at the age of five. The councillors' power to initiate policies and to nominate candidates for office increased greatly during regencies.

The principal councillors of Louis XIV in 1643 were his mother, granted regency powers by the Council and the Parlement the day after Louis XIII's death; Gaston d'Orléans, the boy king's uncle and the sometime plotter against his royal brother in the 1620s and 1630s; the Prince Henry II de Condé (father of the future "Grand Condé"), the king's blood relative and an immensely wealthy and influential peer who was governor in Burgundy until his death in 1646; and Chancellor Pierre Séguier, whose office gave him sweeping control over the judicial and record-keeping officials throughout the realm.

There were also lesser councillors who had come up through the ranks and had held administrative offices such as secretary of state, but only two of these officials dominated power during the Fronde. The first was Particelli D'Hemery, the superintendant of finance. An experienced, hard-headed, and ambitious man who was eager to use the powers of his office to gain control of the Council, D'Hemery had proposed both the tax increases that had prompted small riots in the Paris suburbs and across the realm and the creation of new venal offices that had led to the strike by royal officials. In a sense, D'Hemery's task was hopeless. The war had devastated the royal treasury to the point that the crown could find few lenders; and very little new revenue was coming in. Bankruptcy had almost been declared in 1638 and would loom again in 1648. Resistance to higher taxes and to increased sales of offices had been building since the early 1630s. Had D'Hemery succeeded in forcing the Parlement and other courts to accept these odious proposals, his power in the Council would undoubtedly have increased. His failure to do so led to his disgrace.

The second and last of the royal councillors who were neither members of the royal family nor senior administrators was Cardinal Mazarin. Born to a Roman family in 1602, his successful diplomatic negotiations attracted Richelieu's attention and quickly placed him in an influential position within the cardinal's little circle of collaborators. When Richelieu died in 1642, the prompt disgrace of this foreign prelate and his expulsion from the Council were expected, as older and more experienced councillors competed for control. But Mazarin had been able to establish solid advisory relations, first with Louis XIII and then with Anne of Austria, the regent. Highly intelligent, observant, sensitive, and incredibly relaxed in the face of terrible political pressure, Mazarin slowly undermined his competitors' power to dominate in the Council of State.

By then Louis XIV was nine years old. Just what did the sensitive and quite intelligent boy think of all the measures and countermeasures decreed in his name? Memorizing the speeches placed before him and reciting them on tense ceremonial occasions, the little king quickly learned to do his utmost to help his mother, for he sensed that she was under great stress. He had a "natural" dignity about him as a child and would never lose it. The infinitely complex task of greeting his subjects, each according to his or her rank, quickly led the king to distance himself from all but a few intimates. Noting the relaxed and supportive role that Mazarin played with his mother, Louis extended his filial affections to this Roman prelate, at first hesitantly and then deeply.

Queen Regent Anne of Austria profoundly loved her elder

son. Her unfailing ability to perceive a tinge of rudeness in a gesture or a hint of indignity in a compliment was communicated to the boy at a very early age. Although Anne gained a reputation for being inflexible, shrill, and excessively devout once the outpouring of affection for her as the persecuted widow of Louis XIII had ceased, she slowly came to project the image of the protective mother and queen that eventually earned her the respect of her subjects and even a certain amount of affection. The French tended to suspect foreigners of all manner of sinister personal and political failings. Anne and Mazarin therefore became the brunt of vicious and scurrilous attacks that would have infuriated weaker individuals or driven emotionally unstable ones insane. Would the Fronde have occurred had Anne been a bit more suspicious of Mazarin's successes at letting his competitors on the Council destroy themselves? The shortcomings and the authoritarianism of Chavigny and D'Hemery, not Mazarin's machinations, account for their disgrace. On occasion Anne missed signals and became confused during the Fronde, but she was guilty of neither the inflexibility nor the ineptitude that would be ascribed to her by the middle-class male historians of the nineteenth century.

Dependent on the Council, but at times proudly independent of it, were the shadowy figures we have already met, the *partisans,* or tax farmers. Through the superintendant of finances, the Council auctioned off leases to collect excise taxes throughout the provinces. The 50 to 60 major leaseholders, their associates, and their agents across France became the focus of intense hatred and ostracism during the Fronde. Reaping enormous profits, the tax farmers earned the public's scorn by displaying their wealth and buying offices that placed them high in the Robe. We have already seen that this group was perceived as a corrosive power in the realm; and a more general description of their activities will be provided in Chapter 2. At the moment, the point to make about their power is that despite the animosity expressed toward them, the *partisans* retained their power and continued not only to contract for tax collecting but to lend the crown money. Opportunities for profit remained high in the risky atmosphere of revolution. Though the tax collectors were perceived as the source of evil, not even the wildest reformer or revolutionary proposed an administration that would free the state of their odious services.

To a Tacitean, ever inclined to interpret great events as

caused by personal rivalries, the Fronde will always be an extension of the duels for dominance of the Council of State that
took place between Superintendent of Finances D'Hemery,
Cardinal Mazarin, and Secretary of State Chavigny, on one level,
and Gaston d'Orléans and the Prince de Condé on another.
The intransigency manifest in harsh fiscal measures and in the
dramatic arrests of judges indeed resulted from the intense
jockeying for power in the Council. But the fiscal situation was
desperate. In the face of these duels for power, and of the harsh
measures proposed by the councillors, Mazarin sat back, listened, and virtually mumbled his own opinions. And his influence increased at the expense of the other administrative
councillors. He did however exhibit intransigence when he
rejected Spanish peace proposals aimed at regaining at the peace
table what had been lost on the battlefield. The Spanish government was counting on a more accommodating French foreign
policy now that their monarch's own sister was regent of France.
Yet Anne followed Mazarin's advice and continued the war while
negotiating with Spain. A cardinal since 1641, Mazarin let his
air of detachment from the issues of taxation and from office
sales work to his advantage in the Council.

He also cemented solid, even friendly, relations with France's
leading general, Louis II de Bourbon, a prince of the house of
Condé whose stunning victory over the Spanish at Rocroy in
1643 earned him the name the "Grand Condé." Only twenty-
seven in 1648, Condé was the elder son of the council member.
Until the elder Condé's death in 1646, father and son cooperated to enhance the interests of their family; and Mazarin gave
powerful support to their every request for money, for supplies
and, until mid-1649, for offices for the Grand Condé. Like
Mazarin himself, the Grand Condé took pleasure in seeing
D'Hemery and Chavigny leave the Council in disgrace, as a result
of the Parisian Fronde. But later on, when Condé's increasing
demands for money and offices became excessive, Mazarin would
turn the tables and order the prince's arrest. Always a great
power in the Fronde because of his client network and his command of the army, the Grand Condé turned toward rebellion
in part as a result of the death of his father, who had been a
moderating influence on his own, and in part owing to the
intensifying competition for money and offices among high
aristocrats.

While the princes constituted no single, cohesive power, they deserve to be mentioned as a power in the Fronde. Henry IV's illegitimate children (among them the Vendôme–Beaufort–Mercoeur line) and the very powerful Bouillon–La Tour d'Auvergne-Turenne clan had been stripped of some of their offices, influence, and provincial properties after having participated in rebellions, first in 1632 and again in 1644. The Vendômes and the Bouillons wanted to regain their governorships and their lands, which had been partially distributed to the Condés and to their close relatives, the Longuevilles. Early in the Fronde the princes, or the "party of the princes," constituted a potential challenge to the crown should governmental control momentarily weaken. The Vendômes and the Bouillons, having been beaten back, stood on the sidelines of high politics until the judges' strike gave them a chance to attempt bargaining for the return of their offices and lands, in exchange for supporting the crown. Mazarin refused to advise Anne to yield to their pressure, causing the Vendômes to join the Parisian Frondeurs, while the Bouillon–Turenne clan were Frondeurs but lay back and waited for an even more propitious moment.

ONE *France in 1648*

FRANCE in the mid-seventeenth century: a population of some 18 million souls stretched unevenly across a land that extended from the Atlantic to the Mediterranean, from the dunes of the Landes and the marshes of the Low Countries to the foothills of the Vosges Mountains and of the Alps. Rich and poor alike, this population was largely located in the countryside, and it was almost entirely occupied with producing sufficient food and shelter to assure life. Some 200,000 who "lived nobly" constituted, along with their judicial and administrative officials, the elite of the rural population. They lived in castles, in manor houses, and in townhouses of various ages and states of repair.

Villagers frequently lived within the shadow of a castle, in mud-walled huts and small stone cottages with thatched or tiled roofs. A parish church and the surrounding cemetery, a rectory, and a village common were the site of various tasks such as threshing or drying beans or wool, and of family and neighborhood gatherings for weddings, baptisms, and funerals. Here also, after mass on Sundays and on saints' days, male villagers assembled to talk about crops, taxes, and one another. On the night of the festival of the village's patron saint, on St. John's Night, and whenever news came of a prince's birth or a victory of the king's army over the Spaniards, almost everyone but the aged flocked to the village common for a bonfire and dancing. Children played fifes and peddlers would play their hurdy-gurdies all night long in exchange for soup or drink. All that was needed was someone to keep a beat (and the arrival of news from the distant world of France, that is from Paris or the king's court) and dancing would begin. Be the news sad or happy, the festivities varied little, although the bonfire was reserved for joyful occasions. Lights and darkness, happiness and sorrow, life and death, were joined in the lives of French rural communities in ways that were very powerfully expressed. Was the emphasis on dancing in the pictures of seventeenth-century village life a visual projection upon the village by an artistic elite? In rural societies of the period, dancing meant a break in the routines of planting, harvesting, gathering firewood, and tending vines—activities that were scarcely memorable enough to be subjects for paintings. The images of dancing villagers that graced Parisian walls in 1648 may have seemed strangely incongruous to their owners, in the light of reports and rumors about armed peasant revolts and pillaging.

Time weighed heavily on the rural nobles' hands. Occasional trips to the provincial capital to discuss a lawsuit, attend a meeting of the local estates, or see a notary about a property settlement interrupted the routines of chateau life, which consisted of supervising the estate, hunting, litigating, visiting neighbors, and attending baptisms, weddings, and funerals. As lords and ladies looked down from chateau windows, the gaiety of the village dance briefly dispelled the boredom of their lives.

The seasonal review of fields, pastures, and vines in the parish by the larger landowners and minor officials working for the seigneur would quickly end in tax assessments for the villages of the parish. The routines here, like the assessments themselves, were almost as immutable as the planting and harvesting. The size and productive value of every piece of land in a parish was known to all the village landowners, no matter how small the plot or vine. There was little secrecy about the neighbors' total annual production and therefore their income. Annual production varied, of course, from year to year as a result of the weather, blight, or insects, but the variations affected small and large landowners alike. To be sure, some neighbors worked harder than others, and some had more children to help with the work, but that also meant more mouths to feed.

Even if the purchase prices of plots of land were kept secret, there was general familiarity with the average productive capacity of each plot, because the units of measurement were visible to everyone. A hierarchy of productive capacity in the village was overtly manifest. In some regions of the South, these hierarchical evaluations were written down in registers known as *compoix*, kept by the local notary. Changes in this register were frequent, as a result of deaths or sales of *lopins* of land. (The *lopin* was a derisory term for a tiny parcel of land, about the size of a vegetable garden.)

In the North, taxes were less directly related to the productive value of the land, and the records kept by the village officials and notaries therefore carried less information. The recollections of neighbors talking on the common after church could resolve differences of opinion about boundaries, ownership, and the neighbors' past tax payments or could end in a majoritarian agreement to override a neighbor. The large landowners who lived at a distance from the village—for example, monasteries, cathedral chapters, hospitals, and high-ranking aristocrats—paid portions of their income from leased properties to the legal professionals in the parish, who supervised the renting, planting, harvesting, and tax assessments of their lands. No matter how specific the leases and tax assessments, these lawyers and tax collectors had the opportunity to increase their own income, as a result of their multiple roles in supervising the property of others. When royal officials or very rich landowners sought "reforms" in tax assessments, the villagers resisted, suspicious of change from past experience. Still, large landowners almost invariably ended up with lower assessments, and the smaller ones with higher ones.

Historians have occasionally inferred that seventeenth-century French peasants were "backward" because they automatically resisted a reform of taxation and of the procedures for raising taxes. Yet peasant resistance to these reformist interventions into their private and communal lives could also be described as very contemporary. Individuals, their families, and their communities lived in close proximity to each other and had slowly learned to accept the perceived inequities that were already part of the laws and customs of the realm. Reluctance to accept changes in these perceived inequities occurred because peasants, nobles, and finally royal officials saw no possible advantage for themselves or their neighbors in these reforms.

By 1648, changing the patterns and amounts of tax assessments—be it the basic tax, the *taille* (levied on persons in the North and on land in the South), or an excise tax such as the *gabelle* on salt or the *aide* on wine—had been accompanied by more than a decade of attempts to increase revenues throughout the realm. This pincers movement on taxes, with its "reform" of assessments and increased tax rates, prompted the Fronde. In those provinces where local estates still voted taxes to be paid the crown, the assessments themselves were no more equitably fixed, and perhaps less so, than in the provinces directly under the control of royal tax officials such as the *élus* and treasurers. The routines of tax collecting in those provinces with estates were familiar to everyone, and they were continued throughout the Fronde. The result was a less excited response to the crown's increased fiscal demands.

I. The Little Kings in the Provinces

In contemporary Western societies, we pay taxes from a sense of civic duty; we tax ourselves because our private interest as individuals seems to accord with the public interest in defense, education, fire and police protection, and support for the needy and sick. We may disagree with the way our governments allocate precious fiscal resources and protest that too much money is going for defense or whatever, but there is nonetheless a powerfully established if scarcely articulated consensus that the common good is served by defending the country, educating the young, extinguishing fires. In 1648 no such consensus about taxes existed in France, or for that matter anywhere in the Western world.

Instead, taxes were infinitely complex bundles of rights or powers to collect certain sums from certain classes of the population. One's place in society, one's rank, was overtly and publicly defined in no small measure by the type and amount of taxes paid. And the higher one's social rank, the less taxes one paid, by *right*. This fusion of rank and "privileges" (rights bringing tax exemption) meant that whenever the king and his Council sought to change tax legislation in any way, they immediately clashed with particular groups holding specific tax exemptions. Beneath the issue of rank lay the inevitable equation—greater wealth = less taxes to be paid—that pervaded French society for centuries and that is perhaps not altogether dead, despite several revolutions carried out, in part, to root it out.

The basic tax that most seventeenth-century French peasants paid (in one form or another) was the *taille*. Until the late fifteenth century, this had been an extraordinary tax levied in time of war, when the need for funds was particularly high; but in the course of the the sixteenth century, which brought decades of war in Italy, it became a permanent annual imposition. In the South, the *taille* was fixed on the land: whoever owned land that was *taillable* therefore had to pay the tax, regardless of his status; but in general this tax fell on the largest segment of the population, the peasantry.

In annual meetings the Council of State would fix a figure to be raised in each general tax district (*généralité*), after which the local officials (*élus*) of the district would, with the help of the treasurers of France, determine just how much each parish would pay. At the parish level, the sum was apportioned in part according to "ability to pay," as revealed by the *compoix* or by property assessment rolls. But over the years, decade after decade, and despite the upheavals of the Wars of Religion in the late sixteenth century, a routine of payments and perhaps a hierarchy of sums due by each member in a parish had become established. Discussed in whispers while gardens were spaded in the spring, the amount each individual paid had become known long before 1648 and was even public information in some areas of France.

In recent years, historians have sought to reconstruct as accurately as possible the accounts of revenue and expenditure accounts kept by the royal treasury. The results are not only confusing, they are contradictory. The principal difficulty has been discerning exactly what the figures in the documents represent. Total revenue from the *taille?* Revenue minus the funds siphoned off by local officials for services rendered? Revenue available to be assigned to an expenditure by the central government? The variations in the figures are substantial, but one thing is evident: a steep rise in assessments occurred during the decade leading up to 1648, first doubling and then tripling the tax burden. A previous rise had occurred in the late 1620s, but only after 1636 would the state suddenly appear insatiable in its strident demands for increased revenues. The correlation between higher taxes and warfare was, of course, absolute. Armies swallowed up royal revenues in huge quantities and, as we shall see, there seemed to be no end in sight to the war with Spain. Eventually, protesters demanded that the *taille* be restored to its level under Henry IV. The language of their protests reveals not only a certain public awareness and an anger at the steep increases, but also a desire to erase the memory of the entire reign of Louis XIII, from 1610 to his death in 1643.

Revenues from the *taille* dropped after 1643, falling to just under 19 million *livres* in 1647, once local collection fees had been deducted. The Council lowered the *taille* just a bit in 1644 and in succeeding years, but these reductions probably were nowhere nearly as great as the actual decrease in collected revenues. Arrears, those taxes that remained unpaid at the end of the year, began to rise at an alarming rate; the *élus* and treasurers reported that try as they might, they could not coerce peasants to pay what they owed. Resistance often took the form of armed revolt. The ministry had responded to these incidents by sending officials into the provinces with vast legal, administrative, and military-police powers, to force payment of taxes. These officials were, in most cases, called "intendants of justice and finance" and held royal commissions empowering them to give orders to local officials, including the *élus* and the treasurers of France, and to arrest, try, and either imprison or execute the guilty parties. The intendant's first task involved forcing payment through "exemplary" action. He usually had only a brigade of troops at his command, or at most a regiment, so it was impossible for him to round up all individuals who had defaulted and force them to pay their debts. Thus he selected perhaps four or five prime cases in a region and sent assistants, accompanied by troops, to collect the tax. If the defaulting family would not or could not pay what it owed, their furniture and their farm animals, if they owned any, were confiscated in lieu of payment.

It will never be possible to determine just how many confiscations of personal property took place, but the use of such highly coercive, overt, and capricious tactics for dealing with non-payment of taxes aroused anger and collective protest in region after region. In many instances peasants and artisans took matters into their own hands, after heated verbal confrontations between local authorities and the intendants. They either waylaid the intendant's assistants in dark streets or pillaged the residence of a particularly zealous *élu* or other royal official. In some provinces a state of war developed between the population and the intendant and the royal officials who carried out his orders. During a particularly intense moment in a debate in the Parlement over whether or not to abolish the intendants, a senior judge cried out eloquently: "They are little kings in the provinces." This remark, which linked the intendants' tyrannical behavior to the monarchical form of government, was a cry of despair—and of revolution.

Hundreds of letters sent back to Paris from intendants to the chancellor, the most important official charged with maintaining public order, have survived, so it is possible to discern how the intendants behaved as individuals when attempting to carry out orders. Recruited from Robe (that is, professional legal) families that often had several generations of experience in royal administration behind them, the intendants were young men (most of them in their thirties) who were expected to "uphold royal authority" in the face of disobedience and verbal threats. Never perhaps in all of French history did a group of officials cover themselves so completely with the fleur de lys and become so sensitive about their dignity as officials. Some intendants delayed or found other ways to avoid confrontations with the local populace; others were zealous, indeed fanatical, in their attempts to coerce the people to obey royal orders.

Isaac de Laffemas, an intendant whose name became familiar to thousands of Frenchmen during the late 1630s, carried the strategy of exemplary punishment, which was designed to coerce the whole population to obey, to a point that can only be described as aberrant. On one occasion he personally saw to it that a nobleman who had allegedly committed a crime was arrested and tried (by Laffemas, of course, with local judicial officials in attendance), then found guilty and sentenced to beheading. Since public executions were a distraction, if not an entertainment, for seventeenth-century Frenchmen, Laffemas chose a time and place for the execution that guaranteed a maximum impact on the population.

Then, without informing any other royal officials, he arranged for a mounted herald to arrive at the place of execution a few minutes before the scheduled event, bearing a royal pardon. In this way, love and respect for the king, and especially gratitude for his clemency, would be enhanced! Laffemas sent an account of this mock execution to Chancellor Séguier, who had himself tried and sentenced Norman rebels to death in 1639. It is not known whether the chancellor reprimanded Laffemas for "excesses" and abuse of his authority. Beyond, or perhaps beneath, the urgent need for money that caused royal officials routinely to violate codes of conduct, there lies a baroque theatricality in the assumptions made about the effects of exemplary punishment. In dealing with the revolt in Normandy, Cardinal Richelieu had ordered Chancellor Séguier to "punish the most guilty" by making "examples." Dramatic executions of one's neighbors, confiscations of property, and numerous other actions were used to disorient villagers, break down routines, and finally to coerce the king's subjects into increased obedience and tax paying. The little kings in the provinces may not have behaved like petty tyrants day in and day out. But as the years went by and tensions mounted, enough stories circulated about their brutal and illegal actions to make an outburst of hatred and a call for their removal almost inevitable by the summer of 1648.

II. *Towns and Cities*

The picturesque walls, gates, marketplaces, narrow streets and alleys, mud, church steeples, houses with overhanging stories and high-pitched roofs, and beggars that form our mental images of the seventeenth-century French town are a creation of artists and writers working after 1750. Very few paintings and etchings of French urban life date from as early as 1648. Some pictures of ceremonial processions through streets and newly built squares in Paris give an idea of the capital, but the details of daily life in these pictures were filled in by the artists without an attempt to portray street life as it actually was.

A painting of a destitute man standing on a corner with his hand extended probably attracted buyers because it reminded them that one must be charitable in order to go to Heaven. But artists refrained from painting scenes of markets, bridges, and streets. Maps of the bigger cities such as Paris had begun to appear (the wife of the English diarist Samuel Pepys would hang one over the fireplace in her bedroom in the 1660s), and scenes of traffic on the Pont Neuf, new churches, the Sorbonne, and the squares known as the Place Royale and the Place Dauphine satisfied the curiosity about the new urban spaces that had been created during the reign of Henry IV; but scenes of life in other cities, showing rich and poor, thieves, beggars, judges, and clergy mingling with artisans, merchants, donkeys, horses, and carriages had not yet captured the artistic imagination.

The image of the Fronde as mobilization of opinion is captured by the etching of a young man speaking animatedly about the Fronde in one of the residential quarters of Paris, across the Seine from the Tuileries. He was probably standing in the Pré aux Clercs or in one of the nearby firewood storage lots that lined the riverbank. Little notes giving places and times for meetings and for speechmaking would circulate from cabaret to cabaret and from law clerk to law clerk in the heady days of the Fronde, and a favorite rendezvous for talking politics and for speechmaking was located near the Rue du Bac and in the fields beyond, far from the commercial and traffic centers of the city and precisely where the Palais Bourbon (National Assembly) now stands. Why this distance from the heart of the city? Judicial and police surveillance of French cities was probably quite effective at repressing free outdoor debate and speechmaking within the city walls. These police controls take us to the heart of what urban life was in the France of 1648.

Towns and cities were congeries of population bound together by elaborate controls over work, play, food, place of residence, and religious practice. Like our image of the jostling crowd, the idea that the early-modern city had a special air of freedom was invented by Romantics during the late eighteenth and nineteenth centuries. To be sure, cities were the haven of those seeking to escape the humdrum exertions of rural life. Towns and cities contained the so-called floating populations of wanderers, prostitutes, beggars, hawkers, and pickpockets, but so did the countryside, albeit in a less visible way. The steady influx of unemployed and unskilled country people, many of them teenagers, kept wages low in cities, and there was a great deal of hardship for the so-called *marginaux* (the beggars, homeless, and underemployed), but only in the biggest cities did something like the possibility of true anonymity in an urban setting exist in 1648.

In 1650, most French towns had populations of between 5,000 and 12,000 inhabitants. Hundred of eyes peering through shutters or squints or from behind sacks in dark storerooms provided a surveillance of the streets and markets of these urban centers, a "policing" of urban space that still can be sensed in many smaller European towns of the twentieth century. A seventeenth-century town might have its own *marginaux,* but their conduct and their searching through rubbish heaps had long since become a routine part of everyday life. On the other hand, a stranger trying the same thing would rather soon feel probing glances on the back of his neck; for towns and cities alike were suspicious of outsiders, and the inhabitants were prompt to report strange goings-on. Might the same point be made about the surveillance in each individual quarter of Paris, Toulon, Lyon, Marseilles, and Bordeaux? It is tempting to say so, but this in no way minimizes the fact that a stranger could move about big cities and stop in at a cabaret more freely and under less surveillance than in a town of 7,000 souls.

Towns and cities were places with strong restrictions on every aspect of individual conduct. Shopkeepers generally kept weapons, and in the streets "young blades" often were eager to intervene in a dispute or an incident involving the theft of food or a purse. The revolution did not take place in free-for-all settings or in an atmosphere where "anything goes." The Parisian militia companies stood firm to protect personal property from pillage, *except* when the property of a hated tax official was involved.

Evidence about the Fronde in towns and small cities has never been systematically gathered. What occurred in Rodez, Auch, Albi, Caen, Angers, Amiens, Reims, Dijon, Grenoble, Bourges, in 1648 and 1649? Like other provincial capitals, these small cities experienced their own tax protests and strikes by the royal treasurers and judicial officials in the spring and summer of 1648. But in the power struggle that was the Fronde, they remained on the sidelines. The inhabitants of small cities watched, grew sullen, and occasionally sent representatives to vent their grievances to royal councillors and to the regent, but that was as far as they went. An exception was Aix-en-Provence, a city small in population and in economic function but destined for intense internal political activity, if not violence and revolution, owing to the presence of the Parlement of Aix and to the divisions among its members over who would dominate provincial patronage in Provence.

The Fronde took place in four of these large cities—Paris, Rouen, Bordeaux, and Toulouse—and, as just noted, in the smaller provincial capital Aix as well. Rural areas suffered from military occupation (notably in Champagne), and others were of strategic importance as blockade points, particularly around Paris; but in general both the countryside and the towns remained calm between 1648 and 1652. The reasons are obvious. In the summer of 1648, the powers of the intendants were terminated by the Parlement of Paris and the other courts joined to it; and so, accompanied by the more coercive tax farmers, or "snakes," as they were called, the intendants either returned to Paris, fled, or kept a low profile in the provinces.

The countryside remained virtually free of attempts to raise taxes once the treasurers and masters of request went on strike. While it is true that peasants in the Southwest and in parts of Normandy, usually under the command of their seigneurs, sporadically continued to harass tax officials and columns of passing troops, these incidents only served to keep anxieties in Paris high, not to intensify them.

Once the treasurers and masters of requests had angrily stopped carrying out their duties, the countryside, the towns, and the small cities waited to see what would happen. Intendants returning to the capital, judges sitting in local courts, and wine and grain merchants trading not only in the Paris basin but also in Guienne and Burgundy knew full well that the countryside was waiting for something to happen during the summer of 1648. What the French cities had in common beyond parlements and other royal courts was the Robe officialdom as a whole, with its hundreds of clerks, scribes, recorders, and advocates. Marseilles and Lyon were exceptions: they lacked royal superior courts.

Still, a commercial city where large numbers of legal officials were present was not an absolute precondition for the Fronde. A certain "insulation" from the harsher, more coercive tax measures of the Council of State may be discerned in regions with local estates that had some degree of power to approve or reject royal tax initiatives. The Fronde was less intense in Rouen, Aix, and Toulouse, which were provincial capital cities with local estates or assemblies. Yet urban revolts in Rouen and Aix prior to 1648 indicate that the potential for disorder was not automatically reduced in provinces where provincial estates met.

During the heady events that took place in Paris during the spring and summer of 1648, the delegates sent by other parlements and courts to express their solidarity *("union")* with the Frondeur judges powerfully reinforced the impression that the entire realm was heading toward a cataclysm akin to the civil war then raging in England. Few members of the Council of State took comfort in the fact that the Lyonnais did not seem likely to rebel. Too many solemn-faced judges were arriving from Toulouse, Grenoble, Aix, Bordeaux, and Rouen to protest royal legislative measures and to express varying degrees of sympathy for the strike by the treasurers and masters of requests.

The Fronde's most active revolutionary moments of 1648 and 1651 occurred in the two large-scale commercial cities, Paris and Bordeaux. Both cities had parlements and large numbers of Robe rebels and sympathizers with the Fronde, and the estates and assemblies in the Paris region and Guienne, the province in which Bordeaux was located, had no voice in determining either the total tax or the individual assessments imposed by the Council of State. The scale of rebellious activity and revolution in Paris and in Bordeaux during the Fronde far exceeded that in any other city or region.

III. The Snakes

No living creature was held in greater contempt in the Christian tradition than the reptile that induced Eve to eat an apple. Always the symbol of the Devil, the snake signified everything that was evil, corrupting, and contemptible. To lash out at a fellow human being by calling him a snake was about the worst slur or epithet imaginable in seventeenth-century French.

A distinguished senior judge in the Parlement used that very word to describe the *partisans:* he implored his colleagues to act in ways that would drive the snakes from the realm. The *partisans* were those well-to-do Frenchmen of merchant and legal-professional background who leased the right to collect excise taxes. The system deserves to be described in detail because it provoked more animosity and contributed more to revolutionary tension in 1648 than any other single aspect of royal government.

The excise taxes, or *aides,* were like our modern sales or value-added taxes, a fixed percentage to be paid on each item purchased, depending on its quality and quantity. The *aides* fell heavily upon urban populations, particularly on consumers and wholesalers of wine, cider, beer, fish, livestock, and wood. For example, three sous were collected on each hogshead of wine at the various gates into the city of Paris, like a customs duty. Taxes on cellars in the city were also collected from wine wholesalers. The *aides* were a veritable labyrinth of excise taxes, in some instances collected several times on the same product, and at differing rates in the various areas of France. Since the royal government lacked officials to collect these taxes, collection rights were leased to private parties who in turn hired toll-takers and tax collectors and posted them along all the main transport routes in France.

Estimates of the annual amount of wine brought into Paris and other regions were, of course, available; so finance ministers could and did project the approximate total income that each *aide* would bring to the crown. The figures supplied by the previous leaseholders of the *aides* were suspect from the beginning; it certainly was against their interest to be honest.

By the 1640s, the practice of offering annual or triennial leases to collect the various *aides* for various fiscal districts throughout France had become routine. The contracts specified the amounts, the dates of payment, and the taxes that could be collected. Those who made bids to collect such taxes had to pay their employees, of course, and take the risk that a crop failure or a war might severely reduce income from the lease. In practice, however, the revenues collected far exceeded the sums paid to the crown according to the terms of the lease. There was room for coercing subjects throughout the excise-tax raising system, from the lowest level of the tax booth, moving up through a series of intermediaries and ending at the top where gifts and "friendship" between royal ministers and leaseholders turned the whole system into an elaborate circuit for private benefit at the expense of the king and his subjects.

For the crown, the principal advantage of leasing taxes was the assurance of regular payment in cash. In an era when efficiency was unknown in revenue collecting, or for that matter in almost any other aspect of society, royal ministers shut their eyes to abuses, especially to gouging by local excise collectors, in return for the regularity of income. The *partisans* did not, of course, possess the large amounts required for the advance payments and the regular installments stipulated by the contracts. They had to borrow money. The actual auctioning of the contracts became somewhat farcical, especially during periods of war and economic stress, when only a single bid might be made, sometimes by one *partisan*, sometimes by a consortium of *partisans*. The ministers who were trying to maximize income for the crown were therefore faced with choosing between no revenue collection at all and a rigged low bid. Moreover, the bidder or bidders used fictitious names. The royal ministers sometimes could and did figure out how the auctions were being manipulated, especially when prospective bidders secretly agreed among themselves to refrain from bidding against each other and to make a series of low individual bids for their mutual benefit; but they were reluctant to use such powers as they had to stop this finagling, for fear the *partisans* would refuse to bid altogether.

The anonymity of the *partisan*, at least officially, prompted a great deal of speculation about who was in fact bidding for huge contracts such as the wine tax. In the 1640s, a kind of witchhunt directed against *partisans* developed in the big cities. But surprises could always occur. The individuals, also anonymous, who made loans to the *partisans* were often prominent nobles, judges, and monastic communities eager to earn the above-average interest rates paid by the *partisans*.

Added to this was the fact that when the crown wished to borrow money, it again had to turn to the *partisans;* no public banking institutions existed. Thus, in wartime, a remarkable and unalterable solidarity developed between the crown, represented by the ministers in the Council of State, and the *partisans* to whom the crown was beholden both for regular revenues and for loans. The leading court of law, the Parlement of Paris, would periodically set up a special investigative chamber, called a *chambre de justice*, to gather evidence and fine any and all *partisans* and royal ministers who had willfully and fraudulently benefited from tax contracts. The judgments usually were very arbitrary, with the conduct of the *chambre de justice* bordering on that of a kangaroo court. Ministers could not be relied on to report accurately what had happened; they resented the Parlement's probing into their affairs. As for the *partisans*, it became impossible for prosecuting lawyers to prove conclusively, and according to the rules of evidence, that fraud had occurred, largely because some of the biggest financial operations were conducted without any written records and relied on the participants' word of honor. And yet everyone knew that fraud had taken place over the tax contracts, that the rake-offs increased during a war because the tax levies increased, and that the government had no clear idea of how much increased revenue any given tax increase would bring in. The taxpayers expected the *partisans* to be "bled," that is, forced to pay heavy fines, and this is usually what happened. Thus, in 1624, 426 *partisans* were fined a total of 6,918,074 *livres*, yet the practice that had been so roundly condemned by everybody went on as before.

In addition to the profits from tax leases and loans to the crown, the *partisans* also carried on a semi-secret business in government bonds, or *rentes*. In periods of dire financial need, the crown raised funds by selling bonds at higher than usual interest; then, as the financial crisis worsened, the market value of these bonds would drop far below face value. The crown had summarily cancelled bonds before, leaving the holders with nothing, and it could do so again. Because the *partisans* had the facilities for accumulating capital, they bought up these discounted bonds and held them until the crown sought to borrow from them. The negotiations for loans to the crown very often included buying back these bonds at *face value*, which meant huge profits for their holders.

During periods of peace and internal stability, these three financial activities—tax leases, lending to the crown, and redeeming discounted bonds at face value—did not provoke mass protest and angry outbursts among nobles and judges. In time of war and financial crisis, on the other hand, profits from these activities increased immensely. And this went on at the very moment when other segments of society were being taxed at ever-higher rates, were being forced to buy more salt than they could use, and were being obliged to make forced loans to the crown that would never be repaid.

The *partisans* were not a social group; they were not formally recognized and had no corporate standing; and they were unlike virtually every other element in French society. The secrecy, the anonymity, and the fact that the financial dealings of the *partisans* appeared to involve foreigners, particularly Swiss and Dutch Protestants, made them an ideal object of public hatred. Nor did the *partisans* hide their wealth: they commissioned the best architects, painters, and sculptors to build beautiful new townhouses during the years when the French were being asked to make sacrifices because of the war. The local rebellions finally became revolutionary in 1648 because in the revolutionary language being used, "corrupt financiers" had come to mean the same thing as *"partisans"* throughout France. *Partisans* were, of course, more numerous in and around Paris, simply because Paris was the capital and more leasing and lending was done there; but the phenomenon was the same, for example, in Bordeaux or in Aix.

Public outbursts against higher taxes and against the financial dealings of a few anonymous intermediaries between the rich and the government were also fed (especially among the elites) by the religious revival that was taking place across France in the mid-seventeenth century. The church's ethical position on interest-bearing loans had not changed: it was a sin to exact interest. In practice, little subterfuges had long since developed in financial operations to make it appear that the lender was receiving no return on his money. If a random sample of sermons preached in any big city were taken for a given year in the 1640s, one would certainly encounter strong language from the pulpit to the effect that collecting interest was a sin. The behavior of the snakes, especially when they flagrantly displayed their profits, confirmed the diabolical presence of luxury, corruption, and fraud. Artisans sitting before their empty glasses in cabarets may not have been very aware of the precise ways in which the *partisans* made their fortune, and they probably did not hear many sermons either, for listening to sermons was largely an elite aspect of seventeenth-century Catholicism; but they did not need to be informed in order to hate the people who had gotten rich quick from the public coffers. Among elite groups a slur about the social origins of the *partisans* would certainly be added: they were "people from nothing." And the judges would add, "people who are poorly educated" or "people with no learning." In the slurs shouted by virtually every social group and quarter of French society, we discern the counter-definition of the sense of solidarity created by birth, by rank in the community over several generations (particularly for merchants), and, of course, by learning (for the judiciary).

All these groups, and many others, had an emphatic idea of what the snakes were doing, but none had a very clear idea of how to remove them from society. Suspiciousness about neighbors who suddenly spent more than they had in the past, or about the new neighbor who had built a splendid house, or about the one who was always offering gifts to the church and seemed to be on unusually good terms with the *curé,* made the atmosphere heavy in the streets of Paris and throughout the realm in the 1640s. The artisans who built houses for the rich or who made their fine clothes, their jewelry, and their furniture must have known that the money they received in payment had, in one way or another, been stolen. To accusations of this sort, the *partisan* would retort that, owing to the rebellious atmosphere in the cabarets and in the countryside, he and his fellow contractors were taking high risks by making bids to collect royal excise taxes. And the crown had not always kept its word. By defaulting on loans and breaking contracts, royal officials had forced *partisans* into bankruptcy on several occasions prior to the Fronde.

IV. Paris and War

The rains were particularly long and heavy throughout northern France during the winter of 1648–49. In Paris, the Seine River overflowed its banks and flooded the Hôtel de Ville and the adjacent streets and houses. Cellars filled with water, and firewood and manure floated among the flyboats that left their usual runs in the channel to transport the inhabitants of flooded neighborhoods to their houses and to the market. As the Parisians struggled to keep dry and warm, stories of scattered violence in the provinces were repeated in cabarets and stables. Tales of tax-collecting, particularly about the seizure of furniture and farm animals in lieu of payment, had been circulating for years. No one had the means to verify whether these stories were true, yet these tales, and still more rumors of new taxes, kept nerves taut. The rural origins of most of the domestic servants and heavy laborers in the capital contributed to the sense of immediacy and anxiety produced by these stories. Were rumors about negotiations to end the war with Spain also circulating in cabarets and markets? Diplomacy, like war (but not paying for that war), was the king's business. Reports by "his" Council and by "his" nobility entrusted with carrying out these functions of state rarely provide information about current affairs. It is very difficult to learn to what extent the French were informed about, or what they understood about, the war with Spain.

Like populations in many nations today, the French only officially learned about the war when the French army won a battle. Nothing was announced after a defeat, not so much because the royal ministers deliberately wished to dupe the population as because they believed that a *Te Deum,* or "Thanks be to God," sung in each and every one of the more than 36,000 parish churches of the realm really helped the war effort. One could not thank God for a defeat. Historians have often remarked that these thanksgiving services were propaganda devices. Whether the worshippers were thankful or not, they attended these services in unusually large numbers, partly because work stopped and partly because the population was eager for a distraction wherever they could find it. Trumpet fanfares, horse guards, generals on horseback, and coaches filled with ladies in lowcut dresses and diamonds instantly attracted crowds in seventeenth-century Paris. The louder the thanks, the quicker God would perhaps grant France another victory. From the memoirs and letters that have come down to us, it is clear that the elites firmly believed in God's immediate and frequent intervention in human affairs. What the rest of the population, the 17 million other French below the elite, believed is impossible to discern.

The justification for higher taxes and for an increase in the number of brutally coercive measures to raise taxes was, of course, the high cost of the war. Members of the literate elite were no doubt familiar with this official justification, but did the majority of the population understand what was happening to the royal treasury because of the war? Certainly not. Government officials often made vague remarks about the extreme necessity of raising money to pay the troops when confronted by delegations of angry peasants, merchants, and artisans protesting the high taxes. As internal tensions increased, ebbed, then increased again in the 1630s and 1640s, less and less tended to be said about the war and its high cost during these encounters—or rather, these confrontations—between officials and protesters. As tensions increased, the immediate day-to-day issues of paying taxes and finding enough to eat so preoccupied the French that the argument about the war effort was rarely brought up any more.

For the Parisians, the war with Spain was nonetheless immediate, even if they ceased to believe (if ever they did) that the war justified higher taxes. Enemy troops were only 120 miles from the capital. A panic had occurred as recently as 1636, when it seemed that the capital might be besieged after the Spanish capture of the frontier fortress of Corbie, just 80 miles from Paris. There were still Parisians alive in 1648 who could remember the Spanish blockade of the city in the 1580s. They knew that if the Spanish broke through again, a mere 6,000 to 9,000 troops could besiege their city, cut off food supplies, starve the population, and force the French king into a humiliating peace settlement. True, the French had been doing quite well in the war of late, but no one could predict when a reversal might occur. The Spanish presence on the northern border helps explain why neither the city fathers of the northern towns nor members of the provincial estates made dramatic appeals to the king for concessions to the Spanish and for peace. By 1648, something like a phony war had developed; the population no longer wanted to make any efforts to carry on the war, and yet there was a vague realization that the enemy was not far away and that he might do immediate and terrifying harm.

Miscalculations of enormous proportions had occurred on both the French and the Spanish sides, not only about the cost of the war but also about its length. There had been no illusions that one or two campaigns would suffice to humble Spain, but thirteen years? Those who thought the war had gone on much too long by 1648 had no way of knowing that a general settlement was still eleven years away. Seventeenth-century warfare had certain clockwork features about it, which ought to have facilitated planning for fixed objectives; but other features, most notably the lack of money to pay troops and the insubordination of generals, prolonged the war for years. By 1648 France and Spain were hanging on, in near exhaustion. Peace negotiations had begun as early as 1639, but it was evident to both parties that these would be fruitless as long as the parties could continue the war. Increasingly arbitrary taxation, borrowing as much as creditors would lend, and pawning precious possessions to raise still more funds to pay the troops had already been going on for so many years that finance ministers literally did not know what to do next. In the last months of 1647, Particelli D'Hemery, the superintendent of finances, proposed ways to raise funds that were so odious to segments of the population that there was a strong possibility that sufficient funds might not be found to keep an army alive on the northern border. The Spanish negotiators at the peace conference knew this. The Spanish financial situation was scarcely any better, but the possibility that the adversary might collapse first kept both sides in the struggle.

The other determining factor in peace negotiations was, of course, internal rebellion. When news of a revolt in Catalonia reached Louis XIII in 1641, the king immediately wrote Richelieu to say that this rebellion, thank God, might make the Spanish more accommodating at the peace table. In Madrid, news of the Normandy revolt of 1639 and of the sporadic uprisings in Périgord, Rouergue, and elsewhere throughout the 1640s nourished Spain's hope that perhaps France would at last be forced to make concessions and sign a peace. To the observer several centuries distant from the peace negotations between France and Spain of the 1640s, it seems absurd that these nations would continue to fight. Fundamental social and institutional structures were threatened on both sides by the continuation of the war. Still, there was little fear of a general peasant revolution to overthrow seigneurialism and monarchy. Both parties fought on in the belief, or the illusion, that one more effort might suffice.

As we shall learn from the calculations made when the Parlement of Paris raised an army in 1649, the cost of troops, munitions, and gifts for the officers was immense. The early-modern army was a parasite that sucked the lifeblood out of states faster than it could be replenished, with little regard for cost effectiveness in any sense of that modern term. To call the seventeenth-century officer corps corrupt is to abandon careful historical research and to turn moralistic. Military expenditures, like taxation and like everything else that has to do with the exchange of money, must be carefully analyzed in order to discern the fabric of power structures within society. The army officers, munitioners, and to a lesser extent the troops themselves had long since come to form a powerful bloc that could blackmail the king or his ministry, could simply choose not to fight the Spanish, or could rebel and blockade Paris, holding it hostage until it was ransomed by a bankrupt ministry. By 1648, the French government faced bankruptcy, a potential army rebellion, rural revolts by the peasantry, and urban tax riots.

What had been won against the Spanish at Rocroy in 1643 and in other battles could be lost in an instant through financial collapse or revolt.

Richelieu, the rationalist dreamer-minister who in the 1630s had set France on a course to curb Spain, had been aware of the dangers of war, but there was no turning back. He initiated a policy of spending every available sum. The so-called "Nupieds" Revolt in Normandy of 1639 had been put down with military force, speedy trials, and executions. Never before, or at least not for centuries, had the power of the state been so brutally and systematically applied to the people of a French province.

This was the lesson to be learnt by any and all who considered rebellion. To be sure, Cardinal Richelieu held certain notions about royal authority that prompted him to be particularly severe towards those who rebelled. In day-to-day administration, immediate considerations of prestige and power usually prompted him to take severe measures. The Norman revolt occurred at precisely the time when rumors about plans for peace negotiations were circulating in various European governments. The repression in Normandy would be studied and discussed in debates of the Spanish royal council.

The war effort, and more especially the effort to create the impression of internal prosperity and stability needed to convince the Spanish about French military superiority, finally stimulated the development of a new type of state that was ready to coerce society and, if needed, terrorize it or repress it in order to acquire the necessary resources for war, in ways that had hitherto never been used on such a scale. What has rightly been described as a "governmental" revolution began to occur during precisely the same years as the deepening of the conflict with Spain. All the traditional principles of morally upright governance, charity, and prudent administration were suspended by a government that seemed to go wild in its tyranny and arbitrariness to extract money from its own people.

V. The Regency

Clues to the crisis that came to a head in 1648 are found in many of the letters and memoirs of the statesmen of the time. The most frequently repeated remark almost invariably pointed out that Richelieu and Louis XIII had "raised royal authority too high." Vague as this notion is, it can nonetheless be intepreted as part of a more general theory about governance and authority. By stressing "royal" as it does, it suggests that other types or kinds of authority existed in the realm, and indeed they did. By raising royal authority "too high," Richelieu and the king had in effect *lowered* the other authorities of the realm, that is to say the great aristocratic houses, the Parlements and other high courts, and the corporations and estates.

What is expressed here, vaguely but powerfully, is the Frenchified and updated theory of government derived from Aristotle's *Politics*. In the body politic, having *one* (a king or monarch) with the greatest amount of authority to order others about did not mean that no other authorities existed. Those who observed that Richelieu and Louis XIII had raised royal authority "too high" did not perceive this as a catastrophe or as something marking a definitive change in French governance. Quite the contrary. Things would right themselves "naturally," and they had begun to do so when Providence left them a child as king. A regent could not be expected to wield successfully the authority of a mature and forceful king. Hence it was considered inevitable that the authorities of the great aristocratic houses, the law courts, and the corporations would increase, restoring the old balance.

Louis XIII had distrusted his wife, Anne of Austria, because she had defied him and had corresponded with her Spanish relatives. He distrusted virtually everyone else as well, however; so his behavior toward Anne was scarcely exceptional. By nature suspicious, Louis XIII wrote a will that would reduce his widow's powers as regent by forcing all major governmental decisions to be passed by a majority of the Council of State. Moreover, the regency council, as Louis envisaged it, would be more than a rubber stamp for Anne's will. It was to include Louis' younger brother, Gaston d'Orléans, who had spent his entire adult life in and out of plots against Louis XIII's ministers and policies. It was also to include the Prince de Condé, a powerful, loyal, immensely rich man. Then there were to be some of Richelieu's creatures—Claude Bouthillier, superintendent of finance; Pierre Séguier, chancellor; Léon Bouthillier de Chavigny (the son of Claude Bouthillier), secretary of state; and Jules Mazarin, one of Richelieu's protégés, who was extremely talented at diplomacy and at understanding how plots might develop.

Governance by such a large council would have been unwieldy at best, but it conformed to certain traditions of government by council, especially during a regency. In an attempt to ensure its establishment, Louis summoned his leading judges from the Parlement of Paris and instructed them to enter his will concerning the regency council into the registers of their court. As he lay on his deathbed in the spring of 1643, the king took a position that probably was entirely consistent with the wishes of Cardinal Richelieu, who had died five months earlier. He attempted to restore a certain balance in the governance of the realm by effectively decreasing royal authority, as embodied in the power of a single individual. The judges solemnly promised to carry out the dying monarch's last wishes and did in fact register his declaration of a regency council, thereby making it the law of the land.

Louis had made Anne a party to all these decisions, and she had vowed to rule with the council he had just established. But within hours of the king's death, and perhaps before he breathed his last, Anne's supporters were carrying on secret negotiations to have her named regent with full powers. The Prince de Condé and Gaston d'Orléans acceded to her wishes, as did the key judges in the Parlement. The other members of the Council did not count for much in such high-level power brokering, though the Parlement had to be included in discussions as a result of its solemn registration of Louis XIII's declaration.

Thus only a day after Louis XIII's death, and with the approval of the key members of government, Anne of Austria was appointed regent with full royal powers in a solemn *lit de justice* in the Parlement. Why did the Parlement agree to such an action? It made itself look absurd by completely undoing the legislation it had solemnly sworn to uphold only a few days earlier. On this point, and on numerous others, we shall find that the blending of "constitutionalism" and "legalism" in France was quite different from what it was in seventeenth-century England. Indeed, in abrogating Louis XIII's will the Parlement seemed to be taking up the absolutist strategy—that is, it was increasing the power of the monarchy, or, in this instance, of the individual representing the monarch, the queen mother. Why did the Parlement lay foundations for perpetuating the very power that had previously been "raised too high" by the late king and his fanatical minister?

The answer to this question is twofold. First of all, the Parlement was legally bound to favor strong royal powers; and second, this corporation of judges was motivated by self-interest. Anne of Austria had suffered humiliation and lack of affection for decades at the hands of her late husband. She had been virtually accused of treason, in various plots at court. The judges responded openly and affectionately to the request of their queen, a woman of virtue whom they "loved as the mother of their sovereign and dear prince." Royalism and respect for maternity, when combined with and supported by relief at the news that Louis XIII had at last died, carried the judges to grant Anne's request. As for self-interest, it was not often that the judges were asked to decide on something as constitutionally important as the powers of a regent. The "makers" of a regent saw themselves as increasing their authority; and who could say: in subsequent regencies, registering the regent's powers in the Parlement might become a precedent. The possibility of gaining power was there, and so was the possibility of losing some. Regencies were not all that fixed in French constitutional law. For example, Louis XIII could have made his brother regent, had he chosen to do so; but needless to say, because of Gaston's record as a conspirator Louis did not trust him. In fact, Louis XIII trusted none of the people he had named to the regency council, except perhaps the young Italian diplomat Mazarin. And Mazarin could only gain in power by being trustworthy, for he lacked the thousands of acres and the hundreds of clients that Gaston and Condé could boast. The other members, Bouthillier, Séguier, and Chavigny, were small fish who might easily be swallowed up by the bigger ones, to use a favorite seventeenth-century metaphor.

The years from 1643 to 1648 brought declining hope and increasing political tension. Aristocratic plots continued, much as before, with the same plotters and the same dire consequences for governmental policy. Jockeying in the Council of State for increased power pitted Gaston against Condé, and Mazarin against Bouthillier and Chavigny. Only those too powerful to be disgraced and imprisoned, and those not powerful enough to pose a threat—Séguier and Mazarin, in this instance— stayed on. Tainted by an overly intimate relationship with

Richelieu and by his involvement with the hated *partisans*, Bouthillier was the first to be dropped. This could be considered a popular decision on Anne's part. His replacement was Particelli D'Hemery, who had a long career in financial operations and was reputed to be effective at "finding money." His probity was not mentioned, for it did not exist. In the early years of the regency, a climate of generosity pervaded the monarchy. There was always the argument, "In finance, it takes someone who is corrupt to bring in revenues." And then, the mere handling of financial operations, or of associating with *partisans*, was enough to taint anyone. In the Council, however, D'Hemery also counted as a supporter of Mazarin.

The correspondence between D'Hemery and Mazarin makes it is quite clear that D'Hemery had been appointed to carry out the Italian's wishes. The latter, of course, continued to feign ignorance of financial and tax matters, just as Richelieu had done. It was better, much better for public opinion, not to appear familiar with or in control of the sordid side of government. In point of fact, however, Mazarin pulled the strings on his puppet D'Hemery, while the latter took it on the chin before the public in his role as corrupt councillor. D'Hemery did not complain; he quickly feathered his nest by making friendly agreements with the *partisans*. The loss of public esteem could be compensated for by money, and by a marvelous discourse about serving the king. Indeed, D'Hemery did everything he could to raise money; he borrowed in his own name and lent to the crown, but perhaps more than anything else, he decided to mortgage the future of the monarchy by borrowing as much as possible against future revenues. The stakes were high. Peace negotiations, military campaigns, tax revolts, and plots in the Council: of the four, Anne and Mazarin judged the rumblings in the Parlement of Paris to be the least crucial. In one sense, they were right; the judges were royal officials. But in another, they were wrong and miscalculated terribly, for if the Parlement rebelled it could speak for the realm as a whole.

VI. The Historical Imagination

In periods of social and political upheaval, there are always individuals who have a sense of what will happen next, because they have a historical imagination and can draw inferences from past human experience and apply them to the conditions of their day. In the events of 1648, a great number of Frenchmen went from day to day, with no clear idea of what was going to happen next, while others saw apocalyptic visions of a revolution that meant the end of the world. Educated Frenchmen busily applied Roman history to the current situation; others, notably Omer Talon and Cardinal Retz, became obsessed by the possibility that the French were experiencing events akin to the civil wars of the late sixteenth century. Parisians doing guard duty or drinking in cabarets would remember the pillaging of cities by rampaging troops, the rapes of women, the desecration of churches, the blockade of Paris, and the hysteria triggered by food shortages. The fears that prompted the building of barricades in 1648 were based every bit as much on an authentic and comprehensive history of the social and military dynamics that the city faced as on the fears of learned judges who always seemed to find an appropriate Latin quotation to explain or to understand their times. The diversity of historical imaginations may have held a greater place in the minds of the Parisians of 1648 than it does in the minds of peoples in Western societies today. And in that diversity lies the explanation for the Fronde's failure to transform revolutionary thought and action into radically different institutional, military, and social balances within the French monarchy.

TWO *The Parisians and the*
Parlement before 1648

Boys breaking windows with slingshots? The act seems
banal and scarcely important enough to be remembered
in history. The window-breaking occurred in Paris in the
fall of 1648, and the streets, markets, and cabarets soon were
filled with people talking about what the boys had done and
what would happen next.

The broken windows were in the carriage house and stables
of the illustrious and eminent Cardinal Mazarin, the principal
minister of state. Deeper feelings of hatred had developed toward
this foreign cardinal who seemed to have sneaked his way into
royal favor by corrupt means and perhaps, it was rumored, by
sexual attraction. Always dressed in the finest red silks and
woolens, Mazarin was driven about in a sumptuous coach surrounded by guards and pulled by the most beautiful of horses.
His Eminence lacked, however, the high-minded power to
communicate to the French in the ways so brilliantly exempli-
fied by his hated yet respected predecessor, Cardinal Richelieu.
Richelieu had mobilized opinion through sermons and cheap
pamphlets that explained, to anyone who could read or listen,
how the kings of France had suffered humiliation from their
Spanish brethren and how the Holy Roman Empire threatened
to become a gigantic unitary state on the other side of the Rhine.
The French of all ranks, including the humblest Parisians in
the artisanal quartiers of the city, may not have agreed with
Richelieu, and they objected to his raising the power of the
monarchy higher and higher at the expense of other authorities in the state; but at least he answered his critics: he impris-

oned or executed his enemies, and he explained clearly why the terrible conditions prompted by the War with Spain had to be endured.

Cardinal Mazarin was just the opposite. In private conversations and public addresses, he replied to questions so vaguely or so briefly that his words were immediately discounted by all but his immediate followers and the hangers-on brought along by family tradition to support the king's principal minister at all times, whether he was convincing or not. Though the boys who broke the cardinal's windows did not become heroes, they were neither punished nor apparently brought under increased supervision by their families and neighbors in the quarter dominated by the Palais Royal. An unexpressed complicity developed between the boys who carried slingshots and a large segment of the Parisian population. In the absence of rhetoric about revolution, revolution can be said to begin with unexpressed complicities about violent acts. Historians cannot determine whether the slingshot incident was the origin of the revolution called the Fronde, but the French word for slingshot is *fronde,* to go slingshooting is to *fronder,* and the person using the weapon is a *frondeur.*

Among his papers, the best known of the Parlement judges, Pierre Broussel, preserved several tiny notes received during the Fronde. They are about as big as the messages that schoolchildren pass from row to row during class. On them is written, in big, awkward letters, "Come slingshooting with Beaufort . . . ," and the hour and place are specified. By the time little slips of paper of this sort began to be addressed to Parisian artisans and their friends, the term "slingshooting" had become a powerful metaphor for political action. Pamphlets began to appear bearing the word "slingshot" in their title, along with promises to describe the "true slingshot" or the "just slingshot." The puns were intentional: these pamphlets aimed to describe in accurate detail a particular vice or a particular enemy of the Parisians, and Cardinal Mazarin came in for the heaviest abuse. To be sure, he hired writers to respond to these attacks, and friends volunteered their help; but he never captured the initiative in the heavy pamphlet war.

The expression *pauvre peuple,* or "poor people," can be found in speeches, letters, royal proclamations, poems, and debates conducted by royal councils and courts of law. In the *cahiers* that provincial estates presented to the king, in sermons, and in pamphlets written to raise money for charity, the "poor people" were referred to again and again. The words "people" and "peoples" recurred. The expression "people of Paris" is often found in the documents describing the revolutionary conditions of 1648, and the implication is clear: the people of Paris were one of the principal actors in the political arena. The other protagonists were the Parlement, the court, and the army.

The vagueness with which the term "people" was used is disconcerting. Historical professionalism and revolutionary theory make us crave precision. We must be content, in one sense, with what the documents say very explicitly—that is, the "people" were a *force* to be reckoned with. All other major forces in the revolution must take the initiatives and the responses of the people into account. Instead of being disconcerted by the imprecision, we should perhaps be struck by the powerful significance suggested by the use of such a general term. The vagueness of such terms as "unemployed" or "minority" in our everyday speech provides a clue to understanding how terms such as "poor people" and "people" were used in the seventeenth century. When an expression is repeated over and over again, its meaning may simply collapse; or it may suddenly become charged with a new meaning and may stimulate fears and revolutionary action. The "people" appeared throughout the Fronde as speakers and actors who were listened to or pandered to by those who did not belong to the people, as speakers and actors whose power was assessed, along with predictions of how that power would be used.

There were a great number of sophisticated and curious empirically minded observers of the Fronde. They scrutinized and recorded a multitude of phenomena such as the color of Anne of Austria's cheeks or the flash of her eyes when she became angry, but none chose to make an occupational analysis of the people. Cardinal Retz, in an offhand remark, asserted that it was the men of "little property" who were the most revolutionary and the most willing to risk what they had. This observation was more a commonplace from ancient Greek political philosophy than an insight into the social origins of the Fronde.

Having only a minimal civic standing in the body politic, the "people" was that vast anonymous political group that members of a divided and quarrelsome elite discussed and often spoke on behalf of. Arguing for tax reduction, the eloquent and learned Advocate General Omer Talon brought tears to the regent's eyes as he vividly described the sufferings of the poor people in the countryside. When he gave this speech before the Parlement of Paris in 1648, all the judges—and perhaps Queen Anne for that matter—undoubtedly believed him. No one rose to say, "The people have hidden their wealth, they really can pay higher taxes." There was a complete consensus about the economic condition of the "people." Everyone not of the people agreed that the "people" had been forced to pay taxes far beyond routine levels.

In rebellious provinces, little placards were tacked up in markets or on church doors. They prove a moving testimony to the authentic voice of the "people" and are exciting reading for us because they put us in direct communication with their feelings of despair, bordering on rage, about taxation. The phonetic spelling of these little protest placards heightens the message conveyed by the words. When a prominent judge spoke on behalf of the "people," the statement had power, to be sure; but when the "people" themselves spoke, this power of speech was intensified.

Before the invention of the daily newspaper, heads of state, ministers, and judges—in short, the governing elite—often tried to communicate directly with the "people" by speeches and by reassuring personal remarks. When riots occurred, the city fathers, dressed in the gowns and caps of their offices, marched through the streets of Paris, of Aix, and of Bordeaux, not only inspecting and assessing the political climate but speaking to the crowds from street corners or church steps. Attempts by the elites to speak to the people directly are difficult to evaluate as speech acts; yet their importance as symbolic gestures of solidarity with the "people," and perhaps with their protest, is definitely apparent. The Parisians became anxious when members of the elite left the city. With amazing rapidity, rumors of a blockade and military occupation would fly from shop to shop and across courtyards. So when the city fathers and, even more, the Parlement ceremoniously manifested themselves before the "people," these were important expressions of solidarity.

Members of the ruling elite, including Queen Anne of Austria, the king's uncle Gaston, and, of course, Chancellor

Pierre Séguier were also stopped in the streets and addressed in no uncertain terms by the "people." As she came out of Notre Dame Cathedral, one day, Anne was immediately surrounded by passersby who began to talk to her emphatically, though not in overtly hostile tones. Someone from the people told her that she had a controller-general of finances who was "spending all her son's inheritance." Anne was reported to have been "astonished" at this remark. For us it is an unmistakable indication that while the "people" may not have had an active voice in deciding affairs of state, they were nonetheless familiar with the fundamental familial and institutional structure of the monarchy. The official referred to was Particelli D'Hemery— the superintendent of finance, not the controller-general; but the error over his specific title does not affect the speaker's meaning or the empathy expressed. Many other incidents occurred in which the "people" sought, either directly or through the institutions to which they belonged or had access, to state clearly and responsibly that their financial situation had become intolerable at a time when corrupt officials were stealing the boy king's property.

The merchant guilds, which certainly were composed of the "people" according to the definitions current in 1648, sent representatives to Montbazon, the governor of Paris, with an emphatic statement that no more money, presumably in the form of forced loans, could be turned over to the king. Asserting that they knew where money could be found, they began to name names. The Fronde had many vigilante features about it. The "people" legitimately wished to take affairs into their own hands, which usually meant confiscating the money and furnishings found in the houses of tax collectors and *partisans*.

Louis XIII, as it was said at the time, "took a long time to die." As the weeks dragged on, rumors about poison began to circulate in Paris. The poisoner had been, the rumors claimed, Richelieu. A suggestion that the "people" go to the Sorbonne chapel, remove the cardinal's body from its tomb, desecrate it, and throw it into the river became so widespread that as a precautionary measure the corpse was disinterred and hidden, so that the "people" could not find it. When the king finally died, surgeons performed an autopsy to establish the cause of death. A routine procedure perhaps, but it is interesting to note that their report took the trouble to state that the king had not been poisoned. The popular opinion may have circulated so widely that it was considered necessary to answer this rumor with a professional opinion. Links between popular opinion and elite opinion would be frequent in the revolutionary summer of 1648. And we shall find judges who spoke on behalf of the "people" as if they had personally heard the voices.

In addition to the night watch conducted by 140 archers, the only important source of security in the Parisian streets was the militia, made up of the Parisian "people" themselves. Quarters were subdivided into districts (dizaines), and in the event of riots or attacks a drum beat, or the tocsin, the alarm bell, summoned the "colonels" or columns of marching citizens to guard duty. The militia was made up of the richer "people": shopowners, merchants, and the wealthier artisans who were listed on the city roles as bourgeois. Each column of the militia was directed by a colonel who was partly elected by the bourgeois of the district and partly appointed by the city fathers to command the men of his quarter. These colonels not only had numerous responsibilities in the city, they were also the political leaders of the "people." Throughout the seventeenth century, a minimum of four or five of the sixteen colonels were also judges in the Parlement of Paris. We can therefore be sure that when the judges rose to speak on behalf of the "poor people," their colleagues in the Parlement were reminded of the offices these judges held in the militia (they say as much), and that these offices gave added authority to these testimonies about the poverty and the mood of the city's "poor people." In other words, as in the traditional societies that survive in today's world, channels of communication existed between the politically "powerless" and the political leadership. Speeches about the desperate condition of the "poor people" had, however, become so familiar that they seemed to have lost their force. Only a rather detailed analysis of the events occurring in the spring of 1648 will enable us to understand why phrases weakened by repetition suddenly took on increased force and meaning and propelled both the "people" and the Parlement into a revolutionary situation.

If the "people" had assembled for one reason or another and were quiet, "respectful," and simply enjoying a holiday celebration, the crowd was called just that, a "crowd." If an assembly became very noisy and began to make threatening or obscene gestures and to display knives or pistols, it was described as a "mob," or *canaille*. The "people" and the "mob" are one and the same social and political phenomenon during the Fronde; but their moods were distinctly different. On numerous occasions, mobs would storm into the *Palais de Justice*, the seat of the Parlement, and collect outside the doors of the Great Chamber, shouting and intimidating the judges who came and went. On occasion these mobs numbered only a few dozen people, but more often than not these assemblies outside the Palais de Justice were estimated to involve between 300 and 500 shouting "people." This mob was something the judges had to put up with year in and year out. When encounters became particularly menacing, the judges would ask the militia to stand guard in the Palais. They also began the construction of a new door that would provide them with another exit from the building. But in general the Parlement tolerated the threatening mob that shouted about excise taxes at its very doors.

At one point, when the tax on suburban property was being considered, a particularly vociferous member of the mob shoved Judge Thoré and may have poked him with a sword. Witnesses supplied the name of the assailant, who turned out to be a rich and well-known merchant named Cadau. Although shaken, Thoré was unhurt. Some of his colleagues may have been secretly pleased when they learned of the incident, because Thoré's family name was Particelli and he was none other than the son of the superintendent of finances. The Parlement decreed Cadau's arrest and prosecution for physically attacking a judge. Some sources say that Cadau was arrested and punished, others maintain that the criminal officials of the Châtelet had been given secret orders *not* to track him down. These conflicting bits of evidence and the uncertainty about what actually happened put us close to the mood that reigned between the "people" and the Parlement. Anne and Mazarin would call it complicity.

Another source reports that a mob threatened to pillage D'Hemery's house. As the narrative of the incident proceeds, it becomes clear that the mob consisted of masons, certainly one of the most respected occupations among the "people." The talk of pillaging houses and shops certainly prompted fear of the mob; some sources say that "if it had not been for the militia of Paris, we would have been lost" or that "they would have pillaged our houses." Incidents confirming this talk were scarcely reassuring. There is little evidence to suggest that the "people" or the mob were beggars and street people. Quite the contrary. The latter groups are mentioned primarily during the blockade of Paris, when the city fathers ordered them to leave the city because they were not "born" there and had no right to draw upon the charity of the Parisians. Indeed, as food supplies diminished, beggars were offered money to leave the city. The mobs feared by the elite were in fact made up of the "people," that is, artisans, merchants, and servants who were as Parisian as the elite and who might begin pillaging tax collectors' houses or become confused about a royal official's title. In a moment of heated conversation and drinking in a narrow street, the judge who had condemned a "poor devil" to prison for non-payment of taxes could be likened to a tax collector. Indiscriminate violence, terrorism, and random pillaging did not occur during the Fronde. Some feared it would, and this was an important motivating fear among the elite. As the study of violence between Protestants and Catholics in the sixteenth century has shown, crowds selected their victims carefully in accordance with their own conception of criminality and justice.

The Palais de Justice was located in the very center of Paris, on the western end of the Ile de la Cité, an immense heap of stone structures punctuated by courtyards, gardens, and a cemetery. It was a five-minute walk from the Palais to Notre Dame Cathedral, barely a ten-minute walk to the Hôtel de Ville, and roughly a twenty-minute stroll to the Louvre. Formerly the principal residence of the kings of France, the Palais de Justice had long since become the main center of judicial and fiscal administration in the realm. Approaching it from Notre Dame, one saw smaller turreted buildings and gates, surmounted by the delicate majesty of the Sainte Chapelle, built by St. Louis to house a thorn from Christ's crown, among the most venerated relics of Paris. Once in the great courtyard, one moved up the principal steps on the right and entered a vast chamber that had recently been rebuilt after a disastrous fire. Seventeenth-century lawyers did not have law offices; instead they discussed lawsuits with their clients in this vast room. Here also stood the most elegant and expensive boutiques in the city. Lace collars and cuffs, gloves, perfumes, combs, watches, books, and "necessaries"—those little cases in which women carried scissors and needles—were all displayed in the galleries of the Palais.

Beneath the boutiques were prisons and guardrooms, closed, of course, to the public. But apart from the courtrooms, a number of rooms in the old royal residence, the upper floor of the Sainte Chapelle with its famous stained-glass windows, and the archives, the Palais was open to anyone who wished to enter.

Only two doorkeepers stood at the entrance to the Great Chamber where the Parlement met in general session. This room was not only the site of numerous dramatic ceremonies such as the *lits de justice,* it also served as a regular courtroom during the judicial sessions. The Great Chamber had been refurbished here and there, but by 1648 the decor was almost three centuries old. The vaulted wooden ceiling seemed mysteriously suspended in the air, since no columns brought the weight down to the floor. Originally a glorious and garish clash of colors— red, green, blue, and yellow overlaid with gold—this ceiling had been darkened by the smoke, the fly-spots, and the cobwebs of centuries. Carved oak benches were arranged around all sides of the room, like bleachers, with those closest to the walls being the highest (and therefore the most prestigious). Little figures wearing outdated judicial gowns decorated the paneling, which framed two small, enclosed balconies, called "lanterns," from which prominent litigants and foreign dignitaries could follow the proceedings below without being seen. On the wall hung a monumental painting of Christ crucified (now in the Louvre), a reminder to the judges that the moral and political order they sustained was a gift from God.

Membership in the Parlement was established by centuries-old rules. The king and the chancellor could attend whenever they wished, as could the princes of the blood (royal princes) and peers of the realm. But the day-to-day business of the court did not attract these "members." To facilitate judicial proceedings, the Parlement had been subdivided into special subchambers of Inquests and Requests, and the Great Chamber, where senior judges met. Jealousies between the junior judges in the Inquests and the Requests and their senior colleagues in the Great Chamber were part of the social and political mind-set of corporatism in late medieval France; but through seniority and the purchase of presidencies, the junior judges could eventually be promoted and also sit in the Great Chamber on a regular basis. These jealousies did not go so far as to break down the constitutionally established principle that the Parlement should "speak with one voice." The junior judges could request to meet in the Great Chamber, in a full session of the Parlement; and when the king came for a *lit de justice* or sent a letter to Parlement, all judges were convoked to the Great Chamber, which was presided over by the first president, the only officer in the Parlement whom the king could appoint. Once they had been officially received into the Parlement, the other judges, 140 strong, remained judges for life; and when they died, their offices were assumed by a son or a nephew. A tax had to be paid whenever an office was transferred in this way, and each judge paid a special tax each year that was in part determined by the market price of parlementary offices; but apart from these rather minor issues, membership in the Parlement was beyond the king's power to change. He could, of course, as we shall learn shortly, create new judgeships and sell them, but the edicts establishing these new offices had to be registered by the Parlement itself, which was reluctant to accept new members.

The first thing to understand about the Parlement, or for that matter about any superior court in the realm, is that each court was the preserve of certain prominent judicial families. Deference to these families within these courts was automatic, and the influence exerted by the members of these families over the other judges was disproportionately high, regardless of whether or not a particular member of the family was intelligent or eloquent. There were very specific laws regarding the acceptable degree of kinship for members of Parlements; in theory, members could not approve brothers and first cousins for service in the same court, but in practice these rules were waived for the leading judicial families. The age requirement also was frequently waived for the sons of these same families, with the result that the superior courts throughout the realm tended to become the preserves of a few leading families.

The purchase price varied for a councillorship in the Parlement (the lowest ranked judgeship). It had begun to rise rather dramatically in the 1630s, despite the new judgeships that Louis XIII had coerced the Parlement into accepting. Presidencies were much more expensive, especially those of the Great Chamber, and one of the puzzling aspects of office sales during the 1630s and 1640s is that prices continued to rise, although the judges believed that their prestige and their salaries were declining as a result of these new offices. Why, if a simple market phenomenon was involved, did prices not drop as more and more judgeships were created? Some of the angrier judges already in the Parlement interpreted the price rise as resulting from the efforts of *partisans* to invest their new wealth securely and in a way that would bring prestige to their children. New-rich families were scorned and publicly ridiculed, as we shall see, especially if their money was tainted by tax farming or tax contracts. In general a new-rich family dared not attempt the outright purchase of a judgeship for a son. It would have been ridiculed and forced to withdraw the offer. Instead they would marry into the Robe families of the Parlement, despite the judges' hostility to new-rich families who wished to increase their prestige rapidly through such marriages.

On questions such as the creation of new offices, the Inquests and Requests invariably requested a meeting with their colleagues in the Great Chamber. Proceedings began about seven in the morning and continued until shortly before "dinner," their term for lunch. If an assembly was convoked in the Great Chamber, it also took place in the morning and, by custom, ended when the clock struck ten. As tensions mounted in the spring of 1648, the more radical judges forced their colleagues to extend meeting times and were more flexible about the order of speaking (eldest first); but their more conservative colleagues rallied majority votes in order to maintain the traditional ceremony and procedures of the Parlement. Threats to boycott sessions and to leave the Great Chamber while the Parlement was in session were frequent in 1648, but unlike the terrible splits and purges that had occurred during the Wars of Religion, the judges did not divide into two groups. Such a split would occur in 1652. Solidarity was maintained in a heated atmosphere, out of a sense that the Parlement's authority must be maintained at all costs.

The first president, the presiding officer of the Great Chamber, owned the most expensive parlementary office and was appointed by the king. The Parlement could not meet unless he was on his bench or, if indisposed, had appointed another president to replace him. After President Le Jay's death in 1640, Mathieu Molé—the "intrepid" Molé, as Retz called him—became first president. Sixty-four years old in 1648, Molé had been in the Parlement since 1606. No procedural thicket was unfamiliar to him; and, combining qualities of aloofness and mystery acquired during decades of speaking before the Parlement, he managed to offer outstanding leadership in a period of crisis. The Frondeur judges attacked him, of course, and on one or two occasions the conflict became so heated that Molé was physically threatened when his colleagues tried to pull him from his lofty seat. As the crisis deepened, Molé's authority over his colleagues nonetheless increased: he too once had been a junior judge and had behaved much as these young men did in 1648. Molé's office required him to "manage" the Parlement on behalf of the crown and see to it that the king's interests and policies were defended at all times. This usually meant that he found himself in the uncomfortable position of having to scold his colleagues and subdue their vociferousness, while at the same time being criticized by the king and the chancellor for lacking firmness. When delegations were sent to the queen and the Council of State, Molé expressed the views of the Parlement. He performed this task forcefully, though he knew that some of his colleagues would criticize him for being too daring and others for not being daring enough. If the old structures of the monarchy and the Parlement survived the revolution of 1648, it was because of Molé, who never once moved from the eye of the storm.

A body of men meeting regularly over several hundred years develops an *esprit de corps*. The judges were "brethren" in the sense that while they might disagree violently with one another and did not hold each colleague in equal respect, they all recognized that they were members of the same *corps* and that sooner or later enemies would become allies, and allies enemies. Being a judge in the Parlement conferred far more prestige in seventeenth-century French society than being a physician, a priest, a merchant, or a banker. The judges were lawyers—that is, they had been admitted to the bar—and were professionals in the sense that they had special training in legal procedure, a lot of it acquired while on duty. But much more important than their legal professionalism was their function as judges in the king's service. After passing a usually perfunctory oral examination, a candidate entering the Parlement swore before his colleagues to uphold the king's laws, the Roman Catholic Church, and the moral and social order. A special court, the Edict Chamber, had been established under Henry IV for cases involving Protestants, and Protestant judges served on that court. Hence the judges in the Parlement could uphold the Catholicism of the French church and often did so. The Parlement censored books and authors for heresy and for scandalous writing or talk; it could and often did order the burning of books and their authors. Judicial power, they believed, had been bestowed on them so that they might decide in favor of the innocent, not simply prosecute the guilty brought before them in the course of routine litigation. It was also their solemn duty to ferret out and repress injustices and evils in society. Their duties made them civic priests in a traditional society. Frequently called upon to sentence individuals to death, the judges of the Parlement constituted both a formidable and a vulnerable authority in society.

The judges' rhetoric about their high moral purpose and their loyalty to the king sounds pompous and shrill to us. We live in an age when moralizing in the form of repeated truisms almost inevitably prompts derision, if not laughter. Why did the judges ceaselessly repeat these phrases about loyalty to the king and about doing good? To be sure, repetition of the commonplace may be described as propaganda, but on further analysis the pompous rhetoric of the Parlement may also have been a sign of its vulnerability, a sort of whistling in the dark. Absolutist statements emanated from the kings of France and their councils principally in times when royal authority was being threatened by the Roman Church, by the great nobles, and by dynastic conflict. Louis XIII had been at his most peremptory and his most authoritarian during the final years of his life, when conspiracy and fraternal rebellion had raised doubt about his ability to make his subjects obey. If we take our cue from this observation, we can understand both the strengths and the weaknesses of the Parlement.

French society in the seventeenth century was highly compartmentalized, and while it was the judges' duty to prosecute subjects who had violated the king's laws, regardless of their social standing, in practice the members of the other strong corporate bodies in the society did not perceive either the king or his courts as their first line of defense. The members of the First Estate, that is, the church and its cardinals, bishops, and wealthy abbots and abbesses, had little reason to respect the Parlement or to look to it to defend their interests. Their authority, like that of the judges, also came from God. Prelates (churchmen above the rank of priest or monk) found that their authority was sufficient to carry out their mission of assuring the triumph of Catholicism and of good in society, and that they need not have recourse to the Parlement. The church had its own courts, laws, and prisons; it only turned to royal officials, and then not to the Parlement, for certain types of cases, and for the execution of heretics. The church constituted not only an enormous institution with authority over society, but an institution that could strongly protect its own members from prosecution in the king's courts for many alleged criminal acts.

The Second Estate, that is, the nobility, also traditionally kept its distance from the Parlement. Accustomed for centuries to resolving disputes among its members by combat, duels, or clan wars, the nobles of the 1640s still questioned the king's, though not the Parlement's, authority to keep the peace. The letters and memoirs of noblemen of the 1630s are filled with slurs directed at the royal justices, who are portrayed as mere scribblers whose courage was limited to spouting Latin phrases and to covering themselves with the mantle of royal authority. For the nobility as an estate, the Parlement's claims to uphold the good and to enforce the king's peace were not only pompous but downright suspect. In some instances the Parlements had enforced royal legislation against duels; but more often the enforcement was left to royal commissions. When the king was uncertain about whether the Parlement had the courage to prosecute a nobleman for dueling (and often, therefore, for murder), he would create a commission of judges drawn from the Parlement. This commission invariably found the parties guilty, and in a few famous cases sentenced the noble to death. Louis XIII's use of these commissions was more of a humiliation for the Parlement than a threat to their jurisdictional-constitutional standing.

These commissions revealed the king's lack of confidence that his own justices would uphold his laws. And though they could never say so, some of the judges in the Parlement must have breathed a sigh of relief when the king decided to have noblemen quietly tried by a commission rather than by the Parlement. It took the pressure off their court. And pressure it was, because condemning a noble to death for defending his honor created a fundamental clash between the alternative and competing ethical norms of seventeenth-century society. To be sure, in the Estates-General of 1614, the nobles had solemnly voted to suppress dueling; they supported the king's laws as written. *But* it was quite another matter to prosecute a noble-man, find him guilty, sentence him, and have his head chopped off. In other words, being a nobleman in seventeenth-century France still meant having the right to protect one's honor in combat, regardless of the king's laws and the Parlement. Not that the approximately 200,000 members of the Second Estate were continually dueling and fighting, but their sense of inde-pendence and their self-esteem depended on their right to duel under certain conditions, without the interference of royal judges.

The more we learn about the corporate social-political structure of early-modern society, the hollower seem the claims to absolute authority put forth by kings and judges. On such crucial issues as conspiracies and rebellions led by royal broth-ers and great noblemen, the nobles had the solemn right to trial by their peers in the Great Chamber of the Parlement. This Achilles' heel of the Parlement was so vulnerable that the judges proved ineffectual in trying and sentencing their colleagues for conspiracy and rebellion. Thus at a time when the king and his Council needed the judges *most,* they knew that they must expect the *least* when it came to upholding royal laws.

Less powerfully, perhaps, but no less effectively, other cor-porations also protected their members. The university, with legal foundations partly in the church and partly in the mon-archy, defended statutes granting special treatment to all its members and graduates. And the claims that professors some-times made to uphold the moral and religious order constituted just one more competing authority for the Parlement. While less prestigious than the university, the physicians and surgeons had considerable strength if one of their members was threat-ened with litigation involving his professional activity. Corpora-tions, not the Parlement, protected professional interests. Granted royal charters that guaranteed monopoly over profes-sional, artisanal, and commercial activities, corporations had elected officers, initiation rites, and fixed rosters of members, and their privileges permitted them to speak before the king or any other authority in the realm. So when a doctor was faced with prosecution for criminal activity of a non-professional nature, he could be certain that some of his colleagues would

speak on his behalf to the individuals assigned to judge him.
And there always seemed to be extenuating circumstances to
account for the aberrant behavior of members of the elite corporations, and anyone who could afford to hire a lawyer.

What is important for us to understand is that the judges
were susceptible to pressures and bribes coming from any and
all quarters of society and concerning any and all types of cases.
The frantic mother of the accused would tell the judge about
her nightmares and her prayers that her son be given just one
more chance. Corporations such as the wine merchants, always
influential because of the credit they extended to cabaret owners, would write and speak on behalf of their members. And on
one occasion when a marquis was litigating with a woman relative over "her" inheritance, the lady sought out and personally
"greeted" every member of the Parlement individually. The
judicial life was, then, a life of pressures—exerted from above
by the king and his councillors, who were forever exhorting the
judges to uphold royal authority, and from below by litigants,
who ranged from the wealthiest and most powerful individuals
in the realm to "poor devils" on the margins of society.

For their routine activities, the judges maintained a very
strict dress code: black silk or serge robes and square black bonnets for the lay councillors, short white surplices over black silk
gowns for the religious councillors, and mortar hats and sleeve
stripes for the presidents. The red wool robes, symbolizing the
immortality of the monarchy and of the king's justice, were by
royal order worn on the numerous ceremonial occasions in which
the Parlement participated—for example, *lits de justice* and
processions in rank to Notre Dame for a *Te Deum,* a "Thanks
be to God" service. One particular councillor asked to be admitted to one of these ceremonies wearing a black serge gown. His
request was denied, despite the "need for haste" prompted by
the revolutionary activity of the summer of 1648. This vesti-
mentary code was, of course, an expression of prestige, and it
should be interpreted as such. But was it not also, like the
pompous rhetoric about royal authority and the moral order,
an attempt to bolster the judges' self-esteem? Certainly many
judges, who because they were political animals liked to please,
needed literally to wrap themselves up in their offices in order
to judge in accordance with the laws of the realm.

Maintaining some consistency of action across the years,

the decades, and the centuries was one of the prime preoccupations of the more learned judges. On laws involving treason or lawbreaking, arguments about articles in the royal *ordonnance* of Blois of 1579 were cited in opposition to articles from the *ordonnance* of Moulins of 1566. In general, however, learning in the world of the law appears only in a councillor's ability to recite rapidly, and in Latin, the first sentence of an article of Roman law. These tags would occasionally be supplemented by others drawn from Roman literature and from French history. One senses that the members were familiar, very familiar, with almost every argument and opinion a colleague might make on a specific point. Since the Parlement and other courts were courts of law, discourse consisted of deliberations, not debates. The distinction is fundamental for whoever wishes to explore the differences between the Great Chamber and the House of Commons in the 1640s. Individual judges gave opinions, once the judge in charge of "reporting" the case had presented it and had given his opinion about the course the Parlement should take in its judgment. Any other justices desiring to speak gave their opinions in turn, starting with the dean—that is, the most senior judge.

To *deliberate* means to consider and to reflect upon the trustworthiness of the testimony and of the other opinions, particularly that of the reporting judge. To *debate*—derived from the French word *débattre* or contend—means to struggle, to reason, to argue. The debates in the House of Commons during the English Revolution were more searching and more fundamental on such questions as the nature of government, society, and man's relations with God than was almost any subject deliberated upon in the Frondeur Great Chamber or in the courts assembled in the St. Louis Chamber after a "union" of the sovereign courts was declared in May 1648. The differences in the function of discourse within these two bodies should not be exaggerated, but neither should they be ignored.

The judges in the Great Chamber did not advise the king; that was the function of the Council of State. Through *remonstrances,* they could humbly point out certain inconsistencies in laws before registering them, but these remonstrances often focused on quite specific and technical points of law. More general principles, such as the Parlement's claim to authority over all legislation involving taxation, could be and were linked to the court's more fundamental claim that one of its prime duties was to review legislation having to do with the royal domain—that body of rights and real property owned by the crown. But throughout the Fronde, articulating these principles remained unnecessary in the face of general agreement about the principles of how institutions functioned. In this context, then, judicial deliberation on a question as vague as "help for the poor people" constituted an immense break in the routine discourse of the Parlement, a break provoked by social conditions that forced the judges to abandon habit and to focus upon the immediate political interests affecting the "poor people."

Historians have often judged the Parlement of Paris harshly because it looked after the interests of its own members and their families first, and only later those of the "poor people." If, however, we bear in mind what has just been said about the church and the nobility—that is, that each major group in the elite had its own corporate force to protect the persons and property of its members—we should not be surprised at the Parlement's priorities. Indeed, the Parlement behaved like all other corporate bodies: it looked out primarily for its own members and did its best to defend the function that assured them dignity and income, in this case the rendering of justice. It would, for example, have been unthinkable for judges suddenly to begin claiming to speak on behalf of churchmen and nobles. These groups could take care of themselves.

A governing principle of this corporation-ridden society was direct access to the king for redress of grievances. Each year the Council of State received hundreds of appeals from both organizations and individuals, concerning the largest possible variety of topics. An appeal to the Council was quite different from a lawsuit; it was an attempt to remove conflict between organizations and individuals *without* determining guilt or damages. If a tanner wanted to install vats along an abbey wall and believed he had the proprietary right to do so, yet the nuns of the abbey did not want these vats because of the noxious fumes produced by the tanning process, to avoid a lawsuit the nuns or the tanner might write and request a decision from the Council of State. This habit of seeking solutions to conflicts without resorting to litigation pervaded the society, with the result that in general the justices of the Parlement assumed that other members of society could protect their own interests fairly well and would do so without judicial interference—unless, of course, the judges were asked to intervene when a suit was opened. In the study of these political-social relations, it is interesting to speculate about why the nuns (or the tanner) chose to write the Council of State rather than the city fathers of the town where they resided. Justice (and the redress of grievances that resulted) was thought to be best performed by individuals with no personal interest in the outcome of the issue. If a royal letter offered the nuns (or the tanner) a resolution of their dispute, it was because the personal interest of the king's councillors was not involved.

While it is dangerous to draw any conclusions on the basis of a single example, the story of the nuns and the tanner could be multiplied thousands of times. It suggests the ambiguous position in which the judges found themselves vis-à-vis the rest of society. In order to perform their duties, the judges had to be disinterested in the technical sense of that word—that is, neither personally nor proprietarily affected by the specific issues in a given lawsuit. Then as now, a judge disqualified himself when personal knowledge (prejudice) and proprietary interest might affect the outcome of the case. This helps us understand why the Parlement carefully and coherently defended the interests of its own members first, and only after that the interests of those presenting appeals. Here the term "appeal" must be understood in two different, but complementary, meanings.

The first meaning of "appeal" is formal. For example, the corporation of the treasurers of France and the corporation of the masters of requests lodged appeals with the Parlement against the king's decision handed down by the Council of State. As fellow royal officials, these corporations formally sought the support of the leading judicial organization of the realm, the Parlement of Paris. The second meaning of "appeal" is less formal but no less powerful. By shouting in the street, talking over a glass of wine with one's fellow militiamen, and participating in organized protests, the "poor people" made it clear that they wanted the judges to take up their cause against the decisions of the Council of State. The judges heard the appeal—this informal appeal—when it had become a powerful roar of public opinion that expressed anger at the tax-collectors' behavior. In other words, when polite discussions failed, aggrieved parties logically turned to the body or organization that was entrusted with hearing appeals against the actions of the Council of State.

Anti-royalist? No. A struggle over different conceptions of the monarchy? Richelieu and Louis XIII had pressed royal authority "too high," particularly when they humiliated the Parlement by forcing it to admit new members and by using royal commissions to convict aristocratic conspirators and their allies at court and in the Parlement. But as we have seen, that conception of the monarchy died when Louis XIII signed his will. All that remained—an overpowering *all*—was the need to find money so that the war could continue. The king's Council reserved the authority to levy taxes, create new offices, and arrest whomever it pleased without cause. And of course it also reserved the undisputed right to abrogate, to have declared null and void, any act of Parlement. The constitutional foundations for that "too high" monarchical authority exercised by Louis XIII had been there all the time. The constitutional foundations of monarchical absolutism were centuries-old, as every judge in the Parlement well knew. Any attack upon these foundations would be revolutionary. And yet one can fairly state that the revolutionary actions of the summer of 1648 stemmed as much from royalism, as the judges understood it, as from radicalism. We noted the social and institutional foundations for revolutionary action when we established how the second meaning of "appeal" came into being. Attempting to mobilize or even to radicalize political organizations by forcefully arguing that "the people support" a given issue is no doubt more modern and more democratic than the emotional pleas to heed the appeals of the "poor people" made by certain judges, but links between the two nonetheless exist. The judges were not elected by, paid by, or in any other way chosen by the people. Their duty to preserve the social order, their fear of violence, and their desire to be charitable finally caused them to heed popular appeals.

I. Venality of Office

In 1515 the royal government consisted of about 4,000 officials and 20,000 soldiers. By 1640 this figure had swollen to 37,000 officials and 60,000 soldiers. Though crude and approximate, these figures shed light on the growth of the French state. More than half of the offices of 1640 had been created before 1600, though the 1630s and 1640s were also years of very rapid growth.

The principal qualification for an office in the royal government was wealth, that is, amassing the money necessary to buy an office. To be sure, there were other requirements, such as literacy; but no special education was required in order to qualify for an office of secretary, forester, doorkeeper, verifier of accounts, treasurer, and so forth. At the very top of the hierarchy, both in prestige and in price, were the offices in the superior courts of law such as the Parlement, the treasury, and the Council of State. The king ostensibly sold offices in order to "improve" services for his subjects—for example, to speed up litigation in the courts; but no one was duped by this official reason. The sale of offices brought enormous sums to the royal treasury, and in wartime the practice was one of the principal ways of obtaining money to pay troops. Years of war were therefore periods of very rapid growth in the state. As jockeying for higher places on the ladder of prestige occurred, families were continually forced to reassess their positions and compare them with the status of relatives and neighbors. The years that brought increased office sales thus were tantamount to years of increased social mobility, always a source of tension within a society.

Once an office had been purchased, an investment was secure as long as the holder was careful to 'pay his fees and comply with the rather simple rules he must observe. He could sell the office, bequeath it to a son, or, if "Nature" had failed to provide that son, to a nephew. A royal office was property, and during the interminable financial negotiations that elite families conducted prior to the marriages of their children, the value of the office was assessed (as if it were a house, bonds, or farmland) and entered into the calculation of the total wealth the young couple could expect to inherit. On the average, offices made up 24 percent of the total wealth of a judge in the Parlement. The figure ran as high as 31 percent for younger judges who had not yet inherited other property, and as low as 19 percent for the oldest and wealthiest judges.

During the reign of Henry IV, a great debate had taken place over the effect that the sale of judgeships would have on the ethical standards of the courts. Did mixing money with a judgeship "corrupt" justice? Sully, Henry's long-time companion in arms and powerful adviser, sought to redress the monarchy's disastrous financial situation by regularizing the sale of offices. He favored selling judgeships and making them property to be transmitted from generation to generation; he asserted that the judge who purchased his office would be more independent and upright than the one who was appointed through political favoritism. After this debate, Henry IV decreed that judicial offices would indeed be considered transmittable property and that the royal legislation legalizing this practice would be renewed every nine years. The repercussions of this law turned out to be far more important than either Henry or Sully had envisaged. What if the law were not renewed? The justices would lose their investments, since the offices would expire when they did. And so every nine years, rhythmically, a major confrontation took place between the Council of State and the officeholders.

The law permitting inheritance of masterships of requests had expired on 31 December 1647. The masters met and voted that if one of them died, the price of his office (180,000 *livres*) would be divided among the 71 remaining masters, who would each give his share of the total to the family of the deceased, thus keeping the heirs from a financial loss. The renewed law for the judges in the Parlement of Paris expired in December 1647. The deliberations of January 1648 include no lengthy discussions of their threatened positions, but the undertow of anxiety about this issue is manifested in the Parlement's readiness to take up the appeals that the treasurers of France and the masters of requests had lodged with the court. The Council of State, and D'Hemery in particular, anticipated that the uneasiness of all these royal officials about the ownership of their offices would eventually make the Parlement approve their creation. The patterns of confrontation over new office creations were familiar to all parties; the effect of discursive battles pitting similar but slightly variant authorities against one another intensifies in repetition.

On 10 December 1635, Louis XIII arrived at the Great Chamber to hold a *lit de justice* and force admission of new officers into the Parlement, without giving the judges so much as a chance to deliberate or to state the reasons for their opposition. Chancellor Séguier spoke at length about the reasons for the king's declaration of war against Spain, stated that the war would be very costly, and acknowledged the fact that the French people could not pay increased taxes. The nobility was paying with its blood, the church was doing what it could, and so must the Parlement.

In the subsequent skirmish, the first president, whose duty it was to defend the king's decision before his colleagues and yet at the same time defend the Parlement during his interviews with the monarch, did his best to avoid an outright collision about whether the judges were entitled to deliberate over a royal decision that had been registered by a *lit de justice*. The precedents were vague, but not for Louis XIII, who simply ordered "his" judges to accept the sale of new parlementary offices and to approve these new members. The following night, those judges who persisted in their determination to deliberate received *lettres de cachet* ordering them to leave the capital within twenty-four hours. The most adamant Parisian *parlementaires*—Laisné and Foucault—were imprisoned at Angers; Sevin, Eaubonne, and Le Febvre were sent to the distant province of Auvergne; and the prominent judge President Barillon was exiled to Saumur.

One can imagine the agitation when the Parlement met the next morning. In the midst of the commotion over what should be done to support and recover the exiled members, a secretary of state arrived with a letter from Louis. It was procedure for the Parlement to assemble with all its members in the Great Chamber to read aloud any royal letter addressed to the Parlement; but the first president, anticipating still another castigating letter about obedience and royal authority, merely called the presidents to meet for a reading of the letter, as deputies from the Inquests and Requests chambers. In this way he avoided an escalation in the conflict between the king and the younger members of the court.

The Parlement resolved to send deputies to the king to request the return of the exiled judges. The first president made the request, adding that new councillors were being received. Louis XIII replied, "When all [the new councillors] have been received, I shall be clement." The first president continued just a bit, when Louis interjected, "I do not capitulate to my subjects and officers. I am the master, and I wish to be obeyed." Astonished by such authoritarian language, the judges took their leave.

When crises of this sort occurred, and they were numerous, various negotiations were conducted to defuse the situation. These negotiations often achieved just the opposite of what they were intended to do, and the confrontation between king and Parlement would involve an increasing number of officials and attract public attention. The issues in these negotiations were really always the same. Did the Parlement respect royal authority? Did the Parlement have the power to meet when the king specifically and emphatically forbade meetings? Ought the king have the power to exile members of the Parlement arbitrarily? In practice, the negotiations ended with solemn promises to respect royal authority, to refrain from meeting, or, if meetings were held, to conduct only legal business. The exiled members were returned. Then the Parlement went right on meeting and, despite the efforts of the first president and other supporters of the king, continued to deliberate about the issues they had solemnly promised not to debate.

In the 1636 confrontation, a stormy interview with Louis XIII was followed by Chancellor Séguier's extending an invitation to all the presidents of the Parlement to assemble at his house. During that meeting Séguier proposed that were the Parlement to get out of hand, the presidents should rise and leave the chamber, having first taken note of which judges had been disobedient. There were doubtless presidents who sided with Louis and the Council of State in 1636, but after hearing this proposal the presidents unanimously agreed that it was unjust to expect them to denounce their fellow judges and that they were obliged to maintain secrecy about the internal proceedings of the Parlement. Séguier replied, "There is no secret for the king."

One of the candidates who had signified a desire to buy an office of councillor in the Parlement was a certain Sieur Colombel, whom the Parlement refused to receive. Colombel was a jurist and had taught law to many of the younger councillors. Nonetheless, during the question period, the poor man was examined very unfairly on inappropriate subjects and in such abusive language that he sat silent. There was, of course, absolutely no doubt about Colombel's competence to serve in the Parlement. The rudeness and rigor of the examination were merely tactics to thwart an expanded membership of the Parlement. The Prince de Condé attended the Parlement and pressed the judges to accept Colombel, having probably been asked to do so by Louis XIII or Richelieu.

Then, during the deliberations, the dean of the Parlement opened a *lettre de cachet* from Louis XIII ordering Colombel's acceptance. This new expression of royal authority consternated the judges. Sensing that the judges were about to disobey the royal order, Condé tried to convince them to accept Colombel, adding that if they did they could be assured that they would be granted satisfaction on some of the other issues that the judges hoped to win, including a diminution in the proposed number of new parlementary offices and a continuation of their right to transmit their offices to sons and nephews. Louis XIII and the royal councillors advising him (Richelieu and Bullion) knew that the judges were particularly vulnerable at that time, for none wished to lose the enormous sums invested in his office. It was therefore the best possible time for an attempt to force the acceptance of new judgeships.

Almost every element in the confrontation of 1635 to 1636 may be found in 1639, 1645, and 1648. The clash that had taken place in 1631 and 1632 was, however, somewhat different, principally because Louis XIII needed the Parlement's approval of his and the Council's decision to annul the marriage of his rebellious brother, Gaston d'Orléans. But in all these clashes we find the language about authority, the use of *lettres de cachet,* the exile of members, and the intervention of powerful individuals such as the Prince de Condé. The trade-off that Condé publicly offered the judges—that is, a reduction in the number of newly created judgeships in return for accepting Colombel into the Parlement—is particularly interesting because it presages the role the high aristocracy would play in the Parlement during the Fronde. Did Condé have assurances from Richelieu and Louis about these proposals? He was a cautious man who had long since made his peace with Richelieu and had agreed to support the cardinal in return for huge pensions and important provincial offices. Still, it is worth speculating that Condé might have promised the judges more than he was authorized to promise, and that he subsequently found himself bargaining with Louis and the cardinal in order to keep his word. He had, in effect, made a commitment in the king's name before the Great Chamber, and he was a prince of the blood and a royal councillor. In this instance it so happened that Condé and the king agreed. This would not be the case in later confrontations with the prince's son, the Grand Condé, victor at Rocroy.

Masters of procedure and of language that they were, the judges noted the possibility that Condé might be exceeding his authority; for when they finally accepted Colombel, their resolution read that it was by "the very explicit command of the king, as brought by the Prince de Condé." In the heat of argument, the younger judges rose two or three times, threatening to leave because their powers to vote had been violated, as indeed they had. But Colombel was accepted, the law assuring the inheritance of offices was renewed, and the number of new judgeships was reduced.

In the negotiations to end the crisis, Louis XIII had insisted that the Parlement humbly request the "return" of their colleagues. On such occasions, a fairly large delegation of judges usually went to see the king, because the judges enjoyed telling their families and friends about the interview with the ruler. But this time, the other presidents found that they had other pressing things to do and left the first president to go alone and humbly request the return of the exiled members. The fight was over, and their release had already been agreed to; but Louis did not miss an opportunity to give the Parlement another tongue-lashing about obedience, even though the Parlement was reduced, that day, to the first president, whose office obligated him to report the royal words to his colleagues.

In this confrontation, as in others, it is impossible to assess the extent to which the judges were acting in accordance with certain principles of government, mainly of upholding the prestige and power of the Parlement, and the extent to which they were acting to preserve their own wealth and their personal prestige as members of a small and elite group of parlementary judges. French political discourse during the 1640s included distinctions between public and private interest, and, as we shall see in 1648, the judges were often painfully aware of how the concordance of their private interests with those of the public diminished their moral authority and political power. But, as noted earlier, corporations gained prestige and power in French society at least in part by their success at defending the private interests of their members. Thus, though the Parlement was perhaps vulnerable to attack from pamphleteers who delighted in pointing out the contradiction between the judges' laments about the "poor people" and their stiff political opposition on a single issue—the increased sale of judgeships—it nonetheless maintained its prestige because it always concentrated its efforts upon preserving that prestige and the wealth of its members.

The links between power, action, and reward were also apparent and immediate. For his efforts to bring the Parlement into obedience, the first president was appointed keeper of the seals of the Order of the Holy Spirit, a post "resigned" by Claude Bullion, superintendent of finances and minister in charge of the creation of new offices and of relations with the Parlement. Had Louis and Richelieu concluded that Bullion had exacerbated tensions between the king and the Parlement? Louis' harsh, authoritarian language remained engraved on the judges' minds, which explains why they thought the king's enhanced authority was responsible for subsequent rebellions; but beneath the language, the prestige and the financial interests of the Parlement came through unscathed. Advocate General Talon believed that the Parlement lost prestige in these confrontations. He was very sensitive to the underlying meanings of deliberations—perhaps too much so. Crises occurred between between judges and king, and peasant rebellions came and went; but it would be incorrect to infer that a general pressure toward revolution was building up. The pressure did not increase with each successive crisis, at least not until the explosion of 1648.

Instead of the modern-day type of revolution—which is partly manifested by and partly reflected in a head-on collision between the discourse supporting the *status quo* and revolutionary discourse that offers a radical alternative to existing social and political institutions—the discourse of the French king during confrontations with Parlement was more like the exchanges that take place during an old-fashioned family argument. The affection that held the parties together gradually peeled away, as the argument heated up and parties on all sides did and said things that they meant intensely and totally at the moment but that seemed less emphatic or appropriate later on. In the long run, the results were of minor "constitutional" importance, as this word came to be understood in England. Of course, once tempers flared and the Parlement seemed to have been humiliated, another round would always follow, perhaps over issues where the king's authority, his bite, would be weaker than his bark. What were Louis XIII's reflections about "his" Parlement as he turned to it on his deathbed and asked it to uphold his arrangements for the regency?

The senior judges of the Parlement had the experience of reign after reign, and confrontation after confrontation. Mathieu Molé, the first president in 1648, had been a firebrand as a young judge during the previous regency. He had participated in the investigation of Marie de Médici's Florentine favorite Concini, convicted of treason by the Parlement *after* his "execution" by Louis XIII. Molé was familiar with all the ministerial crises and conspiracy trials in the early years of Richelieu's administration, and while vastly knowledgeable about the interests, and the psychological and familial quirks, of every member of Parlement, he kept his distance from his colleagues in order to carry out his role as first president.

Similarly, the other leading presidents (assuming that the amount of verbiage and the acuity of their words are a reliable indication of their leadership) each played a role that was in great part determined by his office. The judges presiding over their juniors in the Inquests and Requests had to maintain a certain discipline; yet at the same time the influence they exerted upon these younger men gave them the power either to support or to stop the course of the Parlement in the Great Chamber. The presidents could be particularly slippery. After setting up the junior judges to oppose an action by the crown, a president could later plead moderation and respect for their elders before these same colleagues, assembled in the Great Chamber. In the Parlement of Paris, "management" was at once explicitly practiced and very ineffectual. President Le Coigneux, one of the parlementary leaders most willing to use the bevy of junior judges to press for what he thought should be done, owed his office as president to the favor of Gaston d'Orléans, Louis XIII's brother. (Someone as well-informed as Advocate General Talon nonetheless thought that Richelieu had been behind this promotion.) In the confrontation of 1648, Le Coigneux favored Gaston's proposals, either from conviction or in remembrance of an old favor. In a conversation with Talon during a particular moment of crisis, Mazarin, casually mentioned that Anne of Austria had approved granting an abbey to Talon's brother. Talon instantly declined the abbey, without even consulting his brother. A rumor circulated that the queen had given Cardinal Retz large sums to pay his debts. Was it true? In his memoirs, written over a decade after the events, Retz denied being offered such a gift. Management—favors, promotions, offers, abbeys, and bribes—was something every judge in the Parlement lived with daily, as did, of course, the judges in the other courts. In the course of the confrontation of 1635 and 1636, Superintendent of Finances Bullion distributed about 30,000 *livres* to judges in the Parlement. Some of the men accepting this money may have turned coat and led the fight against accepting new judgeships. There was no breakdown of management in the 1640s: a change occurring in deeper, more structural political and social conditions rendered ineffectual the giving of bribes and other favors and the caucusing of the King's Men (whose duty it was to "manage" the Parlement).

In the networks of family interest and patronage, some judges gradually accrued more authority than their colleagues. These model judges were genuinely popular, not only among artisans and merchants but also among their fellow judges. Indeed, their years of experience, combined with the complexity and variety of issues with which they had to deal, tended to make these judges cautious about overt conflict or fundamental splits with any colleague. An intense fight, even name-calling, might break out between two judges over a specific issue; but two weeks later they might well cooperate and ally on another question. Mutual respect and mutual wariness, rather than affection and friendship, bound them together into an immortal corporation. President Barillon, whose unassuming manner, modest life style, and courage during deliberations permitted him to stand up to the king or his representative, was the most popular judge of the Parlement during the 1630s. As previously noted, he had been exiled in 1631 for opposing Richelieu over the politically delicate dissolution of Gaston's marriage; in 1636 he was again exiled; in 1638 he was exiled for accepting a plea from bondholders against the royal administrators of the salt tax; in 1641 he was exiled for opposing the creation of new judgeships; and in 1645 he was exiled for opposing the edict that would have forced suburban landowners around Paris to pay real-estate taxes.

The frequency of Barillon's exiles made him a popular hero. When he was exiled to Saumur in 1636, he was received with honor into the city. His popularity was so widespread that in exasperation Louis XIII exiled him to Pignerola, a fortress in an isolated Alpine valley near the Italian border. There Barillon died, becoming a martyr for the parlementary cause. He had acquired a reputation for piety, probity, and charity, all virtues in themselves; but, as Madame de Motteville observed, "he was an honorable man, but also one of those tortured fellows who always hate those in positions of power and who believe that loving is only to love the destitute."

Perhaps still closer to the prime element that enhanced Barillon's prestige was his contentment with his life as a distinguished member of France's highest court of law. He seems not to have sought to enrich himself dramatically either by secretly investing his capital through *partisans* or by arranging marriages for his children with families that were socially less prestigious but far richer than he. Le Coigneux would, on the other hand, stoop to accepting a marriage proposal from a tax farming, royal-treasury family in exchange for a dowry purported to total the fantastic sum of 600,000 *livres*. How many times did the recollection of this marriage agreement and dowry come to his colleagues' minds as they listened to Le Coigneux implore them to do something for the "poor people"? The professional boundaries between the private and the public were familiar to the elite circles of seventeenth-century France; and one's authority among colleagues, as we shall see in the case of President Broussel in the 1640s, depended in no small measure on the delicate balance between social conduct and available wealth. Indeed, misconduct in financial matters must have been frequent enough; but all that was required was that appearances be kept up. Moreover, the leading judicial families basked in the affection and respect of their colleagues. If a Judge de Mêmes, a de Thou, a Harlay, a Nicolaï, a Talon, a Pasquier, a du Tillet, a Pithou, or a Molé broke the code by accepting gifts or royal favors, the matter was hushed up and perhaps forgotten. The less prestigious and newly arrived magistrates felt a strong need to believe that some families were above corruption. Sexual promiscuity was perhaps talked about in hushed tones, but it damaged a judge less than bribetaking.

The judges cherished their reputations and, as we shall see, were extremely reluctant to enact a law that would threaten either their personal popularity or the prestige of the Parlement. Masters at delaying certain cases, they could, if they wished, act with the speed of lightning and cut through months of chicanery. When popular disturbances began to shake Paris, they brought to trial those who had started the riot with their insulting language. But if public attention became focused on the person to be indicted, the *commissaires* charged by the Parlement to make the arrest rarely got around to doing so personally. In other instances, the arrested rioters waited months, perhaps years, for their trial, a punishment and an injustice by our standards, to be sure, but better than being tried, found guilty, and executed?

THREE *Constructing Solidarities against Council Authority*

Louis XIV, age nine, fell ill with smallpox on 11 November 1647. His younger brother Philip, heir to the throne in the event of Louis' death, likewise came down with this often deadly disease. Followers in the entourage of the king's uncle, Gaston, made insinuating remarks about how the Duke d'Orléans might soon become king, should the two children die of the pox. Public prayers were ordered. Ministers in the Council whose sole support came from the regent who had appointed them knew full well that not only might they lose their posts should Gaston become king, they might also be tried and fined for having become rich quickly as a result of their links to the royal treasury. Strong expressions of affection and support for the queen mother came up from the Parisians, especially the various families in the royal government; but beneath this show of sympathy could be felt the anxieties provoked by a government that appeared to be on a collison course with society. The boy king would be out of danger by mid-December, but he remained very weak.

In Münster, in the German province of Westphalia, French diplomats were trying month after month to negotiate a settlement to the war that had ravaged Germany for nearly thirty years. France's allies, Sweden and the United Provinces of the Netherlands, had their own interests to defend. The common war effort against the Imperial Hapsburgs and their German arch-Catholic allies had in large part been forged by massive cash subsidies that the French paid the Swedes and the Dutch. The terms of the alliances had not been kept. France had not made all the promised payments, and the Hapsburgs were waiting for a crack in the alliance. In December 1647 it was becoming obvious that still another large-scale military operation would be necessary in the spring, if the previous gains were to be consolidated into a peace settlement. The Hapsburg monarchies, German and Spanish, could be particularly intransigent around a negotiating table. In a sense they had been defeated militarily; but the powers that had defeated them were so exhausted by their efforts that they risked losing in negotiations what they had gained in battle. The strains of war were terrible throughout Europe in 1648. And in England, the civil war had led to the triumph of the Parliamentary army and the arrest of King Charles I, news the continentals could scarcely believe.

Already stunned by the flooding Seine and the bitter cold of early 1648, the Parisian elites soon reeled at the announcement of the new round of tax proposals that the Council had put forth to raise funds for the spring campaign. It was absurd to wait until January to raise funds for an army that was expected to fight in May or June, but there seemed no way out. The bad planning resulted from the refusal (and the inability) to legislate fundraising during previous years. Attention oscillated between the peace negotiations and the tax-proposal negotiations during the winters of 1641–48, and on into 1659, when peace with Spain was finally achieved. In fact, Superintendant of Finances D'Hemery hoped to borrow immediately against the newly levied taxes and then forward the money, in coin and as letters of credit, to the generals and intendants on the northern and eastern fronts. Troops had gone unpaid, and munition- and food-suppliers had advanced essential commodities, in effect lending the crown money in the hope of being handsomely repaid for their cooperation. Thus the war effort hinged on the Council's ability to legislate some taxes and create new purchasable offices that creditors would take seriously. The timing was terrible. It resulted from earlier attempts and failures to increase revenues, not from lack of administrative competence or of political acumen. The Council of State sat squarely in the middle, between Hapsburg doggedness in Münster and parlementarian doggedness in Paris, Aix, Rennes, and elsewhere.

When governments are functioning in a more or less effectively routine fashion, and the pressures from society and from foreign powers are at routine levels, very little debate usually takes place about the nature of power and the foundations for authority. To be sure, philosophically inclined ministers now and then come to power, with visions about what relations between government and society ought to be. These visions are only very modestly realized, if at all, *unless* established patterns of authority and governance come under challenge.

The so-called absolutist government of seventeenth-century France developed as a result of persistent challenges to the king's authority in Council by the Roman Church, the parlements, and other corporate bodies eager to defend the interests of their members. The policies of the monarch and his minister threatened established power relations in society and, in the ensuing conflict, would lead to a great deal of debate about political authority. Still, the debate about authority was not the most important feature in the confrontation. Instead, the confrontation was like an old-fashioned family quarrel in which the father uses categorical statements to thunder about what children may or may not do, and children reply with equally absolute statements about what they will or will not do. Like the family after a dispute, the parties combating one another during the Fronde made up and lived on together, as the dust settled during the 1650s. There were no ineluctable shifts of power or authority. This said, we should by no means minimize the intensity of feeling produced by the Fronde or the real threat to social stability created by confrontations.

In early 1648, various groups of royal officials and leaders of the Parisian bourgeois began to reach out for support beyond their own membership and family relations, because their own limited powers were proving inadequate to force Anne and her ministers in the Council of State to cancel the tax proposals that their members categorically found unacceptable. Direct appeals went unnoticed. The pressure on Chancellor Séguier, the official customarily assigned to receive such appeals, brought no results. Séguier listened, but the tax proposals remained. And as D'Hemery presented his new tax proposals for the spring campaign of 1648, it became clear that protest, indeed intense pressure to have these proposals withdrawn, was forthcoming.

There was a great deal of coming and going at the Luxembourg Palace, Gaston's Parisian residence. Appeals sometimes were made formally—that is, they were drawn up, printed, and presented to the prince by officials representing their corporations. At other times, appeals were personal, whispered or based on warmed-up old ties of affection. Gaston must have watched his long career as conspirator and army general flash by as, over and over again, groups of royal officials and private individuals told their tales of woe. While not regent, the prince was very influential: he was the king's uncle and a member of the Council. When pressured to force changes in government policy, Gaston carefully repeated the official line about the dire military situation and the need for money. The prince who had once sought Hapsburg support for his conspiracies against Richelieu and Louis XIII remained surprisingly loyal to the regent and to official policy as established by the Council of State. True, he would occasionally let slip a phrase about the unbearable and odious new taxes or about the terrible extortions carried on by revenue farmers, but he insisted that for the moment nothing could be done.

The other magnet for these appeals was, of course, the Parlement of Paris and to some extent the provincial parlements. Since they insisted on their right to register all royal tax legislation, they were the institution on which to apply pressure. Cardinal Mazarin received a number of protest delegations, but he was spared much of this pressure in 1648 because his role in the Council was, quite incorrectly, thought to be limited to diplomatic affairs. In addition to Gaston, the other prince of the blood on the Council, Condé, was absent with his army on the northern frontier and inaccessible to protesters. Gaston and the parlements were therefore the targets of the pressure and the protests. D'Hemery and the other members of the Council of State were counting on Gaston and these judges, as integral parts of the government, to legislate and enforce acceptance of the new tax proposals.

One of the most fascinating aspects of the study of political behavior in a complex and interlocking power structure is the way in which parts of the structure can suddenly switch from being enforcers of government policies to opponents of those policies. Enforcers of policies suddenly become intermediaries between conflicting parts of the government, or between government and a society that is moving from protest to confrontation and finally to revolution. The duties and powers of Gaston, an individual prince, and the Parlement, a collective body of judges, would seem very different. Yet as France moved toward revolution in 1648, they assumed similar roles as intermediaries between what—when the labels are peeled away—can be called the crown and society.

The three proposals arousing the most tension in early January of 1648 were the creation of twenty-four new masters of requests; the *franc alleu,* a special tax on a certain type of landed property; and an increase in the excise taxes on such products as foodstuffs and wine entering Paris. Numerous rather similar revenue-raising proposals were also being made, but they affected less powerful groups such as court recorders or the citizens of small towns. So, although D'Hemery was sensitive to the test of strength that his proposals were sure to trigger, he had little reason to expect an explosion. If things followed their usual course, after protests from particular interest groups or segments of society the Council would reduce the total taxes slightly and the new revenues would become law.

Before a revolutionary moment can occur there must be a number of breakdowns in the boundaries separating particular interest groups or social classes. Common grievances must be discerned, and the frustration over failure to obtain a change in government policies must develop within a climate of general anxiety. In January, the masters of requests began paying the expected round of calls on Gaston d'Orléans, and on 8 January the bourgeois of Paris assembled to oppose the levying of new and higher taxes. It would be very interesting to find specific information about the persons who assembled that day and about what was said. Delegates from the six major merchant guilds, and probably the city government, certainly were present.

The seventy-two masters of requests also convened several times in early January to organize their protest against the proposed creation of new masters. In addition to agreeing to reimburse any widow of their number who risked losing the property of her deceased husband now that the "annual fee" had expired, they also proposed paying a higher tax than their office was worth when renewing that "annual fee"—sweetening the pill, as it were, for D'Hemery and his colleagues on the Council.

The "annual fee," or *droit annuel* (also referred to as the *Paulette*), was the key contractual arrangement linking the value of offices as property to the individual who owned the office. A tax of one-sixtieth of the purchase price had to be paid every year if an officeholder wished to retain his office. The decree that established the annual fee in 1604 applied to a period of nine years. Nine years therefore became the customary duration of each contract, causing a crisis between the Council of State and the Parlement approximately every nine years: 1613, 1621, 1630, 1639, and 1648. Before the royal councillors mentioned the possibility of non-renewal, the judges would become very nervous about the money they had invested in offices. As negotiations heated up in the spring of 1648, D'Hemery saw that the impending renewal of the annual fee could be a highly coercive instrument to bring the judges to accept the new offices. The parlementaires, in turn, met to ensure that any member dying after the expiration of the contract would be reimbursed for the price of his office by a collection among the justices. The pending expiration of the annual fee certainly heightened tensions in the spring of 1648, for it made the judges feel very insecure.

As it turned out, the measures proposed by the judges did not suffice. Those pillars of royal authority, the masters of requests, were "betrayed" by the colleagues they had instructed to negotiate for the group as a whole. The masters were unaccustomed to acting together as a body, least of all to launching a protest against the Council, the supreme governmental body to which they usually reported. Chancellor Séguier complained that it would be impossible to negotiate with a body of seventy-two officials, but the masters stood firm and refused to appoint a delegation. A stormy session in the Council pitted some of the masters against the chancellor. Séguier was forced to leave his seat and retire, lest he lose his dignity. At almost the same time, the masters called upon Gaston d'Orléans, Mazarin, and Condé (who happened to be in Paris), with reassurances that they were certainly not going to stop work to protest the proposed creation of new masters. Yet that is exactly what they did. The routine proceedings of the Council of State ground to a halt, because the masters of requests refused to present cases before it. Even when Séguier summoned them, they declined to appear. A new and much stronger solidarity was developing among the masters of requests.

On January 10, 1648, the four most senior masters of requests entered the Great Chamber of the Parlement and took the seats to which they were entitled. All masters had the right to sit in the Great Chamber, but since only four of them could vote the rest of these officials had no reason to attend routine legal business conducted there. Since many of the masters had been junior justices in the Parlement earlier in their careers, they knew and were often on very good personal terms with the councillors of the Great Chamber. Indeed, several judges of the Parlement had sons who were masters of requests, while others, whose sons were serving as provincial intendants of justice, had likewise been masters of requests. Master Laffemas made the brief, polite address appropriate to the occasion, and in reply First President Molé stated that the masters had poor memories about their services in the Parlement, since they seemed to attend only when it was convenient. Molé nonetheless accepted the masters' plea for the Parlement to represent them in a juridical, procedural sense: the Parlement's own prestige and the personal property tied up in their offices inextricably linked the councillors to the fate of the masters of requests. Solidarities were being renewed and extended between otherwise competing and hierarchically separate segments of the government. And, by taking up the masters' cause, the Parlement in effect moved from being a royal institution that enforced laws to an intermediary institution that stood between contesting parties. This case and others suggest that as a result of strike and protest, a hierarchically divided and competitive social-institutional structure suddenly was being transformed into a monolithic bloc during the first months of 1648.

D'Hemery's only trump card was, of course, a *lit de justice*. The earlier protest scenarios were so familiar to all parties, including possibly the bourgeois leaders at the Hôtel de Ville, that rumors began to circulate about the date when a *lit de justice* would be called. Various officials, including Omer Talon, the advocate general, warned D'Hemery and Mazarin that a *lit de justice* would be most inopportune; it could only be perceived as a *coup d'autorité*, a brittle and authoritarian stroke that would arouse anger and polarize the judges of the Parlement. D'Hemery insisted on pushing ahead, in the firm belief that his proposals were just, since the families whose fortunes were most affected by the sale of additional masterships—that is, families already possessing these offices or those with the means to do so—ought legitimately to make an increased contribution to the war effort.

As advocate general, Talon had the anomalous duty to represent the crown's interests and communicate its views to the Parlement. Consciously seeking compromise and a middle way, instead of confrontation, he often found himself scorned by the queen regent and her councillors as too inclined to favor the Parlement, while the Frondeur judges in the Parlement felt he was too accommodating to the queen and Mazarin. A perceptive and philosophically and historically minded judge, Talon made numerous powerful speeches and conducted many negotiations to keep the peace, largely in vain. He died in 1652, a discredited and broken man who fully realized that he had failed.

I. The Arrival of Troops

Soldiers began to file into streets such as the Rue Saint-Denis on 11 January 1648 and take positions where soldiers normally were not deployed. Why? Some anxious officials in the Parlement sought information from the Council of State, which replied that security had been increased as a result of the attack upon President Thoré. Rumors about the arrival of still more troops circulated rapidly, and it was said that the capital had not seen so many soldiers since the Day of the Barricades in 1588. Who could have made this observation? Someone from a learned judicial family? Or an elderly habitué of a cabaret on the Rue Saint-Denis?

Though the Catholic League and the Wars of Religion certainly meant something quite different for a rich merchant, a judge, and an elderly beggar, the common experience of the League permitted them all to refer to "the Barricades" when speaking to one another. In this case, "the Barricades" referred to 12 May 1588, the day when Henry III flooded the city with troops and the Parisians responded by arming and by building barricades throughout the city in order to protect their property, their wives, and their daughters from pillaging and rape. One soldier had taken a few sausages from a stall in 1588, just enough to set the merchants on edge. Would other soldiers do the same thing? The population had not waited to find out.

Merchants had closed their shops and had stood in their door-
ways, muskets ready.

As the rumors about troops swelled and spread across the
city on 11 January 1648, the provost of merchants and other
city fathers rushed to the Palais Royal and "requested" that Anne
remove the troops lest shops be closed and barricades built.
During the night, many troops were seen in the vicinity of the
Palais Royal and around D'Hemery's house. Merchants on the
Rue Saint-Denis sent neighbors to the belfreys of the three
churches along that street to watch for the approach of columns of marching soldiers. Throughout that night, the population of this very populous street remained on the alert and
armed to the teeth. Thousands of musket shots echoed in this
quarter as bourgeois tested their weapons by shooting into the
air. When troops were ordered to withdraw from that quarter
of the city at eleven o'clock on Sunday morning, everyone
breathed a sigh of relief. Judges did not, of course, live on the
predominantly commercial Rue Saint-Denis, but their residences stood within earshot of the shooting practice that tore
the blanket of quiet that descended over the city each night.

We shall have occasion to explore in depth not only Parisians' collective memory about troops and barricades, but also
the dynamics between men in power, such as the provost of
merchants, and the members of the Council who commanded
the military. But for the moment it is important to stress the
unifying effect on the populace of an incident such as the threat
made earlier to President Thoré and his father, D'Hemery. The
Parlement had, of course, immediately ordered the protester
arrested by the *commissaires* of the Châtelet who were supposed
to carry out judicial orders of this sort. Believing that they possessed sufficient authority and troops, the *commissaires* took full
command of the situation. Someone in the Council had, however, become convinced that troops would intimidate the
neighbors of protesters along the Rue Saint-Denis and would
at the same time express overt support for D'Hemery and his
son by encircling the superintendent's house.

The links between the Council and military force would
haunt the Parisians throughout the Fronde. The bourgeois
believed that they could defend their city against a royal army,
and they never hesitated to do so. But if the Council ordered a
blockade of the capital, the arrival of bread and meat would

cease. The bourgeois were divided over whether or not they as militiamen had the necessary firepower to break an eventual blockade. Such issues seemed remote to the judges and tax protesters from the Rue Saint-Denis in January 1648, but they were very much a part of the collective memory of everyone who was exerting pressure on the Council to cancel the new tax proposals.

Would the Council and the Parlement reach an impasse over these new laws? The rumors about an impending *lit de justice* had been circulating for over a week when suddenly, on the afternoon of 14 January, orders were received to prepare the Great Chamber for the king's arrival at nine the next morning. Once these clashes between the Council and the Parlement had begun, escalation to the ultimate legal instrument of power, the *lit de justice,* became inevitable. Beyond that, the Council's only weapons for imposing laws upon the Parlement were military force and orders to exile either individual jurists or the Parlement as a whole.

The boy king was carried into the Great Chamber in the arms of a duke and peer. Anne, Mazarin, Gaston d'Orléans, Séguier, and various other councillors, dukes, and prelates occupied the high benches to the king's left and right. When everyone had found his proper place and was seated, young Louis began his speech, faltered, and started to cry. He had memorized his speech but under the gaze of 200 subjects forgot it. No matter. Chancellor Séguier knelt before him and then spoke about the reasons that had brought the king to "his" Parlement: six edicts about the creation of new offices and taxes were to be registered as laws of the realm. The first president then spoke, advocating registration. He stressed that in this instance the additional financial burden did not fall on the "people."

The provocative speech of the day was made by Omer Talon, who not only summed up the history of changes in the ceremony of the *lit de justice,* but went on to stress the impoverishment of France because of governmental policies. In the past, he argued, *lits de justice* were not acts of sovereign power that "sowed terror everywhere," but were instead deliberative assemblies and councils. He had made these arguments before, and to little effect. But tears welled up in Anne's eyes when Talon compared France to the kingdoms of the Medes and Per-sians, impoverished by the effects of despotic power, and stressed how people were being forced to sell their furniture in order to pay taxes. To be sure, he continued, the costs of war are high, and quiet prevails in the provinces. Listeners could almost hear what Talon was *not* saying: If the Council continued on this collision course, provincial rebellions would break out. Constrained by the duties of his office, Talon, as advocate general, nonetheless concluded in favor of registering the edicts. Chancellor Séguier, who was conducting the ceremony, moved around the Great Chamber to record affirmative opinions, first asking the boy king's opinion and those of his mother and his uncle Gaston, then questioning in turn the presidents of the Parlement, the dukes and peers, and the younger judges in the Inquests and Requests chambers. The atmosphere was heavy and sullen. As the young king left the Great Chamber, there were no shouts of *Vive le roi!* Several observers considered this fact very significant and ominous.

In a later private meeting, Mazarin reproached Talon for the boldness of his speech. It had weakened the French diplomatic position abroad. Indeed, Mazarin showed Talon an annotated version of his speech published by the Dutch that made France appear to be in desperate straits and on the verge of political upheaval. Other versions had been edited to provoke revolt in the provinces. All Talon could say in reply was that he had stressed the misery of the people in order to make the Parlement register the edicts, since their economic impact affected the rich, not the poor. Mazarin interrupted him to observe that this argument was "very subtle." Talon seems not to have been very shaken by this encounter; the realities of human suffering and the Parlement's authority would always be stronger in his mind than France's strength abroad in war and in diplomatic negotiations.

II. Strategies for Opposition

The Parlement felt rebuffed, stymied, and humiliated by the *lit de justice*. It did not know what to do next. Pressures intensified for it to assume greater authority and halt the perilous course that the regent and her councillors were taking. How could the

Parlement carry out its function as guarantor of royal authority yet simultaneously oppose legislation explicitly promulgated by that authority?

The ceremony of the *lit de justice* had given D'Hemery the legislation he needed to carry out his fiscal policy, especially the creation of new masterships against which he could borrow in order to pay troops. But would lenders bid for offices that might not, in fact, be accepted by the masters themselves? There always seemed to be prospective purchasers for such offices, regardless of the difficulties they might encounter in gaining acceptance by the corps of officers involved. But the masters of requests were still meeting and refusing to work. Anne summoned them all to the Palais Royal, where another verbal confrontation occurred. She had thrown down the gauntlet. Throughout her years as regent, she would, in a shrill and haughty voice, accuse her opponents of attacking royal policy.

Historians have been harsh on Anne for her apparent inflexibility in early 1648. She would have been shrewd to sustain royal authority without referring to it or without evoking it in an adamant tone of voice; but that was not Anne's or her century's way of doing things. Verbal contests with the masters of requests brought little change, however. The important fact was that the masters had now united in their opposition to the new offices, had ceased working, and had won the Parlement's support. Tensions were also increasing in other royal courts, particularly in the Chamber of Accounts, because officials believed that since the Council had dared humiliate the masters and the Parlement, and had gotten by with it, their turn was next. In January 1648, the various corps of royal officials certainly had every reason to anticipate the domino effect.

The *lit de justice* provoked hesitation and soul-searching in the Parlement. The time was ripe for a long and intense debate about the nature of royal authority, justice, and public life within the monarchy. Lawbooks, accounts by Roman historians, and the writings of the eminent jurists of the preceding century (Jean Bodin, François Hotman, and the du Tillet brothers, John I and John II) were dusted off as the judges sought a way to counter royal authority without at the same time claiming to have any authority themselves other than royal authority. The speeches made that year during the spring session of Parlement provide us with a full account of the possible ways in which the Parlement might oppose the regent and yet remain an instrument of the royal government.

Not wishing to name Louis XIII, Talon had alluded to a recent change in the legal status of the *lit de justice*. An institution for seeking advice and counsel had become a pro forma instrument for gaining approval of the king's decisions because, during the almost entirely ceremonial gathering of opinions carried out by the chancellor, none of the dukes and peers nor the judges was willing to stand up and say, "No, I respectfully object." Talon would repeat his argument on several occasions, but during the deliberations of January 1648, First President Molé and President de Mêmes answered him in ways that probably quite effectively ended any effort to build a case for opposing the Council or any effort to return to the earlier type of *lit de justice* ceremony. Molé recognized the historical accuracy of Talon's remarks but argued that *lits de justice* of the sort the judges had just experienced had been going on for at least eighty years. He thus denied a recent increase in the use of absolute power, or the foundations for the use of absolute power, through the *lit de justice* ceremony. Since it was Molé's duty to defend the regent's views, his historical analysis of the *lit de justice* was suspect to Talon's supporters. But Molé's success in refuting Talon is indicated by the fact that no formal attempt to reform the *lit de justice* and return to what it had once been occurred during the Fronde. Still, as a technique for forcing the peers and the Robe judges to obey the royal will, it would be effectively undermined by the Parlement's decision to debate what would be declared law by the *lit de justice* of 31 July 1648.

Taking quite a different tack, President de Mêmes first rehearsed the medieval foundations for royal authority—indeed for absolute authority—and pointed out that from the earliest *lits de justice* until the present, the chancellor always sank to his knees before the king and requested permission to speak. For de Mêmes, this detail of the rite was an explicit indication that it was the king's word that counted, not the consent granted by the dukes and peers and other members of the Parlement. That consent would have been impossible had the king not granted the chancellor's request.

The judges may well have pondered at length de Mêmes' remarks about kneeling, because this rite was a central element in many other ceremonies where, indeed, it was formally stated that the king was the sole source of authority, law, and action. Royal officers of various ranks, among them the first president of the Parlement and the masters of requests, knelt before the chancellor to repeat their oaths of office. Kneeling in such a variety of ceremonies, including knighting, may have been recognized as a gesture of such importance that the judges could find no way to refute de Mêmes and support Talon without raising other issues about the origins of their own judicial authority. Though Talon's views did not in the end provide a foundation for action that would force the council to alter its course of action, they nonetheless provided the context for discussions of various fundamental issues of governance. After research, reflection, and speechwriting, each leading speaker believed that his way out of the dilemmas confronting the Parlement was superior to the solutions proposed by his colleagues. No real parties, programs, or scenarios had as yet been worked out by the judges.

In a more philosophical moment, that pillar of probity, Pierre Broussel, argued that the Parlement's authority would not be diminished if it opposed the king's authority, since their authority was the king's. Logical arguments of this sort rarely convince deliberative bodies. No one doubted the truth of Broussel's words, but this paradox did not bear strongly on the fundamental issues at hand. Broussel's argument also presented a serious inconvenience: it led to the reflection that in opposing the king's authority the Parlement was not only diminishing the king's authority, but its own. This was not a very pleasant prospect for the judges.

Some days prior to the *lit de justice*, President Le Coigneux had developed an argument for opposition based on the venerable concept of the king's two bodies. Did not the office of king reside in all the institutions and legal instruments that bore his name? The powers of initiative were royal in public affairs, just as they were in rendering justice. How could these be said to depend on the will of a boy king—the king's human body—when the monarchy itself had divine foundations? This argument gained some support here and there, perhaps as much because Le Coigneux was Gaston's point man in the Parlement as for the soundness of the argument itself.

Arguments about the nature of the regency itself were stated again, and refined. They had been suspect to most judges ever since the Parlement had abrogated Louis XIII's will. For, once explored, these arguments almost inevitably led to the recommendation that since the Parlement had given the regent "full and entire power," all it therefore must do was revoke the act conferring that power. The solution to the problem of curbing the regent's power seemed simple enough to proponents of this strategy, but this course was in reality fraught with perils. The legal precedents concerning regencies were confused enough as it was, and the judges did not wish to contribute to this confusion by undoing, then doing, then undoing what they had done, since it was also clear that there was no *status quo ante*. Such machinations could only diminish the continuity of the Parlement's own actions, and nothing then would stop the Council from promulgating a decree nullifying the Parlement's statements on the grounds that they lacked royal consent.

Related to this, of course, was the argument that the power to create law resided solely in the king's body, and that this power was in effect suspended during the prince's minority. Regents did not therefore possess "full and entire power" to govern, nor did the Council. This more abstract expression of the argument over the nature of regency government no doubt had implicit support not only among the judges but also among elites in general, because it accorded with general attitudes about wardship and parentage. But here again, there seemed no way to formulate the argument and convert it into action without forcing the Parlement to undo what it had already done.

All along, Anne had defined the issue as one of royal authority. Séguier and Mazarin followed the speeches in the Parlement daily. As early as 17 February 1648, Anne requested, through the King's Men, that the Parlement state whether it believed it had the right to modify an edict that had been promulgated by a *lit de justice*. How to answer? The speeches continued. Anne's maneuver worried Talon, who requested his instructions in writing, because he feared divisions and repudiations in the Council in the event of a confrontation. In effect, Anne's question encouraged the parlementaires to try harder to find a justification for reaching the harsh and categorical definitions of royal authority that the queen shared with the councillors. Also, it is important to note that Anne and the Council continued to hammer away at the Parlement and the masters of requests, by asking them to come to the Palais Royal and give an account of themselves, so that the Council could manifest its own unity and firmness. Needless to say, the judges were familiar with all the arguments about royal authority, and they resented their articulation by the Council.

Le Coigneux went through his king's-two-bodies argument again and ended by stressing the need to do something to relieve the "poor people." Suddenly things were moving in the Parlement. Precedents had been found, or invented, and the argument of "necessity" had been invoked, not for themselves or for the masters of requests, but for the poor people. The Parlement still hesitated to answer the queen's question. The argument of necessity had venerable Roman legal-political origins. It was certainly familiar to royal councillors and parlementaires alike. Simply stated, this line of argument held that prevailing conditions required actions with or without precedent, in the name of a majority of judges.

Some historians assert that de Mêmes was a royalist, and others that he was an "absolutist." While it is correct to say that he often rallied to First President Molé's position, and therefore supported the crown, de Mêmes remained entirely independent and at critically important times often contributed bits of argument that enhanced the Parlement's authority. In February 1648, he pointed out that they were dealing with a boy whom they referred to as "king," and that the adamant statements about royal authority made during the *lit de justice* had not come from this lad, whom they all loved and cherished. Had not the royal councillors precipitated the king into a *lit de justice*, "like a theatrical machine"? The analogy in itself is very interesting, for it contributed to making the Parlement pluck up its courage, to take up the laws that had been promulgated by the *lit de justice*, deliberate about them, and present their remonstrances. De Mêmes concluded in favor of a remonstrance that in the end was tabled. This part of his speech, and the speeches of many of his colleagues, contributed both to sustain royal authority and to encourage the Parlement to deliberate on the objectionable edicts promulgated by the *lit de justice*.

In a long and incoherent speech, Corbeville stressed that there was no doubt whatever about the absolute authority of kings. Nonetheless, he argued, that authority should be considered a right never to be invoked in full, any more than a father should use his full power over his children. Councillor Theles reminded everyone that the king was a minor acting only according to the intentions of some ministers, and that his will therefore carried less weight.

On 20 February, Le Meunier asserted that all the powers of kings were limited, since they themselves were subject to certain fundamental laws. Broussel reminded his colleagues of the terrible tyrannical powers over the Senate that Tiberius had assumed in Rome. Corbeville spoke again, saying that the power of the Parlement was in no way separable from royal authority. Quite the contrary, royal power was at its center *in* the Parlement.

The speed and intensity of the deliberation increased, and still there seemed to be no firm sense of direction. Le Coigneux described the odious laws as an effect of the king's anger, and that, as such, the laws should not be responded to, but simply sidestepped. De Mêmes agreed, comparing anger of this sort to Zeus' wrath as described by Homer. The phrase "relief of the people" was repeated day after day, and with increasing frequency. It was something everyone could support, a moral statement that, when coupled with the argument of necessity, could lead the Parlement into unfamiliar waters.

Finally, the issue of whether or not to deliberate the laws promulgated by the *lit de justice* was stated as a resolution. The first and second readings produced a tie vote. On the third, Le Meunier changed his vote, and the resolution carried. As often happens in deliberative bodies, the debate had been so long and difficult that no one quite knew where he stood when it was all over. They had resolved to deliberate, but did their decision apply to all the edicts, or only some? Had they agreed to submit remonstrances? Further discussion led to a decision to deliberate about each edict separately. Only when the Parlement began to debate excise taxes, however, did it break new ground, largely because the judges were very reluctant to violate governmental procedures in favor of what were coming to be defined as personal interests, such as their own income from the crown (*gages*), the inheritability of venal offices, and the creation of new offices. Increasingly wary about pleading on their own behalf, the judges moved to the edict on the excise tax, because it was the one issue where they were disinterested as a corporate body.

Broussel turned out to be the reporter for the excise tax

edict (10 March 1648). This may have been no accident. Presidents and senior councillors such as Broussel could ask to report on any case they wished. Thus, barring competition among the judges, a case was assigned to the individual who requested it, especially if the judge had as much personal prestige among his colleagues as Broussel did. Beginning his report with something he could say as a self-evident truth, Broussel stated that

there was no financial need in the State, as had been inferred, to keep up the luxurious ways of a few individuals, and to criticize the usury of the *partisans*. Indeed, the financial needs of the State certainly had not appeared to be so great as to oblige the Parlement to weigh down the poor people by forcing them to buy food at higher prices.

He concluded by recommending that the Parlement table the edict. It is very difficult to translate texts of this sort. Terms such as "luxury" and "usury" have lost in English the force they exerted upon seventeenth-century listeners. Broussel powerfully joined together and articulated in emphatic ways not only Christian thought about such vices but also the writings of such Romans as Cato, Livy, and Cicero, who described luxury that had corrupted the body politic. Heir politically to the martyred President Barillon, the parlementaire who had been exiled by royal order and who had discussed in no uncertain terms the vices of wealth, Broussel repeated such points from time to time. His persuasiveness, however, focused on the constitutional issue, saying that "the Parlement would be worthy of eternal praise for having resisted the Sovereign Will, because the Sovereign is best served by being disobeyed." Furthermore, some of the barons of the realm had done the same under Charles VII.

President Novion followed Broussel the next day. After repeating the point that the Parlement must protect the property of all the royal officials, he turned to the edict on excise taxes and attacked the *partisans* as *canaille*. Listing some of the nefarious actions of the provincial intendants, he ended his speech by observing that the people were leaving Paris because they could not afford to live there.

It was difficult for the Council of State to respond to these speeches. Indeed, the only remaining defense for the edicts was the fact that they had already been made law by the *lit de justice*. The voting after the deliberations need not be described here, save for one detail. The Parlement had examined each edict separately, registering some but for others voting to present remonstrances about others to the queen. The edict creating still more lower-ranking royal officials was registered, a fact that some historians have interpreted as an indication of the partiality and self-interestedness of the judges. This does not appear to have been the case. The edict increasing excise taxes was not registered. The judges responded to a very difficult situation by giving the councillors some of what they wanted but countering them on the very points where the Council was feeling the greatest pressure, from the masters of requests and from the people of Paris. And to the political pressure was added the opposition by judges such as Broussel and Novion, who had become genuinely provoked by the *partisans'* corruption and wanted to force the Council to join the Parlement in "rooting out" the evil traffic in royal revenues.

As the weeks passed, the judges dug deeper and deeper for precedents, searching not only the past but also moral philosophy. The official registers of the Parlement do not record all that was said, usually because the speeches were repetitive. One anonymous account nonetheless adds that

M. Talon has wished to omit from the speech that he has recorded in the register, that place in his speech where he states that the Parlement was the head of people with the character of sovereignty, in order to manage their interests and represent their necessities, and with that quality it [the Parlement] may oppose the will of kings, not, however, by provoking their anger, but by imploring their justice by remonstrance.

Talon did not become the leader of the Parlement in the crisis, and it is impossible to claim that his arguments, indeed his constitutionalism, had gained adherents. Nonetheless, in his search for a way out of the clash between the Council and the Parlement, Talon frequently raised general issues for deliberation, thereby encouraging further suspension of the very rigid rules that determined what could be discussed. This little anecdote is an example of how he could lead the Parlement toward opposing the Council and yet remain a "king's man." After more than hinting at a theory of popular sovereignty, he then specifically requested that his remarks about parlementary sovereignty not be recorded in the registers. Then he also concluded that remonstrance was the way to oppose the king's command, a seemingly banal remark but not so in reality, at a time when the Parlement was groping for a mode of action to circumvent a *lit de justice*. Talon nonetheless opened alternative procedures for the Parlement, even though the judges did not adopt his ideas or recommendations; he raised issues and used phrases that carried the judges out of the procedural thickets of the law courts and into the more explicitly political issues of the Fronde.

It is more difficult to evaluate the force of Broussel's arguments upon his colleagues' actions than Talon's. Broussel's poise, his disinterestedness, and his astuteness during deliberations sustained his rank as an undisputed leader in the Parlement. Paradoxical formulas for action appealed to a certain number of colleagues who had studied logic in school. Broussel, of course, also led his colleagues by his ability to quote just the right tag from Roman law. Cardinal Retz's *Mémoires* depict Broussel as bordering on senility, but all the other sources suggest that he was an astute parlementaire who was both respected and liked. His leadership during the spring of 1648 was crucial in building a force to oppose the Council in Parlement.

The same search for the foundations for opposition was taking place in other superior courts of Paris, Aix, and Rennes. The Fronde leadership often came from the most eminent families. The Nicolaï family had held the first presidency in the Chamber of Accounts in Paris ever since the court's creation in 1506. With its vast geographic and administrative jurisdiction over both the royal domain and titles of ennoblement, the Accounts competed with the Parlement in prestige and power. Like Molé, First President Nicolaï expressed the collective opinion of his court, and his own, when he accused the Council of acting tyrannically:

They [the councillors] close our mouths, they take speech away from us, they treat us as if we lacked the ability to know what is useful for the State, and as if we lacked loyalty and affection in contributing to the prince's glory, and for the benefit of his affairs. The power and this absolute authority with which they are taking away the liberty of our feelings, has always been rejected in the most healthy and most just of governments. And, in fact, it is overthrowing the foundations of this state by breaking the link between the Sovereign Powers and his subjects.

Nicolaï coupled together the courts of law, the Council of State, and the people as sovereign powers. Whether they were prompted by the constraints of tyrannical government itself, particularly in the loss of liberty to speak, or whether they were inspired by Cato and Tacitus, Nicolaï and the other judges who sought to analyze the power structures in their monarchy relied on familiar definitions of the forms of government. Imposed silence and the denigration of civic competence were two of the principal features of tyranny, as classical republicans defined it. This position should not, however, be interpreted as anti-absolutist, or as an attack upon the notion of sovereignty as such. Nicolaï was not a political philosopher, but he found that his point about the existence of sovereign powers—rather than sovereign power, in the singular—provided a way to describe the traditional arrangement of powers in France. To be sure, all authority was derived from the king; and when past kings had granted nobles, law courts, and other officers the power to act in his name, they had effectually done his will. Any attempt to violate these arrangements was tyrannical, and especially so if the prince was a minor. Nicolaï gave this speech before Gaston d'Orléans on a ceremonial occasion. Gaston had become involved in efforts to calm things down, and the Council thought that the prince's presence in the court and his presentation of a short speech about royal authority might incline the judges to "obedience." Gaston did try to perform the task assigned to him, but if Nicolaï's speech is indicative of the mood of the Chamber, the duke's remarks must have been quite ineffective.

Presidents served as spokesmen both for their colleagues and for themselves and maintained their authority with their more radical colleagues by using their office to express feelings and positions—collective expressions—that were bolder and more daring than what had been the "sense" of the chamber. Molé often surprised his colleagues by taking positions more radical than theirs, or nearly so, when he addressed the queen as spokesman for the court. In some ways, Molé's role as spokesman for the Parlement enhanced the authority of what he said, for he would make a fair and accurate statement of the "sense" of a deliberation. On occasion his speeches were, on the other hand, discounted as merely ceremonial, because they represented only a minority of the members.

At this moment in the crisis, the conclusion of Nicolaï's

speech before Gaston is particularly important. First of all, Nicolaï
was First President Molé's brother-in-law. And then, lest Anne
and the councillors of state discount the content of his formal
remarks, he assumed personal responsibility for his words in
the following way. Having remarked that he did not want his
children and nephews to say that he had diminished the virtue
inherited from his ancestors, he then alluded to the fact that
the previous four generations of his family had also been presidents in the Chamber of Accounts. Nothing could have been
more painful for a member of a Robe dynasty than the prospect that his descendents would refer to him after his death as
a weak member of the family. Nicolaï also implied, of course,
that the Nicolaïs knew something about royal service and were
not about to be pushed off-course by a regent and a few councillors led by an Italian prelate of inferior birth. In institutions
where Robe dynasties commanded the deference of colleagues
and socially inferior families, it is possible that the authority
conveyed by invoking a dynasty, as Nicolaï did, was more powerful, and more convincing, than religious conviction. For while
the Robe was a quite precise group of families, some of these
families were more prestigious than others, partly because of
their greater wealth, but also partly owing to their generations
of service in a given court. In Nicolaï's speech, we discern the
links between family, courts of law, and royal service that were
peculiar to the Robe.

Such phrases as "he defended the Robe" or "a terrible day
for the interests of the Robe" appear with increasing frequency
in the deliberations of the law courts during the spring of 1648.
A collective actor, the Robe, was being forged for the Fronde,
as individuals and families perceived themselves threatened by
the actions of the regent and her Council. For "Robe" meant,
in simple terms, office-holder, someone who held a purchased
office. In the Parlement, there were occasional expressions of
support for what were called "inferior offices," and while the
Parlement might approve the creation of still more of these
"inferior offices," it increasingly became perceived as the
defender not only of the prestigious and the rich, but also of
the inferior and the not very wealthy. Pressure from the masters of requests had provoked weeks and weeks of parlementary deliberations; the same thing was taking place in other
sovereign courts as a result of pressure being exerted by other

corps of officials. Anne and her councillors were perfectly aware of the changing mood in the courts, and of the rise of a Robe solidarity that was beginning to break down the traditional rivalries between the courts and between the various corps of officials. There was a great deal of sparring back and forth, particularly over the annual fee *(droit annuel)*, which if not renewed would provoke huge financial losses for Robe families. Instead of intimidating the officials, Anne's actions prompted their increasing solidarity. The pressure from this Robe solidarity made itself felt first in the procedural battles unifying the Parlement, then in the unification of the other superior courts with the Parlement. But "interests of the offices" and "relief for the people," not agreements about the nature of political authority, would carry the judges along.

In the Parlement's routine work as a court, the chambers of Inquests and of Requests met separately from their colleagues of the Great Chamber. This speeded up legal business, at least ostensibly; but it also impeded the Parlement from developing a common view or policy about political issues. When the Chambers of Inquests wished a general meeting of the Parlement to discuss something, they had to make their request to the first president, who consulted the members of the Great Chamber about granting or refusing that request. Hours upon hours, indeed weeks and weeks, of the spring of 1648 were spent in parlementary maneuvers to set up general and frequent meetings in which to deliberate about political issues. Molé often succeeded in gaining the Great Chamber's support for denying the Inquests' request for a general meeting. But when Anne and the Council issued a decree that "insulted the Parlement"—and the Parlement was easily insulted—the judges of the Great Chamber invariably voted to receive their junior colleagues for a general deliberation. D'Hemery firmly believed that if he maintained his pressure on the Parlement long enough, and refused to renew the annual fee, the judges would finally knuckle under and accept the new masterships of requests. In the spring of 1648, D'Hemery outmaneuvered himself. He granted the annual fee to judges in the other courts, but not to those of the Parlement, expecting the Robe to once again be divided. Just the opposite occurred. The judges in the other courts adamantly declined to "betray" their fellow judges in the Parlement, and the conflict so deepened during April and May that Molé finally had to abandon the procedural devices that permitted him to prevent general assemblies in the Great Chamber.

More direct types of pressure were no doubt exerted on the judges as well. President Broussel's son, who was an officer in the royal army, learned that he would not be promoted to lieutenant "owing to the opinions expressed by his father in the Parlement." Those who had taken bribes in the past probably continued to be paid, but in the atmosphere of division and anger over charges of government corruption, it became increasingly difficult for D'Hemery and Mazarin to offer payments to judges who had not previously been bribed. The judges who always voted in favor of the proposals put forth by the Council may have started to form a solid bloc as early as March or April. For when tie votes occur in constituted bodies, blocs become inevitable and parties form in those bodies. Rumors were also circulating to the effect that D'Hemery's friends in the Parlement had stated that opposition leaders would be arrested or exiled if they persisted in their opposition.

Life was becoming uncomfortable for the judges. Pressured by the crowds in the Palais de Justice and by Anne and the councillors, anxious about the provincial revolts that were appearing on the horizon, and viewed as the solid pillar upon which a whole corps of royal officials in rebellion could lean for support, the judges groped their way through procedural thickets to find some way to meet as a body should the first president deny their request. When nothing else could prevent a meeting, Molé would simply get up and leave. On more than one occasion during the next few months, however, he was firmly and forcibly kept in his chair or even held in place by hands reaching out to grasp his gown. At one point, the judges of the Inquests occupied their benches in the Great Chamber for several days, with "nothing happening." In fact, of course, a lot was happening as the judges sat in silence. Strategies were being worked out, and solidarities were deepening into a coherent opposition to Anne's regency government.

After particularly stormy confrontations between the Council and the Parlement, the other courts would send delegates to meet with judges from the Parlement and express their solidarity. These encounters between the judges of the various courts gradually began to prompt thoughts of a "union" of the sovereign courts. The term "union" was certainly familiar to many of the justices involved: it was an important inheritance from the days of the Wars of Religion. D'Hemery's attempts to keep the judges divided had been both a response to their increasing solidarity and a powerful force prompting them toward "union."

III. *13 May 1648: The Act of Union*

The attempt to divide the Robe by giving the annual fee to every sovereign court except the Parlement had failed, not so much as a result of a dramatic new escalation of the Council's and the courts' refusal to cooperate as because of another shift by D'Hemery, still greatly in need of funds. On 30 April, the annual fee was granted without further ado to *all* the courts, the Parlement included, on condition that the judges receive no salaries for four years. D'Hemery was simply trying to extort money from the judges in a different way. Would he succeed in borrowing, the next day, against the revenue sources that customarily paid judicial salaries? The credit market remained very tight all spring, not because there was a lack of capital but because lenders feared royal bankruptcy. Anne's speeches about the importance of maintaining royal authority were always partly prompted by the need to reassure potential lenders to the Council. Since January, the growing opposition in the Parlement had raised the specter of bankruptcy, for the crown could borrow only at extremely high interest rates, using jewels and relics as collateral. And the refusal of the moneylenders—that is, the *partisans*—to loan money to the crown enraged the more civic-minded parlementary judges, especially those, like Broussel, whose modest wealth permitted them to wrap themselves up in togas of virtue as far as all high finances were concerned.

The maneuver to separate the Parlement from the three other sovereign courts—the Great Council (not to be confused with the Great Chamber), the Chamber of Accounts, and the Court of Excises—had effectively prompted ties of solidarity among these courts. In all the courts there was talk of the need to protect the *gages* and privileges of the lowest-ranking judicial and financial officers, for their *gages* had also been cancelled and they faced loss of revenue as a result of the numerous new offices created during recent years. The deliberations of the Chamber of Accounts, and in the Parlement as well, make few allusions to their own cancelled *gages*. Instead, they repeatedly talked of helping inferior officials—evidence of widespread discontentment over this lost income. Deputies from the Chamber of Accounts, the Great Council, and the Court of Excises had been meeting during early May. Their first task was resolving how they might sit together without raising the thorny issues regarding each body's relative prestige. By an ingenious compromise in which the hierarchy of seating intersected the hierarchies of the courts, none of the courts staked claims to gain or lose prestige through these meetings. Their next important task was sending deputies to the Parlement to request that court to send delegates to the St. Louis Chamber. The principle that each of the superior courts had its own sphere of competence, a jurisdiction, and that each was "sovereign" within that jurisdiction and had direct access to the Council of State and to the king did not seem to be jeopardized by an assembly of delegates from each court. The Parlement of course claimed to be more prestigious than the other courts, and some judges asserted that it constituted the estates of the realm whenever estates-generals were not in session; but proponents of Estates-Generals refuted this claim. In any event, none of the essential prerogatives of the various courts nor their hierarchy seemed directly threatened by a meeting of delegates in the St. Louis Chamber. The Council, however, and D'Hemery in particular, saw that the still inarticulate but growing Robe solidarity could become an institutional foundation from which opposition could be coordinated within all the superior law courts. And since the delegates meeting in the St. Louis Chamber had already begun to discuss the need to preserve the salaries and privileges of all low-ranking officials, it was becoming apparent that the entire judicial and financial machinery of the government would soon go on strike and coordinate its efforts to force D'Hemery to change his policies.

The deliberations in the Parlement of Paris suddenly became quite predictable. Broussel took the trouble to write out an outline for his speech, because he wanted it to reach a larger public. He pointed out that there were "bad councillors who lack education and a sense of public order. . . . They wish to gain reputations as politicians with finesse, but they do not under-

stand politics at all. All they have is money as the basis for all
their policies." Broussel turned each theme over and over again,
ending on a crescendo of moral outrage.

Judge Lainé, who would develop into a radical leader within
a few weeks, stressed the fact that the judges in the presidial
courts (royal provincial courts of the first instance) and the treasurers of France had also not only lost their *gages* but had been
obliged to supply 45 million *livres* in forced loans in order to
get the annual fee for their offices renewed. The message was
clear: if the judges did not fight for their *gages,* they would be
forced to lend the king money. Lainé's speech seems illogical
until we recall certain features of seventeenth-century government. The Council had just renewed the annual fee and had
cancelled the judges' *gages* for four years. Nothing prevented
the Council from in effect changing its mind, revoking the annual
fee and asking at the same time for forced loans. This had happened before and would happen many more times. We have
only to recall how the Council abrogated its own decrees when
attempting to raise ever-larger sums of money, after it had solemnly promised in a royal charter—that is, had given the king's
word—that no additional funds would be sought for ten years.
Indeed, Lainé's speech was perfectly logical if we understand
the context in which it was given. In fact, no judge rose to his
feet to say, "You are wrong. We have the king's agreement that
the annual fee remains in return for four years' *gages.*" No one
dared make such a speech, because the king in Council had
broken his word too often in the past.

Judge Tambonneau insinuated that there were "politicians" in the Parlement—that is, men who were collaborating
with D'Hemery and the Council. The notions of politics and
politicians in both Broussel's and Tambonneau's speechs imply
immorality or at least amoral thought and action. In one way,
Tambonneau's remarks were a portent of events to come. Would
the Parlement be required to purge itself of members who
favored D'Hemery and the Council? The pieces of the puzzle
were on the table; those who were wealthy and linked to the
partisans and who had voted and spoken in the Council's favor
could be accused of constituting an immoral political element
within the Parlement. Tambonneau also pointed out that it would
be precipitous to act, since members of the Chamber of the
Edict were not present. This was a special division of the Parle-

ment, composed of both Protestant and Catholic judges, which tried cases involving Protestants who feared that their religious beliefs might prompt discrimination by Catholics. These pieces of the puzzle had not yet been put together, but they were there as early as May 1648.

The very influential President de Mêmes, whose family traditions of learning, probity, and wealth gave him power to sway his colleagues' opinions, favored "union," although he recognized some obstacles to it. At this point, Molé realized that he could never stop his colleagues from voting for "union," once de Mêmes and Broussel had come down in its favor. He maneuvered shallowly in stormy waters, saying that the Parlement ought to recall that there were other parlements in the realm, that indeed it should reflect on how a union with the other superior courts of Paris would affect their relations with these provincial parlements. There is no evidence to suggest that Molé's argument carried the slightest bit of weight with his colleagues. The Parlement solemnly voted a "law of Union" on 13 May 1648. The action came as a severe shock to D'Hemery and probably to Mazarin. Had the two men believed that rivalries among the various courts would always permit them to divide and rule? They were failing to assess the growing Robe solidarity that had been prompted by the massive office sales, the forced loans, and the cancelled *gages*. Anne remarked in a shrill voice: "They [the judges] are trying to make a republic in a monarchy."

During the last weeks of May, the Council took up arms against the judges. In an obvious attempt to get some of the leading activists out of the city, it dispatched several of the masters of requests on missions in the provinces. Chancellor Séguier scurried about in meetings with various judges, first trying to stop a favorable vote on the "union" and then trying to convince the judges to revoke it. President Blancmesnil, of the Inquests, had either taken to reading the registers of the Parlement himself or was having his young clerks do so; for he reported that in 1594 and again in 1597 deputies from the four supreme courts had met together to discuss public affairs. For absolutizing judges who remembered their history, these precedents must have been a nightmare: these had been years of division, revolution, and civil war. Further research revealed that deputies had also assembled in 1618, that time in the context of a scrap with the Council over the renewal of the annual fee. There were indeed scenarios or patterns of push and shove in the struggles between the judges and the Council, and awareness of earlier struggles may have heartened the judges and strengthened them to go on.

Chancellor Séguier would sometimes tell officials he was receiving news about the terrible turn of events in England, where royal authority had so recently collapsed. There is no doubt that these bitter lessons about English politics were designed to sober his listeners and make them back away from "union." Omer Talon favored "union," despite the fact that his official duties as advocate general forced him to stay on the sidelines. He wanted Anne to be informed about the precedents that Blancmesnil had found, and when he finally reported them to her he stressed how the Parlement's authority helped maintain order in the realm.

Poor Chancellor Séguier! When informed of the meetings in 1594 and 1597, he could only reply that he was familiar with these precedents and that the meetings in question had not been held against the express command of His Majesty, Henry IV. He also pointed out that delegates may have met before—indeed, there were precedents for such meetings—but that never before had an Act of Union been signed.

As a result of the Act of Union, the Council promulgated a royal edict revoking the annual fee for the judges of the sovereign courts. The councillors were eager to promulgate an act nullifying the Parlement's Act of Union but hesitated to do so for the moment, preferring direct pressure (in the form of cancelled inheritability of office) to a showdown over which body could abrogate which royal acts. And since the Council had, after all, promulgated the first annual fee act, it could, it claimed, now abrogate it.

Then a rumor began to circulate to the effect that several treasurers of France had been arrested and put in the Bastille. These officials had been behaving like the masters of requests until that point—that is, they had been on strike and had met sporadically to maintain their solidarity in opposition to the new offices and the cancelled *gages,* both of which they had experienced in recent years. The treasurers of France were very prestigious officials and should in no way be confused with the *partisans* or other individuals vaguely but powerfully castigated as being "in finance." Like the masters of requests, the treasurers were loyal servants of the crown; for decades they had done their best to enforce royal policy in the provinces, only to find themselves recently displaced by the intendants. There was little evidence of corruption in their fiscal operations. There was also very little evidence of their willingness to use military force, imprisonment, and confiscation of furniture to extort taxes from the peasantry. These officials had inherited their administrative routines from the sixteenth century, and there probably was no way they could be brought to use the more coercive tactics that Richelieu and Louis XIII had tolerated in the name of the need to win the war against Spain. Since their prime function was supervising the collection of the *taille*, their duties, and their decision to strike, placed them in the interstices between the royal government and the peasantry.

After writing about their protests to their subordinate colleagues in all the financial offices of the realm, the treasurers sought to come before the Parlement. Having been received, they lodged a "request," that is, a legal act asking the Parlement for its support against the Council and against the use of intendants. Their brief against the intendants was printed and sold throughout Paris in a clear extension of the debate to an ever-increasing number of officials. Before May, the Council had been able to count on carrying on its fights with the parlements of Paris, Aix, Rennes, and to a certain degree Rouen, without fearing that these courts would join in a common front of opposition. By writing to the entire provincial administration, and to areas where there were no parlements, the treasurers of France extended specific terms of protest to the realm as a whole. Up to the time of their appeal, only occasional allusions had been made in the various parlements to the coercive actions of the intendants. Now their criticisms became a slogan that everyone agreed with. In a revolutionary situation, such slogans can suddenly provoke urgent and provocative action.

Was the Council aware of the effects of its policies? These tests of will, and the Council's use of authority, were transforming a congeries of competing and jealous royal officials into a powerful Robe solidarity. The Robe indisputably shared views on property, office, royal service, and family inheritance; and as the old corporate rivalries of the officials were peeled away by fears and anxieties, common action became possible. To be sure, some members of the Robe blindly supported the Council's actions and asserted that this was the only way to uphold royal authority. But by late May thousands of royal officials had rejected this loyalty to the crown and were arguing that by opposing the Council *they* had become the true defenders of royal authority. The king was but a boy; the Council had fallen into the hands of men linked to the *partisans*. Such an idea had begun to appear as early as March and April of 1648; but it did not, of course, square with Gaston d'Orléans' presence in the Council. The authoritarian actions of the Council would continue to be interpreted as caused by the regent's bad temper, triggered by D'Hemery and Séguier, who had learned their odious conduct from Richelieu. But anxiety about offices and *gages* precipitated the Robe into increased solidarity and therefore pressed the Parlement further into opposition.

No one has ever accused Anne of Austria of running from a confrontation. She responded by summoning the entire Parlement to the Palais Royal. The judges disliked the "invitation" because they knew full well that they would once again be dressed down. Blancmesnil argued that they ought politely to decline, but when presented as a motion the suggestion received only seven votes. Instead the justices hit upon the idea of marching to the Palais Royal, in robes and bonnets. Though Parisians were accustomed to witnessing all manner of processions, at this early point a few of them may have wondered why the judges were going fully robed to the Palais Royal. The gesture may have been intended to enhance the judges' prestige, but it also revealed their insecurity. Still more important,their presence in the streets manifested some solidarity with the peo ple of Paris. Before departing—and this decision was very important—the judges agreed *not* to take with them the registers in which the "Act of Union" had been recorded and witnessed by the court recorder.

As soon as the judges reached the Palais Royal, they were asked whether they had brought the "Law of Union." Molé replied, "No." Anne, who was only an antechamber away, quickly met with her councillors and decided that no interview with the Parlement could be held until the document was brought to the Palais Royal. The judges were herded into a small, chairless antechamber, to await the return of the person who had been sent to the Palais de Justice to fetch the register. The situation had become quite ridiculous: a fight over a piece of paper was becoming a distinct possibility. Suddenly Anne and her councillors, shifting tactics once more, requested the judges to enter the throne room. There they found the councillors standing about a seated boy king and his mother. Anne ordered a secretary of state to read the Council's decree declaring the Parlement's Act of Union null and void. Such an impasse no doubt caused mental anguish for all the jurists, regardless of the sides they were taking. The monarchy had gone off-course: one part of the government ought not be obliged to declare that a law promulgated by another part was null and void, for both parts, indeed *all* parts, were acting in the king's name. Was the king's authority higher or greater in the regency council than it was in his Parlement? The old attitudes about hierarchy held by the various segments of the royal government were being challenged on every front; the intendants were acting over the heads of provincial parlements and treasurers of France; the law courts had joined in an act of union; and now it no longer seemed clear that a few men and the Regent could take actions in the name of a boy king, in ways that were provoking opposition throughout the realm.

Talon hoped that the Parlement would find a "middle way." Oblique procedures existed by which the Parlement could resist the Council. But how could it do so squarely and categorically, against the Council's explicit orders? He recognized that historically the Council had powers that he wished the Parlement possessed. And, as always, Talon feared an "emotional upset in the peoples' minds," akin to the upset that had occurred in the terrible crisis of 1588. He was certainly atypical of governmental officials, because—historically, logically, and juridically—he tried hard to understand what was happening in France in 1648. The majority of judges continued voting with their feet in the Parlement, expressing Robe opposition almost without knowing how it could be perceived as "anti-royal." The clarity of vision of a few analysts such as Talon should not distort our understanding of the crisis, else we lose the vagueness and confusion that compelled the judges on. Mazarin knew full well that Talon was pursuing a "middle way" and that he might influence Parlement; and for this reason he tried to be candid with Talon and bring him into his confidence about diplomatic negotiations and about the difficulties he was encountering in keeping Gaston and Condé satisfied with their pensions and offices. On one occasion Mazarin went too far, from Talon's point of view, when he casually mentioned that the Council had, that very morning, decided to give Talon's brother an abbey. Without a moment's hesitation, Talon declined the abbey. He recognized the gesture for what it was, an attempt to soften his opposition to some of the Council's conduct.

The conduct that appalled men of Talon's stamp were the arrests and exiling of judges simply because they seemed to be leading the opposition. Royal decrees forbidding the courts to meet were considered so ridiculous that the judges invariably ignored them.

On 5 June 1648, five treasurers of France were imprisoned, for the Council still believed that this form of intimidation would work. Late one night someone sneaked around the Pont Neuf and, sounding threats in the very heart of the city, condemned the regent's favorite minister to death if the copies of the Act of Union were not returned. Were the Parisians recalling the fate of Concini, whose body they had unearthed, dismembered, and burned in 1617? We have no way of knowing. But someone found a copy of Concini's death sentence for treason, had it reprinted, and glued it to walls throughout the city, openly suggesting that Cardinal Mazarin deserved the same fate. Another Italian had somehow captured control of the Council. If he were removed from power, would not the confrontation between the Council and Parlement subside?

FOUR

The King's Council:
From Absolute Power to Brittle
Authoritarianism

URING the nine weeks that separated the confrontation
at the Palais Royal over the Act of Union of 13 May
and the Day of the Barricades of late August 1648,
the Council's power to govern the realm diminished with astonishing rapidity. An almost unreal, or phony, state of affairs had
developed by late June and would last for several months. The
Council continued to promulgate royal decrees, and the chancellor would affix his seal to them, making them the law of the
realm. On the surface, nothing seemed to have changed; but in
reality the Council was merely approving texts submitted to it
that indirectly emanated from either the St. Louis Chamber, via
the Parlement, or from conferences at the Luxembourg Palace
held on Gaston's initiative. The new legislation was entirely and
completely legal. To a foreign observer uninformed about recent
events, the French government would therefore have seemed
stable and working smoothly.

The only confrontation arose over whether the delegates
from the various superior courts who assembled in the St. Louis
Chamber would cease their meetings, as Anne and the Council
had insisted. Indeed, numerous concessions were wrung out of
the Council, in return for the Parlement's promises to cease all
assemblies other than routine legal business. But the judges broke
their word and continued to meet; circumstances had changed,
they argued, so these meetings were necessary. More fundamentally, the Parlement, unlike the English Parliament, believed

in its solemn right to assemble whenever it chose, and to deliberate on any subject it wished, except, perhaps, foreign policy. Anne could neither prorogue Parlement nor summarily close it, as the English sovereigns did, or tried to do, with Parliament—until the Revolution broke out in England.

In the Luxembourg Conferences that were held under Gaston d'Orléans' aegis during the summer of 1648, the justices were informed in great detail about the dire state of royal finances. When the judges arrived at the Luxembourg Palace, they were ushered into the gallery, at the end of which stood a table covered with an Oriental rug. Small folding stools had been set up for them, while Gaston had an armchair and the other councillors chairs. The judges did not fear arrest. Strong, almost paternal feelings of affection linked some of the older presidents to Gaston d'Orléans. This younger son of Henry IV had committed the crime of treason during plots to change his brother's policies; but, as is often the case in quarrels between brothers—especially brothers of royal blood—right and wrong had not always been clear in those terrible trials that Louis XIII had brought before the Parlement. The judges also were eager to find a compromise solution for the conflict with the Council. Thus, in June 1648, Gaston had the opportunity to change the direction of the highest level of government. Gaston insisted that the judges keep their hats on before him, an explicit signal of his respect for them and his willingness to confer with them. The prince opened the conference on a purely personal note so characteristic of princes who have spent their entire lives in the labyrinth of court conflicts. The queen had been "worrying," he observed, as a result of the clash with the Parlement, and this was not good for her health.

Gaston encouraged the judges to make proposals for meeting the crisis and promised that the Council would weigh their advice seriously. Confronted with the mass of figures about one account or another, the judges faltered. Some of them may have lacked experience in complex budgetary matters; others may have been made to feel uneasy about the discussions over the tax contracts. The Council, or at least some of the councillors, had made a sincere attempt to drive a hard bargain when the collection of the king's revenues had been put up for auction. Thus the judges attending the Luxembourg Conferences peered for the first time into the abyss of wartime bankruptcy. The

costs of each military effort were staggering, and the deliberations of the Parlement made it clear that some of the judges
were naive and that others possessed only a rudimentary
knowledge about financial issues affecting the monarchy's power
to carry on the war.

True, the judges had only been exhorted to approve new
revenue-raising measures; they had never really been given the
facts about the disastrous condition of the royal treasury. To
his credit, Richelieu had been amazingly candid about both diplomatic and financial conditions during the late 1630s. Though
he had defied the judges to meddle in any way with foreign and
fiscal affairs, he had at least kept them informed. Ten years had
passed since the Parlement had been given any solid figures;
and now, having suddenly been provided with the terrible facts,
they were being asked to propose a solution.

In revolutionary movements, one party or another usually
offers, stridently and forcefully, a number of simple solutions
to complex problems. The Fronde was no exception. The Frondeur judges saw the king's financial collapse as resulting from
theft, fraud, and corruption within the Council, all of which
had benefited such superintendents of finance as D'Hemery and,
of course, the "snakes" who held both the royal debt and the
tax-collecting contracts. The simple solution to the kingdom's
financial problems lay in confiscating the property of the *partisans* and in clapping these financiers in prison. Would this not,
in itself, provide sufficient funds? The Frondeur judges reached
this conclusion despite the hard facts about the costs of the war.
The sums paid out were enormous. The judges simply could
not believe that money was lacking; it must simply be going to
the wrong place, that is, to the rural castles and country estates
being built by the *partisans*, rather than to the army. And it was
also apparent that taxes had been far too high; the rebellions
in the provinces and, as the judges said, the "impoverishment
of the people" meant that higher taxes were not the answer.

When the presidents returned to the Great Chamber of
the Parlement after the first Luxembourg Conference, they had
the makings of a compromise that seemed simple enough. The
Parlement had merely to send deputies to the queen mother to
express their good intentions and loyalty. Molé soon discovered, however, that the Parlement had grown much more radical as a result of the Luxembourg Conference. Only after a

fairly long deliberation did the judges accept motions to thank Gaston for his initiative and to send deputies to Anne. They interpreted Gaston's initiative in the conference as weakening the Council's power.

Through the King's Men *(gens du roi)*, Anne eventually informed the Parlement that she found it "good" for delegates from all the sovereign courts to meet in the St. Louis Chamber. She accepted the Act of Union and ordered the decree abrogating it revoked. She also wished the Parlement to "consider the fact that the king's army was on the frontier and in the presence of an enemy army only two hours away . . . and that armies cannot survive without money." Gaston had quietly promised the Parlement these concessions in return for their assurance of good intentions and loyalty. Imprisoned royal officials were also freed.

No minutes of meetings of the Council of State (or, more specifically, a subdivision known as the Conseil d'en Haut) were taken during the late 1640s. This council (composed of Anne, Mazarin, Condé, D'Hemery, and Séguier) met several times a day in periods of crisis. And because all its members except Condé were near at hand, we have no correspondence reporting in detail the positions various councillors took during their meetings with Anne. Although the surviving letters from Mazarin to Condé are very interesting, they unfortunately do not include detailed analyses of the various options pursued by the Council.

Gossip circulated about these meetings, of course, mostly to the effect that Anne had pressed her ministers to approve the use of force against the judges. Gossip may be accurate; or it may be false. Cardinal Mazarin's influence over Anne seems to have grown stronger than ever, but this should not be interpreted as the reason for the compromise that he and Gaston worked out with the judges at the Luxembourg Palace. The clash at the Palais Royal that was triggered by the Act of Union had to be answered in some way, and Gaston did just that. The reasons behind Anne's and Mazarin's acceptance of the prince's proposal were twofold. First, something had to be done to reach an accommodation with the Parlement. Second, at the end of the summer-autumn military campaign, or by the early winter of 1649 at the latest, the Council could order the army to move south, toward Paris, to clip the Parlement's wings by a show of force. Anne's acceptance of a compromise with the Parlement was insincere; nor would she accept in good faith any of the reform legislation coming from the St. Louis Chamber and from subsequent conferences held at the Luxembourg Palace over the next few months.

This is one more reason for describing the political situation after mid-June 1649 as unreal, or phony. Expressions of compromise and affection flowed from both parties, but only the naive believed them. The key principle of royal authority that Anne and her councillors always sought to preserve was the power to repudiate past agreements. The Council held that the king was bound neither by the laws of his ancestors nor by his own. Thus, when the time was ripe, the decrees so carefully drawn up during the summer of 1648 and promulgated with the royal seal could simply be torn up. Mazarin and Anne viewed the situation in the same way. Did the Council's acceptance of the Act of Union therefore count for all that much? Some of the judges in the Parlement perhaps believed that a change of heart had occurred. The majority, however, were entirely capable of suspecting that the Council would not so easily give up its centuries-long defense of royal authority as defined by its power to ignore earlier contractual agreements. For that reason the majority, while saying one thing and emphasizing their loyalty and good intentions, were quite willing to act quite differently.

Was Gaston sincere? In traditional societies, powerful princes might feel affection for individuals; they might understand questions of principle such as royal authority and "constitutionality," but they rarely acted on them. Gaston watched out carefully for his own interests (he received over 1,000,000 *livres* from the royal treasury in 1648), yet at the same time he probably was genuine in his quest for harmony within the realm. The prince was loyal to his sister-in-law; and because she seemed to trust Mazarin and needed him if she was to govern, Gaston cooperated with the Italian. But none of this implied that the shrill talk about the undermining of royal authority influenced Gaston in one way or another.

And lest we think that Gaston's initiative derived in some way from his heritage as an opponent of arbitrarily used power, it is important to observe that it was triggered by the head-on collision between the Parlement and the Council. Something had to give. The dynamics of confrontation between institutions competing for power at the highest levels of government necessitated Gaston's action. The standoff between the Parlement and the Council could not continue; one side or another must either admit defeat or resort to force. Gaston's initiative came almost as part of the process of confrontation itself, and the conferences encouraged some of the judges in the Parlement to explore issues that they had hitherto mentioned only in passing. Indeed, viewing the first conference at the Luxembourg as a victory for the Parlement, some judges escalated their demands.

The participants in the revolutionary moment that would occur only a few months later were now in place: the Council, the Parlement, and the people of Paris. The new structures for action had been established with little discussion and certainly without the intention of those who created them. It will be very exciting to observe how these apparently minor shifts—a few meetings in the St. Louis Chamber, a procession to the Palais Royal, a conference at the Luxembourg—unleashed a revolutionary moment.

Fear of a popular upheaval was shared by both the councillors and the Parlement, but owing to that fear, neither would give in to the other. A revolutionary moment may occur at any time, once the huge power blocs in the state and society become aware of their interests and begin to watch each other. No observer at the time could quite state the obvious, as we can from hindsight: that the Council had the army behind it, and the Parlement was backed by the people of Paris. The new structures for action would be productive of new clashes between the Council and the Parlement.

St. John's Day, celebrated on 23 June, was one of the greatest and oldest of French popular festivals. At dusk, great bonfires were always lighted, and individuals bearing the saint's name would place lighted candles in the windows to honor their patron. The official bonfire of the city of Paris was lighted on the Grève, the famous public square in front of the Hôtel de Ville. Dressed in splendid laces and silks, Louis XIV and Anne, accompanied by their court and their guards, made their way to the Grève to light the bonfire. Anne made a special point of talking with some of the leading officials of the Six Corps of Merchants and assured them that interest on government bonds would be paid.

It was a ceremony like so many other ceremonies in a traditional society. But the atmosphere of the St. John's bonfire of 1648 was particularly buoyant. Anne and her councillors had deigned to participate and had been especially cordial toward the merchants. Indeed, the duel for the support of the people of Paris had already begun. And like the majority of the judges in the Parlement, the merchants of Paris would avoid applying logic to the analysis of political authority. They basked in the pleasure of the royal compliment and noted the promise that interest would be paid on government bonds. Could the Parlement offer the same assurances? What is striking about traditional societies on the eve of revolution is their attention to hard economic issues and their concern about preserving property. The ceremony at the Grève, and the silken garb of the court, appear to have aroused strong feelings of love and a willingness to sacrifice.

By mid-June, the new structures for action were in place. Should further confrontations take place between the Parlement and the Council, the results were predictable. The Council would resort to military force, and the people of Paris would lend even stronger and potentially coercive support to the Parlement. Historians have often debated the question of *when* the Fronde began. The answer lies in identifying the time when certain actions would immediately and powerfully prompt other actions. This does not mean, of course, that a revolutionary moment was inevitable by mid-June of 1648. Nor can the appearance of the new structures of action be said to be revolutionary in itself and certain to decrease the Council's power by their mere existence. Quite the contrary. Ironically, an increase in the Council's strength, or presumed strength, would set things off. A military victory over the Spanish at Lens brought the new structure of action into play in just the ways we have observed. But before we examine the resort to physical force, we must look at the principal issues debated during the summer of 1648.

I. Dismantling the Richelieu State

In the days immediately following Anne's acceptance of the Act of Union, the parlementaires meeting in the St. Louis Chamber began the task of dismantling the state, or para-state, created by Richelieu and Louis XIII. The meeting of 30 June had something jubilant about it; a dike of obstructions raised by the Council had given way, and the St. Louis Chamber worked very quickly over the next few days. The principal articles put to the Parlement were:

1. provincial intendancies and other officials acting by special commissions that had not been verified by the Parlement would be revoked;

2. the *taille* would be collected by officials established for that purpose (the *élus* and the treasurers), and not by tax farmers;

3. the *taille* would be reduced by one-eighth for the year 1648;

4. all *tailles* in arrears would be cancelled;

5. no subject of the king, regardless of his status, would be kept in prison more than twenty-four hours without being brought before an appropriate judge;

6. there would be no reduction in the *gages* paid royal officials; and

7. payments on royal bonds would continue.

Still other proposals were discussed in the St. Louis Chamber and would be modified by the chamber itself in the course of its move toward increasingly radical measures, and by the Parlement as well. The first measure—the abolition of the intendants—was deemed crucial. It was in the air in all the sovereign courts by late June. By 4 July, the Parlement took the preliminary step of asking the queen to revoke the intendants. Observers from both sides were astonished at the Parlement's speed on this issue, and by the Council's virtual collapse.

As with all other issues, backing and filling took place over the revocation of the intendants. Once a vote had been taken, the Parlement did not traditionally drop an issue; a second or even a third round of debates and votes on the same question could occur if the opponents had been particularly strong or if the act was vague about dates and implementation.

In July, the Parlement assumed the characteristics of a revolutionary assembly. Superficially it seemed to be its staid old self, but the dynamics of a popular assembly gained strength during frequent meetings and intense debate. The customary holiday breaks were ignored, and the rules ending sessions at ten in the morning were sidestepped, if not actually broken. There was a dramatic rise in the number of judges wishing to speak. The Parlement usually relied on the report made by the "reporter," a colleague in charge of presenting a case to a chamber of the court, and would reach its decisions after a few clarifying questions. In July 1648 the judges began to talk on and on, and no one was quite sure what topic was being discussed, or whether specific proposals were being presented before the Great Chamber. As this flood of words poured out, ever more fundamental issues about the nature of politics and society began to be raised. Once this occurred, still more discussion was, of course, required. The tissue of attitudes and assumptions that had characterized the routine life of the Parlement was suddenly being questioned and, in some instances, attacked.

In the deliberations over the revocation of the intendants, a consensus quickly formed favoring their recall; but there was strong disagreement over how this could best be done. The dean of the Parlement—that is, the most senior member—boasted the privilege of giving his opinion first; and on this issue he stated that though he certainly believed that the intendants were corrupt, he favored leaving the necessary reforms to the queen. Broussel made a long speech against the intendants, critizing their luxurious life-style in the provinces. Why, they lived like the great aristocrats! This did not mean, of course, that Broussel was attacking the way great aristocrats lived. (We are not in 1790.) Rather, he criticized the pretentiousness and luxuriousness of socially middle-ranking men who, thanks to corruption, were living on a level far above that appropriate for their status. We shall have numerous occasions to observe how the Fronde of the Parlement came to be articulated in a classical republican ideology about property, power, and the way money corrupts the ruling elite.

Insecurity about their own social status in a still aristocratic society was the source for a powerful Robe weapon against both the members of the Council and the tax farmers. The intendants were presumed by the judges to be clients of the council members. Some judges sought to understand what the intendants were doing to destroy the balance of force within the monarchy. Pithou, for example, presented a history of the arbitrariness of certain officials acting in the king's name down through the centuries. Starting with the *misi dominici* under the Carolingians, these officials had been a burden on the people and had abused them, so it was time to rid the monarchy of these "melancholic and harsh" men who oppressed the people.

Then, leaving the topic at hand, one judge rose to announce that he could name four judges in the Great Chamber who had been approached about bribes in return for voting to maintain the intendants. He ended by hoping aloud that his colleagues would join him in imploring the king to cease attempting to bribe the judges in return for votes. This plea was seconded by another judge, who, in a moment of self-pity and confessional power-seeking, added that he had never personally taken any money from the king beyond his *gages*. The judges who made such confessions enhanced their power within the Parlement; those who did not eventually felt the eyes of the former trained upon them, as if sitting in silence were evidence of their guilt. The Parlement was becoming an excited forum for deliberation; and as votes were often close, the inevitable tactics for attacking subgroups or individual members came into play. After long hours of speeches about the intendants, two proposals finally came up for a vote: (1) the Parlement should make remonstrances to the queen about the intendants' conduct; and (2) the Parlement should act to revoke all officials serving by royal commissions that had not been approved by the Parlement. The second proposal was by far the more radical, not only in regard to the intendants, but also in general, because parlementary approval would curb the Council's powers to initiate administrative and judicial changes in the realm. The second proposal also effectively tied the Parlement of Paris to the demand being made by the other Parlements of the realm, namely that Parlements be given power to prevent the Council from appointing officials to serve in a given jurisdiction without the approval of the local Parlement. The second proposal passed 106 to 66.

Still more radical judges began to call for the publication of the acts of Parlement and their distribution in printed form to every parish within the court's jurisdiction. The sense of urgency increased: the Parlement must act quickly in order to prevent a disaster. Small clusters of peasant protesters who had come in from the country gathered at the door of the Palais de Justice off and on during July. Gaston d'Orléans was almost assailed by protesting women as he entered the Parlement, but it is difficult to determine whether the urgency felt by the governing elites was the result of fears of violence from the population, or stemmed from a deep, collective fear prompted by the judges' obsessions about property and status rather than from any precise perception of events in the countryside or in the streets of Paris. The presence of small groups of protesters angrily shouting and making threats outside the room where an assembly was conducting a heated debate about property issues may have had a very disquieting effect.

On the morning of 7 July, the judges learned that Gaston d'Orléans had come to the upper chapel of the Sainte Chapelle (just adjoining the Great Chamber) and sought to attend the Parlement. Several presidents rushed to meet him and escort him to the high bench reserved for princes of the blood, dukes, and peers. After a few opening remarks, the prince made it clear that he had come to ask the Parlement to postpone enacting the revocation of the intendants. Having made it clear that the act itself met with his approval, he added that given the dire conditions of the royal finances and the already tense situation in the provinces, it would be best to postpone this revocation until things had calmed down. Some judges, at first very obliquely and then with increasing clarity and explicitness, argued in favor of the immediate revocation of the intendants, regardless of Gaston's statement. A see-saw deliberation over the intendants began to develop. The king's uncle realized that he would be unable to delay implementation of the act for more than a few days. He then called for another conference at the Luxembourg and in effect defied the judges to implement the revocation while this conference was being held. Gaston still exerted a great deal of influence over the Parlement; the judges had little choice but to accept his proposal.

After many smaller preliminary meetings in the Parlement, however, it was decided that this time the presidents attending the Luxembourg Conferences should be accompanied by councillors and by representatives of the other sovereign courts. Gaston could easily understand what was happening here: he was creating another body that would be increasingly difficult to control. Yet he could see no other alternative, for the Parlement itself was out of control. A general sense of the gravity of the situation developed. We do not know for certain that judges who were meeting in the St. Louis Chamber now sought to attend the Luxembourg Conferences as well. But it is significant that Gaston had to stipulate that no member of the sovereign courts currently serving in the St. Louis Chamber could attend the conferences being held at his residence—a pretty good sign that Frondeur judges were becoming known and that measures were being taken to curb their influence. To enhance the chance for a compromise, Gaston also ruled the exclusion of judges known to be favorable to the Council. This was not the last time the prince would seek a *via media* and fail.

Having spent a part of the initial session at the Luxembourg reviewing the issues, Gaston realized that the body of judges facing him was more determined than ever to revoke the intendants at once. So he rose and announced that they would reconvene some days hence, on 10 July. The judges may have been surprised by his move, but they had already lost some of their awe at being in the presence of this prince and being permitted to glimpse the splendors of his palace. Gaston wanted to gain time. He was not the first manager for the crown—for that was the role that Gaston was in effect playing at that moment—who had sought to win precious hours or an overnight lull and thus give the Council time to put together the changes, the concessions, or the dramatic announcement that would turn the Parlement around. The descent into revolution, however, had begun.

As early as the confrontation over the Act of Union, Superintendant of Finances D'Hemery, who had been in charge of applying the pressure on the Parlement, showed signs of losing his nerve. One night he frantically sought a meeting with Talon and in an abrupt about-face attempted to change the Council's policy of intimidation. Michel Le Tellier, a young secretary of state, informed D'Hemery on 9 July that the queen requested him to leave the capital immediately. The news of D'Hemery's disgrace was received with jubilation by the radical judges of the Parlement—and perhaps by the conservative ones as well, for no one in the Parlement had supported the use of coercion to make the Parlement approve the new masters of requests. With D'Hemery's disgrace a policy of intimidation and arrests was, it seemed, abandoned.

The situation for young President Thoré, D'Hemery's son, having become intolerable in the Parlement, he too withdrew to private life. D'Hemery had been carrying out time-honored policies to "bring the Parlement to heel." They had worked under Richelieu and Louis XIII, but times had changed. Did the disgrace result from D'Hemery's failure of nerve? Men involved in intense political conflict may crack (as Richelieu almost did in 1636), or they may suddenly become convinced that the policies they have sought to carry out are fundamentally wrong. The question cannot be answered at this point, but raising it provides a clue to the thinking of the council members.

For the time being at least, no more dramatic confrontations would take place between the queen and the Parlement. They had ended in standoffs, not in the resolution of the issues at hand. Chancellor Séguier's endless thundering about royal authority had lost him his credibility in the Parlement. Mazarin still wished to remain in the shadows, as always, negotiating quietly and exhorting such men as Talon and First President Molé to keep up their fight to maintain the Council's power. But as a result of the Luxembourg Conferences, Gaston d'Orléans held the power to initiate a resolution in the conflict between the Council and the Parlement. The great liability at this point was, of course, D'Hemery. After his disgrace, the Council's policies became increasingly erratic. It would veer from conciliation, or what on the surface appeared to be conciliation, to intimidation or coercion, using arrests and threatening military force. The Council's balance wheel seemed to come off, at roughly the time of D'Hemery's disgrace, just when the Parlement was becoming a radical assembly where everyone agreed about membership and the right of each member to cast one vote.

D'Hemery's successor as superintendent of finances was Marshal de La Meilleraie. This was not the first time the crown had turned to a military man to fill that office in time of crisis. La Meilleraie was known not only for his firmness but for the way he had intimidated the Parlement of Brittany during conflicts over new offices being created in that province. He was Richelieu's relative and was tied to all the late minister's clients and relatives, who had remained in their high positions after the cardinal's death. One observer concluded that La Meilleraie might be harsher and more coercive in dealing with the Parlement than his predecessor had been. Still, D'Hemery was gone, and some found it more pleasant to see a hated individual leave in disgrace than to imagine that his successor might be worse.

The Council also appointed two directors of finance to "help" La Meilleraie. Both came from prominent Robe families that were noted, at least in recent times, for their probity in financial affairs. Would the little "understandings" between the superintendent and the *partisans,* which had led to so much corruption involving councillors and tax farmers, continue? With Robe families countersigning La Meilleraie's orders, the cat seemed to have been belled before she started to hunt.

The second Luxembourg Conference, which was part of a series that began in July 1648, opened on schedule on 10 July, with La Meilleraie attending. Lacking the time to learn about the fiscal situation, he asked Tubeuf, an old-line administrator in the treasury, to report to the judges. As a maze of figures and accounts were read aloud, the judges' minds wandered. Some of them may have realized for the first time that the French state was bankrupt. Their lack of expertise in financial administration also made them prone to look for simple solutions for the problems at hand. Hours and hours spent poring over figures—chiefly debts and revenues already borrowed against—gave the Luxembourg Conference a quality that must have seemed unreal to the parlementaires. In their deliberations they were accustomed to using figures for a rhetorical effect. For example, Broussel asserted at the time of the second Luxembourg Conference that the crown had "eaten up" 200 million *livres* during the past twenty-five years, and that much of this money had come from tax-paying families. The Parlement felt comfortable with figures of this sort—almost pulled out of the air—and would talk passionately about the potential role their body could play in reforming the fiscal administration of the realm. When confronted with real figures, however, they turned away or ceased listening. The Robe's attitudes toward money and fiscal administration, like their attitudes toward tax farmers, remained fixed in a moral and familial context. They felt a sort of taboo about focusing on the fiscal administration, and this despite the fact that they could be excessively candid about such family matters as marriage negotiations and property evaluations. And of course precise knowledge of the bankruptcy facing the crown sustained the Council's contention, which Gaston now frequently repeated: it was time for the rich parlementary families to contribute to the war effort by approving the creation of new offices.

In the Great Chamber the deliberations turned to reducing the *taille*. A one-eighth reduction had initially been mentioned, and this seemed to have the approval of the St. Louis Chamber; but by the time the subject came up before the Parlement—that is, in the Great Chamber—a strong party favoring a one-fourth rebate had taken shape. The dean opened the deliberation and spoke in support of a rebate of this magnitude. The reasons behind this shift merit more research; but the known facts make it appear that La Meilleraie's first general attempt to come to terms with the tax farmers and head off bankruptcy in this way had ended in his being forced to make further concessions in the form of higher interest rates on loans from the snakes. When the judges in the Parlement learned this, they pressed for a larger reduction in the *taille*.

II. Descent into Revolution

In the deliberations over the *taille,* phrases about the need to "relieve the people" were heard again and again, and with ever-increasing emotional intensity. President Novion was not alone when he stated, as a fact, that lowering taxes on the people was carrying out God's work in the realm. The mid-July meetings in the Great Chamber would be critical for the stability of France, and all the participants knew it. The people of Paris watched and listened to the Parlement. So did the Council. Proposals continued to flow from the sessions being held in the St. Louis Chamber, and discussions with Gaston continued at the Luxembourg Palace. An abrupt shift in the power to govern France could occur at any moment.

Until then, these exchanges had been sober and just deliberations, not debates; but throughout July the judges sometimes ended up shouting at one another. Speeches would be interrupted by hissing and by stamping feet. It was no longer possible to state the absolutist principles so dear to Richelieu, or to defend the intendants on the grounds that they were loyal officials who were carrying out the orders of the king and the Council. Entire approaches to discussing political action had to be abandoned. Intimidated and afraid of being ridiculed by their colleagues, judges who supported Richelieu's principles were forced into silence.

The presidents, especially those sitting in the Great Chamber, occasionally tried to reassert their control over debate and agenda; but the other judges ignored them or found some way to make concessions. Whenever the presidents of the Great Chamber refused to convoke a general assembly of the Parlement, a block of radical judges would simply *occupy* their accustomed seats in that chamber. As a result, the presidents often refused to preside and the whole Parlement would sit silently, in their robes, staring one another down hour after hour, day after day, until the presidents gave in. Divisions did not occur entirely according to age and rank, in themselves two quite distinct divisions. Some presidents were in fact quite young, indeed as young as the councillors, that is, the more junior judges in the Inquests, which was reputedly the radical center of the Parlement. On every close ballot, at least one senior councillor or president always seems to have joined the radical younger judges. There was no party discipline, and the independence of each member was at least officially maintained. In the balloting over the *taille*, which pitted a one-eighth reduction against a one-fourth reduction, the Parlement divided 87 to 87. In subsequent discussions and votes, Gaston finally convinced some of them to change their position, permitting the one-eighth cut to win, 89 to 85. The victory proved to be pyrrhic. Those delegates to the Great Chamber who had espoused the losing position simply brought the issue up a few days later during the Luxembourg Conferences.

When divisions were this close, attempts to denigrate the opposition were inevitable, first taking the form of oblique allusions to supporting the Council and the intendants through personal interest, and then escalating to insinuations about bribes or about family ties to tax farmers. Epithets of this sort increased the Robe obsession with the classical republican thought about the relationship between money and independence. Any judge who sincerely believed in the Richelieu state, or who believed that the intendants were necessary or that the peasantry really could and therefore must pay the *taille*, was accused of family involvement with the tax farmers. In moments of heated debate, some judges publicly expressed regret that their father or uncle had married the daughter of a *partisan* or a governmental financial officer. Vulnerability of this sort could not be overcome, and it would silence a fairly large segment of the pro-

Council members of the Parlement. In his advice to his son, the ailing Omer Talon remarked that his father had told him never to arrange a marriage between a Talon and a family tainted by service in the royal finances. On his deathbed in 1652, Talon now gave the same advice to his son, having first observed that family ties of this sort had rendered a portion of the Parlement impotent during the late 1640s.

If not driven to silence, the tainted judges attempted to prove their detachment from sordid financial dealings by increasingly radical leadership. The Le Coigneux, father and son, were both in the Parlement thanks not only to Gaston's patronage but also to immense dowries brought by tax-farming brides, which had permitted the men to purchase offices, among them a presidency. We should not be surprised to find the senior Le Coigneux leading the fight to revoke the intendants and even calling for a special judicial chamber to prosecute the tax farmers for peculation. With great feeling and with sighs of pious despair, Le Coigneux would prayerfully repeat: "We need to give the people relief." Needless to say, his colleagues aggressively pointed out this president's inconsistency: how could he profit from the wealth of tax farmers yet call for their prosecution? His projection of a certain lack of self-esteem, which took the form of appeals for radical reform, permitted Le Coigneux to play a considerable role throughout the summer of 1648. And his proposals were no more consistent than those of his patron, Gaston.

On 23 July, President Blancmesnil carried the allusions to money and to tax farmers a step farther. He solemnly asked those members of the Parlement who were in any way involved in the king's debts or in their administration to abstain from debating and voting. An abstention of this sort, he asserted, had occurred in 1597. Was Blancmesnil thinking of his colleagues who had actually participated in the tax-farming administration? Or was he including those who had lent the crown money through the tax farmers? Strong objections to Blancmesnil's proposal resounded in the Great Chamber, and President de Mêmes ironically observed that if his colleague was referring to persons who had lent at high interest, he was asking two-thirds of the Parlement to disqualify themselves.

First President Molé made a compromise ruling: judges who had invested money in loans to the crown would not automatically be disqualified, but they could voluntarily absent them-selves. At this point, the Parlement was close to a purge, which was nonetheless avoided when some forty or fifty councillers voluntarily withdrew from the following day's debate.

On 12 July 1648, some prisoners "escaped" from the Con-ciergerie. It was difficult for persons worried about the possible outbreak of riots and violence to accept the excuse that the escape had occurred without the jailers' complicity. Next, a peasant came to the St. Louis Chamber offering to make a deposition about the place where one tax farmer had buried his silver dishes. Some of the judges eagerly pressed to have his testimony recorded and to send officials to dig for the buried treasure. Calls for speedier action became increasingly frequent. Indeed, judges who made lengthy speeches were accused of slowing down the Parlement and impeding it from giving "relief to the peo-ple."

Judge Boullanger, one of the older members of the court, made a long speech that rambled on far longer than the more radical judges could bear. As Boullanger reached his perora-tion—a quote from Cicero about how "Italy would not be des-poiled"—the younger judges burst out laughing. Someone had turned the Latin words around and had whispered that the "spoils were going to Italy," an allusion to the belief that Maza-rin had been sending money to his native land. As the old judge tried to shout down his hecklers, he collapsed in the arms of a nearby colleague, who barely had time to make a sign of the cross over him before he breathed his last. Deliberations in the Great Chamber ceased for the day.

The incident is particularly interesting because it provides evidence that as early as mid-July hostility toward Mazarin lay just beneath the surface of parlementaire debate. The terms for an attack on the cardinal were already familiar. A play on words in any political assembly may indicate a great deal about the terms for future radical directions. Judge Pithou had already asked whether or not Particelli D'Hemery had sent huge sums of money to Italy. Over the centuries the Parlement had expe-rienced numerous bouts of xenophobia about Italians, partic-ularly when these Italians were involved with money. The Particellis had left Italy a century earlier and now considered themselves French; yet in the minds of some of the radical judges the family name revealed the man's "true" origins: "common, base, and filthy money." For judges such as Pithou, who saw the intendants as originating from a "corruption beginning under the Carolingians," a century of residence in France did not suffice to remove the stigma of Italian blood. Only a few days earlier, when two judges had sought to defend the intendants against these charges of "corruption," Pithou had retorted that he was not surprised to hear the intendants defended by the two judges in question. Were they not going to inherit a great deal of money from tax-farmer relatives? The knotty web of radical ideas about corruption, tax farming, Italians, intendants, and general moral depravity would eventually tighten in the overt attack against Mazarin; but all these themes appeared as early as the debate over the intendants.

For the rest of July 1648, and indeed throughout August, September, and October, the three centers of debate—the Great Chamber, the St. Louis Chamber, and the Luxembourg Conferences—continued to work on legislation to "restore public order." A confusing but nonetheless predictable pattern developed in the debates and proposals. The radical reform proposals coming from the St. Louis Chamber were first modified in the Great Chamber and then modified again in the course of the conferences being held with Gaston d'Orléans at the Luxembourg. To be sure, the judges sitting in the Great Chamber clashed with the representatives attending the Luxembourg Conferences. The key figure attempting to brake reform was now Gaston, and the more he sought to modify radical legislation, the more his prestige in the Great Chamber declined. He also experienced great difficulty in modifying proposals at the Luxembourg. During this period, Anne accepted whatever Gaston favored; but she and Mazarin sincerely believed that the reforms the prince was striving to achieve in the Council diminished the king's authority. Anne and Mazarin suspected that making concessions to the Parlement would simply embolden that body and encourage it to delve deeper and deeper into the affairs of state and to claim increasing authority at the expense of the king's Council. Prior to the *lit de justice* of 31 July, Gaston had believed in the Parlement's good intentions and was convinced that if the Council made sufficient concessions, the Parlement would step back into line and vote through the laws providing money for the war.

Gaston was, as we shall see, wrong. By August he was embittered and hostile and had become convinced that certain leaders of the judges had betrayed him. And in a sense he had indeed been betrayed. Mazarin remained almost totally absorbed with the diplomatic and military effort against Spain. His relations with Condé, France's commander on the northern border, grew increasingly close and became genuinely intimate over the summer. In late July, Condé made a quick trip to Paris, causing some of the more historically minded judges to wonder whether his presence had been prompted by the radicalization of the Parlement. As a deliberative body, the judges had become quite absorbed with their own perception of French political life. There is no evidence to suggest that at this point any of them could imagine that Mazarin might order Condé and his army back to the Paris basin in order to reduce the Parlement's power. Each day the judges listened to speeches extolling their corps' moral rectitude, wisdom, piety, and charity. The judges' purview of political-military realities became so categorical and shortsighted that facts were simply ignored when they did not confirm that purview.

For the judges, supporting this parlementaire view of political reality became not only a civic duty but an act of piety. A key feature in the judicial purview was the agreement among the judges that the conditions prevailing in France under Henry IV must be restored. The amount of the *taille,* the number and duties of royal officials, and the relations between the Council and the Parlement—in short, the judges' reform program—consisted of returning France to what it had been in 1610. The judges were fleeing the present, with all the complexity of moral and political issues that had been provoked by the war and by money's "pollution" of the body politic, and were extolling conditions they believed had prevailed under Henry IV. Had he not given them security? It was no accident that the Parlement sought to return France to that moment when the *paulette*—that is, the ownership of their offices—first became secure.

Returning to the conditions of 1610 meant, of course, dismantling the administrative innovations forced upon French society by Louis XIII and Richelieu. For the judges, the innovations and the arbitrariness with which these innovations had been established were parts of the same thing. The judges did not reflect about the power shifts that had occurred within the realm as a result of those innovations. They found it difficult to see beyond the hated intendants, who were few in number and who did not really pose a difficulty, because they could eventually be integrated into other royal offices. They could not perceive the power of hundreds of upwardly-mobile families that in one capacity or another worked for the tax farmers. The tax farmers belonged to some twenty-five families, a small number indeed; but their recorders and the subordinates working in the tax-collecting administration that depended on the farmers extended across France. How could such a vast network be dismantled? If every serpent's head is cut off, the race will die— or so the Frondeur judges thought.

More serious still was the judges' inability to perceive that the tax farmers held not only the crown hostage, but the Parlement as well, along with every Parisian who had invested in government bonds. During times of widespread anxiety about property, the Parlement believed it could legislate the maintenance of the credit market and guarantee the payment of government bonds. But this time the serpent refused to play dead, and the Parlement experienced increasing difficulty in adjusting its ideal of a France of 1610 to the realities of the bankruptcy of the crown and therefore of every institution and individual who had purchased bonds. These factors went beyond the judges' purview as they struggled on with the more immediate goals of revoking the intendants and decreasing the *taille*. Occasional allusions to credit conditions and to bond payments nonetheless began to crop up in speeches before the Great Chamber.

Late in July, a virtual pandemonium of debates about reform broke out in the St. Louis Chamber, the Great Chamber, and the Luxembourg Conferences. Except for short-lived attempts to stop them, this speech-making continued at an increasingly frantic clip into late October. What were these radical proposals that went beyond dismantling the Richelieu state? Historians have often stressed the initiative establishing a special judicial chamber to prosecute and fine tax farmers, for this measure was carried out. By late July, the Great Chamber and the Luxembourg Conferences had agreed on the need for this special court, which—thanks to Gaston's approval—was quickly set up in the Council's name. Prosecuting the rich for corruption, however, was neither new nor radical. Numerous special courts of this sort had existed in the past and had fined tax farmers.

In Chapter 6 we shall see in more detail these operations and the work of this special court and the way it carried out the judges' moralistic impetus to purge the body politic of the individuals who had polluted it. But in the political and social context of the 1640s, prosecuting corrupt tax farmers was scarcely at odds with prevailing values. Although men such as Richelieu, Gaston, Condé, and Presidents Molé and de Mêmes had very different social origins, they could agree that the tax farmers were a base and common lot who ought to be prosecuted. Gaston said as much in the Great Chamber, and Molé decried the tax farmers' immorality in his speech at the *lit de justice* of 31 July 1648. When historians describe these prosecutions as radical, are they themselves not yielding a bit to the classical republican impulse to attack corruption? It is certainly clear that prosecuting the tax farmers was not logically linked to a "soak the rich" impulse, for the "rich" were the judges and the princes, and both groups sat in the Parlement.

The more radical proposals dealt with legal and civil rights. They were fundamentally political in nature rather than economic or social, and they derived from the Parlement's sense of power as a sovereign court. At one point the judges debated about whether the king should have the power to pardon someone who had been sentenced by a court of law. Venerable arguments were made to the effect that magnanimity and charity were among the highest attributes or marks of sovereignty, and the proposal was killed. The proposal nonetheless suggests the tenor of these civic and legal reforms: the reforms represented attempts by some of the judges to curb the king's power over individuals.

Lettres de cachet were orders signed by the king and validated by a small private seal. These letters were not subject to review before being sent out by the chancellor or a secretary of state. When the king wished the Parlement to come before him, he would send a *lettre de cachet* requesting their presence. When used this way, these letters were almost a sign of respect, or even of intimacy with the monarch. In public opinion, however, these letters had a different meaning. When the king wished to have someone arrested or exiled, he sent a *lettre de cachet* to the appropriate officials or guards, requesting them to carry out his order. There was no appeal to an order by *lettre de cachet*, nor an avenue of appeal through the courts. When a great noble was thought to be conspiring against the monarchy, he was usually arrested by guards bearing a *lettre de cachet* and led off to prison. The Frondeur judges' attempt to eliminate these letters was prompted by the arbitrariness of their use in civil relations. Numerous judges of the Parlement had been exiled by *lettre de cachet*. The Council had also used these letters to arrest prominent judges in the Court of Excises in May 1648, and a number of treasurers of France who had circulated a letter to colleagues to rally opposition to the increased sale of offices had likewise been arrested in this way. The Council's resort to the *lettre de cachet* was clearly odious to the judges, not only for these personal reasons but because the letters could be used to nullify their own jurisdictional authority to arrest and to prosecute. Indeed, when a judicial official ordered someone's arrest, the king could, by *lettre de cachet,* order the individual released without having the charges against him presented in a court of law.

When the proposal to abolish these letters came up for debate, Gaston quickly mobilized all his forces to defend their use. Throughout the Fronde, Gaston brought his personal influence in the Parlement to bear on only two or three issues, and this was one of them. Why? He himself had suffered the use of *lettres de cachet* directed against some of his friends. In his speeches aimed at persuading the judges to maintain this arbitrary power, Gaston said he could not imagine the survival of the state without the *lettre de cachet*. The judges, who themselves often referred to the "mysteries of state," believed that these mysteries existed and ought to exist. Gaston's firmness finally led them to drop the proposal to abolish the letters. Images of conspiring princes and heretics may also have been lurking in the backs of the judges' minds. The state might really collapse, they concluded, if the king could no longer order such arrests.

Other principles to limit the king's power over individuals remained couched in the legal language of the court. In the sixteenth century, certain clauses in royal ordonnances had curbed royal power over individuals, and these clauses had been violated by Louis XIII. The judges were very adamant about respecting the ordonnances of Orléans, Moulins, and Blois, and about the Council's previous solemn promises to abide by them. The crown always claimed the power to abrogate its own laws. The long-term duel between kings and parlements over this issue continued throughout the Fronde as the Parlement sought to bind the Council to "keep its promises." Kings—particularly Louis XIII, of recent memory—had questioned the Parlement's ability to keep its word: it had, after all, broken the conditions stipulated in his testament within days of solemnly promising to uphold the will. But this did not prevent the Parlement from trying to force the king in Council to keep his word.

Nineteenth-century historians sought to capture the realities of power balances within the state by analyzing and assessing violations and enforcements of royal ordonnances. The results were often abstract. For beneath seventeenth-century debate about fundamental laws, and the charges and counter-charges between kings and Parlement over promises and "word-keeping," lay the realities of power and the patterns of support and opposition that alternately led from solidarity to conflict. It was part of the order of things that in a period when the Parlement had entered the political arena farther than ever before, that body should test its new power and attempt to force the crown to obey every law or ordonnance that upheld the Parlement's legal status within the monarchy. While neither particularly new nor particularly radical, the effort was in this instance also part of the general attempt to bring about reform by reducing the sphere in which the king or his Council could exercise arbitrary power. In short, the Parlement wanted the old guarantees about the rule of law to be honored. The judges could not, of course, attack the power by which the king ruled as a sovereign, because they themselves acted on that same royal authority; but they claimed that royal authority in law and in the fullness of king and parlement was more complete and noble than royal authority expressed, say, in a *lettre de cachet*.

The one reform proposal that would have a somewhat longer life in the heady debate over public order stated that none of the king's subjects could be detained for more than twenty-four hours without being indicted by the appropriate judge or court of law. This proposal was more extensive than the one abolishing the *lettre de cachet* and went part way toward accomplishing the same aims as that reform. The king could not have someone arrested without cause and then allow him to rot in jail for weeks or months. Nor could seigneurs in their courts, or for that matter the watch (*archers du guet*) or the *prévôt* of Paris.

The number of legal and police jurisdictions entitled to make arrests always seems strikingly large in traditional societies, but it has remained just as large in many contemporary societies. This reform proposal did not attempt to reduce the number of jurisdictions making arrests; it attempted to enforce the court's role once the arrest had been made. The vagueness of the term employed in the proposal—"appropriate judge or court of law"— is evidence of its radical significance. Drawing up an explicit statement about which court was the appropriate jurisdiction for a given crime would have kept the judges hard at work for the rest of the century, drafting reform legislation. Could a thousand years of legal history be cast aside in one revolutionary moment, or even in a revolutionary decade as turbulent as 1789–99? The impetus to curb the abuses of arbitrary arrest is apparent. Gaston accepted the proposal, and it eventually appeared in the declaration solemnly promulgated during the *lit de justice* of 31 July 1648.

Gaston had presided over the Luxembourg Conferences and attended many of the key debates in the Great Chamber. He was on familiar terms with a great number of judges. As each issue was debated, what he saw as give-and-take, as compromise, developed. There is no doubt about his sincerity: he wanted to work within the Parlement and to accept a reform that would dismantle some of the governmental features initiated by his late brother. Having become accustomed to giving his word to the judges and to winning concessions from Anne, Gaston also got into the habit of assuring her and the Council that the judges would go no further once certain concessions had been made. Put in tactical terms, Gaston—as lieutenant general of the realm and uncle of the king—had assumed the role of intermediary between the Parlement and the Council. His plan was to sum up all the reforms that were hammered out in the Parlement and agreed to in the Luxembourg Conferences; to have them reviewed again and yet again by parlementary leaders; and to submit them to the Council and make sure that that body would accept them. Then the reforms would be presented as the law of the realm by His Majesty Louis XIV and his mother the regent—and also by Mazarin, those peers who were in the capital, and the judges of the Parlement, all solemnly gathered in a *lit de justice*. The resolution of the conflict between the Council and the Parlement seemed to have the

characteristics of a "fundamental" reform and a sincere resolution of the crisis.

The judges spent weeks on the text, modifying it and delet-
ing words with Gaston's help. This prince had gotten the Council to accept many concessions in return for the Parlement's
cooperation. There was no more talk about increasing the
number of masters of requests. The annual fee had not yet been
renewed, but some judges expected signs of the queen's "good-
ness" on this issue. Much had been accomplished toward restoring French government to what it had been under Henry IV.
All but three provincial intendants had been revoked and the
treasurers of France and the *élus* had gone back to work. The
taille had been reduced by one-eighth for the year ending 1
January 1649 and would be reduced by one-fourth for the following two years. The clause stipulating that no new taxes would
be levied on the people without parlementary approval was
particularly important to the judges. In the eyes of some of
them, it brought a return to fundamental law.

Another clause in the reform legislation reiterated an oft-
repeated demand: revenues from excise taxes and other dues
specifically raised to pay the interest on government bonds must
be reserved for this purpose. In addition, the law proposing an
assessment on suburban properties in the Paris basin was also
revoked. Some newly created offices in the sovereign courts and
other branches of the administration had never received parlementary approval. These were cancelled. Another provision
made the export of gold and silver illegal. The *déclaration* also
promised that a council consisting of princes of the blood, other
princes, dukes, councillors, and the "principal members of our
sovereign courts" would be called to advise the king. The final
and key clause stated that the meetings in the St. Louis Chamber would cease and that the Parlement would resume its labors
as a court of law.

The *lit de justice* of 31 July 1648 was very well attended.
Chancellor Séguier spoke about the greatness and antiquity of
the French monarchy and about the divine support it had
received over the centuries, especially in times of peril. First
President Molé's speech impressed everyone by its forthright
and almost brutal discussion of certain issues, regardless of the
queen's presence. He stressed the legitimacy of the Parlement's
effort to restore "public order" in the realm. He also remarked

that the tax farmers had threatened that order by embezzling the king's revenues and living in luxury. As he spoke these words, the eyes of the younger judges turned and scrutinized Mazarin's face, seeking signs of discomfort. The Italian remained composed.

After these principal speeches, the chancellor knelt before the young king and requested approval for gathering the opinions of everyone attending the *lit de justice*. Louis approved, so Séguier turned first to the presidents of the Parlement, who assented, and then to the princes of the blood, to Mazarin, to the other princes, and to the marshals of France. Then, moving down into the Great Chamber, he approached the bar and asked the councillors—the often obstreperous younger judges—for their approval. Murmurs could be heard to the effect that judgment should be reserved until a debate the following day, but Séguier ignored them. Climbing back up to his place near the king, he waited until the doors of the Great Chamber had been opened, as custom dictated, and then solemnly pronounced the *déclaration* to be the law of the realm. The *lit de justice* was over.

While everyone was waiting for the king and his mother to leave the hall, Séguier announced that His Majesty and the regent had graciously renewed the annual fee for the members of the sovereign courts, on the same terms as in the past. This was a major concession. It was supposed to consolidate the work that had been summed up in the *déclaration* just approved by the *lit de justice*. Since the fall of 1647, the judges had been nervous about the fate of their proprietary claims to their offices. After 31 December of that year, they were not sure whether they would be able to transmit their offices to their heirs. Gaston—and very possibly Molé, de Mêmes, and other parlementary leaders who sought a compromise with the Council—now had every hope that the descent into revolution would cease. He and the Prince de Conti (Condé's brother) attended the ceremonies held in the other sovereign courts to confirm the settlement and consolidate opinion in its favor.

As in earlier attempts to reach a settlement between the Council and the Parlement, the *lit de justice* and the dramatic concession involving the annual fee were meant to silence political debate in the Parlement. The backlog of law cases had increased over the months. Would the judges now resume their legal duties? The answer lay in the murmurs of the councillors during the *lit de justice* and in the fact that the customary shouts "*Vive le roi!*" had been conspicuously absent at the end of the ceremony. The atmosphere in the Chamber of Accounts and in the Court of Excises was sullen rather than joyous.

After a few hesitations, a general assembly of the Parlement in the Great Chamber was requested for 5 August, signaling a showdown between the radical judges and Gaston and his supporters. The prince arrived ahead of time and talked privately for a time with Broussel, the popular Frondeur. Rumors circulated among the judges to the effect that their venerable leader had been offered handsome positions for his sons. The accuracy of these rumors matters less than their possible effect upon the assembly in the Great Chamber.

As was customary in such sessions, the dean gave his opinion first: he quickly and strongly came down in favor of remonstrances to the Council about the *déclaration*. In the heady days of Louis XIII's reign, with its harshly applied royal authority, the king and his Council would have deemed a remonstrance about a law promulgated by a *lit de justice* both illegal and unacceptable. Any judge proposing such a course of action would have been promptly arrested and exiled.

The procedural issues had become less clear by the summer of 1648, especially after Anne's announcement, during an earlier effort to reach a compromise with the Parlement, that she would always be happy to receive remonstrances from the judges. On the other hand, the delegates to the Luxembourg Conferences had reached an understanding with Gaston: the *déclaration* would be accepted and the Parlement would resume its legal business. The dean's proposed remonstrances would certainly involve the judges in lengthy debates and, if accepted, would signal Gaston's failure to stem the tide of revolution in the Parlement.

At this decisive moment, the Parlement turned to Broussel, an undisputed leader in the debates and a judge who often proposed innovative and significant courses of action. When Broussel spoke, his colleagues waited on every word. He expressed "concern" about the newly established judicial chamber that would prosecute the individuals who had introduced corrupt practices into the king's financial administration. There was nothing in the *déclaration* to indicate that the Council would really cooperate with the Parlement's effort to clean house by prosecuting the tax farmers. As Broussel continued, Gaston interrupted him and insisted that everyone had agreed that the Parlement would stop debating public affairs. Quietly and courteously, Broussel stood up to the prince and recommended that a committee of four judges be appointed to review the work being carried out by the new judicial chamber.

The critical point in the debate had been reached. Attempting to stop it, Gaston and Molé resorted to a variety of parlementary tactics. But after Broussel's speech it became apparent that many of those assembled in the Great Chamber wished to speak. When his turn came, Gaston began by reminding the judges of all he had done for them and of all the advantages they now enjoyed, despite the objections of those who opposed "assemblies of the Parlement." He then implied that he and the judges, working together, had avoided an "entire revolution" by the people, but that now "the people no longer wanted to pay any taxes at all." Recognizing that many of the parlementaires were faithful and prudent, he affirmed that the stubborness of others was leading to opinions that he considered contrary to royal authority. Gaston rose to leave, saying that "he could not approve of this debate by his presence." First President Molé urged him to stay and thanked him, on behalf of the Parlement, for all he had done for that body. Gaston resumed his seat, saying, "I cannot favor any course of action other than interrupting the course of the assemblies of the chambers and reestablishing the ordinary course of justice."

Yet again Councillor Laisné made the emotional appeal that he had been repeating for weeks: "More relief for the 30 [sic] million Frenchmen driven into poverty" must be forthcoming from the Parlement. Du Hodic, his voice dripping with emotion, asserted that he could not, "in good conscience," favor the cessation of debates in the Great Chamber. This was a venerable argument, used in the sixteenth century to support this very sort of debate about where authority rests in the state. At this point, however, it was probably less convincing than the halting and logically flawed speech by President Le Coigneux that followed.

A long-time friend of Gaston's, and someone who could correctly be described as the prince's "client" (Le Coigneux owed his appointment as president in the Parlement to Gaston), Le Coigneux gave the only other really decisive speech in the debate that followed Broussel's remarks. Le Coigneux was aware of his patron's aim to cut off parlementary debate. After announcing that he saw two issues before the Parlement, the president stated that since no objections to the *déclaration* had been raised during the *lit de justice*, it was correctly and properly the law of the realm. At the same time, he continued, it was also true that no law could be promulgated in France without verification, that is, approval, by the Parlement. The Parlement was therefore obliged to debate the *déclaration*. His second point stressed that it was impossible to postpone parlementary debates, or even end them, until that body had treated all the proposals that had been presented to it for debate and approved by the St. Louis Chamber.

Numerous observers during the Fronde remarked that Le Coigneux lacked courage, though they never quite called him a coward. In his efforts to avoid confrontation, Broussel often became enmired in parlementaire subtleties and roundabout tactics, yet he was always described as courageous in debate. But when Le Coigneux used similar tactics, people interpreted them in exactly the opposite way. The reasons for this difference lay primarily in Broussel's independent stance with his colleagues, and in Le Coigneux's dependence upon Gaston and his connections with tax farmers. The breakdown of patron-client bonds of the sort that had existed for over a decade between Gaston and Le Coigneux accelerated over the next few months.

Le Coigneux's speech seems unnecessarily paradoxical, even contradictory; yet it accurately expresses the issues facing the Parlement. A majority wanted to find a moderate way to express their approval of legislation promulgated *solely* by the ceremony of the *lit de justice*. There was also a party seeking to deny altogether the approval of legislation by the *lit de justice*. Before discussing the implications of these two positions it is useful to summarize the outcome of the debate. At one point, Gaston intervened and asked Le Coigneux why he suddenly found it necessary to debate the issues in the *déclaration*, since he had participated in writing the text and had approved its every word prior to the *lit de justice*. This had, of course, been Gaston's strategy: get the Parlement to approve the text *before* the ceremony took place. Le Coigneux could think of no reply. The debate was over. When the vote was taken, the dean's proposal to make remonstrances received a sizable majority, thus winning out over Broussel's review committee. Master parlementarian that he was, Broussel had in reality won on the key issue: the Parlement would continue its debates, just as he had hoped. Superficially he seemed to have been defeated, but Gaston was not duped.

What would have occurred had Broussel used his influence to have the *déclaration* stand without further remonstrances or debate? This question cannot be answered; it is a question quite out of bounds for history, because it deals with something that did not take place. Yet our asking it makes Broussel's key role in the Fronde explicit and easier to measure. This in turn will help us understand why Broussel would be the crucial figure in the revolutionary moment that was to take place in late August of 1648. Gaston had been defeated. As he left, he told some of his followers that he would attend no further debates in the Great Chamber. He nonetheless returned, only a few days later— probably at the request of Anne and Mazarin, who realized that, despite his failures, the prince had helped stem the tide in the Parlement.

Or had Gaston's intervention facilitated its advance? The judges had actually descended further into contestation while working together on the *déclaration* that everyone approved. Why did they reject Gaston's attempts at accommodation? The personal issues motivating the judges had largely been solved. They were no longer faced with a challenge over new offices or over the annual fee. And they had woven into the *déclaration* a clause that assured them that no new taxes would be levied without their approval. Taxes had been cut considerably, though perhaps less than some of the judges had wished.

The reasons behind the Parlement's rejection of Gaston's strategy were now much more specifically political and, in a sense, constitutional. The evidence is scanty but very significant. During the recent weeks of debate, motions had been made from time to time to add the phrase, "with the liberty to vote" to acts of Parlement. The judges making this motion sought to undermine the customary power of the *lit de justice,* be it in its more harshly absolutist form or in its more modified one, by denying the constitutionality of the ceremonial consultation and acclamation. A debate had taken place over whether the phrase "with the king's good pleasure" should be added to an act of the Parlement. Those judges who wanted to add the phrase "with the liberty to vote" objected strenuously to Gaston's proposal to retain the phrase "with the king's good pleasure" and claimed that the words were superfluous. Indeed, everything the Parlement did was accomplished, they said, "with the king's good pleasure," a phrase that had, for centuries, routinely appeared in royal legislation to uphold the direct and personal authority of the monarch.

A lengthy debate about the nature of royal authority, the *lit de justice,* and voting in the Parlement might conceivably have taken place at this point. The elements were certainly present, and the judges were forming parties to support what were developing into party cleavages. Just below the surface lay thoughts about the power to discuss or debate any matter they pleased, whenever they wished. Habits had been formed during the past weeks, and they would prove difficult to break. For the time being, the *lit de justice* had obviously ceased to be a weapon that the Council could wield against the Parlement. It had been tried too often. In addition, Molé quietly dropped Gaston's fight to have "with the king's good pleasure" incorporated into acts of Parlement. Without the first president's support, this issue could not be a rallying point for those who sought to stop the Parlement from descending ever deeper into conflict with the Council.

In mid-August, attention turned to the new judicial chamber set up to prosecute the tax farmers, and to proposals to further reduce the *taille.* Then, on 22 August 1648, news reached Paris that the French army under Condé's command had dealt the Spanish forces a major defeat at Lens. This was the news that the Council had been waiting for. It would immediately resort to brittle authoritarianism.

FIVE *The Joy of Revolution*

THE debates in the Parlement growled on about the sale of offices and the cancellation of *gages*, issues of no interest to the merchants and artisans in the capital, and of no interest whatever to the peasantry in the countryside. Though the judges occasionally ended their speeches on poignant notes, alluding to the need to order relief for the poor people, there seemed no reason to think that what they said in the summer of 1648 would be more effective at undermining the Council's authority than what they had said in the past.

There were no revolutionary parties or organized protest groups trying to mobilize popular support against the policies of the Council of State. True, angry posters were glued to walls and bridges in the cities. And news that yet another peasant had committed suicide as a result of his inability to nourish his family circulated quickly from stall to stall on market days, and among drinkers in cabarets. But this did little more than feed the mood of resignation. There was no doubt about the feelings of discontent, protest, and despair, but there was no focus for these feelings. How could mass protest and revolution manifest themselves in such a hierarchical and compartmentalized society?

The historical study of revolution is the search for the origins and understanding of collective action. What weakens the barriers that separate classes? What prompts people to abandon their routines of work, food preparation, eating, and sleeping? What violence focuses opinions to create fears, panic, and collective action? Only careful analysis of the moments when large-scale collective action occurs permits answers to these questions. Revolutionary moments merit careful investigation in order to discern what the principals are doing and what they may do in the future. The barricades of 26 August 1648 mark the dramatic intervention of the Parisian people into the deadlocked balance between the queen regent and her councillors, and the judicial elites led by the Parlement.

The revolutionaries of 1648 used a very rich social vocabulary to understand how each group entered the conflict. The principal terms were "Robe," "bourgeois," "artisan," "noble," "people," and "vagabonds." More precise terms were used to denote the special interests of officers such as the masters of requests, the intendants, the governors, and the royal household guards.

The historical meanings of such words as "bourgeois" and "people" will always be a subject for debate among social scientists. In providing an analysis of revolution, however, the precise meanings become evident as a result of the high degree of specificity in the contexts of thought and action in which these words are used. Up and down the streets of Paris on the Day of the Barricades, the word "bourgeois" could be heard, and it meant militiamen marching about in columns or standing guard at the city gates. The terms "noble," "bourgeois," and "artisan" have social meaning because individuals used them when drawing up marriage contracts, wills, apprenticeships, and financial transactions before notaries. There will always be a need to generalize beyond the usage found in these legal acts, in order to describe how the bourgeois, for example, act collectively. Describing a given group as bourgeois and as acting collectively in a revolutionary movement is a sound historical practice, because contemporaries interpreted events such as the Day of the Barricades in just this way. Toward the end of this chapter it will be necessary to question some inferences about the behavior of the bourgeois during the week following the barricades.

The temptation is always very great to begin thinking of any collective actor in a revolution as a class. The meanings of such terms as "noble" and "bourgeois" found in non-legal sources provide the possibility for a slight corrective to the legal meanings—or if not a corrective, an enrichment of the meanings, but without making the leap toward post-1789 class interpretations. Put simply, the bourgeois certainly intervened in the stormy events of 26 August 1648, but why they did so and what prompted their withdrawal are fundamental questions, which must be answered in this chapter.

I. The Day of the Barricades

By late August 1648, relations between the Council headed by the queen regent and the united sovereign courts were at a complete impasse. Concessions had been tried; high-level mediation had been tried; arresting the judges' leaders had been tried. The stalemate was such that the routines of legal proceedings in the courts were completely stopped and royal tax officials went out on what would in the nineteenth century be called a strike. Still more important, the rebellious officials from the courts were moving toward offensive measures and away from what had been essentially passive resistance to the royal will. A special judicial chamber created to issue subpoenas and charge and judge the men who had grown rich by collecting royal taxes had not yet begun its work, but the Council had approved the creation of such a chamber. This court would have the power to prosecute, fine, and execute persons guilty of peculation in the king's finances. Indeed, on Saturday, 22 August, the charges that an obscure royal official made about Catelan, one of the tax farmers, had been reported out to the Great Chamber of the Parlement. It was charged that false tax-assessment rolls had been used to collect millions more than the crown had ordered, and that the difference had been pocketed by Catelan and his associates. Charges and countercharges were printed and distributed, and the reporting judge who summed up the case and gave his opinion was the very respected Frondeur, Broussel. With this case in mind, and stirred by rumors of corruption, the judges decided to hear witnesses against three of the most notorious tax farmers, among them Catelan. How many judges sincerely believed that if the tax farmers were forced to bleed a bit, they would lower their interest rates and become more cooperative about the royal treasury's desperate need for ready cash to pay for the military effort against Spain? A majority of the judges believed that the courts had the moral duty to prosecute these tax farmers and others who had grown rich at the expense of the peasantry, the artisans, and the royal government.

This situation was seen very differently by the government officials and the tax farmers. Threats of prosecution prompted the tax farmers to cease all offers to loan money to the royal treasury, regardless of the interest rate offered by the crown. Bankruptcy appeared inevitable. The royal councillors around Anne accused the rebellious judges of disloyalty and selfishness and maintained that they were financially very able to help the royal treasury by approving decrees that would bring in revenues from such quite new taxes as the *toisé* in Paris and of course the sale of more offices.

During this evident stalemate in Paris, news arrived from the northern border that the French had decisively defeated the Spanish army at Lens on 20 August 1648. This news was certainly welcomed by all the Parisians, because memories of Spanish invasions remained strong in the capital. The implications of this military victory for the internal political stalemate quickly became a subject for discussion in both the Council and the Great Chamber. For Mazarin and the other councillors, the victory appeared to enhance the possibilities for breaking the deadlock in the diplomatic negotiations with Spain. This time, they thought, such a devastating defeat, combined with the difficulties of supplying troops so far north, would at last make the Spanish soften their terms for peace.

The evidence about how the rebellious judges interpreted the Lens victory is very scanty. Some judges had believed that Mazarin actually wanted to prolong the war because, were a peace signed with Spain, his chances of maintaining his position in the government would be dramatically decreased. Criticisms surfaced about the way peace negotiations had been conducted in the past. In general, however, the judges had formulated no alternative to the Council's policy of conducting the war. We know that on 26 August, during the ceremony of the *Te Deum*, or "Thanks be to God," the judges turned out in greater number than usual, because they did not want anyone to infer that they were unhappy because the victory enhanced the Council's position. To the more historically minded judges, however, Lens raised possibilities that Condé and his troops might now be free to swing southeast, blockade Paris, and force the rebellious judges to obey the royal decrees being issued by the Council. In the days that followed Condé's brief and unexpected visit to Paris in July, the specter of a blockade of the Seine River and of the roads leading into the capital prompted serious reflection.

Still more inarticulate were the reactions in the markets and cabarets. Was cynicism about the victory claims strong among the Parisians? Had the defeat of the Spanish army actually taken place? Here the crucial role played by couriers and returning camp-followers is evident. News of victories and defeats may well have prompted incredulous shrugs after a decade of war, yet the events on the Day of the Barricades certainly suggest that the *peuple* knew about the victory at Lens and believed it to be a decisive military action. Why pay more taxes on wine and salt if the victory over the Spanish had in fact been decisive? The threat of an invasion by Spain seemed diminished, so why not suspend extraordinary and arbitrary taxes? The possibility that both the Council and the rebellious judges misinterpreted popular responses to the victory cannot be confirmed; but it is evident, not only in the Fronde but over the centuries, that the people of Paris had explicit ideas about their own defense and believed that all armies were dangerous to the welfare of the capital.

The policy debate in the Council after Lens is reported in the sources. Though not a member of the Council, Retz was always eagerly hoping to oust Mazarin and assume the high degree of power the cardinal wielded. He claims to have suggested the possibility of harsh repression against the judges, prior to Chavigny's proposals to that effect. The victory was certainly considered likely to improve the crown's ability to borrow money, not an unimportant fact in itself.

Arresting rebellious judicial officials had often been attempted in the past, in order to intimidate them into obedience; and this is the step that Retz claims to have discussed with Mazarin. The recent arrest of several rebellious royal treasurers had gone without a hitch, but arresting a judge admittedly brought a greater risk of riot than arresting a treasurer. Chavigny, secretary of state and a veteran councillor from the days when Louis XIII and Richelieu were carrying out high-handed and authoritarian measures, proposed arresting the leading Frondeur judges, causing the massive collective action of 26 August 1648. Within the Council itself, Cardinal Mazarin's power was very great; but there were still contenders for the power that Richelieu had once exercised. Had Chavigny's proposal been accepted and successfully carried out, it would no doubt have been a repressive action sufficient to have stopped the Fronde. It would also have enhanced Chavigny's power in the Council. As usual, Mazarin simply lay back, letting the Council decide on a course of action that he knew to be risky. And failure was sure to weaken his rival, Chavigny.

II. The "Te Deum" Mass

As was customary after major military victories, a solemn service of thanks to God, a *Te Deum*, was ordered to take place in Notre Dame Cathedral, to be attended by the queen regent, the boy king, the councillors, and the judges of the sovereign courts. According to the drill for such ceremonies, royal guards posted themselves along the route that the royal coach would take from the Palais Royal to the cathedral on the Ile de la Cité.

Dressed in his pontifical vestments, Retz, the coadjutor bishop of Paris, officiated at the service of prayers and music. According to custom, the flags and trumpets captured from the Spanish regiments were solemnly offered to God before the high altar as material expressions of thanks for the French victory. The crown periodically ordered services of this sort conducted in every cathedral of the realm and occasionally in the 35,000 French parishes. These ceremonies strengthened the perception of strong signs of favor bestowed by God upon the king and the French. As the *Te Deum* service for the victory of Lens broke up and the royal coach headed back toward the Palais Royal, some of the judges attending the service noted that the guards did not break ranks and follow the coach.

Our modern eyes may no longer be attuned to little changes in routine, especially in ceremonies; but those judges who noted that the guards had remained at their posts realized that something terrible was about to happen. They began to run for their lives away from the cathedral, scurrying into hiding down narrow streets and through obscure courtyards. Why? Because in recent years arrests by *lettre de cachet* had been made on several occasions immediately after a ceremony at Notre Dame.

While the *Te Deum* was being sung, a coach accompanied by only four royal guards had drawn up before Broussel's house on the Rue Saint-Landry, a narrow street lined by high, over-hanging medieval houses located between Notre Dame Bridge and the cathedral itself. A captain of the royal guards summarily ordered the seventy-three-year-old judge to rise from his meal and enter the coach. For a few minutes neighbors watched, incredulous, and then the shocking news of Broussel's arrest spread like wildfire through the densely populated Cité. This island, like the Latin Quarter and the quarters of Saint-André-des-Arts and Saint-Merri, was inhabited by royal judicial officials. The name of Broussel, leader of the protest against royal fiscal policies and opponent of the tax farmers, was certainly familiar to his neighbors. "The guards have taken Broussel," neighbors shouted from house to house and from street to street.

A *tocsin* or alarm bell began its wild ringing on the Rue Saint-Landry, and within a half hour the entire population of the Cité knew that something very significant had happened. They did not wait to find out what it was before closing the shutters on their shops and stalls. Barricades made of barrels, paving stones, lumber, carts, and wagons suddenly blocked intersections, and chains were stretched across streets to prevent the passage of horses, troops, and crowds. The Parisians went on the defensive before they knew what the threat was—a typical, indeed centuries-old, structural response in the capital.

Broussel was not the only one scheduled to be arrested. President Charton, who had spoken openly in favor of tax reductions, escaped the guards by jumping over his garden wall. President Blancmesnil, in Saint-Merri parish, had been less quick; he was arrested and trundled off to imprisonment in a royal chateau outside the city. The sources indicate, however, that the names of these two judges were unknown to the Parisians; only Broussel's name would be shouted, and only his portrait and speeches would be hastily printed on cheap paper and hawked for a few *sous* on street corners.

When merchants and artisans finished locking up their stalls and shutters, they reached for their muskets, swords, and cudgels. Several observers were surprised by the number of armed men from bourgeois and popular backgrounds who quickly mobilized in the streets; but these were in fact the militiamen charged with keeping the peace in each quarter and defending the population of the capital against any armed threat. The militiamen usually waited for the orders from their colonels or the provost of merchants, commander of their "columns," as the units were called; but this time the shouting and the ringing of the tocsin had been enough to mobilize them. Watching shops close and barricades go up on the island was enough to prompt neighbors on both sides of the river to do the same. News that the Cité was barricaded quickly reached the Hôtel de Ville, where the provost of merchants immediately ordered all militia columns to arm and post guards at the city gates. He then mounted a horse and attempted to calm things down, but with little success.

After the coach carrying Broussel drove away (only to break down a few minutes later), the royal guards who had remained in position on the bridge and along the streets throughout the *Te Deum* were ordered to form columns and march to take control of the Palais de Justice, at the other end of the Cité. As they approached the Palais de Justice, a volley of musket balls was fired their way by Parisians occupying the Palais de Justice and paving stones were hurled down on them from the roofs. Obviously outnumbered and the target of both stones and musket fire, the guards beat a hasty and humiliating retreat, moving back across the Notre Dame Bridge and down the Rue Saint-Honoré, to the Palais Royal. As they retreated, they were joined by comrades posted on the bridge and along neighboring streets and formed a quite formidable force—which partially accounts for why the guards were not pursued by the populace. But there is still more important reason. The bourgeois militiamen's deeply defensive patterns of action are evident throughout the Fronde. Rarely moving beyond the confines of their street-corner defenses or the city gates they were defending, the militiamen did not take the offensive unless ordered to do so by their officers.

The significant question at this point is, why did the militia prevent the guards from occupying the Palais de Justice? The Council had dispatched the guards to the Palais de Justice to prevent the Parlement from gaining access to the Great Chamber and, above all, to the St. Louis Chamber, where representatives of all the sovereign courts had been meeting since May. Did the bourgeois militiamen suspect the Council's plans? Some of the militia colonels were themselves judges in the sovereign courts, so it is possible that Robe leadership and bourgeois militiamen combined forces at this crucial juncture. The next day the colonel from the Notre Dame quarter appealed to the provost of merchants for support, because the militiamen would no longer obey him. Only lengthy research may turn up documents indicating the reasons for this insubordination. A reasonable speculation would be, however, that the particular colonel encountering insubordination was more partial to the Council than to the rebellious sovereign courts. After all, the judges were split into pro- and anti-Mazarin parties. A certain Desroches was colonel until 8 February 1649, when he was replaced by Champlâtreux, an intendant and Condé sympathizer who was certainly devoted to the Council. The son of Mathieu Molé, first president in the Parlement, Champlâtreux was known for his loyalty to the Council's cause in the duel with the sovereign courts. The bourgeois would slander Desroches contemptuously during the winter war of 1649, because he had dared drive about the Cité behind his beautiful horses. Now, the militia captains of the Ile de la Cité who reported directly to the colonel included none other than Broussel himself! If we wonder why the bourgeois responded so rapidly after his arrest, it is important to recall that one of their officers had been arrested.

The militiamen's blockade of the city streets was a defensive move; the boatmen and the artisans, by contrast, did not hesitate to go on the offensive. Assembling somewhere between the Palais Royal and the Place de Grève in front of the Hôtel de Ville, they began to move toward Notre Dame Bridge, smashing windows, doors, and carts as they went along and shouting, "Long live the king, and liberty for Broussel!" Artisans massed on the Left Bank. What they set out to do remains unclear, although the presence of large masses of men here and there in the capital constituted a powerful political force, even if they had no specific aims.

How many bourgeois militiamen were now in the streets and guarding barricades? Estimates range from 12,000 to 60,000 for the bourgeois militia as a whole during the Fronde. Each of the sixteen quarters of the city had its own quite independent column commanded by a colonel; and each *dizaine*, or subquarter, had its own group commanded by a captain. The precise territorial demarcations of each militia troop remained stable in this period. There was, however, a fairly high turnover among the officers of this period, with the result that most of them were quite young and inexperienced at handling moments of tension and riot in the capital. Nonetheless, the militia companies were stable and constituted a manifest presence throughout the capital at the time of the Day of the Barricades. In times of crisis, "the companies," as they were called, might swell to include as many as 60 or 70 neighbors. In periods of calm, perhaps only six or seven men turned up in the shop or cabaret that served as their headquarters and as a depot for the chains, muskets, powder, and shot allocated to them and paid for by the Hôtel de Ville.

The troops and guards in the capital, as distinguished from the bourgeois militiamen, made shopkeepers, their families, and their neighbors very uneasy. Despite all the harsh royal legislation forbidding troops to pilfer shops and force women, so many crimes of this sort had taken place over the centuries that the Parisian shopkeepers had lost all confidence in the royal legislation outlawing such infractions. The inevitable had occurred too often. A guard reaching across a stall to cut down a little sausage with his sword would prompt defiant shouts from a *charcutier*. Shopkeepers hearing the shouts would rush to support their neighbor; other guards would hasten up to stand by the equally defiant guard who had stolen the sausage. The watch, a body of 140 men, attempted to prevent crime by patrolling the city of some 225,000 inhabitants, but the pilferer would often make sure they were not in the neighborhood before committing his illegal act. When large bodies of soldiers were quartered in the city, many shopkeepers and artisans who were militia regulars joined their neighbors to defend their property and families. What occurred in the countryside—that is, a tightening of neighborhood bonds and defense when faced with outside threats from tax collectors or troops—also occurred in the different quarters of Paris.

III. The Barricades

Barrels filled with paving stones are strong enough to prevent cavalry and milling crowds from moving down a narrow street. Omer Talon, the upright advocate general of the Parlement, estimated that within hours of Broussel's arrest 1,260 barricades built of barrels, carts, and beams had been placed across the street crossings of the capital. Some of these intersections were barely 120 feet apart; some had ditches dug in front of them; others had water run into the ditches to create moats. Caught up in the thrill of collective action, neighbors speedily came forth with the labor and material to build the barricades. Exhilaration and even joy filled the hearts of the bourgeois as the militia columns were called up.

Throughout the night the militiamen kept their muskets loaded and matchlighted as they guarded barricades, shops, houses, and families. The Parisians did not feel sufficiently protected by the chains stretched across the streets in threatening times; they needed in addition the protection of a barricade in order to load and fire their weapons. Near the Palais Royal the first barricade of militiamen stood just ten feet beyond the sentry posts of the royal guards. Throughout the afternoon and into the evening of 26 August 1648, it was evident that the slightest move by the royal guards or the appearance of a column of troops from Erlach's army, stationed outside the city, would have triggered salvos from behind the barricades. Up in the many church towers, neighbors took turns watching for the slightest sign of moving lights along the river or in the suburbs. All city gates were locked, and militia guards watched from the walkways above them and from nearby windows.

After the *Te Deum* service, Coadjutor Bishop Retz barely had time to reach his residence—and had not even removed his pontifical cape and lace surplice—before his householders rushed up to him and recounted what was happening in the streets around the cathedral. Some of Retz's more flippant advisers urged him to go outside immediately and attempt to restore calm. Retz thought about it a moment, then acceded to their wishes, probably with relish, for he had a taste for the theatrical. Joining a venerable tradition of clergymen who had walked among the Parisians in their vestments, attempting to "restore order," Retz sallied forth, gave blessings, and shouted that the queen regent would "settle everything." The object of jeers at first, but gradually winning respect as he made his way to the Palais Royal, Retz began to be perceived as a peacekeeper and negotiator for Broussel's release. Amid the excitement of shooting and running crowds, the wounded and the dying lay here and there. Marshal de La Meilleraie and troopers on horseback dashed about, trying to disperse the huge crowds;

but they merely exacerbated the situation by wounding bystanders. Retz stopped to hear the confession of a man who lay dying in the street, probably wounded by La Meilleraie or one of his cavalrymen. The coadjutor was astonished by the rapidity and intensity of barricade-building in the central city.

No doubt looking shaken by the time he reached the Palais Royal, but also exhilarated by his procession through the crowded streets, Retz was immediately ushered into Anne of Austria's presence. Having made the proper reverences, he began to speak in the hope of persuading the queen to release Broussel. But he was promptly interrupted. Retz later claimed that Anne gave him a cold stare, which implied that by processing through the streets as he had Retz had increased the intensity of the riot. His report about the exact words exchanged that day cannot be entirely trusted, but it is certain that Retz was still hoping to win Anne's favor and would therefore have avoided being rude. He had gone through the streets trying to calm the popular outburst; now the queen accused him of worsening it. How could the activities of a prominent ecclesiastic who was sincerely trying to calm a tumult be seriously interpreted as inciting to riot?

The first element in a revolutionary moment appearing at the level of political decisionmaking is the confusion over duties and the roles played by established political leaders. By his evident political ambition and his activist preaching on behalf of the poor of Paris, Retz gave Anne the impression that he had been aiding and abetting the opposition in the sovereign courts. By late August 1648, she and her councillors felt isolated from entire segments of the royal government. Hundreds of officials had solemnly refused to obey the king's orders. The feeling of being besieged and yet of following a policy that was absolutely right appears in Chancellor Séguier's speeches of this period, but he was not being listened to by rebellious royal officials. Retz had presented himself before the crowds as an authority figure with influence over the queen. Always theatrical, his role this time had been a sincere attempt to calm down the Parisians and take credit for it in Anne's eyes. He expressed surprise at the intensity of the riot. A moment of collective panic in the streets could have been turned into a religious procession. But the Parisians had other ideas. Over the next thirty-six hours the crowds would allow prominent figures such as Retz to approach the Palais Royal, almost as if they knew that should he be arrested, they would clamor for his release. It was entirely beyond Retz's power to create a panic; still, Anne had good reasons for perceiving the prelate as someone who intensified the angry mood of the crowd.

Advice given by a high-ranking clergyman was customarily taken seriously, though not always followed, by councillors. If Retz recommended Broussel's release, it was in order to spare the city from bloodshed. For this he was coldly but politely dismissed from the royal presence. The claque of courtiers and lesser councillors around the royal persons asserted that the coadjutor was exaggerating the danger of riot and that everything would soon calm down. But by going through the street dressed in his pontifical robes and blessing the crowd, had Retz not legitimated the rioters and in some way associated himself with them? Anne sincerely believed that he had, and she was right. In a revolutionary moment, a speech or activity may be perceived in a number of very different ways. Anne often scorned Retz as a Frondeur, while he sincerely believed that he was strengthening public order. The same contradictory perceptions would be the Parlement's fate in a matter of hours.

We have already noted how the royal guards failed to reach and secure the Palais de Justice on the Cité. The Council had aimed to close all the entrances to the judges and thereby impede them from meeting in their accustomed chambers. After Anne had rejected the advice to free Broussel given by Retz, and by others, a council meeting was held and it was decided that Chancellor Séguier should go to the Palais de Justice the next morning and, by royal order, cancel all judicial proceedings.

Bravely setting out by coach, Séguier was confronted by bourgeois who refused to lower the chains and remove the barricades so that he could pass. He tried by various routes to reach the Palais de Justice but was finally surrounded by an increasingly threatening crowd that recognized him for what he was: the chancellor of France, a person of great power. Intimidated by the menaces, Séguier ordered his coachman to drive into the first open courtyard along the Quay of the Grands Augustins. Fleeing from the coach with the crowd at his heels, the chancellor, his brother the bishop of Meaux, and his daughter ran into the house, dashed up the stairs, and hid in closets. While searching for the Séguiers, the angry crowd tore off doors, broke windows and stole any household item within their reach.

News of what was happening to the chancellor quickly reached the Palais Royal, and La Meilleraie set off with some cavalry to rescue him. By the time La Meilleraie reached the house where the besieged chancellor was hiding, the tormentors had moved on, carrying their booty. The damage to the house and its furnishings was extensive, but within three days virtually all the stolen property had been returned. The point is important in itself for the study of the Fronde, for it reveals the rationality and moral uprightness of the Parisian crowds and neighborhoods in the mid-seventeenth century.

What prompted the return of the stolen property? Thus far, sources have not been found to answer this question; but it is interesting to raise the possibility that this incident is a further indication of the effectiveness of militia control over neighborhoods. The one known journal of a militia officer for this period indicates not only great familiarity with every house and street in a quarter, but the strong discipline that the bourgeois companies exerted on their neighbors. Did the bourgeois militiamen realize that pilfering the house tended to associate the movement to release Broussel with common theft, and therefore pressure the people who had carried valuables home to return them? In other words, did the militia possess both the moral force and the armed control of the neighborhood required to bring this about? The owner of the house had been in no way responsible for Séguier's taking refuge there. Why then should he suffer such a loss of property? It so happened that the owner was a prominent aristocrat, and it is also possible that, through his servants or his charitable deeds, he had some favorable standing in the quarter that was entirely independent of the militia. Still, pilfering a house and subsequently returning the stolen items is a remarkable example of the moral economy exercised by a crowd on a day of great emotional uproar.

IV. The Parlement in the State

The Council's strategy to prevent the Parlement from meeting had failed. At six that morning, First President Molé had begun to listen to litigants. The other judges, some 150 strong, arrived by eight o'clock and quickly resolved to set out as a body and, robed and bonneted, march to the Palais Royal to ask the queen regent for the release of Broussel and of Blancmesnil, his less popular colleague who had also been arrested. As the judges headed across the Seine in a column led by their doorkeepers and clerks, it became evident that they possessed every bit as much a sense of the dramatic as Retz did. The chains and barricades were promptly opened up by the bourgeois all along their route, even in the heavily barricaded area around the Rue Saint-Honoré and along the Rue de la Croix-du-Trahoir. A noisy crowd of some 20,000 Parisians followed them "in procession," certainly to lend support by their presence to the cause that had prompted the procession. The Parisian people were in political action.

Upon reaching the Palais Royal, First President Molé requested that the entire court be permitted to see the queen regent and was told to wait on the ground floor while she consulted with her household officials. It was customary to arrange a royal audience in advance; and it was equally customary for the Parlement to send a delegation of three to five judges, rather than arrive *en masse* as they had that day. Immediately after hearing the request for an audience, Anne decided to refuse their request. Then the Queen of England, Henrietta Maria (daughter of Henry IV, sister of Louis XIII, and wife of the defeated Charles I of England), asked to speak to Anne. Her experiences in and around London had left her embittered and virtually destitute, but in this instance she vigorously and successfully strove to convince Anne to receive the judges.

First President Molé's speech was long but very explicitly requested the release of the two judges who had been virtually kidnapped by the crown. President de Mêmes, certainly the second most prestigious judge in the Parlement, also spoke in favor of Broussel's immediate release. So did President Bailleul, known and respected by Anne. After some immediate conferring with Séguier, Mazarin, and Gaston d'Orléans, Anne informed the assembled judges that she refused to order Broussel's release unless the Parlement agreed to stop meeting with the other sovereign courts and to cease meddling in political affairs customarily reserved for the Council of State.

Now it was the judges' turn to reply. They had come as a corporate body, and their numbers certainly added force to their request. Many of them quickly indicated their opposition to such important concessions. One member suddenly remarked that it was impossible for them to discuss such weighty matters outside their own chambers. And so, after the customary courtesies, the judges took leave and headed back down the Rue Saint-Honoré, led by Molé and Mêmes. As they approached the first barricade, the way was opened for them; but as they moved along the narrow streets under the eyes of thousands staring from streets and windows, jeers and taunts began to be heard. Defiant questions were then shouted at them, asking whether they had secured Broussel's release.

When the procession reached the intersection of the Rue de l'Arbre-Sec and the crowded Rue de la Croix-du-Trahoir (where Henri IV had been assassinated), the bourgeois refused to open the barricade. A butcher suddenly pushed through the crowd and stuck a pistol (some sources say it was a knife) under President Molé's chin, demanding to know whether or not Broussel's release had been granted. When Molé said that it had not, the butcher (some sources call him a bourgeois, and there is no contradiction between the two terms) attempted to drag Molé into an adjoining house at gunpoint—explaining that the first president would be the hostage for Broussel, because "the chancellor escaped" that morning. Mêmes and Molé argued that there was no point in taking a hostage. Though the butcher was finally calmed down by his neighbors (fellow militiamen?), there was still no question of opening the barricade. The entire Parlement was left with nothing to do but turn around and march back to the Palais Royal. To break ranks would have meant suffering a tremendous public humiliation—and possible loss of life. Still, in the shuffle of the crowd, and while all eyes were on Molé and the butcher, quite a few judges, in fear for their lives, dropped their bonnets and gowns and blended into the crowd. Of all the leaders of the Parlement, only presidents de Mêmes and Le Coigneux stayed at Molé's side.

When the judges reached the Palais Royal, they were served food and drink in a ground-floor room, for by this time it was mid-afternoon. They quickly dropped the issue of whether deliberation could only take place in their chambers and turned to the terms Anne had offered for Broussel's release. Despite a minority that refused to give in, the judges, now something of a rump parlement, voted to accept the conditions. The chancellor was informed and a courier bearing royal letters was immediately sent to the prisoners' families, informing them that release was imminent. Couriers also set out for the châteaux outside the city where Broussel and Blancmesnil were being held. After this, the Parlement broke up and each judge made his way home as best he could, and as inconspicuously as possible.

Royal town criers, carrying letters bearing royal seals, went about the city announcing the decision to release Broussel. But for the second night in succession, the bourgeois militiamen remained under arms and the barricades remained in place and guarded. The provost of merchants had learned that the bourgeois of the Cité had refused to obey their colonel, so he rushed over to try to resolve the dispute. More serious, "vagabonds"— that is, the "riff-raff" or non-bourgeois Parisians—had formed a vigilante militia and were blocking the Marie Bridge with a barricade. Reinforced by some companies of bourgeois who were loyal to him, the provost of merchants made his way to the bridge and broke up the barricade, a powerful indication of how coordinated and tightly disciplined the militias of the various quarters were, and how each barricade had in a sense been authorized by the militia and by the provost of merchants, their commander-in-chief.

The night of 27 August 1648 was just as quiet as the previous night. Occasional shots rang out in the dark, but the population remained calm and the bourgeois remained awake and on guard. When Paris awoke the next morning and learned that Broussel had not yet returned to his house, rumors again began to circulate and tensions mounted. Finally, at about ten in the morning, Broussel arrived in a coach. Crowds lined the streets to welcome him, shouting loudly as he passed: "Long live the king and Monsieur de Broussel!" The barricades along the route were immediately and ceremoniously dismantled so that his coach could pass through the city in triumph. Plans were made to sing a *Te Deum* at Notre Dame in thanks for Broussel's release.

The elderly judge remained modest in the face of this popular acclaim. Returning to his house, he spent some time with his family before heading to the Parlement in the afternoon. His fellow judges greeted him warmly. First President Molé, who took a position contrary to Broussel's on most issues, gave the old judge a welcome greeting that was so sincere and so deeply felt that Broussel kept a copy among his judicial papers, where it can be found today.

Rumors of troop movements still circulated about the city. At one point the barricades that had been torn down were hastily rebuilt. By early afternoon, however, they had all been dismantled and shops and markets were open for business for the first time in two days.

V. Interpreting Militia and Popular Actions

Jean Vallier, the author of an eyewitness account for the Fronde, asserts categorically that the barricades had been built to preserve the private property of the bourgeois and other well-to-do residents of the capital. Fear of looting is a fairly frequent explanation offered in the sources as a motive for the bourgeois' behavior. Vallier also claims that no rebellion against the king was involved. Thus he, a first-hand observer, offers two separate and general explanations for the conduct of the bourgeois during these two days.

A few days after Broussel's release, Anne of Austria invited the provost of merchants, other city officials, and the militia colonels to a royal audience, where she publicly thanked them for having kept order in the city. Contemporaries hostile to Mazarin and to the Council immediately interpreted this action as a ploy to curry favor with what was admittedly a powerful political force. Like a sleeping giant, the bourgeois had intervened in the contest between the queen regent, her councillors, and the rebellious royal officials headed by the Parlement and the other sovereign courts. But more significant at this point is the fact that Anne's expression of thanks confirms Vallier's interpretation of the barricades. Fear of disorder, especially looting and burning by "vagabonds," "*canaille*," and "*coquins*," remained a very important determinant in the conduct of members of the ruling elite. They might be deeply divided over such issues as taxes and office-sales, but parlementaires and councillors alike shared a perception of the city population founded on fear of looting and burning. This dismantling of the vagabonds' barricades, like the return of property to an owner who was not known to have profited in the king's finances, con-

firms the impression that the bourgeois, as expressed powerfully in their militia, were aware of the explosive situation in
the capital and that they used neighborhood persuasion and
paramilitary force to protect their own property and that of
their fellow citizens. And they wanted Broussel's release.

During the evening after Broussel's release, the order was
given by some member of the Council to deliver powder and
shot from the Arsenal, which stood on the edge of the city, to
the Palais Royal, in its center. Seeing these carts laden with arms,
the people in the Saint-Antoine quarter immediately blocked
their advance, pillaged their contents, and began to build new
barricades. Numerous incidents occurred over the next few
weeks, in which carts and sacks suspected of concealing arms
were searched by the people. They did so less to prevent supplies from reaching royal guards than to keep defensive equipment from leaving their section of the city, and in many instances
their quarter, and being put to use elsewhere. As this type of
pilfering for self-defense went on, rumors circulated to the effect
that troops would be arriving in the night to capture the king
and take him from the capital.

The Day of the Barricades ended in a "transport of joy."
Streets were filled with deliriously happy people celebrating
Broussel's return. At the same time, the ever-suspicious Parisians kept an eye cocked on the royal guards and on the roads
along which troups might arrive. The Day of the Barricades
had been an exhilarating occasion, a common effort to defend
the king and the capital. But it also was much more.

The Parisians had prevented the guards from occupying
the Palais de Justice, and they had forced the Parlement to return
to the Palais Royal and vote the concessions laid out by Anne
and her councillors. In these two dramatic actions, the Parisians
had not only intervened to prevent the queen regent and her
councillors from carrying out their plans to intimidate the
Parlement, they had also intimidated the Parlement. To be sure,
Broussel's praises were sung, and so were the Parlement's once
the old judge was safely back in his house; but during the confrontation between First President Molé and the butcher on the
Rue Saint-Honoré, the Parlement had proved to be easily
intimidated and as powerless as the Council of State.

The pursuit of the chancellor and the attempt to take Molé
hostage form elements of a sub-plan of defense carried out by

the Parisians on the Day of the Barricades. We will never know exactly what would have happened to Chancellor Séguier had he been caught by his pursuers; but we do know that no barricades were removed as his coachman tried to make his way to the Palais de Justice. And the butcher who attempted to take Molé hostage commented on Séguier's escape. Seen from the distance of several centuries, almost uncanny rationality and planning seem to have been at work in the popular mind of 1648. Far from being aimless pillagers, emotional and uncontrolled, the Parisians of the Day of the Barricades appear as disciplined and in command of carefully worked-out plans for self-defense and political action. Against an intimidating act on the part of the government, and in the face of the possible use of large-scale armed force, the Parisians offered a measured defense and a plan to take hostage the chancellor, that prominent member of the Council of State, and then exchange him for Broussel, or should these plans fail, to capture the first president of the Parlement.

More difficult to interpret is the pillage. The royal carriage that broke down while carrying Broussel out of the city was torn to pieces and thrown into the river by angry bystanders. In a day when wood was the only source of fuel, and expensive, it is significant that the wooden frame, tongue, and wheels of the coach were thrown into the Seine, not carried home for firewood. Casting polluting objects into the river was typical behavior for the Parisians, who gave the same treatment to the bodies of hated criminals or to the tax farmers' furniture and account books they had seized in riots.

The stolen household goods were returned to the residence in which Séguier had sought refuge. The owner seems to have been absent during this unpleasant incident and the only damage he incurred was the cost of replacing and repairing broken windows and doors. And what about the damage to doors and shutters caused by the boatmen (we would call them "dockers") as they moved up toward the Rue Saint-Honoré? The sources do not specify the extent or cost of this damage, but had it been excessive one of the memoir writers certainly would have mentioned it. Perhaps as many as four or five lives were lost as a result of the mêlée and accidental musket fire. When all the damages and casualties were added up, it becomes evident that the Parisians had carried out a massive militarized protest to recover Broussel. The crowd activity was fundamentally defensive, yet the pillaging constituted a solemn warning to the queen regent and her councillors that the power to sack the city might be unleashed if the bourgeois militia failed to mobilize or stand firm. This message did not go unheeded. Before the Day of the Barricades, fear of Parisian crowds had been evident in both the Palais Royal and the Palais de Justice; but now some councillors and judges were seized by near hysteria. The people of Paris had dramatically intervened in an elite dispute over taxes and venality of office. The judges accepted defeat at the hands of the queen regent when they agreed to cease meeting with delegates from the other sovereign courts and discussing public affairs. This did not mean, however, that they would simply knuckle down and return to trying cases. Relying on centuries of precedent and parlementary ingenuity, the judges would find ways to carry on activities they had solemnly promised to avoid.

The subsequent withdrawal of the bourgeois militia from participation in street demonstrations and processions has been interpreted as evidence of an increased fear that their shops and houses would be damaged by the pillaging *canaille,* or vagabonds. While it is premature to offer an alternative interpretation to this conclusion, it is important to stress what can only be called the solidarity of all the popular elements in the capital on the Day of the Barricades. And Jean Vallier's assertion that the bourgeois had mobilized not to protest the queen regent's action but to protect their property and families provides an important clue about bourgeois motives for action that merits further analysis.

If the bourgeois came out in force to protect their shops and provide security in the streets, how can it be argued that their subsequent fears of popular riot and pillage led them to stay inside, that is, to remain demobilized? Like an army, the colonels and captains of the bourgeois militia closed off streets and built barricades after receiving mobilization orders from the provost of merchants. While it is true that on the Day of the Barricades they acted before their orders arrived, those orders followed rapidly on the heels of their action. And the tocsin bell was a mobilization signal in itself.

With uncanny coordination, the Parisians manning the barricades between the Cité and the Louvre opened them to let pass persons of authority who wanted to plead for Broussel's release before the queen regent and her councillors. They allowed Retz to return to his residence after his failure, but they did not do the same with the Parlement. Prior to the Day of the Barricades, frequent allusions to what the Parisians *might* do had been made in the king's Council and in the Parlement. The Day of the Barricades revealed what they *could* do: intervene by massive civilian military force in support of efforts to gain Broussel's release.

When the whole Parlement went in procession to the Louvre to request an interview with the queen regent, their numbers were clearly manifested as political power. Their mass supported the formal appeals for Broussel's release that their leaders were making. In a similar way, the "procession" that followed Retz functioned politically to enhance his message and give it force. The Parisians made their numerical force felt in order to heighten tensions between the Council and the Parlement. The Council's strategy of intimidation failed because of popular pressure. The most important result of all this was that the Frondeur parlementaires concluded that they must prosecute tax farmers as forcefully and as rapidly as possible, to partially meet the demands of the capital's *peuple*.

Protest demonstrations and riots were localized during the months that immediately followed the Day of the Barricades and in no way risked becoming mass movements that might end in burning and pillaging entire streets or quarters. A coercive claque that troubled nervous judges who feared for their lives, the protesters at the Palais de Justice in no way threatened private property. Put another way, the bourgeois militia and other Parisians mobilized in order to contain gangs of pillagers and to defend their quarters against possible attack by an army approaching the city. The orderly conduct and the collective discipline of a city of perhaps a quarter of a million inhabitants impressed contemporaries at home and abroad. Broussel was freed by a government that deeply feared its policy of intimidation would bring about a cataclysm. The Parisians acted in self-defense, and in defense of the Parlement. They still expected tax relief, and their interpretation of the victory of Lens may have been to live, and let the Spanish live, on the northern borders, even if this meant returning some conquered territory to the defeated. And large-scale collective action had been successful in support of the Parlement.

VI. The Declaration of 24 October 1648

The use of arbitrary force to arrest Broussel and Blancmesnil had not only been unsuccessful, it had mobilized Parisian property owners, or bourgeois, to intervene on the side of the Parlement. Broussel the hero, Broussel the fighter against high taxes, Broussel the critic of the tax farmers, became a popular figure known and admired by virtually all the Parisians. Celebrated as a judge who stood up for the *peuple,* Broussel became known as the virtuous, incorruptible judge who was not himself particularly rich.

That the Parisians had intervened in the struggle with the Council deeply affected the parlementaires. The phrase "relief of the people" had been heard with increasing frequency in their debates ever since the judges had decided to forge ahead and debate the articles that had been declared the law of the realm during the *lit de justice* of 31 July 1648.

The decision to continue debate and in effect to violate the terms of the *lit de justice* as the Council attempted to define them was of enormous significance in the revolution that was the Fronde. Like the decision to have judges from the sovereign courts meet together in the St. Louis Chamber, the Parlement's decision to continue the debate despite the *lit de justice* attacked the Council's power head on—and Anne's power in particular.

In this decision to continue its debates, the Parlement was not unaware that it would need issues of more immediate interest to groups outside the Robe, not just the sale of new offices. From the first debates in August 1648 to the promulgation of the 24 October Declaration, the cry "relief for the people" would be heard in crescendo proportions.

The negotiations that took place between the parlementaires and the Council in September and October 1648 had harsh, frank, and unreal features. The judges' habit of tossing figures about for rhetorical effect disconcerted the royal officials who supported the Council and prompted panic among the tax farmers. Broussel and his supporters had set the terms for the

parlementaire negotiating position: a tax increase was unnecessary, in their strident opinion. All that was needed was to force
the tax farmers and their supporters in the Council to relinquish the huge profits they had made from collecting the royal
revenues. Then there would be enough money to pay the troops
and give "tax relief for the people."

The negotiators from the Council of State really sought
only one concession from the Parlement: that it stop meeting
on political matters and resume its judicial duties. As the negotiators haggled over tax percentages and over whether or not
the Parlement would cease politicking, the suspicion that neither party would honor its commitment pervaded the entire
political climate of the capital. The mood of the negotiators was
altered by the suspicion that there would be a resort to force, a
suspicion that becomes inevitable when powerful bodies on a
collision course no longer believe in each other's good faith.
Would the queen regent and Mazarin respect any agreement
that might be reached? Anne and the cardinal sincerely believed
that the parlementaires had violated the Luxembourg agreements by their continued meetings and their discussions of
matters reserved for the Council, namely tax measures.

The judges pressed forward under cover of the need to
"relieve the people." The first article of the Declaration of 24
October 1648 begins by summing up the tax concessions wrung
from the Council in July and August, and continues by granting a 20 percent cut in the collection and assessment of the *taille*
for the entire realm. The second article grants substantial rebates
and reductions in the excise taxes, mainly those on the meat,
wine, and salt brought into Paris. Broussel believed these
reductions indispensable to the maintenance of public order in
the capital. The last lines of this article read:

We [the king in Council is speaking in the Declaration] very strictly
inhibit and forbid our tax farmers, their clerks, and others to increase
in the future the said duties and taxes, upon penalty of [arrest for]
peculation.

The Parlement would press forward its charge of corruption
against the tax farmers and their allies in the Council of State,
against Mazarin, and finally against some of their own members. Could the entire Robe and the Parisian merchant elite be

mobilized in revolution by a violent attack on the tax farmers, their assistants, and those who profited by lending them money? This would be the central rallying cry of Broussel and his supporters. The ancient Roman principles of judicial virtue and probity would be re-articulated in the Fronde and would be promoted as the idea that would bind the Robe to the bourgeois militiamen and to the property-holders of the capital.

The other articles in the Declaration of 24 October restate the content of many of the articles contained in the Declaration of 31 July 1648: venality of office, amnesty for the Frondeurs, jurisdictions for the Parlement and the other sovereign courts, and protection of all royal officials from imprisonment by *lettre de cachet*.

Like the 31 July Declaration, the 24 October Declaration was quickly printed and hawked on the Pont Neuf. Some of the more technical articles may have gone unread by the elite Parisians, but those articles affecting tax assessments and rates certainly became known to a fairly large segment of the population. Did people who owned *rentes* and who were already beginning to feel the pinch of the Council's failure to pay interest on their investment find satisfaction in the sixth article of the 24 October Declaration, which placed the legality and the certification of certain bonds entirely within the jurisdiction of the Parlement? Broussel and his allies in the Parlement no doubt hoped to stop tax farmers from profiteering by purchasing bonds below par and then having them redeemed at par by the royal treasury. Were the judges so naive as to think that by mere words they could undermine the practices that permitted the tax farmers, and through them well-to-do investors, to engage in such highly profitable activities? As the Fronde deepened into the blockade of Paris and into civil war, the Brousselian program for restoring virtue to the royal government would become increasingly phantasmagoric. Royal finances had always been "corrupt," even in the reign of that much eulogized monarch, Henry IV.

Part Two

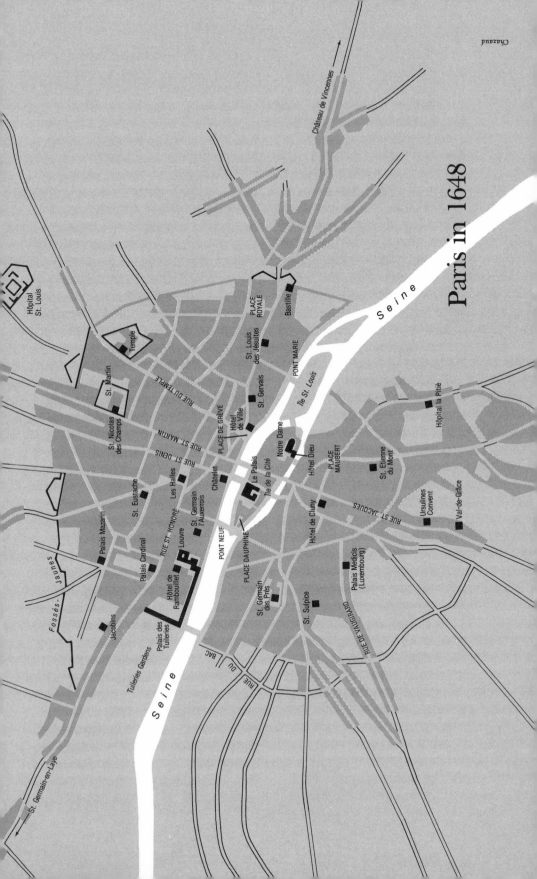

Paris in 1648

Chazaud

Château de Vincennes

Hôpital St. Louis

Temple

St. Martin

St. Nicolas des Champs

RUE DU TEMPLE

St. Eustache

RUE ST. DENIS

RUE ST. MARTIN

Palais Mazarin

St. Gervais

St. Louis des Jésuites

PLACE ROYALE

Bastille

PONT MARIE

Les Halles

Palais Cardinal

Châtelet

PLACE DE GRÈVE

Hôtel de Ville

Notre Dame

Île St. Louis

Seine

Jacobins

St. Germain l'Auxerrois

RUE ST-HONORÉ

Louvre

Le Palais

Île de la Cité

Hôtel Dieu

PLACE MAUBERT

St. Étienne du Mont

Hôpital la Pitié

Hôtel de Rambouillet

PONT NEUF

PLACE DAUPHINE

Hôtel de Cluny

RUE ST. JACQUES

Ursulines Convent

Val-de-Grâce

Palais des Tuileries

Tuileries Gardens

St. Germain des Prés

St. Sulpice

Palais Medicis (Luxembourg)

RUE DE VAUGIRARD

RUE DU BAC

Seine

Fossés-Jaunes

St. Germain-en-Laye

General Perspectives

T HE Fronde became an intense revolutionary force in Paris during the period between the Day of the Barricades of August 1648 and the signing of the accords of Saint-Germain-en-Laye in March 1649, owing to the alliance between the people in the capital and the Frondeur judges in the Parlement. The critical issues forming the alliance had been, of course, defense of the city and reduced taxes, particularly excise taxes on wine.

The Fronde in Paris was certainly not ended by the agreements signed at Saint-Germain-en-Laye, but the alliance between the people and the Parlement had disintegrated. Elite Frondeurs, particularly the younger and more strategically minded ones, would spend the next three years trying, through various techniques, to restore the alliance. But again and again the Parisians declined to be mobilized in any massive way. The two principal techniques used were essentially theatrical and cooptive. The first involved staging a phony physical assault on a lesser magistrate and then running about the capital, shouting that the lives of the parlementaires were in danger and that the Parisians must rush to their defense. This theatrical-political tactic would be tried several times, in slightly different guises, but without success. As a young man, Cardinal Retz had written about staged mobilizations of opinion of this sort in his *Conspiracy of Fiesque*. And for later historians, it is interesting to study these attempts to mobilize opinion by theater; but in point of fact, the Parisians failed to respond.

The second and essentially co-optive technique involved flooding the capital with pamphlets. Given the name *Mazarinades* at the time of the Fronde, these pamphlets likewise failed to mobilize opinion into a large-scale, massive movement to intervene on the side of the Fronde. The result was that, in a sense, Parisians ceased to be potentially revolutionary once the accords at Saint-Germain-en-Laye had ended the winter war. The popular-parlementaire alliance could not be revived.

But what of the princes? All the principal *loci* of the Fronde as a fundamentally revolutionary force capable of altering the structures of power and of social rank were situated in cities with sovereign courts, that is, parlements similar to the one in Paris. The massive forced loans and the increased sale of judicial offices had offended and outraged parlementaires all across the realm. The provincial judges had been faced with the same high-handed, coercive, and arbitrary decisions as their colleagues in Paris. Expressions of solidarity flowed back and forth between these prestigious courts in 1648, and on into 1652. Had Mazarin been less cool-headed, he might have believed that the entire monarchy would explode in revolution and resort to arms as a result of the royal judges' strikes. Indeed, contemporaries saw the situation in the spring of 1649 in apocalyptic terms, but not Mazarin.

As the parlementaire army in Paris demobilized in March 1649, judges in Aix and Bordeaux were raising troops to challenge the Council of State's arbitrary decisions concerning taxes and office sales. Negotiations eventually broke down completely. Specially empowered royal officials were sent to attempt mediations and thus avoid civil war, but to no avail. While Paris calmed down and returned to worrying about a Spanish invasion from the north, the remote provinces of Provence, on the Mediterranean, and Guienne, on the Atlantic coast, reached structurally just about the same point the Parisians had occupied late in December of 1648. There was, however, one major difference in Aix.

The structural similarity consisted of, first, the raising of troops by Frondeur judges, and second, the buildup of troops by commanders loyal to the Council and Mazarin, in order to blockade the cities and force the Frondeurs to negotiate. From January to March 1649, Condé had commanded that military force for Paris. Governor Alais would perform exactly the same function in Provence, as would Governor Épernon in Guienne. Protests and confrontations also occurred in Toulouse and Rouen, but the threat of blockade and civil war that had just been lifted in Paris in March 1649 in the end intensified only in

Aix and in Bordeaux. Mazarin was forced to divert precious tax revenues and resources away from Condé's army in the North, in order to increase the strength of the forces commanded by Alais and Épernon.

Despite these important political and military similarities in structure, there was one important difference. In Aix, the *peuple* did not support the Frondeur judges in that parlement in 1648, as the Parisians had supported theirs and as the Bordelais would do in the summer of 1650. The buildup of troops quartered within Aix prompted neither a fervent movement to civic defense nor a popular identification with the Frondeur judges. The reasons were both military and political. Alais brought hundreds of troops into the small city, so many perhaps that militia resistance became unthinkable. It is also plausible that despite the fact that some of these soldiers came from as far away as Antibes, the Aixois did not perceive these troops in the ways the Parisians had viewed Condé's or Erlach's hardened regulars. Made up largely of nobles from Provence and their clients and servants, the royal army commanded by Alais seems not to have mobilized fears of pillage and rape in the Aixois population.

The important political difference between Aix, Paris, and Bordeaux was that the parlementaires were not particularly respected by the Aixois. A very divided city with competing networks of clients and co-optive networks of rival judicial families, Aix in the end failed to support a parlement that protested against increased office sales and the suspension of judicial salaries. The Frondeur judges distributed small amounts of money to win support among the Aixois, but when they resorted to military force, the *peuple* did not join them. When the judges and their troops attempted to take the Town Hall by force in 1649, there was almost a sense of *déja vu* among the inhabitants. Put succinctly, the Fronde in Aix never became revolutionary because the judges failed to mobilize popular support for their cause. There were, to be sure, revolutionary implications in the generalized protests made by Frondeur judges across the realm, including those in Aix. The impression that civil war might well break out, not only in Aix but also in Bordeaux and perhaps in Rouen as well, exacerbated Mazarin's diplomatic efforts to reach a settlement with Spain. But for the cardinal and for the ever-diligent Michel Le Tellier, secretary of state for war, who was in charge of distributing money and military resources, it was only the confrontation in Bordeaux that risked breaking into revolution and civil war. The crucial precondition—solidarity between the *peuple* and the parlement—appeared in the guise of civic defense to preserve a degree of autonomy from Paris.

s I x *The Winter Wars of 1649*

T HE army that defended the northern cities of the realm against Spanish raids could reach Paris in less than a week of forced march. The commander of this army was the still very young Prince de Condé, victor at the Battles of Rocroy and Lens. The annual military campaigns in the 1640s gave him increased stature as a commander and increased power among nobles and aristocrats through patronage. The recognition and popularity that his victories earned him confirmed the highest ideals of princely conduct of his day. While his father was living and actively participating in the Council of State, young Condé had had little reason to be interested in the political machinations going on in the capital, except insofar as these might affect payment of his troops.

Cardinal Mazarin had sought a genuine friendship with Condé, and the prince had responded in kind. Their letters contain expressions of trust and a willingness to share personal feelings about affairs of state. Mazarin knew that he must maintain Condé and his army in the North to avoid the collapse of his diplomatic efforts to reach a peace settlement with Spain. He also knew that his personal survival as a minister might eventually depend on whether or not the king's army, commanded by Condé, fought for the king, Anne, and Mazarin, her principal minister, or whether it too went into rebellion. Rumors flew, off and on throughout 1648, about how Mazarin and Condé were coordinating the war against Spain, the diplomatic negotiations, and the military buildup around Paris, in order to permit a quick march south to blockade the capital and force the Parlement and the Parisians to cease their revolution. The rumor mills also cranked out an old adage: Paris would be on its knees in three weeks if bread supplies were cut off.

The Parlement had voted a law forbidding any army to come within twenty leagues of Paris. A small army loyal to Mazarin and led by the German commander Erlach was, however, already in the region and had broken this law when taking up winter quarters during the fall of 1648. The Parlement's belief in the powers of its legislation increased rapidly during the weeks that followed the 26 October Declaration. There is no evidence to support the claim that Mazarin believed Paris could be blockaded and forced to capitulate within three weeks. Indeed, it was not like him to speak or write so explicitly about such questions. But beneath the harsh tone he used in his correspondence about attacks on royal authority may have lurked plans about an eventual resort to force to restore that authority. The Frondeur judges certainly believed that their conduct in the Parlement and in the streets of Paris, while legitimate and fair, might provoke the crown to use force against them. Put another way, neither Mazarin nor Anne suffered illusions about the nature of power and of the state, or about the need for power great enough to bridle society. They accepted the possibility that force would be employed to repress revolution. Condé's brief, mysterious trip to the court in July 1648 for talks with Anne and Mazarin prompted further rumors about how and when the capital would be besieged.

Throughout the autumn of 1648, the activist judges in the Parlement, led by Broussel, exhorted their colleagues to vote in favor of raising an army and to order the repair of the city walls. Their speeches were scarcely listened to at first. In the seventeenth century, soldiering was the business of professionals—that is, the nobility of the sword and the marginals of society impressed into infantry regiments. Indeed, armies were made up of the aristocratic elite and the dropout elements of society. Lawyers, judges, merchants, and artisans were practically never recruited and were rarely promoted to officer rank. As possibilities for a compromise with the crown diminished, some of the radical judges in the Parlement and their clerks stated clearly that they looked forward to a war that would consolidate the gains the Fronde had made in the Declaration of October 1648. For example, Judge Deslandes-Payen, who had acquired some military experience while rebelling against Marie de Medici in the early 1630s, exhorted his colleagues to raise troops. When he volunteered to coordinate the military effort, ironic smiles must have appeared on the faces of some of his colleagues. A judge who volunteers in court to raise an army? Deslandes-Payen had often captured the mood of the younger judges from the Chambers of Inquests during the heady days of debate that marked the summer of 1648. Now he may have sensed that some of the other judges were eager to prove themselves as warriors. President Viole categorically and repeatedly stated: "We are not afraid."

Joining an army and doing active service in battle may have been considered not only a proof of virility for some young noblemen of the Robe, but also in some ways a proof of their eligibility for membership in the nobility of the sword. The Parlement was, according to historical metaphor, the ancient Roman senate, a governing body that had been passed on to the French, who had adopted its functions and duties. Roman senators had marched in the legions. For some of the judges in the Parlement, the chance to prove themselves in war not only coincided with their social aspirations to join the nobility of the sword, but confirmed the ideal of the virtuous parlementaire. Several of the judges already served in the militia, so at this point the links between the Parlement and the popular military forces in the city implied that preparation for war meant extending and consolidating already established roles and duties, and not innovating beyond contributing to a paid force raised and funded by the judges.

The mobilization to defend the Parlement and the king (never once did the Parlement or its army deny their obedience to the king) therefore involved first strengthening and training the militia columns that already existed in each quarter of the city, and then recruiting a certain number of cavalry and infantry regiments that would be quartered in the capital and paid and provisioned with funds raised by the Parlement. In the initial discussions of these very important issues, there was an ambiguity about whether the forces to be raised were primarily destined to defend the capital, or were to go out beyond the city gates and stand firm under the fire of any army that was attempting to impede the delivery of grain and bread to the city. Could bakers, candlestick-makers, and lawyers be trained to combat a royal army commanded by Condé? The history of the efforts, failures, and victories of "citizen" and revolutionary armies doing battle with professional troops is one of the more important and poignant chapters in Western civilization.

I. The Flight to Saint-Germain-en-Laye

The Festival of the Three Kings, also called Twelfth Night or Epiphany, was one of the most popular holidays in seventeenth-century Europe. Parisians still celebrate it today. Each January 6 a cake is baked, and in it a dried bean is hidden. When the cake is served, the person receiving the bean is declared king or queen. Then everyone at the table sings and makes numerous toasts to "his majesty." Rich and poor alike enjoyed this inversion of roles that brought the Christmas holidays to an end.

On the morning of Twelfth Night, 1649, the Parisians woke to what were at first thought to be merely wild rumors: the king had left Paris during the night. From our twentieth-century perspective, it is tempting to say, "So what?" But the rumor sent shudders up the mental spines of the Parisians of 1649. In some powerful and scarcely understood way, the king's presence was a guaranty of security and protection. He was a holy figure, an idol that radiated well-being and security. For the more military-minded Parisians, his departure also meant that nothing could now prevent the blockade of the capital. As the shouts echoed up and down the streets, memories of cities that had been put to sack by invading armies transformed anxiety into near-panic. The fear of robbing, pillaging, and raping soldiers struck the Parisians in an instant trigger reaction, regardless of their social class or their place of residence. Suddenly the city seemed to be one single body of people, and every member of that body felt threatened.

The departure of Louis and the queen regent stunned the Parisians. The provost of merchants and the *échevins* rushed to the Hôtel de Ville; the judges of the Parlement ran to the Great Chamber in the Palais de Justice. For the first hour or so, they merely sat on their benches, not knowing what to do. A powerful sense of urgency came over the city. Its very life blood seemed threatened. By dawn, runners were carrying messages through the streets, ordering militia colonels to meet at eight that morning in the Hôtel de Ville. What should be done?

The judges in the Great Chamber finally came to order after Molé arrived to preside. And of course those among them who had talked about the need for military preparedness suddenly had a great deal of influence. Deslandes-Payen and Broussel immediately proposed raising an army to defend the city and sending out regiments to requisition food and bring it into the city walls. This was the moment Deslandes had been dreaming about. In his strong voice he boldly stated: "There is no reason for fear." Paris had an inexhaustible supply of men. He urgently recommended that the Parlement order at once the raising of an army of 10,000 foot and 2,000 horse. He assured the judges that such an army would cost but a tiny sum. Continuing in an increasingly passionate vein, Deslandes added that if necessary Paris could raise 90,000 foot and 3,600 horse. Moreover, there would be no lack of officers. "For myself," he continued, "I wish to live and die for the Parlement. I am a native of Paris, and I offer myself to her, to carry out any order she wishes to give me." Deslandes' speech was well received by a body of men increasingly eager to take action. The panic in the shops and the streets was gaining the Great Chamber. As the debate went forward, rumors reached the judges that the Parisians were closing up shop and were starting to build barricades in the narrow and densely populated streets of northern Paris.

An urge to take immediate action quickly developed. Several senior judges chimed in that they knew men of illustrious birth who would willingly take command of the city's defenses and of any army the Parlement raised. One mentioned a son of Henry IV who might be willing to serve. These vague allusions to aristocrats such as Vendôme, Elbeuf, Beaufort, and Bouillon indicate clientage ties between the judges and these nobles. At many points in the Fronde these ties certainly were a factor; but they cannot be described as determinant in revolution, owing to the many breaches of loyalty and the overlapping ties of friendship and loyalty that prevailed at the highest levels of the elite in French society.

Judge Le Coigneux (joined by Bachaumont) moved that the Bastille, the Temple, and other fortifications in the capital be seized and placed under parlementary control. Client of Gaston d'Orleans' though he was, in the heat of the debate over how to respond to the king's departure Le Coigneux had little

chance of receiving orders from Gaston or of learning about
the position the duke had taken concerning the queen regent's
departure. Gaston had accompanied Anne and Louis XIV on
their flight from Paris and his signature appeared, officially at
least, on the thundering edicts that would soon be issued against
the Parlement. But this did not mean that Gaston really favored
the decision to have Louis XIV, and in effect the court, leave
Paris. In this emergency situation, Le Coigneux and his colleagues in the Parlement could only second-guess their various
patrons' wishes.

The proposal to seize all Parisian fortifications was quickly
approved, and debate then began about issuing a decree that
declared Cardinal Mazarin an "enemy of the state." This too
was promptly passed. It authorized any and all persons to capture and kill the cardinal, to intercept any and all correspondence from him or to him, and to confiscate all his property.
The ink was scarcely dry on this law than the Parlement's porters and criers went out before the crowds that had assembled
outside the Great Chamber. Shouts of joy and relief greeted
the reading of this law, and their reverberations carried into
the Great Chamber, where the judges were still seated. Many
parlementaires no doubt believed that by declaring Mazarin an
enemy of the state they were saving the city from a bloodbath.
The streets were filled with people preparing to defend themselves against an army. Would the beggars, the jobless, and the
petty criminals of the city take advantage of the situation and
loot and rape?

While the Parlement was deliberating, the city fathers had
ordered the militia to post guards at the city gates and stand
ready to repress any outbreak of disorder in the city. Night fell
on a Paris that had abandoned agitation in favor of calm, thanks
to the Parlement's speedy action and to the calling up of the
militia columns. The commander of the Bastille had a son in
the Parlement, though there was some question as to where his
loyalties lay. Montbazon, the governor of Paris, came from a
long line of aristocrats who had conspired against royal ministers. Instead of trying to hold the fortifications of the city for
Louis XIV, he quickly surrendered them to the Parlement, after
only symbolic resistance.

The next few weeks were among the most exciting in the
history of a city that has a long and very exciting history. Did

the Parlement raise an army and declare Mazarin an enemy of the state *primarily* because it wished to pursue by force its own constitutional and office-holder grievances against the crown? Or was it *primarily* responding to a deeper, more popular revolutionary movement in the population? The king's departure and the expected blockade and sack of the city unleashed a new dynamic among Parisian elites. The reports about what the "people" were saying suddenly assumed an authority that no cynical judge, sceptical about the attitudes of the people, could deny.

Some rich Parisians ordered their servants to load up coaches and wagons with furniture and other household goods and attempt to drive them out of the city. Disguising themselves as beggars and peasants, they attempted to escape but almost invariably were caught and turned back by the militia guards and the crowds at the city gates. More than a change of clothes was required to conceal an elite education. Their gestures and their physique gave them away. In fact, on the day the king left Paris, the elite became prisoners of the people of Paris. During the brief parlementary debate over the declaration against Mazarin, someone had said that the judges were "hearing the voice of the people, and that the people demanded the cardinal's head." Molé had retorted: "We should not take the demands of the people into account, but should do what is just." The collective fear being felt by the judges prompted them to do something dramatic in order to maintain their public accountability. Not a few of them also took personal satisfaction in voting Mazarin a public enemy. The moderate and very influential President de Mêmes remarked that "force must be met with force." He then continued by asking whether the commissions and laws promulgated by the Parlement should now be issued in the king's name alone, in the name of the king and the Parlement, or in the name of the king, the Hôtel de Ville, and the Parlement. Such legal niceties were always significant to the Parlement. And so, try as they might, people wishing to influence it during the years of the Fronde—be they from the streets or from the Council of State—tripped themselves up in debates because distinctions, precedents, and formulas impeded their attempts to influence the judges.

The first rush to action by the Parlement and the Hôtel de Ville had not prompted a discussion of the coordination of the city's response to a new situation, but by mid-morning some of the more activist judges took steps, in the name of the Parlement, to assume the authority of the provost of merchants and the *échevins*. This move would prove more difficult than they expected. Arriving breathlessly at the Hôtel de Ville, the parlementaires found that after their first meeting the city fathers had voted to send a delegation to the queen regent and ask the reasons for the royal family's departure from Paris. The Parlement judges consequently tried to stampede the remaining city fathers into voting an act that would relinquish their powers to the Parlement. The city fathers stated that they would do nothing of the kind and that they would in fact do nothing at all, until the delegation returned from seeing the queen. Tempers flared, but the city fathers refused to be coerced into precipitous action. For a time it was doubtful whether the Parlement would gain control of the city militia, an absolutely crucial element in the capital that could be the deciding factor in the division that had appeared in the Hôtel de Ville. Some of the city fathers still wanted to stand for the king and Mazarin, while others favored the Parlement.

The governor of the Bastille was du Tremblay, the brother of the late Father Joseph, Richelieu's famous Capuchin adviser. The Bastille sheltered a few prisoners and a handful of guards, but if the commander chose to resist and ordered the heavy gates closed, only artillery could force it to surrender. A man appointed by Richelieu could have been expected to choose to fight and to sneer at any judges shouting that the gates must be opened in the name of the king and the Parlement. But du Tremblay's son was a master of requests, and it quickly became apparent that father and son were on the Parlement's side. The fall of the Bastille was hailed as a great victory by the Parisian crowds. A debate would ensue about whether to dismantle this symbol of royal authority, this fortification that could always be used to coerce the city into submission by raking streets and squares with cannon fire. In fact, once under parlementary control, the military security that it provided won out over the popular impulse to tear the fortress down. Broussel—and, soon, his son acting in his name—was appointed governor of the Bastille by the Parlement, an act that certainly assured the crowds that the fortress had gone over to the revolution. The Arsenal also yielded to the Parlement, removing from the capital any military presence loyal to the king and Mazarin.

Meanwhile the uneasy wait that had followed the flare of tempers at the Hôtel de Ville dragged on. News of the standoff circulated through the streets, and crowds began to form before the Hôtel de Ville. The city fathers who were holding out grew uneasy as shouts that they should join with the Parlement penetrated the windows and into the chamber where they were sitting. At last the deputies returned from their interview with the king (sources say "the king," though they may have meant the chancellor, Anne, or Gaston). In closed session they informed their colleagues that the king would be pleased to return to Paris on condition that the Parlement leave the city. On hearing this, the city fathers were "greatly perplexed." Only after the arrival of royal orders addressed to the Parlement did the meaning of this reply become clear. The Council of State, in the names of the king, the queen regent, and Gaston d'Orléans, ordered the Parlement as a body to leave the capital and take up its judicial duties in Montargis, a small city on the Loire River, some 60 miles south of Paris.

There was a centuries-long history of royal orders transferring the entire Parlement to another city during a confrontation between the Council and the Parlement, and this history would not end with the Fronde. In practice, however, instead of actually obliging the Parlement to change residence, the gesture forced a split between the judges and, as recently as the late sixteenth century, led to the formation of two separate parlements that thundered away at each other via decrees claiming that each was the one true parlement. Evidently Anne and Mazarin hoped that a splintering of this sort would take place again and weaken the Parlement of Paris as a political force. The judges rejected the royal decree out of hand. Indeed, had a judge sought to leave Paris, the crowds and the guards at the city gates would have forcibly restrained him. The Parisians did not want their "protectors" to depart, any more than they had wished the king to leave. As long as these powerful and rich authorities were present and surrounded by their families and their wealth, the chances were minimal that an army would invade and sack the city.

The provost of merchants wanted to remain loyal to the king and the Council, but there seemed no way to turn opinion around in the capital, after Louis and Anne had fled the city.

Though the provost offered to resign, that tactic, as always, did not alter the realities of the situation. Gunshot pierced his carriage several times as he went about the city, but he held on until the question of who would control the military forces of the capital had been at least partially resolved.

II. *The Duel for Command of the Parisian Military Forces*

As the Duke d'Elbeuf walked through the streets on his way to the Hôtel de Ville, his followers and the crowd shouted, "Long live the king and the Duke d'Elbeuf!" Cordially received by the city fathers, Elbeuf offered his services as commander to protect the city on behalf of the king and the Hôtel de Ville. Elbeuf belonged to the House of Lorraine, the same family as the famous Duke de Guise who had led the Parisians in revolution against Henry III at the head of the Catholic League in 1588. All the former Guise clients and their sons and friends may well have recalled the importance of the Lorraine family in the past history of the capital. The city fathers could do little but thank him for his willingness to help defend the capital and grant him command over the militia and other military forces.

Elbeuf was angry with Mazarin for what he deemed brutal and tyrannical punishments meted out to his family, way back in the early 1630s. He was also very jealous of the power and notoriety that the Condé family had been receiving in recent years. Lacking the acuity and moderation that could have made him a formidable contender for power among the great nobles, Elbeuf slipped easily into rebellion, while protesting his loyalty to Louis XIV. The respectable men of the capital, be they members of the law courts, the administration, or the mercantile and artisanal communities, were in many instances exceedingly deferential and obsequious toward someone of such high birth as a Lorraine. In addition, fears that widespread panic would break out were a factor with which the city fathers were forced to contend; and they knew that the name Lorraine would carry a great deal of weight in popular opinion. With Elbeuf in command of the militia, the issues of treason and rebellion also became ambiguous. By expressing his willingness to serve, Elbeuf was also virtually ordering the city fathers what to do.

Though Elbeuf had hundreds of supporters in the city, he also had his opponents. Just when it seemed that not only the Hôtel de Ville but the Parlement as well would accept Elbeuf as commander, coadjutor bishop Retz and a group of anti-Elbeuf judges in the Parlement plotted deep into the night to curb Elbeuf's rise to power in the Parisian revolution. The structures of aristocratic rivalry will be discussed in a later chapter; here the essential feature to be recalled is the fact that other prominent aristocrats, and Retz himself, feared that Elbeuf would become too powerful through his control over the city's military forces. Allusions to several prominent aristocrats had been made in the Parlement only a few hours earlier. Every prince had his followers in that body, and perhaps as many as three great nobles had a larger following in the Parlement than Elbeuf did— although this scion of the house of Lorraine undoubtedly had more followers at the Hôtel de Ville than they. A struggle for control of the capital's military forces was inevitable. The wily Retz served as a catalyst, not as a creator of the plot hatched during the night that followed Elbeuf's acceptance of command of the militia. According to the plot, the Prince de Conti would leave Saint-Germain-en-Laye, where the court was installed, and make his way to Paris to contest Elbeuf's command during a meeting of the Parlement and the other sovereign courts that was scheduled to be held the next day in the Great Chamber. Retz and his allies convinced Conti and his brother-in-law Longueville, the Norman governor, to ride hard and fast into the city. At first the guards at the gates refused to let them in, not only because they had been ordered to allow no one into the capital but also because suspicions had already been aroused about a plot to challenge Elbeuf's control over Paris.

Elbeuf and Conti were entitled to attend sessions of the Great Chamber of the Parlement whenever they wished, for they were peers of France, and in Conti's case a prince of the blood. These great nobles usually were present only on ceremonial occasions, but in times of crisis, when law suits were no longer being tried and political issues were the order of the day, they could and did attend sessions of the Parlement. To Elbeuf's surprise, Conti made his entry into the Great Chamber and was duly escorted to his very prestigious seat, indeed to a seat higher than Elbeuf's. First President Molé greeted Conti, thanked him for coming, and, having recognized that "royal blood boiled in his veins," all but offered him the command of the army the Parlement was planning to raise. Rumors buzzed through the court that Conti was willing to serve as commander.

When it came time for Elbeuf to speak, he first stated that he honored Monsieur the Prince de Conti because of his high rank and birth. Then he politely but firmly stated that he would execute the commission of commander of the Parisian militia forces that had been given him by the provost of merchants and the *échevins,* and that he "could not share his command with anyone." At that point, Elbeuf prepared to leave, putting the judges into a flurry. A confrontation between the two princes threatened to take place in the Great Chamber; and if anything could disturb the hierarchically minded and deferential judges, it was hosting a quarrel between two persons of high birth. Molé intervened at just the right moment and in a strong voice appointed a committee of judges to meet with the two princes in private chambers to work out an arrangement that was "consistent with the interests of their highnesses and in the Parlement's interest." While the judges breathed sighs of relief, the princes and the newly appointed committee of judges withdrew. Debate about raising an army resumed, but the committee (which included the very prestigious President de Mêmes) soon returned and announced that Conti would be "generalissimo" of the Parisian forces, and Elbeuf the "general," with particular and exclusive command of the cavalry. Difficulties almost immediately cropped up over the command structure of the army, but it was agreed for the time being that Conti and Elbeuf would command on alternate days.

This struggle over the command of the army would deeply affect the military effort to consolidate the Parlement's political power. Elbeuf had in fact stood little chance of winning. His base of support in the capital was small, because it was focused on the less powerful government at the Hôtel de Ville, rather than on the Parlement. It had been relatively easy for Molé to use the powers of his office as first president to facilitate Conti's rise to command, because Conti was a prince of the royal house of Bourbon. Retz and his allies in the Parlement had wanted a commander whom they believed would be easier to control than Elbeuf, whom they despised because of his independence from them. Molé's quick initiative in favor of Conti had not, however, been the result of collusion with Retz and his followers. Quite the contrary. Molé wanted the Parlement to be the controlling vector in the military buildup, and with his customary acuity he wished to keep as many rebellious actors as possible within the royal family, and Conti was a Bourbon. The Parlement had to concentrate its activities on the most important issues: maintaining order in the city and maintaining its own authority. In fact, by Conti's appointment the Lorraine supporters in the Hôtel de Ville and the more militant judges of the Parlement lost ground in the struggle to control the military forces that would either consolidate the revolutionary movement in Paris or break it. Molé had moved in several directions at once.

Conti was a Bourbon, but this did not necessarily mean familial and political unity. Rivalry between the senior and reigning branch of the Bourbon family and the Bourbon-Orléans, the Bourbon-Condés, and the Bourbon-Vendômes had from the outset formed the real backdrop for the Fronde. How this rivalry expressed itself in constitutional terms can best be understood by examining quarrels over membership in the Council of State. And as the Fronde deepened into civil war, the power of the Condé branch increased. As one acute observer put it: "The Dowager Princess de Condé should be very happy to see her children as chiefs of the two parties." That is exactly what happened, thanks to Molé's maneuvers to reduce the influence of the house of Lorraine.

Having Conti join the parlementary forces of the Fronde and command its troops seemed, to everyone who thought about it at the time, a way to increase the pressure on Mazarin, Anne, Gaston, and even Condé to change their tactics about Paris. As far as we can judge from their actions, the Parisians also hailed Conti's appointment. The more princes on the side of the Fronde, thought the typical Frondeur, the stronger the Fronde. They were, of course, being duped. Would Conti ever effectively and fully use the military power put at his disposal by the Fronde? And would he do battle against his illustrious brother? The answer would become apparent during the next few weeks; but no one, except perhaps Molé, was thinking that far ahead. The Frondeurs, including that would-be impresario of the revolution, Retz, were only thinking from hour to hour. As plans for raising troops were elaborated, and as the money to pay them began to pour in, it seemed to the Frondeurs that their cause was assured of victory.

Retz had wanted Conti as commander, because he believed the prince to be more easily manipulated than Elbeuf; and in this he was probably right. Also in Conti's baggage, as it were, came his brother-in-law, the Duke de Longueville, the illustrious descendent of Dunois. Most of the judges in the Parlement attributed Longueville's failure to conclude a peace with Spain at Munster to Mazarin's machinations. Longueville had joined the rebellion in Paris in hopes that the Parlement would grant him a higher status within the aristocracy that would permit him to sit as a member by right; but the judges had not forgotten that when they satisfied the demands and pretensions of one member of the high aristocracy, they usually discontented five or six others. Longueville soon left Paris, empty-handed, in order to maintain control over Normandy for the Fronde. His pregnant wife remained in the capital, a virtual hostage to assure the Parisians of Longueville's support for the Fronde. Or did his wife wish to join the rebellion and therefore decide, all on her own, to remain at the Hôtel de Ville? This brilliant and beautiful woman was every bit as politically engaged as her two brothers: Condé, commander of the king's army, and Conti, the new commander of the Parlement's army.

Elbeuf and Conti were both inexperienced generals, but it was never quite possible to predict how they would behave on a field of battle. Even a novice could win a brilliant victory. Elbeuf occasionally seemed more preoccupied with selecting the colors and the buttons for the uniforms of his crack noble cavalry regiments than with actually disciplining and training them. Whenever the war council's discussions about engaging in a battle required decisiveness from their commander, Conti showed indecisiveness. From what is currently known about the two men, it does not seem that either could have been counted on to fight decisively on behalf of the Parlement. (Nor could Fairfax, the general serving the English revolutionary parliament.) Was Conti genuinely skillful and therefore aware from the outset that the army of bakers and lawyers under his command would never be a match for the troops that had been facing the Spanish infantry, year after year, since 1635? An answer to this question is impossible. Had Elbeuf been made commander-in-chief, not only would he have had a somewhat freer hand in military decisions than Conti did; he might also have provoked a split between the Parlement and the Parisians by favoring a more radical revolution in the capital.

The Duke de Beaufort, who had recently made a dramatic escape from prison, also volunteered his services to the Parlement and requested that this court lift the judgement that had sent him to prison. This fiery and bragging grandson of Henry IV and Gabrielle d'Estrées quickly upstaged the other princes in overt combativeness and courage. The Parlement annulled its judgment against Beaufort for treason and conspiracy and gave him a command in its army, as a "son" of France. Thus the Parlement and the Hôtel de Ville created an army that reflected the traditional social order, not only in its command structure but in its cavalry, which was drawn largely from the nobility, and in its infantry, which had popular origins.

After the Parlement had, by a simple voice vote, declared Mazarin a "disturber of the public peace," it turned to discussing how to raise funds to pay the army. There was the unpaid militia, but the judges knew from the start that they could not rely on the militia alone. After his speech declaring that "force must be met with force," President de Mêmes volunteered to send his silverware to the royal mint to be melted down and used to pay infantry companies. In the seventeenth century, as much as a fifth of a prominent family's capital might consist of silver. De Mêmes' offer came at just the right moment. It prompted others to stand up and offer their money and silver for the army. President Le Coigneux contributed 50,000 *livres*. Soon a scheme for raising 500,000 *livres* was proposed. A suggestion was made to follow the procedures for raising special military funds that had been worked out during an emergency effort in 1635, when virtually every corporate body, beginning with the Parlement and reaching down to the lowliest guilds, was "assessed" according to its presumed wealth.

The fourteen newly created masters of requests whom the Parlement had stubbornly refused to admit into their corporation or allow to serve in the Parlement were now officially received in exchange for 300,000 *livres*, which they were to collect among themselves and offer to the Parisian army. This rapid settlement of an issue that had caused so much strife between the crown and the Parlement marked a bittersweet victory for Mazarin and his supporters in the Parlement, who had asserted all along that the issues dividing them were primarily fiscal and social (decline in the monetary value of offices) rather than constitutional. Now the Parlement needed money, and it had to raise these funds in the wake of the crown's long effort to increase revenues from Paris. The new masters of requests must have talked a great deal among themselves before six of them (Le Camus, de Poincaré, Colombet, Maupeou, Feydeau, and Verthamont) agreed to pay at least 20,000 *livres* each. Others (Guillon and Maugis) contributed as little as 4,000 *livres*. Treasurers (including the publisher Cramoisy) were appointed by the Parlement to keep the funds in their houses or shops and record all disbursements.

On 10 January 1649—that is, only four days after the king's flight—a large group of law clerks called upon First President Molé at his residence and offered to serve in the parlementary army. They estimated themselves to number 1,200 strong. Molé requested a dozen representatives of the group to appear before the Parlement and, after hearing their expressions of willingness to fight and their request for a commander, advised them to report to the Hôtel de Ville.

The University of Paris, represented by the rector, came to the Great Chamber and, after a long compliment in Latin, informed the judges that it had raised 10,000 *livres* for the army. The social history of the university has never been written, so it is impossible to estimate the degree of commitment to the Fronde by professors, chaplains, and students that this sum represented. It would also be interesting to compare the amount the university offered in 1649 with its donations during the league of the 1580s. The formal discourse by the rector clearly indicates that the university could act as a corporate entity and that in this instance it placed its prestige and wealth on the side of the revolution. Through representatives of its Assembly, the clergy would try somewhat later to mediate between the Parlement and the king's council but would find neither party willing to discuss compromise. In fact, some of the richer prelates found that they were "treated like everyone else"—that is to say, they could not enter or leave the city freely.

The prestige of the parlementary judges, who wore their customary long black robes as they moved about the city, gave them a certain independence to act without commissions or instructions from any collective authority. It should not come as a surprise that some judges took initiatives that did not meet the unanimous approval of their colleagues. The Parlement thanked those who began taking inventory of the weapons, powder, and shot available in the Arsenal and stored in other caches throughout the city. This zealousness, however, was questioned when judges began searching private homes for money. The residences of some prominent tax officials, tax farmers, and bankers sat empty or were barely protected by servants. The popular hatred for these men spilled over into the Parlement, which asked: "Have these men not become wealthy by stealing royal revenues?" The residence of Contarini, Mazarin's banker, was one of the first searched by a group of judges. In this instance, the anticipated bags of coins failed to turn up under loose floorboards or behind barrels in the cellar; but in other cases silver and jewelry belonging to families that had abandoned the capital were dug up in gardens or recovered from behind hastily plastered walls, usually with the complicity of servants.

The search for money became a fairly extensive activity. It strengthened popular support for the Parlement and may in the long run have reduced the impulse to pillage the houses of tax collectors and financiers. In late January, the Parlement received almost daily reports about further discoveries of jewelry and bags of money. Since nearly every judge in the Parlement had family ties to ministers and tax farmers, the practice soon became a subject for debate. Movements to confiscate hidden wealth continued throughout the Fronde, but during these early weeks of the blockade around Paris it focused almost entirely on the immense quantity of household effects, books, and ecclesiastical revenues belonging to Mazarin and his immediate collaborators, among them the banker Contarini. When the Parlement finally ordered Mazarin's library sold at auction in 1651, to raise money for the army, the cardinal's supporters surreptitiously bought most of the books with their own money and hid them away. Objects belonging personally to the king and the queen regent were the only ones allowed to leave the capital, and this was only possible because a heavy militia guard surrounded the carts carrying the items out of Paris.

The time had come to choose sides, and, as in any hierarchical society, high-ranking aristocratic personages were wooed by the Frondeurs. When Madame de Longueville, sister of Condé and wife of the governor of Normandy, joined the Fronde, she asked the city fathers for a place to live that would in effect make her a hostage to the Fronde, for she wished to convince everyone of her loyalty. She moved into the Hôtel de Ville with much fanfare and gaiety—and promptly gave birth to a son. No performance could have better curried public favor. The public baptism held in the square before the Hôtel de Ville was one of the important moments of the Fronde. The event had a theatrical dimension; but for the thousands who witnessed it the hopes of victory and the passion to protest government policies united in a fête that was both aristocratic and popular. Retz, the coadjutor bishop of Paris—always a star performer— baptized the infant aristocrat. Among his baptismal names was Paris, chosen to demonstrate his parents' solidarity with the Parisian Fronde.

No less dramatic was the decision to join the Fronde made on 11 January by some 150 of the king's guards who were stationed around the Palais Royal. Their oaths of fidelity to the king and the Parlement were received with particular solemnity because although the Parisians could be raucous and violent, they were not uninformed about the religious and still quasi-feudal bonds that held the monarchy together at its highest levels. The Parlement and the cabarets of the capital rejoiced at the news that the Council had posted guards around the royal chateau of Saint-Germain-en-Laye and ordered them to capture any servant, regardless of his rank, who attempted to make his way to Paris and join the Fronde. This news confirmed Frondeur views about the tyrannical character of Mazarin's government. By 8 January it was no longer possible for any person of rank to leave either Paris or Saint-Germain-en-Laye without a passport signed by Conti or Elbeuf, on the Parisian side, or Gaston d'Orléans or Condé on the other side. Two armed camps now faced each other. The Parlement renewed its decree that no army should come within twenty leagues of Paris. This seems to have been the most fitting reply the Parlement could make to the royal order sending it to Montargis.

The judges continued to make calculations about the size of the army they would raise, and about how much it would cost. Knowledge about raising an army seems to have been extensive; no one judge seems to have claimed that he was more informed about the subject than his colleagues. Agreement was soon reached: there should be an army of 8,000 troops, with 4,000 infantry who would be paid a total of 7,000 *livres* per day, and 4,000 cavalrymen, who would receive 8,000 *livres*. These troops, their officers, their horses, their drummers, and their boys would cost an estimated 465,000 *livres* each month. It soon became apparent that if the army were to have some chance of success, the original plan to raise funds according to the procedures outlined in the parlementary order of 1635 would have to be legislated and enforced.

The Parlement therefore decreed that each house in Paris and its suburbs with a *porte cochère*—that is, an entrance wide enough to admit a coach—must either furnish one horseman or pay a one-time fee of 150 *livres*. Each house with a "small" door was assessed one foot soldier for each household residing there, to do guard duty wherever required. If the soldier was not forthcoming, the household would have to pay 50 *livres*—a sum soon reduced to 30 *livres*. Families with men already serving in the militia were not obliged to pay. In the debates about this legislation, the estimates of the money that would be collected varied considerably; but by early January 1649 it was evident that the Fronde leaders entrusted with raising the army were planning for a well-paid force that would bear arms for several months. At some point—it is impossible to say when— First President Molé noted in his memoirs that the city had become so committed to the war effort that neither he nor anyone else could do anything to strengthen the king's authority in the capital, *until* there was a shortage of money to pay for the army.

III. *Food Supplies*

What the populace feared most—and they were perhaps joined by the judges—was a food shortage. Condé's forces took up positions at every bridge and road into the capital. The more radical among the Frondeur judges moved quickly to legislate controls over the bakers and to fix the price of bread. The grain stored in the various monasteries of the city was not overlooked; but there was plenty of food during the first weeks of the blockade, and the army was taking shape. On 11 January, 500 cavalrymen lined up for review in the Place Royale, obviously a public display ordered by the Frondeur commanders to convince the Parisians that they were receiving defense in return for their tax money. On 29 January, President de Nesmond informed the Parlement that the number of infantrymen had reached 11,000 and the cavalry 4,000.

In the face of public pressure to increase food supplies, the Duke de Beaufort made a sally to the south, to open up the roads. Two cavalry regiments were supported by militiamen who had specifically volunteered to support the maneuver. An attack on Condé's forces was planned for the town of Corbeil, some eighteen miles south of the city; but by the time the Frondeur troops reached Juvisy, the halfway mark, it became apparent that they were inferior in strength to the royal troops and were in no condition to dislodge the other army. Beaufort and his men returned to the capital without food, dejected because the battle had seemed altogether too risky a proposition.

This tiny military setback worried the judges in the Parlement. President Le Coigneux blamed First President Molé. Had he not delayed things? Was the whole military effort now going to fail, because the first president had refused to keep the Parlement in extra sessions immediately after the events of Twelfth Night? Now that Beaufort had returned empty-handed, the Frondeur judges began to plan not only how to mount a stronger military force but also how to ration the food supplies stocked in Paris. Rumors began to circulate to the effect that the regiments stationed around the capital were pillaging, stealing cattle, and spoiling vineyards and fields. The country houses of rich Parisians circled the capital. Properties belonging to the judges of the Parlement therefore suddenly became particularly vulnerable to pillaging; and the Council at Saint-Germain-en-Laye soon decreed a special tax on their owners. The heavy rains of December continued on into January. The Seine overflowed its banks in many places around the city and even inundated the center of Paris. This meandering river seemed to have a stranglehold on the capital, almost as if it were an ally of Condé's army. By late January it was becoming obvious that the only major bridge and road in Frondeur control was at Charenton, a small town southeast of the capital. Could the troops commanded by Conti hold it? This was the principal question being asked during the last week of January and during the first days of February 1649. But the time to test the Frondeur forces had not yet come.

Guards were posted at every city gate, and at night the militia supplemented the regular watch that roamed the streets to maintain order. Several of the eyewitness accounts of this stage of the Fronde stress the importance of "containing" the people; that is to say, military force must be made sufficiently apparent in the popular quarters to impede breaking into houses and shops. By mid-January, shopkeepers on some of the key streets around the Halles, and especially in the Saint-Denis quarter of the city, refused to open on market days. They feared that their shops would be pillaged should food supplies prove inadequate in the nearby Halles. The Parlement therefore ordered Lamoignon, the militia commander for the Saint-Denis district and the area north of the Halles, to be present with his men on market days.

Throughout the blockade, Lamoignon carried out his orders very faithfully, with the result that no major food riot occurred in that area, despite evidence of food shortage and despite a steep rise in bread prices that the price controls voted by the Parlement were powerless to stop. In fact, every market day was a kind of barometric indicator of the sense of security and well-being in the city. If food supplies were adequate and prices were not unreasonably high, shops opened and business was conducted normally. If food was scarce or prices had soared, shops remained shut.

In the narrow and crowded streets of the northern quarters, and around the thriving market at the Place Maubert, neighbors would confer and make a joint decision. We can imagine the women herring-sellers, the roasters, and the butchers signaling to each other across the narrow streets or in little back courtyards and deciding, by gesture, whether business should be conducted that day. There seems to have been a great deal of solidarity among merchants of the capital, at least about opening and closing shop at a particular hour, even though the time was not always clearly specified by city or guild rules. In times of crisis, rumors of pillaging and food shortages affected the decisions taken by Parisian merchants each day at dawn. The sources on which to build a detailed description of the day-to-day life in the capital during the blockade of 1649 are difficult to interpret; but it is evident that the populace and the Parlement responded quickly and nervously to rumors, riots, food shortages, and shouts of alarm that troops were nearing the city gates. The judges and the city fathers frequently rode up and down through crowded streets, or walked two by two up the Rue Saint-Denis, to provide a visible presence of support and order in the capital. Lamoignon observed that the regular watch and the judicial commissioners who patrolled markets and streets during periods of calm lost the respect of the *peuple* during the blockade. During moments of tension, only the militia could maintain order while bread was being distributed. Bakers, and their storage bins and ovens, had to be protected from the mob on days of shortage. The routine attacks on bakers prompted by the quality of the bread, the weight of a loaf, and the price were exacerbated by the shortages resulting from the blockade.

While any conclusion about the state of public order in Paris can only be impressionistic, it is evident that the Parisians remained quite calm and resolute as they faced growing food shortages and possible military attack. The emphasis on defense, which included stretching chains across every intersection, contributed to the sense of security and order. The drums that always accompanied marching regiments were heard frequently, and at odd hours of the day and night. The sound would make people jittery, until friends shouting from steeples reassured the crowds below that "their" troops were making the noise. Past experience suggested that Condé would set up the blockade and wait until a food shortage forced the Parlement to open negotiations; but there were occasional fears that a zealous army captain might try to seize a city gate, pillage nearby shops, and then withdraw. After all, Condé's troops were also short of food.

The rhythm of food supplies, if it can be called that, was broken by late January. Passages had been closed off beyond Charenton, so little food came from the South. Nor could the Parisians reach the crucial town of Gonesse, some ten miles northeast of the city, where much of the cheaper bread consumed in Paris was baked. Bread prices tripled in the course of a single market day, and meat was scarce. The canonical rule that one must fast by eating only fish and eggs during Lent was conveniently suspended by Retz, the coadjutor bishop of Paris.

Anti-Frondeurs greeted this proclamation with derision. Though Catholics could now eat meat during Lent, there was none to be had.

The effects of Condé's blockade, and speculation about what would happen next, unleashed a flow of pamphlets on an extensive variety of ethical, religious, and political subjects. Often sold on the Pont Neuf, these pamphlets diagnosed every aspect of the individual, civic, religious, and familial life of the blockade. The writers of these pamphlets, which were soon to be called *Mazarinades*, rarely signed their names. Chiefly individuals without patrons, these authors expressed what they thought their fellow Parisians should hear.

These pamphlets are remarkable evidence of the existence of public-spiritedness during the parlementary Fronde. Diagnosing the ills of the realm and offering remedies that rarely follow easily recognizable ideological inclinations, the *Mazarinades* are an authentic expression of the variegated, deeply engaged political culture. Some writers placed their hopes in the Parlement, others in the crown, still others in God and the king, to overcome the anxieties created by the court's absence and the blockade. Still others pointed fingers at various evils that must be rooted out before the overall health of the body politic would improve. Between early January and the end of the blockade in March 1649, some 1,200 pamphlets would appear. Explorations of the nature of monarchy, and of the French monarchy in particular, and the relations between its parts, became more thoughtful and genuinely philosophical as the feeling of defeat increased and the eventual humiliation of Paris and the Fronde loomed imminent.

These vitriolic attacks against Mazarin, the tax farmers and their agents, and the other profiteers erupted soon after the start of the blockade. Sometimes accompanied by learned parallels with such evil councillors as Concini or Sejanus, and sometimes pure *ad hominem* attacks against the Cardinal's social inferiority, his nationality, his seducing of the queen, and his rapacity, these *Mazarinades* testify to the presence of the traditional argument so often found in early-modern political cultures: if the "polluting element" is eliminated, all will be well.

The purely literary element was also present in the *Mazarinades* from the beginning, for after all the seventeenth century witnessed the birth of literary criticism. Some *Mazarinades* were admired for the quality of their prose, for their rhetorical brilliance, for their learning. Quite independently of their political or ethical messages, verses were evaluated as *"bon"* or *"mauvais."* There is no doubt that some of the authors published their *Mazarinades* every bit as much to enhance their reputations as writers as to give advice about what to do in time of crisis. In French political culture of the seventeenth century, no boundary line would be drawn between writing as a civic action and the pursuit of *gloire* by writing, and certainly not during the exhilarating political activism and literary vitality of the 1640s.

Just how much hardship the blockade caused is a matter of controversy. When prices rise steeply, those segments of the population with very low incomes, or no income at all, suffer the most. In his memoirs written many years after the Fronde, Retz claimed that food supplies never really became inadequate. This Frondeur who claimed to act on behalf of the people's welfare would certainly never have admitted that food shortages had caused the Parisians great hardship. Yet the blockade occurred during a period of very unstable conditions in the food market. Bad weather had affected not only the harvests but also the transport of grain and livestock.

In fact, Fronde or not, the Parisians never knew from one year to the next, or even from one season to the next, what foods would be available and how much they would have to pay. And, as we shall see, once the stop-gap measures to assure bread supplies began to fail in late February, the almost unthinkable prospect of negotiating with Mazarin became thinkable for the judges of the Parlement. Paris did not become increasingly revolutionary as food supplies diminished.

The Parlement instituted additional supervision of the weighing and milling of flour and the baking and selling of bread. Direct contact between the judges and the Parisian populace, if it ever really was lacking, increased dramatically as a result of their personal presence at scales and ovens. There is little doubt that the Parisians told the judges exactly what they thought about the troublesome times in which they lived. Were the judges who were most zealous for the Fronde, particularly the men from the chambers of Inquests, the first to help maintain security and see to the fair distribution of bread? It is tempting to speculate about how these frequent contacts with anxious and occasionally angry crowds prompted reflections about the Fronde in the minds of the judges who had voted, time after time, to heighten the challenge to royal authority.

Parlementaire committees were appointed to take inventory of all the grain and other food supplies stored in the numerous monastic houses of the city. The religious were known to sell grain on the open market, but what if the grain they held were simply confiscated or paid for with promissary notes that could not be cashed? Reports about the large inventories found in the monasteries cheered the judges, as they fretted over the effects the blockade was having on the city's mood. Hand mills, and a few mills powered by donkeys, were set up in cloisters and in the cemetery of the Holy Innocents to grind these grain supplies into flour, which would be transferred to the bakeries of the city under the surveillance of the militia and baked into bread, again under the supervision of the militia. Opportunities for cheating—and for very high profits—abounded during periods of scarcity.

Was this grain confiscated from the monasteries simply because cash was short? Discussions of paying for grain are not extensive in the reports of parlementary sessions. Far more frequent are calls for new legislation ordering all "beggars and useless eaters" in the capital to be rounded up and escorted out through the city gates to fend for themselves. Legislation of this sort was eventually voted, and the militia and watchmen attempted to implement it. The Parlement's attempts to control bread prices through legislation, punish profiteers, reduce hoarding and illegal measuring, force beggars from the city, and confiscate all monastic grain were part of a routine moral-economic response to the food shortages in Paris. In this instance, these measures were prompted by the blockade, but they could just as well have been triggered by crop failures. Le Tellier, the secretary of state who worked closely with Mazarin, reputedly said that Paris would hold out for only two market periods, that is for approximately two weeks. If Mazarin and others in the Council of State believed this, they were mistaken. Morale remained very high in the capital for at least a month after the king's departure. As February dragged on, both sides began to play a desperate game. In the spring Condé's army would be needed again on the northern border, to intercept a predictable Spanish invasion. If Mazarin assumed that before the start of the spring military campaign against the Spanish, the Pari-

sians would agree to his harsh terms in return for lifting the
blockade, he was pretty daring. In fact, he had no choice but to
hope and to plan on forcing the Parlement to capitulate, or else
to fight to uphold royal authority as he defined it.

The number of military parades and troop reviews increased
in late January in different parts of the city. These events served
not only to reassure the Parisians that they were receiving protection in return for their taxes, they also were the only means
available to ascertain whether regiments were up to strength.
Some quartering of soldiers was ordered by the Hôtel de Ville,
but most of the troops lived at home, for they were Parisians.
A few of the great houses owned by tax officials and royal councillors were opened up for use as barracks. The milling about
of so many soldiers after each muster contributed to feelings of
uneasiness as well as to feelings of security. When a number of
small riots by unpaid troops took place, the uneasiness increased.
Six hundred infantrymen joined together one day in front of
Elbeuf's house on the Rue Saint-Antoine to shout demands for
payment. This occurred on 21 January. Elbeuf had already
received sizable sums from the Parlement's treasurer to be used
for troop payments; but, as was customary prior to the great
military reforms of the later seventeenth century, what a commander did with the money he received was largely his own
decision. Elbeuf may have used these sums to pay his personal
debts and the debts of his relatives and clients. Uniforms, arms,
horses, grooms, boys, and women were probably given priority
over infantrymen when Elbeuf began disbursing these funds;
but if such was in fact the case, his conduct was typical.

Some of the most aristocratic cavalry regiments appeared
for musters in brightly colored uniforms and shiny steel breast-
plates. Matched bridles and saddles also contributed to the pan-
ache of these elite troops; but there is evidence to suggest that
some Parisians deemed these expenses superficial, if not ridiculous, in such a time of crisis. It can be said in Elbeuf's favor
that he and his captains faced the crucial problem of holding
the loyalties of young aristocrats, for whom the issue of the
number of masters of requests in the Parlement remained
unimportant. And the Parisian tailors and harnessmakers were
given work by making this equipment.

There is little evidence of tension between Elbeuf's crack
troops and the militia. Petty rivalries occasionally surfaced

between them, but there was also a great deal of solidarity. The city fathers decreed that representatives from each militia column would be able to attend meetings of the war council, so the militia was perhaps kept better informed of plans and military threats than were the soldiers and cavalrymen paid by Elbeuf. Colonel Lamoignon worked out a plan for rotating the representatives of his militia column. Several men would serve on a weekly basis, after which the rotation would start again. This procedure suggests that not only was there a great deal of consultation and solidarity in the militia columns, but that they also were prepared for a fairly long period of service in this specific crisis. In mid-January, one or another of the colonels attempted to convince his colleagues to promote him to the rank of major, with the approval of the city fathers. All of the colonels were ordered to attend a meeting at the Hôtel de Ville on this question. After some debate it became clear that there was strong opposition to creating still another layer to the militia command structure, and the proposal was rejected. Was this simply someone's attempt to gain a more elevated rank? Or was it an attempt to lead the militia toward a more overt military role? The question cannot be answered until further research has been completed in the disparate sources dealing with this most popular of Parisian military institutions.

On 27 January 1649, Lamoignon received the order to be present at the Temple with the volunteer fighters of his company. The entire northern rim of Paris feared an attack at several points. It was better defended by fortifications along the southern rim, but there were also a greater number of weak points in that area as a result of the construction of suburban houses and shops. The city fathers ordered the demolition of flimsy structures such as lean-to storage facilities and wooden houses. The troops undertaking this demolition carried out their task under the protection of armed infantry. Owners, renters, and squatters disliked the disruption and damage that this demolition brought into their lives and on several occasions did not hesitate to protest to the city fathers and attack the demolition teams.

From the moment of the Parlement's decision to create an army, the more strategically minded judges warned that extreme rapidity was necessary. Defenses must be secured and control of the bridges and roads must be maintained by fairly large military forces. By late January there was a growing feeling that a showdown was inevitable. One January night, Lamoignon received the order to "keep your column in arms this night, and at the sound of the first shot from the Bastille, march toward the Place Royale." Regular couriers ran from the Hôtel de Ville, keeping the colonel of every quarter informed. In addition, a plan had been drawn up for a general mobilization of the city's entire militia. Beaufort's failure to break through at Corbeil had, as we have seen, prompted gloom and failure among the Frondeur judges, who now pressed for more vigorous military plans.

In the first few days of February, rumors flew about that Condé and part of his army were preparing to march upon Charenton, the one town the Frondeurs held along the perimeter of the capital. Conti, Elbeuf, the provost of merchants, Retz, Deslandes-Payen, and presumably officers from each militia column held a war council. The first plan agreed upon was for all the paid troops and militiamen to occupy the area between Charenton and the Vincennes woods during the night and repulse Condé and his troops should they attempt to reach Charenton. After more debate, this plan was dropped, presumably because it involved mobilizing too many men, and for too long a time. Since the projected army of 15,000 to 18,000 men would not be able to live in the open country for very long, Condé needed only to wait for them to withdraw to Paris.

Then, early in the morning of 8 February, an order went out for all the militia columns to assemble as soon as possible and march to the Place Royale, near the eastern rim of the city. Once a few of the columns had arrived, every possible attempt was made to force them to march towards Charenton. The paid army and the entire Parisian militia thus marched out of the capital, an operation that took approximately eighteen hours. Colonel Lamoignon remarked that had all the companies been up to strength, the army of the Parisian Fronde would have totalled 12,000 infantrymen and between 4,000 and 5,000 cavalrymen. But, he added, there were only about half that many. Still, an army of 8,000 men was a sizable force. Condé was reputed to have only 6,000 men. Lamoignon also remarked that almost all of the colonels and other officers were there in person, which suggests that this mobilization had the support of the militia elite, certainly, and of about half the regular militiamen.

By the time the Parisian army had wound its way through the narrow streets of the faubourg and out into the country, Condé had almost captured Charenton. The Fronde garrison in that town fought valiantly to hold the bridge, even after the town was lost; but they were overcome by overwhelming odds. Frondeur general Bertrand de Clanleu remained faithful to the king and the Parlement to the end: he was killed on the bridge at the head of his troops. When Conti and Elbeuf learned from their scouts that Charenton had fallen and that Condé was now consolidating his position around the bridge and city, they held a hasty war council and concluded that they would not attempt to retake the bridge. Orders were given to the army and the militia to turn around and march back into Paris. The Fronde army was larger than Condé's by perhaps as much as 2,000 men, and it was fresh. The decision not to fight sealed the fate of the Fronde in Paris.

Now the city was entirely surrounded and blockaded by Condé's army. In a strictly military sense, the war was over. Never again would the Frondeur generals order out an entire army or prepare to fight their way through the blockade. What had gone wrong? Certainly Condé's army was strong, but after the Charenton attack its position was not overwhelmingly powerful. Conti's hesitation about using an inexperienced army and militia against a royal army is understandable. Divisions within the war council and quarrels between generals may have increased the risk of defeat. The judges in the Parlement and the militia colonels who were armchair strategists had concluded that their cause was practically hopeless after the fiasco at Corbeil. The fall of Charenton to the forces of the king and the Council gave Mazarin an important victory. It was now only a matter of time before the Parisian Frondeurs would be forced to negotiate the terms of their defeat.

Almost from the beginning, First President Molé, Omer Talon, and other parlementaires hostile to the Fronde had called for negotiations to end the war. Their initial calls for peace negotiations had been shouted down; but after the disaster at Charenton a majority of the judges still sitting in the Great Chamber approved the selection of a delegation to explore the possibility of a settlement with the queen regent and the Council of State. A silence fell over the chamber during the days after Charenton. The time for speeches seemed over, and talk of further taxes to strengthen the army fell on deaf ears. Still, as the judges picked their negotiators, it became evident that the Frondeurs were not going to give up easily. In fact, some of their leaders—Le Coigneux, Nesmond, Viole, and Longueil—were appointed to the negotiating team that was drawn not only from the Parlement but also from the Chamber of Accounts, the Court of Excises, and the city council. Mathieu Molé, intrepid as ever, led the whole group by reason of his high office as first president of the Parlement.

The talks lasted almost a month. The slowness almost inevitably resulted from the large body of negotiators and from divisions among the Frondeurs. The desire to punish the Parisians, and the Parlement in particular, was also very strong among some of the royal councillors. Had the Parlement not received a royal order transferring it to Montargis? Should it not then go to Montargis, now that the army it had raised could no longer assure food supplies for Paris?

On the Frondeur side, the negotiators refused to sit or listen to terms until Mazarin had been disgraced and expelled from the Council. This was an impossible condition, but it helped strengthen the Frondeur position and enabled them to accept a compromise: the cardinal would be excluded from the room in which talks were held and negotiations with him would be conducted through go-betweens. The fiction of Mazarin's absence had to be accepted by the Council, a humiliating defeat that Gaston d'Orléans and Anne accepted in order to hasten the settlement.

A lengthy discussion of these negotiations would be inappropriate here, but it is important to note that they deserve careful study in the light of some of the recent studies of the possible influences of internal revolt and protest, and of general negotiations to end international wars. Nineteenth-century scholars of the Fronde had little patience with the frustration that peace proponents faced during negotiations to end civil wars and revolutions. In what seemed like hours of endless talk during March 1649, some of the Frondeurs in the Parlement and the Hôtel de Ville, and even some of the Frondeur princes, insisted on being included in the negotiations to end the civil war—and also in those to end the war with Spain.

Virtually from the moment when Louis XIII drew his last breath in 1643, Mazarin had been attacked over France's negotiations to end the war with Spain. Many sincere and well-intentioned judges believed that the cardinal actually was preventing a peace settlement, and they claimed that he did so because his services would be unnecessary should the war end. This argument had made it possible to infer, of course, that joining the Fronde meant advancing the cause of peace with Spain. Retz, who played an important part in arranging the appearance of a fake Spanish diplomat before the Parlement, probably had no illusions about the difficulties Mazarin actually faced in negotiating with Spain. The wily prelate accused Mazarin of almost every type of duplicity and crime, but he understood that the revolution in Paris would encourage Spanish diplomats to seek harsher terms in their exchanges with the French. The Fronde in Paris had encouraged the Spanish to hang on longer; and while a military victory seemed beyond their reach, what they had lost on the battlefield might well be regained around the negotiating table. Retz was, however, rather special in his lack of idealism. The judges who negotiated at Saint-Germain-en-Laye to end the blockade of Paris, however, may have sincerely believed that they were advancing the cause of international peace by insisting that the Parlement be represented in any further negotiations to end the war that France had been waging with Spain since 1635.

The princes who had commanded the Frondeur armies, and who have so often been described as petty and entirely corrupt in their coming to terms with Anne and Mazarin, also wove specific conditions into the negotiations for a general peace settlement with Spain. Conti, who had appeared so ineffectual in war, now insisted on rapid negotiations with Spain, both in his public statements and in the secret proposals for a settlement that he submitted to Anne and Mazarin. Sincere? Naive? Duped? Did men such as Conti cloak their personal ambitions for additional titles and pensions in the garb of public motives favoring peace that were deemed Christian?

The truth lies in the subtle balance of all these elements. Princes were public figures in the seventeenth century. Two points are evident and deserve to be reiterated: the conduct of rebellious princes who allied with France's foreign enemies in order to increase pressure on the crown was part of a centuries-old pattern of political activity on the part of the great aristocratic families of the realm. The Fronde has many structural affinities with the Hundred Years' War and the Wars of Religion, on every aspect of the political, diplomatic, and military roles played by the great princes. This will become still more evident in subsequent chapters. In the negotiations to end the Paris Fronde, however, we have the paradoxical situation of one prominent prince (Conti) pressing for a peace settlement with Spain at considerable risk to his own prestige and wealth, while another prince (his brother Condé) was commanding the French army's annual campaigns against Spain and feeling pleasure about all the renown his victories gave him, both in France and all over Europe.

The negotiators representing Mazarin (Gaston d'Orléans and Condé) held to a very intransigent and humiliating set of conditions for the Parlement and the blockaded city, until the news reached them that the Spanish army had invaded France and was holding the town of Pontavert, north of Laon. The invasion may have been more symbolic than militarily important, but its diplomatic consequences were enormous. Laon had surrendered to the Spanish out of pro-Fronde sympathies. What other towns in the North were so tired of the war that they would do the same? Condé and his army, which was still deployed around Paris, must immediately head north. Equally devastating was the news that Marshal Turenne had rebelled and was seeking to join the Fronde in Paris.

Mazarin received the news of these momentous events a few days, or in some instances only a few hours, before the Frondeur negotiators did. The harsh conditions were dropped and an agreement was rather hastily worked out. The Frondeur judges kept warning that anything they accepted might be rejected by their colleagues back in the Great Chamber; but in fact a fundamental shift of opinion had taken place among them. These mature and experienced men suddenly perceived that Mazarin's repeated statements about the Spanish threat had some basis in fact. Their mood changed as well, and the patriotic current that ran deep in the hearts of all noblemen of the Robe prevailed. An agreement was signed, with the following principal terms: (1) the Parlement would attend a *lit de justice* at Saint-Germain-en-Laye; (2) there would be no further general assemblies of all the sovereign courts in 1649; (3) the decrees promulgated by the Great Chamber since 6 January 1649, especially those directed against Mazarin, would be annulled;

(4) the troops raised by the Parlement would be cashiered; (5) the Parisians would lay down their weapons; (6) the Spanish envoy would immediately leave the capital; and (7) the Bastille and the Arsenal, and the munitions they contained, would be restored to the king.

In return, the Council of State agreed to declare a general and complete amnesty for the princes, royal officials, gentlemen, towns, and corporations who had taken part in the Fronde. They also solemnly reconfirmed the Declarations of July and October 1648. The blending of foreign and civil war that Richelieu had so dreaded occurred in 1649.

How can the end of a revolutionary movement be recognized? For several months after the lifting of the blockade, the Parisians slowly resumed the routines that had been disrupted by the Fronde. The Frondeur army disbanded. Retz and Beaufort, and their allies in the Parlement, still occasionally tried to mobilize the populace and begin the Fronde anew; but they failed every time. On one occasion, the effort was more theatrical than revolutionary. While riding through Paris in a carriage, a lesser magistrate became the target of prearranged gunfire. To simulate a wound, he cut himself, then shouted for help. A number of his allies rode through the streets, trying to mobilize the city against Mazarin's henchmen who, it was claimed, were murdering the Frondeurs. Though the whole thing had been carefully staged to resemble an assassination attempt, the crowds remained entirely calm. The judges in the Parlement who attempted to mobilize support for yet another round of attacks on Mazarin were shouted down. Instead, a judicial inquiry was established to investigate the participants in the plot. The failure of these attempts by their former leaders to rally the Parisians signaled the end of the revolutionary moment in the capital. What is interesting about this plot is that it had been partly modeled on the arrest of Broussel and his colleagues in August 1648 that had led to the Day of the Barricades. But the climate of opinion had changed.

The anti-Frondeurs also accused the Frondeurs of attempting to monopolize bread and grain supplies and control their prices in order to drive them up and create a climate of panic. But these accusations failed to mobilize public opinion. There seemed to be no way to confirm or deny the charges, and as long as bread was available on market days the issue failed to take hold. Retz and Beaufort probably no longer had the financial resources required for carrying out such a complex and costly market operation, but Mazarin, Maisons, and their friends in the grain trade may have had the money to do this. The issue declined in importance, but it and the repeated attempts of the Fronde leaders to arouse the Parisians to join them suggest that well-to-do Frondeurs and aristocrats had little fear of the lower classes and of the Parisian crowd. In fact, once the blockade had been lifted, the occasional instances of pillaging and of physical violence occurred in the capital at about the same level as before the blockade. The houses of tax farmers, supporters of Mazarin, and royal officials known to be administering taxes were still subject to being defiled, broken into, and in extreme cases set on fire.

One of the important internal factors that had broken the revolutionary spirit of Paris had been the collapse of bond payments. The owners of these bonds, or *rentes,* were almost legion in Paris. Well-to-do merchants had invested tens of thousands of *livres* in these bonds and were now fearful of losing not only the interest due them, but the capital itself. Widows of small retail merchants and better-off artisans often had invested as little as 25 or 50 *livres,* but the security of their investments counted as much for them than it did for the wealthier Parisians who had invested far larger sums. The money used to pay the interest on *rentes* came from excises such as the Cinq Grosse Fermes and from numerous other excise taxes collected not only in and around Paris but virtually everywhere in France.

Interest payments had dwindled in January, then ceased in February 1649. Angry crowds of bourgeois marched to the Parlement to demand justice and an investigation into the maladministration of the *rentes.* The non-payment of interest was, of course, also causing losses for the judges, because virtually all of them owned large numbers of these bonds. The Fronders blamed Mazarin and the war with Spain for this non-payment, but these accusations did little to quiet the anxieties of bond-holders. In conjunction with the officials at the Hôtel de Ville, who were nominally in charge of administering the bonds issued under their authority, a committee of city officials and parlementary judges was established to investigate the administration of the bonds and to attempt to restore the interest payments. While the committee investigated the accounts, it was becoming obvious to everyone that these payments had not collapsed exclusively as a result of the blockade, but that the bankruptcy of the royal treasury and the tax revolt in the provinces were also at fault. Nothing could have had a more counterrevolutionary effect on the Parisian Fronde than the collapse of interest payments on the *rentes*. And on the level of almost unconscious thoughts, the departure of Condé's army also had a profound influence. It was now impossible to threaten the city with a military invasion or a sack.

Out at Saint-Germain-en-Laye, where the court was residing, and later at Compiègne, attention focused once again on the war with Spain and the growing tensions in the Bordeaux area. Merchants from Paris went out to the court to present a humble supplication to the queen, to return to the capital with the king. Their aims probably were more economic than political. Condé, who pressed hard for the return of the court to Paris, also argued that commerce and manufacturing in the city would not pick up until the court returned. The court's presence in Paris would inspire confidence and strengthen France's negotiating position with Spain. A peaceful, joyous return by Louis XIV and Anne would also improve the monarchy's ability to borrow money at a time when munitions and food supplies for the army were running low.

As the great, lumbering coaches approached Paris, the city fathers and guild officials went out to greet Their Majesties, as custom dictated. The crowds took up the customary shouts of *"Vive le roi!"* as royal guards, city fathers, and judges from the Parlement accompanied the king and queen back into the capital. Some of the more calculating among the Frondeurs were stunned by the joyous reception. They had expected sullen crowds to gather. Retz remarked that the crowd was indeed as fickle and mindless as the writers of antiquity had said. He was delighted to be able to observe, however, that Mazarin was not received with the same joy and cordiality as the king and his mother. There was indeed a difference in the crowd's reception of Mazarin, but he and his guards succeeded in moving through the very streets where thousands had shouted death slogans only a few weeks earlier.

A few days later, at a ceremony at St. Eustache Church, great candles were being prepared for a procession. Each bore the arms of the individual who had donated them. Anne's and

Louis' candles were gladly accepted; but when the crowd attending the ceremony saw the clergy approaching with a candle decorated with Mazarin's coat of arms, they tore off the symbol with a quick and overpowering gesture. Hostility against Mazarin would surface in Paris for years to come, especially when his name or his coat of arms was attached to a sacred object. During the Fronde, the populace had deemed him to be defiled; and nothing ever completely removed this taint. A few days after the ceremony at St. Eustache, Mazarin rode about the city in his coach, surrounded by a mere handful of guards and livery men. He was not attacked. Did his coat of arms appear on the coach doors? The sources do not provide an answer. The crowds being jostled in the streets by the horses and the coach perhaps had no way of knowing that the "Italian viper" was passing within easy reach, but such is the nature of urban social life. Anonymity and powerfully overt recognition are both characteristic of urban politics.

The crown's financial situation improved somewhat as a result of the obviously successful restoration of the monarchical presence in the capital. Still more important, the committee appointed to determine what should be done to restore interest payments on the *rentes* had succeeded in inspiring some public confidence. Further crises involving these bonds would occur, but some of the political tension over them began to diminish. Historians have frequently asserted that the financial system of the French monarchy was extremely awkward, confusing, primitive, arbitrary, and ineffective. Selling offices to help balance the accounts in the royal treasury, tax-farming practices, and last but not least the sale of *rentes* have all been described as examples of this inefficiency and backwardness. Nothing like the Bank of England would be founded in France, on a permanent basis, until the late eighteenth century; but in one way or another, the sale of offices and of *rentes* sustained both elite and popular support for the respect of fiscal solvency and private property. If the Frondeur judges during the blockade of Paris in 1649 had not only paid large sums to raise an army but had also ensured that small investors would receive the interest due them for their *rentes,* they would have had a far greater chance of consolidating their gains into some sort of parlementary regime of government by revolution.

SEVEN

The Fronde in Bordeaux

WITH a population of about 35,000 inhabitants, Bordeaux combined all the possible functions of a seventeenth-century port city and provincial capital. It occupied a key position on the Garonne River, which was navigable deep into one of the most prosperous wine-producing regions of Europe. Bordeaux was inhabited in the seventeenth century by a population that shared common agricultural and commercial aims and that hoped for favorable weather for the grapes and for high prices from Dutch and English wine merchants. The city's economic activity turned on winemaking and export, and on the investments that elite families made in vineyards. Even low- and mid-income merchants and artisans used their savings to purchase a few rows of grapevines in the country. Stavemakers, coopers, stevedores, boatmen, and wholesale merchants watched for the rhythmic arrival of foreign ships in the port and of barrel-laden flat-bottomed boats from farther up the river. These Bordelais worked intensely for short periods of time whenever it became evident that the size of the crop would require additional barrels, or whenever a time lag between wine deliveries from the country and the arrival of export ships required storing the wine in city. Weeks, if not months, of almost leisure time for urban workers may have separated these periods of intense labor in the wine trade. Did this period of leisure occur in the summer? It is tempting to speculate on the possibility that the barrelmaking and other preparations for a grape harvest were usually over by late May or mid-June, and that summers in Bordeaux were periods of relative leisure and also of anxious waiting for the wine harvests and winemaking.

This leisurely period, if it existed, should not be thought of as unemployment in the modern sense of that word. When a huge grape harvest was imminent, all hands were needed, and an almost festive atmosphere of hard work combined with play would prevail during the fall and winter months. According to excise tax records, some 77,652 tons of wine were exported from Bordeaux to other regions of France and to foreign countries in 1651. Grain too came down from the *haut pays,* or high country, as did prunes. The economic importance of this export trade cannot be overemphasized; but it must be remembered that there was (and is) a special cultural dimension to winemaking and drinking in the regions where wine is a principal product. As in the Fronde at Aix, the new special taxes on wine, particularly those on wine produced for everyday consumption, prompted riots and rebellion in Guienne. As of 1635, taxes on the little *barricou* of wine brought into the city by the artisan who regularly obtained it from a country relative, and taxes on the wine sold in cabarets, created an atmosphere of rage among the men of the city's popular quarters. In Bordeaux the Fronde occurred in rhythmic pulses during June, July, and August 1651. This intense climate of riot and political activity usually did not continue past mid-September; for as the grape-harvest approached, the Bordelais calmed down and prepared to go back to work.

July and August were also months spent anxiously watching over the wheat fields that dotted the region, almost up to the city walls. The possibility of a poor crop, or a rumor that storms had damaged fields higher up the Garonne, immediately brought higher bread prices in Bordeaux. In June, July, and August, grain merchants coldly calculated whether to raise prices and in effect save stocks for the approaching winter season, or whether to sell them quickly at a lower price since prices were sure to drop even further after a good harvest in August. The high-risk situation of almost endemic or chronic grain shortages occurring in Paris in the mid-seventeenth century did not obtain in Bordeaux. Poor people there were, to be sure. In 1622, some 1,000 paupers regularly received some sort of direct "hospitalization" as a result of their aimless wandering about the city; and while a great number of them were children, it is evident that considerable poverty and marginal destitution were a permanent fixture in the city. In 1649, during the early phase of the Fronde in Bordeaux, two riots were sparked when crowds amassed on the quay refused to let grain be exported from the city, strong evidence for occasional crises in food supply. This overturned the delicate balance between the authority of the government and that of the Parlement, giving the latter the upper hand. The "moral economy" prevailed among the poor of Bordeaux and among the marginally employed, just as it did in other European cities.

In addition to its role as an exporter of wine and grain, Bordeaux was also a provincial capital. One of the principal law courts of the realm, the Parlement of Bordeaux—whose jurisdiction extended to the north, to the south, and far to the east—conferred prestige upon the city and provided income from its legal and administrative activities. Approximately ninety families maintained residences in the city as a result of their membership in the Parlement. The bevy of lawyers, clerks, scribes, and recorders that swarmed around a major court of law in the ancien régime were also a source of pride and economic and political vitality to the city. During the Fronde, the legal jargon used in some of the most important "popular" manifestos suggests the existence of a very important link between the minor, marginal, or occasionally prestigious legal professionals and the intensified political activity that is revolution in the early-modern centuries.

Bordeaux was also an archbishopric, with a sizable ecclesiastical administration in addition to the customary small crowd of canons, deans, deacons, scribes, and servants, whose residences in the archepiscopal palace and around the cathedral constituted an important social and political presence in the city. There were also numerous monastic communities, which provided the Bordelais with important social and spiritual services, as various as offering housing (for a price) to unmarried children, especially daughters; primary schooling; and health care for orphans, the sick, the hungry, and the dying.

Clues to the overall economic well-being of the citizens of Bordeaux are difficult to find, but the high consumption of meat may be one of them. Always an expensive source of protein, meat was virtually absent from the diets of peasants and most urban residents in the France of the ancien régime. Judging from the excise taxes paid on livestock brought into the city on the hoof to be slaughtered and sold, a considerable portion of the Bordelais possessed the means to purchase meat regularly.

No systematic study of the Bordelais elite of judges, wholesale merchants, and well-off artisans and prelates has been carried out. That the elite functioned effectively can be inferred from the powerful institutional cohesiveness of the city, and also from the patterns of riot and Fronde activity between 1649 and 1653. The families at the top of the social scale were, of course, the ones holding the offices of presidents in the Parlement. The same was true in other parlementary cities such as Toulouse, Dijon, Grenoble, and Rouen. In Bordeaux, these families owned large townhouses, country houses or châteaux, and country estates consisting principally of vineyards. Almost invariably the descendents of prominent wholesale wine merchants, these families proudly controlled the city's political institutions and stood up to the king and his representatives when the latter interfered with the political or economic lifeblood of Bordeaux.

That these families competed for promotions in the Parlement and also in the city's governing body, the *jurade*, should come as no surprise. Urban elites in all French cities of the seventeenth century ranked themselves according to a hierarchy of prestige based on titles, offices, and wealth. But rather than being viewed as symptoms of deep divisions within Bordelais society based on class or wealth, the disputes among elite families and the riots and armed combat that took place in the streets during the summer of 1651 can be better understood if viewed as evidence of the existence of a self-confident, proud, and precisely delineated elite that controlled the principal political institutions and lifelines of the city. So self-confident was this elite that when it split and parties fought for control of the city, leaders did not hesitate to co-opt artisans, tavernkeepers, and lesser merchants to do battle at their side in disputes over physical control of the town hall or one of the city gates. The Fronde in Bordeaux was a particularly intense period of party factionalism, with parties reaching up to gain support from the governor and the crown on the one hand, and from artisans and "social riffraff" on the other.

Owing to a centuries-old tradition of great independence from control by the royal central government, the Bordelais paid very low taxes. Freed from the *taille*, as were most urban residents in the realm, the Bordelais had successfully fought off attempts to assess them heavily for a salt tax and for excise taxes. The Bordelais must have known that their Norman brethren, for example, paid far higher taxes per capita than they did, but this fact seems not to have pricked their consciences at all. In an attempt to recoup for past political defeats, the crown had long ago begun collecting a heavy tax on each barrel of wine that was exported from the region. When this tax, known as the *convoy*, was abruptly increased by six *livres* on the barrel, causing taxes to account for about 50 percent of the cost of common quality wine, there was a political explosion in Bordeaux. The increasing fiscal demands caused by the wars waged in the 1620s against the Huguenots in the South and at La Rochelle and against the Spanish in Italy brought steep tax increases to Guienne. The steep rises in taxes after the declaration of war against Spain in 1635 further increased tensions.

Despite frequent claims about devotion to their king and a willingness to die for him, the Bordelais fought a century-long rearguard battle against any and all tax increases proposed by the crown. This adversarial relationship between the crown and the city cemented solidarities across groups and occupations that were widely divergent in status and wealth. The Fronde in Bordeaux was more socially cohesive than anything that occurred in Paris. For that reason the Bordelais Fronde was all the more explosive in the coordination and planning fostered by cabaret familiarity.

Garbed in their expensive gowns, the city government—that is, the *jurade*—was composed of co-opted prominent judges from the Parlement, nobles, and bourgeois born in Bordeaux. These rich city fathers commanded honor and respect. As long as royal officials left the electoral process free from interference, thirty "prudent men" carried out the frequent procedure of consultation and then selection of new *jurats* from among the three prominent "professional" groups in the city. The *jurats* had the power to assess and collect taxes on their fellow citizens, raise troops and build fortifications, regulate manufacturing and market activities, and administer a first degree of civil and criminal jurisdiction in the city. An even larger co-opted body, the so-called "130," met only occasionally—usually when emergencies required broader, more popular political consultation.

During the 1630s, frequent quarrels broke out between the provincial government and prominent judges in the Parlement of Bordeaux. Governor and Parlement each attempted to control the selection of *jurats* and to have his clients and relatives chosen. The Fronde created the political instability that permitted minor lawyers and artisans to seek election to the *jurade*, commissions in the regiments commanded by the governor and captaincies over the city's fortifications. During periods of stability, these posts normally were available only to the prestigious Robe and merchant families of the elite.

When the crown, through the Council of Finances, issued still another edict to raise taxes on the Bordelais, the Parlement of Bordeaux almost invariably failed to register it or went so far as to vote to protest in the form of a "humble remonstrance." The *jurats*, for their part, would send a delegation to Paris to complain and protest the new tax measure. And more important, at least during the first stages of the tax increases of the 1620s, these delegates would begin quiet negotiations to, in a sense, buy out the tax by offering the crown hard cash in lieu of the contested tax proposal. Always desperately in need of ready cash, the king's ministers rarely possessed the flexibility needed to turn a deaf ear to the figure the *jurats* proposed in return for cancelling the edict. The ministers invariably found the sum proposed by the city fathers to be too low; but the Bordelais knew that once the ministers made this predictable reply, the crown would eventually strike a bargain and order the hated new tax stricken from the books in return for a cash payment. This procedure certainly created tensions, and, indeed contradictions, between the "state as lawgiver" and such constituted authorities as the *jurade* in Bordeaux. Indeed, the procedure amounted to negotiations between equals—the crown and the city fathers of Bordeaux. There is no doubt that the Bordelais possessed sufficient political subtlety to realize how much their success during negotiations with the crown enhanced their prestige and their political influence among everyone who felt any political interest in the city, that is, not only the elite but also the lesser merchants, the prominent artisans, and the tavernkeepers.

For the Parlement of Bordeaux, the proposed creation of new judgeships prompted a crisis, as it had done in Paris. The sitting judges charged corruption of justice. And they feared that their prestige and income would be diluted by an increase in the total number of judges sitting in the Parlement. During the 1630s, the judges, like the *jurats*, pooled their resources and negotiated with the royal ministers to purchase newly proposed

judgeships themselves for a flat fee that usually was considerably lower than the total that would have come to the crown
had the offices been sold to individuals. The prospect of ready
cash and the desire to end the confrontation with the Parlement usually ended in a settlement, with the judges buying the
unwanted offices and either leaving them empty or selling them
to "favorite sons" for an amount inferior to the price the crown
had initially asked. At the very center of the "state as lawgiver,"
harsh negotiations once again took place over the sale of new
offices that amounted to a special sort of tax and that created a
situation in which the Bordelais judges negotiated with the crown
as virtual equals. New tax upon new tax was proposed, and an
increasing number of offices were offered for sale during the
late 1630s and the early 1640s. Could this procedure of buying
out the crown's demands on the Bordelais continue? The
breakdown of this escalating confrontation into a revolution
occurred as a result of strategic military considerations, grain
riots, and a brittle Council of State.

The powerful, wealthy patrician class of merchants and
judges governing Bordeaux reminds urban historians of a host
of great medieval and early-modern cities. To the seventeenth-
century observer who reflected on what politics might be beneath
the oath of loyalty to the king of France, Bordeaux must not
have seemed all that different from Venice, Geneva, Toledo,
Amsterdam, and Hamburg. When a French king died, the Bordelais hastily sent a delegation to his successor, to request
reconfirmation of his predecessor's oaths that the privileges and
charters of Bordeaux would be respected. Louis XIII had
reconfirmed these oaths; so would the Sun King. Terrible stresses
and civil war marked the intervening years, as a result of the
monarchy's apparently insatiable demands for money. And the
Bordelais had long memories.

I. Long Memories: The Revolt of 1548 and Beyond

In the Parisian Fronde the historical memories of the violence
and disorder that had marked the Wars of Religion acted like
a brake upon attempts to pursue more radical fiscal and social
reforms. In Bordeaux, the memory of the riots and civil war of
1548 still weighed heavily on the parlementaires and the prin-

cipal wine merchants. The revolt of 1548 had to a large extent resulted from royal demands upon the Bordelais for tax revenues, and it had not been forgotten. The Hapsburg-Valois wars of the 1540s had brought France to bankruptcy, as the war with Spain would do after 1635. Viewed from the perspective of an official on the Council of State in Paris, the Bordelais seemed to be refusing to assume their share of what seemed to be a realm-wide effort. Bordeaux was far away from the northern frontier and had little to fear from a Spanish invasion. The special arrangements that prevailed in commercial relations between the Bordelais and the Spanish assured the former of relative freedom from military or naval encroachment. Royal armies moving south to "liberate" Catalonia or protect the border that stretched between the seaports at either end of the Pyrenees were largely financed by the central government and by taxes voted by the Estates of Languedoc, rather than by Bordeaux.

Throughout Cardinal Richelieu's and Chancellor Marillac's administration, intendants with full judicial and financial powers were appointed to assist the governor of Guienne. Difficulties over tax payments were, of course, encountered throughout the province, not only in Bordeaux, and the *convoy*, or excise tax on wine, had to be carefully supervised to make sure exporters actually paid the tax. But as tax demands increased during the 1630s, the tensions between the Bordelais and the governor and his intendant quickly came to a head. Intendants such as François de Verthamont quickly found themselves lending legal and military support to tax collectors, particularly to those who collected for a tax farmer who had purchased the right to collect a given tax and who was, strictly speaking, not a royal official. When the intendant arrested someone for tax evasion or for threating to murder a tax farmer, he would find that the courts—chiefly the Parlement of Bordeaux—were unwilling to recognize his judicial authority to try, sentence, and if necessary order the execution of a lawbreaker. During the 1630s, the parlements of numerous provinces refused to register an intendant's commission, and thereby recognize his authority, or to uphold his judgments in civil and criminal cases. This was a signal of deeper divisions to come in royal authority.

As already noted, the selection of *jurats* was always a test between the degree of influence the governor could command in the city on behalf of the crown and the amount of influence the Parlement could exert. In the sixteenth century and its years of civil war, the Bordelais had almost completely lost control over the selection process as a result of riots and disputes. In the 1630s, the selection process had once again become relatively free, but the duel for political control of the city tipped in favor of the Parlement and against the governor, owing to protests over new taxes and over the intendants' attempts to carry out their collection. In addition to occasional riots, tax collectors' houses were pillaged from time to time and the collectors themselves were either forced to flee or murdered. During these apparently spontaneous attacks on property, the speed and precision of crowd action was accompanied by the complete inertia of the municipal militia or their armed bourgeois militia neighbors. As in Paris, an unspoken complicity developed between pillagers and the militia-bourgeois segment of the population. Indeed, as tensions developed during the late 1630s, it became evident that instead of dispersing or suppressing a pillaging street crowd, the city militia might join it instead. With no real police force to protect tax collectors' property, the *jurats* could do nothing but appeal to the governor to maintain order.

As in Provence, where governor Alais became the focus of attack by both the parlementaires and the people, the Duke d'Épernon's attempt to uphold royal authority in Guienne aroused collective protest and hatred for what was perceived as an arbitrary attempt to manipulate the selection-election of the principal city officials, the *jurats*. The Parlement of Bordeaux wanted to control the city by selecting-electing these officials; and so did the governor. But beneath this surface issue was the duel for the political control of all of Guienne. A mature and well-established figure, Épernon had assumed the governorship of Guienne in 1643, a year after the death of his swashbuckling father at the age of eighty-eight. At the head of his troops the elder Épernon had frequently ridden against Bordelais militia companies and protestors, for he was eager for a fight that would redress perceived humiliations that pro-parlementaire *jurats* had meted out to him and, through him, to the king. As the son of this forceful figure, Bernard de Nogaret d'Épernon had little choice but to assume the fight for political control of Bordeaux, keeping more or less unchanged the governorship his father had left to him. There was little room for compromise, for each step and symbol had been defined as either dominance or humiliation. And worse, during the 1630s the Condé family had benefited from Épernon defeats in war, as at Fontarabie, and at home, in a clash with Archbishop Sourdis. It is therefore just possible to perceive the Parlement's attacks against Épernon throughout the years leading up to the full resort to arms in the late 1640s as gestures favorable to the Condé family. The judges made several solemn requests for Épernon's disgrace and replacement. Was it entirely accidental that the new governor appointed after Mazarin's humiliating defeat at the hands of Condé and Gaston d'Orléans was none other than the Prince de Condé himself?

Governor d'Épernon controlled small companies of men garrisoned in the great medieval châteaux of Trompette and du Hâ, which had been built centuries earlier, both to offer some protection to the port from any enemy ships attempting to cannonade the city and to maintain the Bordelais in royal obedience. In the course of the round of pillaging that had occurred as early as June 1627, one house had been saved when the guns of the Château Trompette opened fire in the pillagers' direction. Like the Bastille of Paris, which the Frondeur parlementaires immediately attempted to take over in 1648, the Château du Hâ and the Château Trompette became the focal points of war between the governor and the rebellious citizens of Bordeaux. The governor also maintained a residence in the city, a group of some sixty well-trained and loyal uniformed guards, and a small force of guards in the Château du Hâ, another medieval fortification built to defend the city from a land army. Épernon's guards would not hesitate to shoot into rioting crowds or cut their way through barricades if so ordered. The governor could also call on his friends, young nobles coming chiefly from back-country families and having nothing do but hang around in hopes of a good meal at the governor's expense. The several skirmishes that occurred during the late 1630s between the Bordelais and the governor ended with the latter fairly effectively in control of the city, owing to the military superiority of his clients and his professional troops over the crowds of rioters.

To Paris it seemed evident that the Parlement of Bordeaux was not using its authority to enforce tax collections and to punish the perpetrators of riots and pillaging. When summoned before Richelieu or the king, the Bordelais judges would say that the situation was beyond their control. Was it? The intendants and the governor did not hesitate to accuse the judges of provoking the riots. As debates heated up under the shade of the elms, there was less and less doubt about the confrontational mood developing among the debaters, who came to be called *Ormistes* because they met under the *ormes,* the French word for elms. Standoff situations of this sort also developed in Rouen, Toulouse, Aix, and of course Paris, as tax protests grew into organized campaigns whose leaders claimed they were defending municipal and provincial liberties against encroachment by tax collectors and intendants. The situation in Normandy in 1639, that is, the so-called "Nu-pieds" Revolt, was not all that different from the situation in Guienne. Richelieu and Louis XIII chose to use military force to end quickly the rebellion in Normandy, and they followed this repression with summary justice meted out by Chancellor Séguier. They did not do this in the Bordeaux area.

Why Normandy and Rouen, and not Guienne and Bordeaux? The crown's military forces, like its financial situation, were very precarious in 1639. Funding and dispatching yet another army to repress a rebellious province may have been temporarily beyond its capabilities. There were also important differences between the customary and institutional identities of Rouen and Bordeaux, with the former having fewer rights and less autonomy. Closer to Paris and one of the first provinces to be integrated into the fiscal and judicial administration of the Capetian government, the Normans, despite their provincial estates, were kept on a shorter leash than the provincials of Guienne. With Normandy once again obedient and paying its taxes, would it be only a matter of time, the Bordelais wondered, until a royal army appeared before the gates of Bordeaux to humble the city and force the Parlement and the *jurats* to do the king's bidding? Richelieu's death in late 1642, Louis XIII's demise in the spring of 1643, and the expectant mood of the regency in a sense postponed a showdown between the crown and the Bordelais. In Paris additional factors were at work to complicate the relations among the people, the Parlement, and the crown, not least the presence of a Spanish army a few days' march to the north. And by breaking Louis XIII's will in favor of Anne of Austria, Gaston, and Prince Louis I de Condé, the Parlement of Paris had initially taken a position of sustaining the crown, while its sister parlement in Bordeaux was making pro forma expressions of loyalty.

A showdown was postponed from 1642 to 1649, but these were by no means years of political inactivity. Accompanying the tax increases of the 1630s were important administrative and military initiatives by the crown designed to bring the Bordelais to heel. None of these initiatives was particularly innovative. Indeed, the so-called absolutist state rarely if ever came up with a new procedure or power. If the Bordelais were proud and were being encouraged to resist new taxes, the royal councillors blamed the Parlement. But how to humble the Parlement? The solution was to establish a nearby court with jurisdictional powers that were similar to if not quite identical to those of the Parlement. Thus in 1629 the crown established a court of excises in Agen, some eighty miles from Bordeaux. Offices in the new court were sold to local families and to Parisians eager to make an investment that simultaneously enhanced their status and earned them a reasonable return on capital. The judges of the Parlement of Bordeaux thundered their opposition but could in fact do little to stop the new court of excises, which had been created by the same royal prerogatives that had established the Parlement of Bordeaux only a few centuries earlier. The crown's edicts establishing the new court claimed that the move was necessary to assure fair and speedy justice for subjects in the region, but no one was duped. The Parlement could not effectively buy out the judgeships of an entire new court, and the judges in Bordeaux knew full well that the court of excises would grow in size with each new round of office sales. In 1638 the new court was transferred to Libourne, where a special court already sat to try civil and criminal cases involving Huguenots. In other words, the new court of excises moved even closer to Bordeaux.

II. From Protest to Military Action

Immediately worrisome to the Bordelais during the years of the regency was the governor's military buildup around Bordeaux, which began in the spring of 1649. Just a few miles above

the city, along the Garonne, stood the impressive castle of Cadillac, the governor's principal residence and fortification. If an
all-out war developed, it would be fairly easy for Épernon to
blockade all river traffic at Cadillac and prevent wheat, other
foodstuffs, and of course wine from reaching the city. With the
Garonne blockaded, Bordeaux would still have access to the
hinterland trade that moved down the Dordogne River and up
the Garonne River from Bourg to Bordeaux. And it was for
this reason that the governor undertook the construction of new
fortifications at Libourne, a strategic point where a blockade of
the Dordogne and the Garonne would choke off virtually all
commercial traffic and all food supplies headed for Bordeaux.
Again there was nothing new in this strategy; it had late-medieval origins, as had the blockade of Paris during the winter war
of 1649.

The new fortifications at Libourne and elsewhere, and the
strengthened regiments and forts under the governor's control, drove the Bordelais to make military preparations themselves. The citizens refused to cower before Épernon's coercive
military power. By 1648 the situation had become explosive.
Opinion in Bordeaux was mobilized by news of fighting between
the peasants and the governor's troops in the Médoc, news of
initiatives toward self-defense among the towns of southern
Poitou, and above all news about the deadlock between the crown
and the Parlement in Paris over the sale of the offices of masters of requests and of the solemn revocation of all the intendants' powers save in border regions. In some towns, the agents
of the tax farmers doggedly went on with their work, but in fact
large amounts of wine were being shipped through ports where
tax collectors no longer dared set foot.

The Parlement of Bordeaux issued decrees against fiscal
abuses and continued to declare new tax measures null and
void—thus putting itself at the head of a growing movement of
protest against higher taxes and "corrupt" taxation conducted
by agents who were not royal officials. The mood of self-defense
accompanied a fear of reprisals by the governor's troops. In the
countryside, soldiers out foraging for food were ambushed by
peasants. For any unarmed or solitary stranger, fields, paths,
and hedgerows became as unsafe as the main roads. The Bordelais believed that no troops had the right to approach the
confines of the city, so neighbors and communities banded

together to protect lives and property from the governor's troops. Épernon came to be hated for defending his troops and above all for his cold calculations about how to blockade Bordeaux. The father had relied on only a few troops and his swashbuckling friends; the son created a substantial army and even without the fiscal clashes would have prompted a growing anxiety and movement for self-defense. Clamors for an attack on the castle of Libourne could be heard in the Parlement of Bordeaux. With the cooperation of the *jurats,* the judges began seriously to raise troops in 1649 and appoint officers for them. They also took over control of the Château du Hâ, expelling the small garrison stationed there. Épernon began amassing troops at Libourne. Preparations for a large-scale civil war could be observed prior to the arrival of the news that the Parlement of Paris had suspended the intendants in July 1648, but those preparations might not have precipitated a military engagement. Only the possibility that Governor Épernon and his troops might win and humiliate Bordeaux made the city take the offensive and resort to military action.

Cayrac, a merchant and minor royal official who narrated the events of 1649 to 1652 in which he had participated, was captain of the bourgeois militia company of the Pont Saint-Jean, in the parish of Saint-Michel, in the very heart of the city. His account of the buildup centers on the increase in the number of militia companies, which went from 12 (that is, two companies for each *jurade*) to 36. The climate of fear prompted by the presence of the governor's troops and by his control of Château Trompette led not only the city's bourgeois but its artisans and shopkeepers as well rush to join the newly founded companies. The co-optive powers of the town militias accorded perfectly with the mood to defend the city. The elaborate system of rotating guard duty characteristic of all urban militia forces may have been more effective in Bordeaux than in Paris, if we can trust Cayrac. Or were the fines charged for absenteeism more effectively collected, thus enforcing participation? This is certainly true from the perspective of a professional army. But Cayrac, like Tronson in the Faubourg Saint-Germain in Paris, testifies to the paramilitarization of an urban population. Some of the parlementary judges, the prominent city officials and merchants, and certainly a great number of artisans and laborers joined together in the Bordeaux Fronde to defend their city.

Cayrac not only narrates the battles in which he participated and describes these events as if a great deal of solidarity prevailed among the Bordelais; he also evaluates the military strategies of the city's leadership, in a series of armchair afterthoughts about Bordeaux's fate in the civil war. This collective militarist consciousness was the central feature of the Bordeaux Fronde. Not only more coherent but more effective than the civic defense expressed by the Parisians during the winter war of 1649, this militarism provided the warp for the more explicitly political and social revolutionary impulses in the *Ormée* (the Bordeaux revolutionary movement of 1652–53). Cayrac is our only witness for some of the principal features of revolution in Bordeaux, which many of the Bordelais perceived their Fronde to be. He must be carefully scrutinized for error and exaggeration, but he must above all be attentively read.

During the Fronde, the militia companies constituted a framework for the large-scale, if not the total, mobilization of an urban population. Possessing bourgeois status in Bordeaux obliged a man either to serve in one of the city's companies or to pay a fee to hire a replacement. Cayrac says that when public executions or some other special ceremony took place and required the presence of armed militiamen, only the bourgeois members of the columns, but not the artisans, participated. The inference is obvious. In a moment of tension the municipality could count on the bourgeois, but not on the artisans, to stand firm before a crowd, show their weapons, and use them if necessary, should the bystanders attempt, for example, to rescue the condemned person. Cayrac makes it evident that the social composition of the militia columns was therefore heterogeneous in two ways. The column became still more heterogeneous whenever threats from an offensive, non-Bordelais army momentarily created conditions that made the admission of non-bourgeois males advisable. It was also very heterogeneous in such distinctly artisanal and popular quarters as Sainte-Eulalie. Cayrac gives the specific boundaries of his militia column, street by street; but he does not remark on whether large numbers of non-bourgeois residents joined it during the Fronde.

Cayrac's silence on this question is significant. He assumed that the "friends" for whom he was writing were familiar with the workings of the militia and with its rapid expansion in times of crisis. Indeed, the absence of lengthy discussions of this phenomenon in town records, individual memoirs, and histories suggests that the social dynamics that gave the militia its form in the early-modern town were so familiar, stable, and routinized that they did not prompt description. Still, interpreting silence is at best a risky business for the historian. And we must recall Tronson's account of the Parisian incident of 1649, in which an upstart militia leader who wanted to establish a new column in the Faubourg Saint-Germain soon learned that the regulars would not hesitate to break it up and use violence against the upstart leader.

A roster of 127 prominent *Ormistes,* or recognized Bordeaux Frondeurs, names nine militia officers. This militia presence, and the list of parlementaires to be exiled from the city by the Ormée, are important clues to the shifting degrees of cohesion and division within the city—all set within a mood stressing the need for defense. In 1649 the Parlement's and the *jurats'* leadership over military matters remained sufficiently strong and deeply enough engaged to ward off splits in the city's overall social and political cohesion. But what issues prompted the bitter divisions and street fighting in June and July of 1650? The answer to this question takes us beyond the first, socially cohesive Fronde. And so while the question must be posed, it can only be answered after a discussion of some precise evidence about early splintering.

The Council of State appointed an official to mediate the conflict that pitted the governor and his supporters against his opponents in the Parlement of Bordeaux. This official, René Voyer d'Argenson, reviewed the governor's military moves and the city's self-defense movement in ways that would permit a de-escalation of the threat of civil war. His report shows unequivocally that the more conservative judges and *jurats* were having trouble managing their more radical colleagues. Particularly revealing was their quite strong and quite exceptional need to call meetings of the town assembly, that is, the so-called "130," to discuss specific points in the defensive strategy. In mobilizing opinion to defend the city, the judges and *jurats* had not hesitated to call on the "130" in the past. Now, during negotiations for de-escalation, neither judges nor *jurats* could ignore the "130" and fail to call on them. In the confrontation of 1649, Fonteneil, who witnessed the events he describes in his memoirs and was himself a militiaman, notes that the "*menu peuple,* who are not attached to the rules of debate, began to act in a certain way, out of an abundance of heart, without pretension or ceremony, to raise its voice." This is powerful testimony of a rising civic participatory consciousness within the city of Bordeaux. In early-modern France, the metaphor for this behavior was always the "voice," and its links to the tradition of *vox populi, vox dei* are evident.

Agendas and dates were set for a meeting of the "130," but as d'Argenson tells it, after a visit from the Ormist Gay, who said many "words tending to sedition," d'Argenson was informed by a councillor of the Parlement, a *jurat,* and the town secretary that the projected meeting could not be held because the "people seemed to be so riled up." A holiday forced a further postponement, but d'Argenson claims that these delays were in fact calculated in order to give time for the "factions to heat up the people." For when the "130" finally assembled, its proceedings were disrupted by the arrival of craftsmen who had no right to enter the meeting. The proposed agenda was totally ignored and the only subject discussed was the cannons that the governor and the city were quietly placing in strategic locations.

The assembly then refused to break up, and despite attempts at pacification by the presiding judge, the *jurat,* and the secretary, the leaders of the assembled crowd rushed back to d'Argenson, saying that only a royal order signed by him could disperse the "tumult." Seeing that these men feared for their lives, d'Argenson hastily wrote a royal ordonnance stating that work on the new citadel of Libourne would immediately cease. With the royal order in hand, the judge, the *jurat,* and the secretary went before the "people" and read the order aloud. The "130" dispersed, and with them all the people who had shown up for the meeting, be they members of the "130" or not.

The account of this incident could be challenged not so much for its veracity as for its implicit bias about the intentions of the municipal and parlementary leadership at this point. Only a few days later, the *peuple* forced the Parlement to promulgate a decree permitting the general arming of the city's population. In the so-called "secret register" of their deliberations, some of the judges recorded that they had voted yes out of "necessity" (a concept in Roman law), in order to save their lives.

It does not seem useful at this point to explore further the specific parallels between the social-political dynamics of the 1649

Fronde in Paris and the dynamics of the Fronde in Bordeaux. It seems evident that some judges genuinely believed that their lives were threatened, and that in both Paris and Bordeaux the Parlement had to resort to military action to stay ahead of a popular revolution that was taking the form of civil defense. That others were willing to press even further the threat of civil war in order to change the membership of the Council of State obtains only for Paris, but the immediate focus remained defense of both cities from besieging armies and opposition to tax increases and to additional offices in the Parlement. That there were still other leaders, among them Gay, who sought to continue the war by moving out beyond the city's defenses and defeating the governor's army is also evident.

The leadership of the Bordeaux Fronde would not remain static from 1648 to 1653. Cayrac recounts how Lavye, an advocate general in the Parlement and who had been a leader at the beginning of the rebellion, "changed party" and was forced to leave the city. Only the presence of the Marquis de Sauveboeuf, and presumably of his armed friends, prevented the pillage of Lavye's house. The residence was subsequently sacked, down to its very door. As the Fronde deepened toward the break that led to the creation of the Ormée, men who were "unknown" to the established leaders suddenly stepped forward to play a role. Their support came primarily from the militia companies and perhaps from the religious confraternities.

Angered and frustrated by the situation in which he found himself, d'Argenson had been forced to draft a royal ordonnance under threat of a riot and possible murder. The possibilities for serious mediation and de-escalation were over. In fact, d'Argenson quickly came to adopt Governor Épernon's point of view, namely that only force would restore order in Guienne. The commonplace about conspiracy and party factionalism held that by placing oneself at the head of a popular outburst, one's strength could be increased to the point that a coup d'état became possible. In this instance, as in the Day of the Barricades, elected, co-opted officials, like the Parlement, *had* to obtain concessions in order to survive politically and physically. But it is doubtful that, following the meeting of the "130," they in fact had a clear idea of the scenario. Still, evidence of their awareness that concessions had to be wrung from the crown if they were to survive exists in the warning given d'Argenson that a riot would occur if the "130" were to meet on a holiday. At this point the Parlement and the municipal leadership put themselves between the *peuple* and a royal official entrusted with the power to sign in the king's name, and popular force intervened to alter the military situation. It is structurally similar to the moment when the Parisian parlementaires were forced to return to the Palais Royal on the Day of the Barricades.

III. *From Self Defense to Revolution*

Just when the blockade of Paris was being brought to an end by the negotiations being conducted at Saint-Germain-en-Laye in March 1649, a military showdown began around Bordeaux. The conflict in Provence between Governor Alais and the Parlement of Aix was also moving rapidly toward the use of force. Following the combined buildup of political and military opposition to the crown, it was clear to everyone that the situation around Bordeaux presented the greatest threat to the internal stability of a weak France in its war with Spain.

By May, Governor Épernon had effectively blockaded Bordeaux's land and water routes to the hinterland. According to strategic plans, the royal fleet would enter the Garonne and prevent any attempt to relieve the city by sea. Though this action by the fleet was sure to be only partially effective, the Bordelais had little hope of breaking the sea blockade of the city.

The newly formed regiments raised by the Parlement of Bordeaux were quite untested, but they counted nonetheless. The militia leaders—or some of them at least—and their prominent merchant relatives and backers in the Bourse—the Exchange or meetinghouse of the merchants—pressed eagerly for expeditionary forays beyond the city. Negotiations by ecclesiastical and royal officials continued, and on virtually every level from house servants to prelates and councillors, but they were pointless. Épernon had taken time and care when putting his forces together, and he wanted to be master of Bordeaux once again—in the king's name. Lack of rapid communications, ineffective liaisons between the commanders of military forces, and various popular military actions such as peasants' attacks upon sleeping or off-guard troops kept the situation very tense. For example, the Bordelais Frondeurs responded to the blockade

by breaking open the sluices that kept the water around Château Trompette at a low level. The resulting flood spoiled supplies stored in the great cellars of the fort. No professional soldier
had taken the trouble to prepare for such an eventuality by
moving the stores into higher rooms. The garrison that still
controlled the château found itself in an increasingly precarious position. Though loyal to Épernon, they were few in number and were a close target for an increasingly militant
population.

The Bordelais from the artisanal Sainte-Eulalie quarter were
primarily interested in gaining control over every fortification
from which Épernon's troops could fire upon them. The Bordelais from the Chapeau Rouge quarter, where parlementaires
and well-to-do merchants resided, sought primarily to break
the blockade of the city by leading an armed force to capture
the still-unfinished citadel at Libourne. These two strategies
complemented each other to make Bordeaux quite formidable
both defensively and offensively. In one sense, the attack being
prepared against Libourne was both offensive and defensive.
The coordination, indeed the control of operations, remained
in the hands of the parlementary leadership and, through them,
control of the Bourse and the Hôtel de Ville as well. Épernon's
aim was to force Bordeaux's leadership to sue for peace, so that
he could once again elect-select the *jurats* who would sit in the
Hôtel de Ville.

With great fanfare, the Bordeaux troops marched out to
besiege Libourne, and they were doing quite well until Épernon and his troops arrived on the scene and by cross-fire drove
the Bordelais into the water. Chambreret, the Bordeaux commander, was killed, and his troops suffered as many as 300
casualties, the most disconcerting and politically important of
which involved the bourgeois militia. This setback prompted
the more pro-Épernon members of the *jurade* to challenge the
Parlement's control of the war effort; and a minority of judges
in the Parlement (also pro-Épernonists) sympathized with them.
No one party—be it pro-government and Épernonist or be it
pro-Parlement—ever entirely dominated the city's politics for
very long. These shifts in control created waves and ripple effects,
as independents and silent sympathizers moved back and forth
from one party to another. At the crucial level for determining
which direction the city's politics would go, namely that of

selecting the frequently rotated militia officers, partial purges of the parlementaire leadership took place as a result of the defeat at Libourne.

Fonteneil, the militia officer and sometime tax collector, took civic pride in announcing in 1648 that the special *conseil de police* had decided to increase the number of militia companies from 12 to 36. In his case, the pride of participating in the defense of the city counted for far more than either pro-Épernon or pro-Parlement political rivalry. Fonteneil was a Frondeur who identified deeply with the city's defense. The new earthworks built at the Bastide, on the edge of the city, and the need for the city to control St. George Island, were of momentous importance to him. With heady military and civic pride, men such as Fonteneil kept turning about in a search for leaders and forces that could assure protection for their families, themselves, and their neighbors.

In late July 1649, Épernon, the proud governor, dared to enter the city with troops riding before and after him. Proceeding to Château Trompette, he thanked its officers and troops for holding firm and announced a meeting of all the bourgeois. The sources say that at least 500 Bordelais should have attended a meeting of this sort; but either because his support was still so weak, or because the bourgeois feared arrest or some other form of coercion (for example, collecting money), only five people showed up.

Épernon's attempt to legitimate his newly regained power after the victory at Libourne failed completely. Sensing trouble, but wanting to hang on to the Hôtel de Ville, he ordered cannon to be dragged into place before the building and mounted in readiness for an attack. He and his troops were suddenly engulfed by an angry and armed population that drove him and what was left of his guard out of town. One source notes that between 40 and 50 people were killed. For the popular quarters, whose main thought was the defense of Bordeaux, Épernon's defeat before the Hôtel de Ville strengthened their emphasis upon guarding the gates and neighborhoods of the city—a down-to-earth street-by-street, and if necessary house-by-house, defensive strategy.

Though defeated and run out of the city, Épernon still held the hinterland around Bordeaux and counted on the blockade to bring the city to its knees. In August he simply confiscated grain as it was harvested and sold it to pay his troops. The fields and granaries of parlementaires' farms were the first to be pillaged.

On August 10, the Parlement ordered the selection-election of new *jurats*. The results were a foregone conclusion. The remaining Épernonists (one had been killed when Épernon was driven away) were weeded out, and the Parlement's control over the city became virtually total. Funds were collected by all the usual methods in order to raise still more troops for the Parlement, the favorite device being the seizure of whatever funds the various royal officials had collected. A new commander, the Marquis de Sauveboeuf, was appointed. Over the next few weeks, he conducted muster parades and made minor sorties through the city gates; but it was evident that Sauveboeuf did not dare go out and face Épernon and his troops in an open battle in the countryside.

More popular elements in the city, with militiamen at their head, undertook to cut off all supplies to Château Trompette and eventually to mine it and force the garrison to surrender. The ingenuity, hard work, and powerful collective effort of the citizens (perhaps led by masons and carpenters) resulted in the demolition of one of the great bastions by explosives. As preparations were being made to storm the remaining defenses, the commander agreed to negotiate and abandon Château Trompette. The bourgeois militia columns were the first to go to the fort, in great ceremony, and watch the garrison march out under the hostile gaze of most of the city's population. The sources are unanimous about this being a great popular victory. Immediately afterward the "people" set about knocking down as many walls of the fort and prying open as many vaults as possible. This hard work was done in an air of festivity, accompanied by heavy consumption of wine.

The capture of Château Trompette quietly increased the influence of anti-parlementaire merchants in the *jurade,* but more especially in the assembly of the "130." The leadership was still in the Parlement's hands, though less firmly than before. Something of a competition developed over which body could more effectively raise revenues for the war effort. The Parlement ordered the confiscated revenues from the *convoy* to be used for the war, and it borrowed 30,000 *livres* on its own credit. A special tax was also ordered: one *sou* on each pound of meat consumed in the city, and fifteen *sous* on each measure of flour, to be paid to the new leaders—that is, the more mercantile leadership of the city government.

The exact relationship between Bordeaux's political institutions and this new merchant leadership remains unclear, though it is tempting to assert that it came primarily from the guild of great wholesale merchants usually referred to simply as the Bourse, or Exchange, the building in which these merchants met and carried out financial transactions. This new leadership moved to increase revenues in its own right; and since it was not the same as the *jurade,* it called an assembly of representatives from all the guilds, including artisans, to hear any and all proposals about fund-raising. A head tax was proposed, presumably one with different rates, according to status, that would inevitably have caused parlementaires and well-to-do merchants to pay a proportionally higher portion of any taxes collected. But as Fonteneil remarked, the bourgeois wanted to avoid this because a tax of this sort could only be collected with a great deal of "inequality and injustice." Fonteneil does not expatiate on the type of tax that was eventually approved, but it presumably was a more traditional type of assessment, house by house, with the principal residents of the house assessing all other occupants, as in Paris. Still, he notes that

Some paid the tax cheerfully, some with pain. Others let themselves be so browbeaten as to go to jail, and still others were so stubborn that they let themselves be devoured by the militamen who were sent to their houses.

Commissions also went out to look for the accounts of all pawnbrokers. Merchants and Portuguese, he says, were also obliged to pay, and some investigations were carried out regarding illegalities in sugar sales.

Any self-defense movement—and, as we shall see, any revolutionary movement—must raise funds when the need for military force is evident. But in a city whose pride and uniqueness had virtually depended upon no taxes at all or on extremely low ones, any taxes levied prompted second thoughts and resistance. For artisans and lesser merchants, their militia service and their evident lack of wealth may have caused them to turn their eyes toward parlementaire or great negociant fortunes.

The venerable equation—personal service for defense, or paying for it—lay at the foundation of popular Bordelais thinking
as they prepared their defense against the blockade. In the
Bordeaux Fronde, many stages of collective action preserved
the city's independence, and each stage involved an increased
reaching out to the lower social groups. The relationship among
defense, tax levying, and creating a sense of public interest among
groups that could scarcely be considered part of the city's political institutions was of tremendous importance between 1648
and 1653. In Paris, the Parlement came quickly to control the
Hôtel de Ville, so no other group assumed the authority to levy
taxes. With its newly constituted committee that had started out
to consolidate its authority by calling in representatives of every
corporation in the city, Bordeaux was taking a new and different course from the one Paris had taken. The Parlement of
Bordeaux was losing control over the situation, and the issue
before the whole city was increased funds for defense. This pattern of action was certainly a harbinger of the Ormée.

As the grape harvest approached, Sauveboeuf, his paid
troops, and a few zealous militia columns headed out from the
city. They could make no more than a show of force. Épernon
replied by capturing small wine properties belonging to his
Frondeur enemies in Bordeaux. His troops broke into cellars
and opened casks, allowing the new wine to run out upon the
ground. In an obvious counter-reply to these hostilities, the
Bordelais attacked and pillaged Puy Paulin, the governor's urban
residence, and began to demolish it.

Épernon had never really tightened the blockade. No profound food shortage had developed. The governor clearly lacked
the power to take the city and impose his authority. And the
parlementary army was not powerful enough to defeat Épernon in open battle or to capture his great castle of Cadillac.
Negotiations had been going on virtually nonstop, but in late
September 1649 they became serious. Beyond the borders of
Guienne, Mazarin and the Council of State clearly were gaining
strength.

In October 1649, the Estates of Languedoc voted the crown
1,200,000 *livres,* to be paid over a two-year period. The Breton
estates had voted 1,700,000 *livres* in late July. True, much of
this revenue had been "anticipated," that is, borrowed against
and spent, but the decisions lent support to the Council of State

by refuting the rumors that the entire realm was in disorder or opposition. Revenues from those provinces with estates were certainly more regular during the Fronde than from those provinces having no estates. And royal troops were improving their coordination between fighting the Spanish in the North and East and repressing rebellious provinces in the West and South. Still, the situation remained more of a stalemate than a potential victory. Like Épernon in Bordeaux, Alais waited for additional military support from Paris to force Aix into submission.

In December, the parlementaire negotiators sent from Bordeaux to the court were no longer demanding Governor Épernon's replacement. And Sauveboeuf and a by-now-established Merchant Committee that supported him called another town meeting, at which it was agreed that force would no longer be used to obtain payment of special taxes for defense. The crucial issue was the fate of the citadel at Libourne, just as it had been when d'Argenson had been virtually forced to sign a royal order cancelling its construction. So long as the citadel stood, the Bordelais knew that the city's life-blood in food and trade could be stopped. The conditions for peace hardened on the question of dismantling Libourne.

The judges were also sensitive to the popular significance of the capture of Château Trompette, but in a sense, like the Épernonists, or for that matter like perhaps any member of the Guienne elite, they could not imagine a governor *without* military power in the Château Trompette. Though the château was in ruins, there is no doubt that occupants of the popular quarters, and especially those living under the broken cannon emplacements, thought differently. Their aim had been to demolish the fort permanently. Cardinal Mazarin was already calculating where he would find the revenues for its reconstruction. And so, perhaps, were the richer masons, whom the crown would commission to rebuild it.

As the blockade became less and less effective, something of a de facto truce settled in, despite strong disagreements about Libourne. In the early winter months of 1650, the *jurade* was more solidly under the Parlement's control than ever, but neither together nor separately did it dare attempt to cashier Sauveboeuf and his troops. As Fonteneil put it, "It is necessary to have arms in hand when negotiating." Like Beaufort, with whom he had not only charismatic affinities but also political ties, Sauveboeuf satisfied the merchants' and shopkeepers' need for a true nobleman to command the troops. (The guards in the quarters of Bordeaux created in late July of 1789 shared the same social fantasy when they appealed to the aged Duras to command them.) Clearly the anonymous author of the *Manifeste des Ormistes,* which will be carefully examined in the next chapter, expressed a minority position when he appealed to his fellow citizens to pick their officers from among their own ranks.

A declaration of amnesty was presented under the chancellor's great seal in the Parlement of Bordeaux on 19 December 1649. And there was a written promise that the Libourne citadel would be dismantled in return for disbanding the hired regiments raised by the Parlement. In the North, Anne, Mazarin, and the Council of State had little choice but to grant the amnesty, especially since Condé had strongly recommended it. Late in 1649 the king's government had almost no choice but to follow the prince's advice. It had become a prisoner, or almost, of its general.

Epiphany season brought a festive air to Bordeaux, for the war had ended; but the more thoughtful parlementaires, like the guards at the city gates or the clerics in the sacristies, knew that the peace was more of a truce than a genuine settlement. Still, if stable relations among the regent, Mazarin, and Condé had resumed at this point, and if the war with Spain had ended, the Bordelais amnesty would certainly have held. Both Governor Épernon and the Bordelais Frondeurs would have gone on squabbling, but neither a continuation of the civil war nor the Ormée would have would have been possible without the political upheavals pulsating from the North toward Guienne.

Seen from Paris, the lack of a genuine peace in Bordeaux also encouraged an atmosphere of truce rather than settlement. Condé dreamed of becoming a virtual sovereign over either Burgundy or Guienne, or perhaps both, while Normandy would be controlled by his aging brother-in-law, Longueville, and therefore by his politically energetic wife, Madame de Longueville. Guienne, Paris, and the northern frontier where the fighting against Spain continued were the loci of either stability or continued civil war and revolution. How each locus turned toward stability or revolution affected the other two loci. The crisis in Aix continued, and Toulouse and Rouen were a continual cause for concern; but here again, the troubles would have quieted down had Paris and Bordeaux not been torn by factions.

IV. *Factionalism and Revolution in Paris*

In the Parlement of Paris, convulsions occurred in December 1649—convulsions of a sort that are only possible in corporate bodies made up of lawyers. The judges divided into camps over a series of accusations and indictments concerning slander, financially corrupt activity, and conspiracy. Each judge tried to reduce the others' influence by challenging their probity and therefore their right to judge their peers. A judge indicted for a crime should not sit in judgment on other cases, especially when the cases involved charges against fellow parlementaires. Accusations against Broussel, Beaufort, Retz, and their followers prompted a concerted attack on the probity of First President Molé. Floods of legal argument and quotations from Cicero burst forth in the Great Chamber. Mazarin (who always kept his distance), Gaston d'Orléans, and Condé—and indeed everyone lacking legal training—were baffled and angry. For days, accusations of corruption and strident assertions of probity were exchanged. At one point, Broussel was obliged to leave his seat and go outside the bar that separated the judges from those spectators not entitled to sit in the Parlement. This indicated that he was disqualifying himself as a judge in the case before the court. At another point, Molé was such a target of attack that he had to give up presiding over the Parlement. Beneath the legal jargon, the issue was one of power.

In their efforts to defeat the leaderships of the pro- and anti-Fronde parties in the Parlement, the judges were battling for control of its majority. Molé won, and as royal policies in Bordeaux were debated, a majority vote eventually sustained the crown's—and Molé's—authority. But as long as the battle raged, the prestige and power of the Parlement of Paris suffered. The issues being debated had nothing to do with the military, fiscal, or political realities of the Fronde. The brutal conflict between Mazarin and Condé over appointments to governorships and over the command of the Norman fortress of Pont de l'Arche was unaffected. In a sense, the Parlement dealt itself out of the Fronde and would never again play an effective role in it.

Had Mazarin dangled pensions and abbeys before the eyes of some of the "independent" and wavering voters in the Parlement? The cardinal was never one to believe that common sense would prevail or that bribes were ineffective. But how to go about buying votes was not clear in a period of debate about plots and bribes (and therefore about judicial probity). In the heady atmosphere surrounding debate about the corruption of justice, Retz and Broussel insinuated that Molé had accepted the treasurership of the Sainte Chapelle for his son as a bribe. One of Molé's sons did in fact hold that office and had done so since May 1649. And Broussel's son was governor of the Bastille, a highly pensioned and prestigious charge. In the professional mentality of lawyers, the boundary between probity and corruption, and between gifts and bribes, could prompt deep, intense, and abusive debates. An individual's self-esteem and political influence could be challenged. But the legal-historical language in which these debates were cast remained foreign to most social groups in seventeenth-century France. Here a distinct and important difference between Anglo-American and French political culture eventually deepened still more as a result of the new discourse produced by the French Revolution of 1789–95. The legal-historical language of the Fronde is more meaningful in Anglo-American political culture today than it is to the French political culture of the late twentieth century.

The political reality was that Condé's effective influence in the Council of State had led to the amnesty in Bordeaux. Though the prince also favored sacking Épernon as governor, because he had been "ineffective and was disliked," Mazarin, with Gaston's support, held on to Épernon. Gaston certainly did not support Épernon out of personal loyalty or even respect for his high-handed measures to assure the crown's influence in Guienne. Instead, he realized that should Épernon be forced out, Condé would have another opportunity to extend his influence in the realm by recommending a peer who was faithful to him. Late in December 1649, Mazarin, Anne, and Gaston decided to arrest Condé, his brother Conti, and his brother-in-law Longueville.

Historians have traditionally divided the Fronde into parlementaire and princely phases. There are significant reasons for doing so and the arrest of the princes indeed marks a turning point; but it is also important to note the continuities in endless duels for supreme power by princes, ministers, and their clients.

V. *The Coup d'Etat*

The years 1650 and 1651 would witness several attempts to break the stalemate that had become evident in the fall of 1649, not only in the North, but also in Guienne. In January 1650 Condé, Conti, and the Duke de Longueville were arrested in what the seventeenth-century French called a *coup d'Etat,* a strong political act that altered the balance of forces in the state. It was a sign of weakness and desperation but also a sign of strength. Royal letters went out to all the parlements and major town councils of the realm, giving the reasons for this decision. The arrest would inevitably prompt Épernon to make another attempt to impose his authority on Bordeaux, using military force and blockade if necessary. In Paris the *Mazarinades* flowed with renewed vigor. (The princes would eventually be transferred to Marcoussis in August and then to Le Havre in November 1650, in part to defuse the efforts of the princes' supporters, who were mobilizing the Parisians on their behalf.)

With the princes imprisoned in the massive keep of Vincennes castle, Anne, Louis XIV, and Mazarin set off on three long trips, going first to Rouen to gain support for the crown in Normandy, then to Dijon in Burgundy, and finally to Bordeaux in Guienne. Royal visits had for centuries been used to enhance the crown's prestige, particularly when a young king approached his majority and coronation. For such visits, cities ordered celebrations and temporary triumphal arches and prepared fountains that would flow with wine. In the lengthy speeches of greeting, sincere expressions of love for the king were mixed with complaints about taxes, the misconduct of troops and royal officials, and purely local disputes. In Normandy, Burgundy, and Guienne, Anne and Louis usually gave brief speeches during the ceremonies held at the provincial parlement and the town hall, leaving the longer addresses to the chancellor or another prominent royal official. These lengthy orations invariably included a promise that the masters of requests or other councillors would investigate the local disputes and propose remedies by a letter-patent or an *arrêt* from the Council of State.

This problem-solving function of the chancellor and Council certainly counted for much of the increasing power acquired by the central government during the later seventeenth century. Coordinating its decisions with the information and recommendations coming from the intendants, who were rapidly reestablished after the Fronde, the Council of State reached ever deeper into local society and in the end fundamentally altered French politics by focusing power in the capital. Marie de Médicis had used exactly the same strategy when her son, Louis XIII, reached early manhood. Like Anne, she had aimed to curb the powers of such aristocratic leaders as the Condés to control various provinces both politically and militarily. The Rouennais and the Dijonnais who addressed their welcome speeches to Louis XIV certainly did not forget that Condé's father had, as we have already noted, spent time in prison. In the spring of 1650, the Condéists did not overtly tell Anne not to take the young king on all these journeys; they instead expressed their fears for the lad's health, another way of making that very point.

While the trips to Rouen and Dijon were unequivocal successes, the journey to Bordeaux had to be postponed owing to resumption of the civil war in the area. Two important developments occurred in Bordeaux early in the spring of 1650. The first was the creation of a strong pro-Condé party in the city; the second was the collapse of the Parlement's and the *jurade* 's control over Bordeaux. These two developments were strongly related. During the heady days of the 1649 campaign, minor legal professionals, lesser merchants, and artisans had spent a lot of time and effort coordinating the city's defenses. From this defensive activism a new political militancy would grow. Put another way, while defending themselves the Bordelais had developed new solidarities that coalesced into the revolutionary Ormée.

The spark that kindled the movement was provided by the dramatic arrival of the Princess de Condé and her young son before the gates of Bordeaux late in May 1650. Her husband and brother-in-law were in prison and her mother-in-law was under virtual under house arrest (but escaped shortly before her death). The Princess de Condé had, on the other hand, disobeyed Anne and Mazarin's order exiling her to a provincial estate and had fled to Montrond, the great Condé fortress in the Bourbonnais, not far from Bourges. From there she made her way to Bordeaux. Claire-Clémence de Maillé-Brézé was the daughter of Marshal de Brézé and Nicole Duplessis-Richelieu, the cardinal's sister. Though her marriage was far from satisfactory (and certainly not a happy one), the princess performed the duties toward her husband that were expected of a woman of her rank: she bore him sons, and she rallied support to free him from prison.

Before admitting her to the city, the Bordelais decided to take up the question of whether she should be admitted to the Parlement. For any parlement or any city, authorizing the admission of an eminent rebel into the city was tantamount to declaring rebellion against the king. With ears to the ground, the Parlement decided in the affirmative, and the princess and her train were received into Bordeaux with an outburst of popular welcome, shooting, fireworks, and speeches. On bended knee she asked the Parlement for protection and security. Completely aware of the political implications of their gesture, the Bordelais coldly calculated the support it would bring in their war with Governor Épernon.

Indeed, in the princess's entourage were two experienced planners of the war against Mazarin: the Duke de Bouillon and the Duke de La Rochefoucauld. Bouillon had been organizing military forces in the Northeast and at Turenne in the Limousin, just east of Bordeaux. Beaten by Condé in the blockade of Paris in 1649, but not defeated, Bouillon had now allied with the imprisoned princes. La Rochefoucauld claimed to have more power and money at his disposal than he actually had. (Neither Condé nor Bouillon were duped.) He nonetheless had supporters and had demonstrated considerable personal courage in battle. The Bordelais immediately viewed the two dukes and the princes as "saviors" who could raise troops and lead them. Preparations began none too soon, for an army commanded by La Meilleraie was moving south to coordinate operations with Épernon.

After successfully defeating almost all the rebel forces that Condé's supporters had assembled in the Southwest, La Meilleraie and his army approached the outworks of Bordeaux. He knew full well that any prior victories would count for little unless he captured the capital of Guienne. Bordeaux's first action against the threat posed by La Meilleraie took the form of a parlementary *arrêt* forbidding the royal army to come within twenty leagues of the city. Parlementaires, merchants, and artisans feverishly worked together to strengthen the city's defenses, the consensus being that the presence of any army was a violation of Bordeaux's privileges.

Were the Bordelais parlementaires really so violently anti-Mazarin, anti-Épernon, and anti-La Meilleraie? A "royalist" party certainly existed among them, but what about the rest? It is tempting to see the majority's renewed plunge into war preparations as an attempt to stay ahead of the strong popular outburst aimed at defending the city, which was in some sense legitimated by the presence of the princess and the two dukes, who all solemnly swore that their sole aim was to restore government in France and to obtain the princes' release from prison. Mazarin's *coup d'Etat* had driven the princes into an alliance, an almost inevitable development. But Mazarin never seemed to understand the genuine and deep sources of support within French society upon which the princes could call. The Parlement did not want to lose its control over Bordeaux to the princes and their petty merchant-artisans supporters.

La Meilleraie understood the terms of Bordeaux politics perfectly; and he covertly offered to see to it that the hated Épernon was replaced as governor in exchange for the princess's and dukes' withdrawal from the city. These terms must have appealed to not a few parlementaires, but those parlementaires who served as captains in the militia, or who had other links to the popular strata of the city, may well have immediately understood the dangers of such a proposal. Accepting it would be suicidal for the Parlement. The alliance between the *peuple* and the Parlement of Bordeaux would, on the other hand, hold if confronted by a dangerous royal army.

The arrival of a Spanish diplomat—who was promptly received by the princess and the dukes—gave the Parlement some room for maneuver. It was one thing to welcome a princess in distress and her son (in whose veins ran royal blood), and to support with words an imprisoned prince of the blood; but it was quite another thing to receive a representative of a government at war with France. The patriotism and fidelity of the various parlements on this question had been tested many times and had on occasion proved faulty, especially in Paris during the Wars of Religion. However, after the delineation of aims and parties that followed Richelieu's return to the foreign policy of Henry IV and the crisis of the Day of the Dupes in November 1630, the parlements of France knew they were duty-bound to stand firmly behind the crown on matters of foreign relations, especially relations with Spain. The Parlement of Bordeaux made known its opposition to opening relations with and eventually allying with Spain during the Fronde. The result was an immediate explosive confrontation between the Parlement and the mass of the city's population. The Palais de Justice was invaded by pro-Spanish militants, and judges were mauled and injured before the town watch could be summoned and restore order.

If La Meilleraie had attacked the city at this point, a popular massacre of the parlementaires would have taken place; but he had the sense to lie back and wait, without withdrawing his troops. He had already attempted one serious engagement and, isolated, had found the city's defenses too much for his men. A stalemate was once again apparent, and the grape harvest was fast approaching.

A peace settlement was negotiated requiring the princess, her son, and the dukes to leave the city. Nothing else was really resolved; but this settlement permitted Anne, Louis XIV, and his younger brother the duke of Anjou to pay an official visit to Bordeaux late in September 1650. Arches of triumph, speeches, banquets, and fountains of wine brought animation to the city. Had anything really changed? Had Mazarin finally given up his support for Épernon? Would the new taxes on wine once again be collected? Had the monarchy really given up the proposed new parlementary offices? The ceremonies suspended, but could not cancel, these issues. Who was master of Bordeaux? The king had arrived via the river, in a magnificently appointed and decorated galley, not at the head of an army.

EIGHT *The Year of the Ormée: Bordeaux, 1652–53*

S TREET fighting and fatal casualties over the right to come together in an informal meeting? As innocent and super-ficial as it sounds, the Bordelais' right to meet and discuss what they wished prompted the most radical, indeed revolu-tionary, movement in the Fronde. The continual squabbles over control of the city among Governor Épernon, the Parlement, and the municipal government or *jurade* inexorably stiffened the rules of procedure and the claims to representation in the city. The debates were intense over who could attend meetings, who could speak, who could attend and speak but not vote, who could attend and speak and vote. Equally contested were the nomination/election procedures, which were centuries old in virtually all early-modern municipal political institutions. But the Fronde reopened all the old contentious issues in Bor-deaux. All it took was a perceived military threat or a new tax proposal to prompt a challenge to the status quo. Indeed, the war with Spain, the tax increases, and the new venal offices that provoked the Fronde in Bordeaux led to considerable sacrifices of money and time by the *less* enfranchised in the city, who built city defenses and did guard duty. Sacrificing time and money increased their demands for greater political power. In a time of crisis, the distance increased between the *jurats* and the guild heads who typically claimed to represent various professional groups and occupations. Straw cockades tucked into hats and bodices symbolically joined Bourbon princely and artisanal movements in a common effort to defeat Épernon, the "Maza-rinist," and to preserve Bordeaux's privileged independent status.

An angry meeting of a group of Bordelais beneath the elm trees after they had been denied admission to a meeting in the Hôtel de Ville set off what is called the *Ormée* or the *Ormière,* the elm-tree movement. The officially recognized city fathers, the *jurats,* scarcely had the authority to prevent assemblies under the elms, but the Parlement of Bordeaux, which controlled several *jurat* votes, thundered an *arrêt* on 10 May 1652, forbidding all such meetings. Would the Bordelais who were no longer allowed to meet under the elms knuckle down to the Parlement's order and cease their assemblies?

The Parlement had survived the growing challenge to its power the previous year, but the situation had changed enormously after Condé was named governor of Guienne. Continuing to meet under the elms could scarcely have seemed an illegality to the group now known as the *Ormistes.* After all, most of them were probably bourgeois, that is, property-holding citizens of the city, and not a few were members of the Parlement. In 1652 and 1653, the Ormistes strove successfully to take over the Hôtel de Ville and enhance the power of their movement by assuming all the titles and functions that conveyed legitimate authority in the city. One Ormiste leader, Villars, sought to become a judge in the Parlement. But as we shall learn, the takeover of existing city offices proved insufficient and could not contain the demands for political participation.

In the interminable rivalry between the governor and the Parlement over control of the city, the Ormée meetings must at first have seemed a welcome development for the governor, for the Ormée challenged the Parlement. But this routine rivalry was radically altered by the presence of the recently released Condé and his party within the city. Both the Parlement and the Ormée remained forcefully anti-Épernon, but there were small pro-Mazarin and anti-Condé parties in the Parlement, although they dared not speak out and declare themselves, so intense and fervent was Ormiste sympathy for Condé. Seen from the distance of three centuries, the pro-princely fervor of the largely disenfranchised urban population in Bordeaux and the ties between rebellious princes and artisans and small shopkeepers were phenomena of *longue durée* in French politics. The divisions in the Parlement corresponded to factions in the city, but the elm-tree meetings quickly reached far deeper into the disenfranchised population than these factions, which gained support from some of the minority splinter groups in the Parlement.

The Ormistes, with Dureteste at their head, drafted position papers to explain and justify their continued meetings. Born into a prominent, respectable bourgeois family of butchers, Dureteste had become a minor attorney or solicitor, that is, someone who seeks to earn his living by defending individuals needing help in litigating against someone else. He possessed the eloquence required for bringing in majority votes or for at least getting an inchoate mass of irritated Bordelais to arrive at a "sense of the meeting" sort of decision. The other major leader, Villars, who belonged to the household of the Prince de Conti, assumed airs and accepted the personal benefits accruing from his role. He loved living in palatial surroundings and would walk about the city accompanied by a company of guards. Villars eventually betrayed the Ormée cause, but Dureteste remained faithful.

The *Manifeste des Bourdelois* was one of the earliest general statements to be published by the Ormée. It provided a firm foundation of principles for a radical revolutionary movement, for current events in Bordeaux were carefully integrated into the long history of the city. No reference is made in the *Manifeste* to the corporate body, the Parlement, that claimed to "represent" the Bordelais. The opening statement marks the pride of being Bordelais, as does the claim that in Bordeaux the zeal for the "public good" exceeds that of any city in France. The *Manifeste* claims that the Bordelais are leading the way in the realm to recover the "liberty" that was lost centuries ago, by "breaking the chains" that fetter it.

The anonymous author assures his readers that the ancient Romans had freed the Bordelais and given the city a special status in their empire. French and English kings had done the same, down to the reign of Francis I, who had tried to impose a tax of one *sol* per *livre,* or 5 percent sales tax. The subsequent revolt of the Bordelais in 1548 ended in the killing of the royal governor and the capture of Château Trompette.

The *Manifeste*'s vision of the city's history was probably familiar to members of professional groups such as lawyers, notaries, physicians, and fiscal administrators; but to what extent was it familiar to merchants and artisans? Pride in the city of Bordeaux and resistance to royal tax levies had prompted strong self-defense movements during the 1620s and 1630s. Thus it is possible to assert that these visions of Bordeaux's liberties in the past were also known to militiamen. For some militiamen, this vision of a free past may have been superfluous or ignored; but for others, the claim to unique liberties and privileges legitimated their attempt to maintain and to recover lost liberty—at the risk of life and property.

The *Manifeste* then announces that the Bordelais have "raised the standard of liberty" and have decided to constitute themselves a "republic." There follows a quotation from the 13 May 1652 Ordonnance of the Ormée—signed, it notes, by several Ormistes and sealed with a "great seal with red wax on which is represented an elm tree filled with enflamed hearts surrounded by two laurel branches, on which is mounted a dove in the form of the Holy Spirit," with the epigrams *Vox populi vox Dei*, "The voice of the people is the voice of God," and *Estote prudentes sicut serpentes et simplices sicut colombae*, "Be ye therefore wise as serpents and harmless as doves" (Matthew 10:16). For centuries, learned historians have been in the habit of scoffing at the iconographic and epigrammatic achievements of popular movements. Instead, this iconography should be taken as a powerful sign evoking unity of purpose and solidarity. The popular familiarity with *Vox populi vox dei* has long been recognized. Perhaps the *Estote prudentes sicut serpentes* . . . phrase was included to inspire support among more educated and elite Ormistes. Did it resound in the manner of a liturgical text or the inscription on a banner in battle, with Latin itself having inspirational force even when not understood? At many points in its year-long history, the Ormée demonstrated its commitment to being a genuinely popular religious movement that excluded no one on the grounds of social rank. In comparison with other mid-seventeenth-century revolutionary movements, the Ormée clearly expressed religious, juridical, and popular concepts in the only "available language" of revolution. The tree represented the community in its maturity; the hearts in its branches were the individual leaves—that is, the affections or loves that provided life for Bordeaux.

The classical republican themes in the *Manifeste* also accorded completely with the vision of lost liberty and past revolt against unjustly levied taxes:

There is nothing which spreads so quickly in a community as military valor. I argue [the author uses the first person] that the restoration of the French state can only be accomplished by the people. The great nobles and magistrates are the accomplices and disciples of tyranny; if the people turn to other military leaders than those who are among them, in order to free themselves, they will prolong their hardship.

The name of the author of the *Manifeste* will never be discovered, perhaps because he did not wish it to be known. Engaged in a libertarian struggle, yet sufficiently distanced from its political realities to perceive its needs theoretically, he chose to cast his text in three distinct but complementary modes: historical, juridical, and political-theoretical. The results are impressive for their brevity and clarity. The author does not invoke the history of past republican movements, ancient and modern, when he asserts that the selection of great noblemen to command the city's defenses would prolong the struggle. His is a theoretical observation that predicts the future course of events as much as it prompts recollection of Machiavellian thought. Perhaps he did not need to mention that Conti's command of the Parisian forces the previous year had been disastrous for the "liberty" of the capital. What a solemn warning the *Manifeste* gave the Ormistes, as they raised Conti to be their general in place of his absent brother, Condé. For Conti had switched sides by early 1651 and acting in the names of his rebellious brother and sister, Condé and Anne-Geneviève de Longueville, had journeyed to Bordeaux in order to hold the city against Mazarin.

The *Manifeste* concludes by summarily presenting the Ormée's top three priorities during the spring of 1652: (1) the right to meet, debate, and in a sense legislate on affairs in Bordeaux; (2) the recruitment of a citizen army and the building of fortifications; and (3) the exclusion from the city of any Bordelais who was suspected of sympathizing with Governor Épernon, even if he were a parlementaire.

While it is apparent that the ideas of moral economy were familiar to the Bordelais (grain imports were frequently impeded by popular action), it is important to note that the focus in the Ormée was much more reformist than the usually almost-Pavlovian reaction of crowds that acted to prevent the export of foodstuffs and money. Outbursts against tax farmers occurred off and on throughout the Fronde in Bordeaux, but by the spring of 1652 the issue of ridding the community of corrupt officials had been abandoned. In its place came a powerful attack against members of the Parlement who overtly supported Épernon or who were rumored to be doing so. It was their political sympathies, not their marriages with tax-farmer daughters, that counted in Bordeaux; and what can be defined as almost autarchically political therefore counted for much more in Bordeaux than did the moral-economic and the social. One of the first to learn this was Conti, whose initial reaction to the Ormée involved an attempt to disband the group and to forbid further assemblies under the elms. Having failed to do so, the prince, like all aristocratic leaders of factions, attended one of the Ormée meetings and, by honoring the group with his presence, began to co-opt it.

Before long the Ormée leadership was receiving regular pensions from the prince, through his agent Pierre Lenet, who would be Condé's plenipotentiary in 1652–53, as he had been Conti's the year before. If Lenet can be trusted—and on this point he is indeed trustworthy—Watteville, the representative of the king of Spain, also pensioned the Ormée leaders. At this juncture, it is tempting to analyze both the advantages and disadvantages of princely participation in the Ormée as a revolutionary movement; but without the facts about the movement itself, the results would be unnecessarily speculative. With the right to meet having been established by the *Manifeste*, if not *de jure*, and solidified vis-à-vis the Parlement through Conti's presence, the Ormée turned to gaining maximum control of the city's defenses, including the militia and the command posts in the city gates and outworks.

The Parlement's *arrêt* forbidding popular assemblies also included an explicit order forbidding new military units. The Parlement clearly wanted to keep all military powers under its control and the Ormée would not accept this. The compromise solution was, of course, to leave to Conti the administrative powers to create regiments and decide on the construction of forts and preside over a specially created council of war. The membership of this council would include several prominent Ormistes, plus other leading citizens, some presumably from the Parlement and the *jurade*. Here Villars carefully enhanced his role as Conti's favorite. A leader during Ormée assemblies, Villars quickly became an influential spokesman in the war council. He became third in rank after Conti and Marchin, the commander of Condé's troops in Guienne.

The Ormée's exact strength in the militia companies at any one time is difficult to determine. A great deal of hard negotiating combined with coercive, putsch-like behavior occurred in several parts of the city to exclude captains who were parlementaires. Some of the latter were hardened fighters in street politics and did not let themselves be run out of town easily. Early in May and again in June of 1652, night patrols under the orders of the Parlement and *jurade* collided with patrols faithful to the Ormée. Shots rang out and casualties occurred. As the tension mounted, attendance in the Parlement thinned to only twenty-five or thirty members, down from the habitual seventy judges. The Chapeau Rouge quarter, where many of them lived, took on the air of a besieged city as Ormistes gained greater and greater control over the militia companies, and the parlementaires began to fear for their lives and property.

On 27 June 1652, a decisive showdown took place over control of the Hôtel de Ville. The Ormistes took it over rather easily, but their subsequent move to gain control of the Chapeau Rouge quarter turned out badly when a blaze of musket fire erupted from the cover of the parlementaire residences. The judges had armed all their servants and were prepared for the Ormiste patrols. According to the *Courrier Bordelois,* the judges lost three or four of their men, the Ormistes sixty. The skirmish, interestingly enough, occurred while Conti was out of town. Judge de la Roche's house was set on fire. Further research might determine whether his house was singled out because of his position in the Parlement or his influence in the neighborhood and therefore over the militia. Conti's uncontested authority finally muted the outbursts of violence aimed at gaining territorial control over the city's streets. The Ormistes escalated their claims of being the only true and zealous defenders of the city against the scourges of the "Mazarinist" troops.

During the summer months that followed, the Ormée's prime focus remained military. To be sure, from the late winter months of 1652, other issues had been raised and debated, such as rights to participate in city elections and attend meetings in which city political issues were debated. (These issues will be explored in due course.) The atmosphere of the city nonetheless turned on defense. The continuity of aims between the early years of the Fronde in Paris and the emphasis upon capturing Château Trompette is evident in the Ormée-sponsored move of 1652 to capture and demolish Château du Hâ, the other major fortification that governors used to intimidate rebellious citizens. In September of that year, Condé approved the demolition of this fortress—and did so gladly, he asserted. But on reflection he wondered whether there might also be an attack on Montrond, his great fortification some two hundred miles northeast of Bordeaux. This tiny afterthought is very revealing. The prince was, after all, not entirely insensitive to fears about popular military action and revolution. Did he have a phantasmagoric vision of a general popular uprising throughout France, aimed at demolishing fortified cities? There is no way of knowing. While tolerating the Ormée because it suited his strategy of opposition to Mazarin, Condé was in fact temperamentally and socially unsympathetic to popular movements.

In late June an attempt was made to purge fourteen militia captains who had ostensibly refused to obey Ormée commands. As the summer wore on and Mazarinist troops did in fact arrive on the scene and open hostilities, the zeal for defense being expounded by the Ormée may have reached such a feverish pitch that non-Ormiste captains never felt entirely in command of the militia companies. In September 1652 Lenet—who always worked hard to assure Condé's (and Conti's) control over the city and used the Ormée to do so if necessary—admitted that some militia companies were escaping his control. Indeed, some were electing officers whom he did not know and in fact had not even heard mentioned, an ominous sign for a *chef de parti* trying to control all the political and military institutions in Bordeaux.

Over the entire city loomed, throughout this exciting year, the shadow of the rebellious governor, the Grand Condé. For Condé was now governor of Guienne. The negotiations and highly coercive tactics employed by Condé to extort the governorship of Guienne from the crown was, as Chapter 9 will show, part of his general attempt to intimidate Anne and Mazarin. The dismissal of Governor Épernon in May 1651 had been a humiliating defeat for Cardinal Mazarin and a harbinger of his own forced exile from the realm. Condé immediately envisaged putting further pressure on the Council by joining rebellious Bordeaux with Spain, his future ally in rebellion. The prince's brief sojourn in "his government" ended in a telling military defeat. Having besieged various small towns and failed to take even one, he headed north to coordinate military operations directed ostensibly against Spain and against the troops mustered by Mazarin. Condé did not need to stay in the South to control it. His sister, Madame de Longueville, ensconced in Bordeaux, remained a supporter almost as fervent as Lenet. Indeed, Bouillon, La Rochefoucauld, and Condé's wife and young son were somewhat eclipsed by Longueville's presence. Condé's brother, Conti, who had taken minor orders and was expecting to be made a cardinal, quite loyally supported his brother's aims, in contrast to the previous years when the two princes had commanded opposing armies. Never a real leader, Conti nonetheless saw that his duty in some sense lay in keeping public order and in calming *les plus excités,* regardless of their political aims. With Madame de Longueville and the Princess de Condé, he intervened many times during angry confrontations in the streets of Bordeaux, to prevent violent actions and lynchings. Marchin, Condé's military commander, was totally beholden to the Prince de Condé. A condottieri type, he fought on in the hope of reward, that is, of being granted land and titles somewhere in France or in what is today eastern Belgium, where he came from.

Because so much evidence is available about Lenet, and because that evidence is so self-serving, it is almost impossible to avoid crediting him for more intelligence and more influence over the Fronde in Bordeaux, and over the Ormée in particular, than he actually possessed. Lenet's reports to Condé invariably depict him as in control of every situation, even though, in the next report, he might note that the *jurats* whom he had proposed had not been elected, or that his hand-picked militia captains had been rejected by the bourgeois. Ever the "manager," Lenet became something of a philosopher about managing all parties in Bordeaux. (He reminds one of Antoine Guérin, a participant in the revolt at Romans in 1580, as reconstructed by Emmanuel Le Roy Ladurie.)

Lenet's key to success was money, carefully distributed to troops, to the politically influential, and even to the confraternities attended by Conté's devout supporters. One of his first tasks had been a journey to Madrid to assure financial support for Condé's military efforts in Guienne. The Spanish treated him with great deference and signed a treaty by which they promised to supply considerable sums for Condé's troops. However, although his Most Catholic Majesty and his officials sent Lenet highly complimentary letters and personal gifts, the hard cash for the Bordelais mercenary regiments remained but a trickle, and some of this money was siphoned off by the rapacious (if we can believe Lenet) Watteville, the commander of the Spanish fleet anchored off Ormiste Bordeaux. There is no doubt that Lenet efficiently raised and distributed scarce funds, although a rival client of Condé's accused him of melting down the Spanish gold coins and pocketing huge profits while at the same time paying the soldiers in devalued currency.

This drying up of Lenet's funds for paying troops and pensions coincided with the decline of Ormiste power in the city. This is an important fact in assessing the intensity of popular fervor for the Ormée. Throughout the Fronde, in Paris and in the various provincial capitals, money was consistently distributed to generate political support. Lenet boasted that if 1,000 to 1,200 *livres* were carefully distributed to the city's convents and confraternities by "devout women," Condé would be assured of supporters. This type of link between "charity" and faction-building was not unique to Lenet and Condé; Retz admits to doing the same thing in Paris, and even to distributing the money himself, in order to gain the maximum allegiance. The networks of religious communities, both for and against the Ormée, played an important role in its demise. They may also have played a role in its rise.

More curious, though less revealing about the social foundations of the Ormée and of Condé's party, was the forced *taxation* practiced by Ormiste militiamen. Though the subject requires more research in order to determine the prevalence of this practice, it is evident that Ormistes went to private houses and collected "contributions" and "loans." There is little doubt that individuals had to pay or be subjected to threats of and actual pillaging of their houses. Were the individuals visited primarily the richest Bordelais? There is no doubt, if we can draw inferences on the basis of the Parisian experience, that moral economic concepts would be influential here, and that some individuals reputed to be rich would be asked to pay high sums. Or were individuals influential in the militia companies that were resisting the election of an Ormiste captain asked to pay higher sums? Only more research in as-yet-unexplored archives can answer this question. The possibility ought not be excluded that these people belonged to one and the same group, that is, to the richer and anti-Ormiste Bordelais. In any event, Lenet—and through him the militia companies he controlled— was accused of using brutality in raising funds to pay for troops and fortifications. Complaints came in from as far as Paris on that score. Condé continued to give Lenet his full support for whatever he did, and in return Lenet was expected to assure the prince of strong Bordelais support against Mazarin's forces.

While it is certainly true that the social-occupational composition of the Ormée may have varied over the year, as militia members changed sides or factionalization broke out within the Parlement, the continuities are very striking. No large purge took place; and so as late as April 1653, when the financial and military situation had become precarious, the plenary powers voted by the Ormée (under Lenet's direction) to send ambassadors to treat with Oliver Cromwell were signed by men from very different social and occupational backgrounds, starting with Conti and moving down to a parlementaire, a *gentilhomme* and a bourgeois, the mayor of the city, militia captains, and other Bordelais simply identified as "bourgeois."

By then the Condé party and the Ormée holding Bordeaux were beginning to feel isolated and let down by the Spaniards. The appointment of diplomats to make the voyage to London took on theatrical qualities that indicate Lenet's desire to shore up the revolt in Bordeaux. Did links exist between the wine merchants in London and those in Bordeaux that could have given this diplomatic appeal for English military intervention a force in the House of Commons? By the spring of 1653 Cromwell held the reins of English diplomatic action firmly in his hands. Neither favorable trade relations nor expressions of a common struggle against tyranny and of union under God counted for much.

Lenet undoubtedly did all he could to make the text seeking English support appear to be the fruit of a legitimate and forceful control of the city by the Ormée—a control the Ormée in fact still exerted—but the city representatives named in this document are less socially eminent than the names figuring on the roster of exiled Bordelais. Cromwell too was familiar with rump representative bodies and exiled elites. The Ormiste proposal arrived at a time when Cromwell was facing division and outright opposition from the Long Parliament. In foreign policy the logical choice for the Protestant was to seek an understanding with France, rather than Spain, which meant that Cromwell received overtures from Mazarin more cordially than those from the Ormistes.

This leaves the question of why so many contemporaries referred to the Ormistes as being only so much *canaille*. This derisive term has social significance but certainly no one could label "riff-raff" a group to which Conti, Lenet, and the mayor belonged. The answer to this question will begin to emerge in the discussion of the Ormée's reformist program, for here a distinctly popular, even artisanal, resonance is apparent.

Something of a consensus in its program continued throughout the year of Ormée rule. Never an inchoate mass, the Ormée's solid bourgeois or property-owning foundations were pulled in somewhat different directions by the factional leaders within it, but it never reversed direction or broke up into rival splinter groups. An assembly of as many as 500 or 600 people obviously could not govern the city, so a standing committee of thirty Ormistes met daily in the Hôtel de Ville to do so. Power relations among this committee of thirty, the *jurats*, the assembly of 130, the council of war, and the rump Parlement are not easy to determine, but is this not always true about the interlocking bodies of officials in essentially oligarchical, co-optive urban governments of the late-medieval and early-modern centuries? By mid-July 1652, the general assembly of the Ormée approved changing half the members of the Thirty, and they apparently continued to do so regularly. At this time, Lenet reported to Condé that the Ormée was establishing special judicial procedures, lending money to the poor and reconciling quarrelsome citizens who (as we shall see) insisted—at the risk of their lives—on their "deliberative rights" in the Hôtel de Ville, that is, with the *jurade*. The order of the subjects that Lenet attributes to the Ormée here is just the reverse of what we will find in the document called the Articles of Union, which—along with the *Manifeste*—is one of the two primary documents most indicative of the Ormée's public image and intentions.

The first phrase of the Articles of Union reads: "We, the bourgeois, *manants*, and inhabitants of the city of Bordeaux, recognize the great favors and special assistance that we have received from God during the still continuing troubles. . . ." Their first aim, then, was in a sense to strike a bargain with God. If they showed great love for one another, and especially for the individuals who had resolved to make further loans, and if they invited all Christians to do the same, God would, they asserted, extend His special favor to Bordeaux. This preamble is characteristic of what could be called seventeenth-century popular Catholicism. There is a literalism bound up in following Christ's command, "Love your neighbor. . . ," and a forceful expectation of special and quite immediate benefit from the divine for doing so. The triad of authors was all-inclusive; the categories "bourgeois" and "*manants*" included everyone living in the city, with *manants* in this instance meaning residents in the immediate suburbs. With this emphasis on residence, civic identity took precedence over all other dignities and occupational titles. The Ormée rejected the deeply ingrained habit of marching *en corps* on ceremonial occasion, that is, with all the parlementaires together, merchants together according to guild rank, and occupations by guild rank. Instead, the Articles of Union emphasized the civic identity over all others. The Ormistes instituted the radical procedure of marching without respect for rank, a powerfully egalitarian action.

The first article of this document is a promise to obey the king, to serve "our" governor, and to be faithful to the well-being and prosperity of our *patrie,* for whose privileges and franchises we will willingly risk our lives and property. Condé was the governor at the time, so it would not be the least rebellious to promise obedience and service to both the king and the governor. There was no recognition of the fact that the two men were engaged in a civil war, and that the king, through his Council, objected to many of the Ormée's decisions. The rest of the first article is a strident claim to have a "deliberative voice," not just a consultative one, in the "Communal House of this city," and to insist on an accounting from the individuals handling public funds.

The next article is a promise to love one another like brothers, to protect one another, and, should "differences between us arise, we promise to seek out arbiters" or to permit the "company" to select them. Note the reference to "company," a term used for any corporate identity in the ancien régime, be it a parlement or a parish confraternity. Interestingly, the text continues by stating that the agreements made by the arbiters would

be "firm and irrevocable." This very important article constituted the Ormiste hope for a more just community, and one
free of litigation. Dureteste's leadership was uncontested during the period when the Articles of Union were drafted; hence
it is tempting to see in it his handiwork as a founding father of
popular justice founded on principles of moral economy. There
is no attack upon the royal courts of law, and no outburst, in
the manner of radical preachers, against the money-grubbing
of lawyers. But in the words "firm and irrevocable" lay a claim
to sovereign power on matters of property. The next article
contains a promise of protection for any member of the company who is "vexed" by litigation or anything else, and a commitment to lend him money if necessary, free of interest.

The four remaining articles are still more reminiscent of
confraternal statutes. The first of them promises aid to anyone
who is sick, after first exhorting him to think of his conscience,
and promising, should he die, to "protect and defend" his widow
and children, if he has any, as if he were still alive. There is also
a promise to aid anyone who becomes poor, by helping him
find an "upright employment." And he will be aided without
revealing his family hardships, a recognition that the needy
require some privacy.

Another article ensures that foreigners who express interest in joining the company may do so and be treated like the
others. "Foreign" in the sense of non-Bordelais Frenchmen, no
doubt, but did it also include immigrants from the Iberian
peninsula? For centuries, small numbers of Spanish and Portuguese, particularly of Jewish origin, had settled in Bordeaux,
so this clause may be a vague allusion to their presence in the
city. This inclusive impulse stood in stark contrast to the usual
exclusivity and xenophobia that typified French (and European) urban societies in the seventeenth century.

The final clause regards the fate of anyone who ("God forbid") should happen to fall into a scandalous and incorrigible
life. His punishment will be banishment as "unworthy of such
a society as ours, and he will be referred to as a traitor to his
honor and to the public good." On this point, the Articles of
Union come to an end.

Taken as a complete text, the Articles have a powerful
coherence and inner logic. Relations with God are expressed
through a promise of love. Obedience and service are then vowed

to the king and the governor. A solemn claim to political rights in municipal governance follows, supported by a vow to fight to defend the city's privileges in the realm.

After man's relations with God and with his superiors, and after his political rights, comes the issue of resolving conflicts within society. The modes for assuring justice derive from consular courts, where merchants customarily resolved disputes over commercial transactions by appointing one or several of their own to make binding decisions and in this way avoided litigation before a royal court. Then come the more confraternal ideas of aid to the individual involved in litigation or to the unemployed, the sick, and the dying. The clause welcoming foreigners is followed by its pendant, an assurance that anyone who willingly leads a life deemed scandalous will be exiled. The clarity and simplicity of the Articles of Union gives it a place among the great revolutionary texts of Western European societies, alongside the Petition of Right and the Declaration of the Rights of Man and of the Citizen.

Were the Articles merely an expression of the mind of Duresteste or some other visionary? Historians seeking to interpret change in social forces will always be able to raise doubts about the degree of genuine popular support for such statements as the Articles of Union. In answer, all that can be said is that the press was not only free but inexpensive in the Bordeaux of 1650, as the flow of *Mazarinades* proves. Yet no body of pamphlets, and no major spokesman, has been found that systematically took issue with the Articles of Union. Though there is reason to be suspicious about their reporting, both the author of the *Courrier Bordelois* and Pierre Lenet (in the letter to Condé to which we have already referred) substantially confirm that the points made in the Articles of Union were central to the Ormistes. Further research will no doubt refine and nuance this interpretation of the Articles, but this brief summary will suffice to compare what the Ormée claimed it wished to do and what it actually did.

Beyond the constant and almost frantic preoccupation with military matters and with raising funds for defense, the Ormistes centered their attention on their enemies in the wounded but far from defunct Parlement. Rumors of parlementaire-inspired plots and conspiracies to overthrow the Ormée were present from the beginning. They were followed by real plots and conspiracies. Why, we might ask, did not the parlementaires simply give up their claims to control the political life of the city, and join or at least sympathize with the Ormée? The immediate reason was, of course, the Ormistes' exclusion of some parlementaires from their assemblies. Dureteste personally singled out some parlementaires and in effect forced them to withdraw from a meeting by evoking the coercive pressure of hundreds of Ormistes. Soon the proposal appeared "in the air" that fourteen members of the Parlement were to be exiled; another rumor circulated to the effect that as many as 300 families would soon be expelled from the city. Several of the parlementaires being threatened with exile had solid Frondeur credentials. Indeed, the pro-Mazarinist ones had either fallen completely silent by June 1652 or had probably left the city.

There is no doubt that, faced with a defeat at the hands of the Ormée, some of the Frondeur parlementaires moved toward accommodation with the "Mazarinists," but the hardened positions taken in the past made this difficult to do publicly. Did Dureteste perceive some of the judges being threatened with exile as personal rivals for control over the Ormée? It is doubtful whether a minute investigation of all available sources would yield an answer to this question. The parlementaires had networks of relatives and clients, and these networks certainly involved merchants and other non-Robe Bordelais. Dureteste and the Ormée were, in a sense, a new and powerful faction that had grabbed control of the city and were now demanding more popular, democratic governance. It was inevitable that former holders of political power within the city would do everything in their power to oust them as upstarts. In the climate of division and war, it is important to note that the primary Ormiste aim was to exile its enemies, not to kill them.

The social composition of the Ormée remained heterogeneous enough to impede the rise of any large-scale totalitarian machine that identified Ormée enemies by professional or occupational group. Some *Mazarinades* attacked the rich for their ill-gotten gains, but the concept of appropriate wealth to sustain one's rank in society—be one a parlementaire, a rich *négociant,* or an artisan—never really came into question. The first three judges of the Parlement whom the Ormée ordered out of the city were Montesquieu (an ancestor of the *philosophe*), Salomon, and du Bernac, who were specifically accused of plotting with the court (Mazarin) to facilitate the Count d'Harcourt's plan to gain a hold on the city. Harcourt was Mazarin's hand-picked commander of the troops sent south to "restore royal authority" in Guienne. In the face of the Ormée's numerical and military strength, the Parlement virtually ceased functioning. In mid-July the Ormée decided to set fire to the châteaux of La Brède (which belonged to Montesquieu), Cudos, and several others, all seats of their parlementaire enemies.

The effort to ferret out and exile enemies continued throughout the year of Ormiste rule. Filhot, a treasurer of France and therefore someone who might be plotting against the Ormée—as indeed he was—tells how he was taken from his home and tortured by the Ormistes to make him reveal the names of his fellow conspirators. His treatment was certainly inhumane, but he was guilty of the charges the Ormée had leveled against him. Yet his life was spared. The lengthy plot that he described seems a bit far-fetched, but it is extremely revealing about strategies and mentalities of urban factionalism and street-fighting during the seventeenth century. This blend of theatrical devices to show a change of power before it happened and tough commando tactics to capture city gates and the Hôtel de Ville confirms the hypothesis that very few street riots or political movements were "spontaneous" in early-modern France—except those triggered by grain exports.

Filhot and his fellow conspirators aimed at rallying opinions against the Ormée and gaining control of what can be defined as the crucial political symbol and reality of the city, the Hôtel de Ville. The party that controlled the Hôtel de Ville, even if it meant with musket in hand, nonetheless controlled it and had the chance either to consolidate its new power, as was the case for the Ormée, or to return that power to previously constituted authorities. The issue is important both for Bordeaux and for other cities with Frondeur factions. As we shall see, the Condéist attempt to capture the Hôtel de Ville of Paris took place during this same period and under the same circumstances. And though Filhot was on the anti-Condé side at Bordeaux, his aims and his means of achieving them were strikingly similar to those of the Condéists in Paris. Neighborhoods became battlegrounds as the parties fought each other.

After the heavy casualties that had occurred in the street fighting between parlementaires and Ormistes, the latter adopted a plan to compensate widows and wounded. But where would the money come from, and who would collect it? A mathematics teacher and priest named Prade made a special effort to raise funds for this purpose. He also assured those who heard his appeal that he had "seen in the stars that Bordeaux would be a powerful republic." Some Ormistes visited Conti and showed him an ancient parchment chronicle where (so they claimed) the rights for the Ormée to meet could be found. This little fact seems insignificant until we realize that the claims to liberty made in the Bordelais *Manifeste* were reputed to be ancient. That some Ormistes would bring Conti a medieval chronicle to support their claims confirms not only that the Ormistes perceived their movement as entirely legitimate, but also that at least part of the Ormée group shared these ideas about recovering lost liberties and were eager to base political action on the principle of recovering "ancient liberties." In mid-July of 1652, the Ormée proceded to select-elect officers, thereby officially displacing the men who had been selected-elected by the Parlement. In so doing, they scrupulously respected the "mixed constitution" of the *jurade:* two parlementaires, two *gentilshommes,* and two members of the legal profession. This information about selection-election seems to be available only from anti-Ormée sources, such as Filhot, Cosnac, and Lenet, and therefore must be taken as accurate.

Under Dureteste's leadership the Ormée set about reconciling conflicting parties in the city and "judging" from a fleur-de-lys upholstered chair and canopy. Not all of Dureteste's assistants had legal training, but two *procureurs* and a lawyer were among his supporters sitting as judges in a popular court of law. This attempt at rendering justice and reconciling conflicts caused the judges of the Parlement to scoff at the Ormistes and to denigrate their efforts; but the mercantile model for resolving conflict no doubt gained supporters owing to the costly legal fees that litigants faced in the royal courts. And it was rumored that the Ormée was planning to legislate the Parlement out of existence and to abolish venality of office. Was it only a rumor? A rumor perhaps started by anti-Ormistes who hoped to make potential officeholders reflect before backing the Ormée?

As already noted, Filhot and Cosnac were anti-Ormée, but the reasons they give for its rise are interesting because they coincide with the popular-justice movement just discussed. Cosnac, a member of Conti's household, asserts that the Ormistes were chiefly artisans who were usually employed by merchants in the city, and that if these merchants ever took a stand against the Ormée it would collapse. Filhot, certainly no friend of the Ormée, comes closer still to a social interpretation of that movement when he claims it was made up chiefly of artisans and merchants who had either worked for or supplied household items to the judges in the Parlement and who had not been paid and were therefore besieged by creditors, to the point that many of them were themselves deeply in debt. In the current state of research about the Ormée, it is impossible to confirm or refute these interpretations. They are nonetheless interesting because they were made by contemporary observers, indeed participants in the events. The history of social interpretations of the Ormée is a long one, beginning with Lenet, Condé, Filhot, and Cosnac, all of whom stress that its social foundations were the bourgeois, the artisans, and the *menu-peuple*. In comparison with the Parlement and the *jurade,* the popular membership of the Ormée struck contemporaries as revolutionary.

Another issue that is particularly indicative of the Ormée's social origins was the movement to lower the rent on houses and apartments. Madame de Longueville wrote Lenet:

I had some deputies come and see me this morning about reducing house rents. The entire Ormée chamber [the Thirty] will soon be coming to ask me for it. They say that the Parlement is not meeting, and that I had promised them this more than a month ago. . . . They are asking for this with extraordinary pressure—and those [merchants] from the Bourse are in agreement. . . . For my part, I think that an ordonnance in specific terms, with the Parlement not intervening, would not be upsetting if it were granted, and we have promised it for a long time. . . .

Lenet clearly concurred with her opinion, so a special ordonnance was drawn up to order a rent reduction. The justification that Madame de Longueville gives in her letter sheds light on the Ormée movement in general. Artisans and merchants had sacrificed their time in order to defend the city, causing their income to decline and making it difficult for them to pay the rent. The movement to reduce rents in Paris had a similar emphasis, being not an out-and-out attack on the owners of these properties but rather an attempt to give immediate and temporary relief that would offset income lost because of the Fronde.

More enigmatic is Lenet's report to Condé dated 14 November 1652 to the effect that the Ormée sought to impede trade. The only policy that would seem consistent with both the Ormée's general views and the actual impediment of trade would, of course, be the export of grain and other foodstuffs. Now this took place in November, when worries about food reserves were at their peak. Yet the news of poor harvests and burned crops, joined to the real possibility of still another blockade of the city, may have prompted opposition to commercial transactions. Lenet was ready to do anything to raise funds on Condé's behalf, and he no doubt had control over the grain confiscated from "Mazarinist" merchants. Money for soldiers may have seemed a higher priority to him than food supplies for the city. In fact, Lenet always reported that food supplies were quite abundant. But were they? Rumors from the hinterland had a way of making a commodity scarce at just the time when it was needed most. Still, to Lenet's credit, he also had plans for appropriating the grain in the various monastic warehouses of Bordeaux, should shortages begin to create panic. He certainly would not have hesitated to confiscate this grain in the name of the "public good," had food shortages begun to threaten Ormiste control of the city. The year during which the Ormée effectively controlled Bordeaux was, however, not a year of dire food shortages or of greatly inflated prices.

The Ormée's solemn appeal to Cromwell alienated some of the ardent pro-Spanish and Catholic Reformation elements in the city that still nourished illusions of getting revenge on the Protestants. But English support was not forthcoming. As the months went by, the lack of money for troops became the principal cause of concern for Conti and the Ormée. The latter lacked the resources to tax themselves and probably would not have done so in any event since militia service was deemed their contribution to defense. As companies and regiments went unpaid, their ranks thinned to almost nothing; and after several years of experience it had become painfully clear that the militia alone could not defeat a professional army and keep the rivers open. As noted earlier, the Ormée became increasingly insecure about its control over the militia. Various plots to over-throw the Ormistes spawned by Mazarin-supported opposition from religious orders were discovered in time; but these plots had an unsettling effect and very probably encouraged the opponents of the Ormée to organize ever more carefully.

Historians of revolution have been interested primarily in origins, with the result that less research has been done on their demise. The myth that the revolution of the Ormée just went away, or that it gently dissipated, has veiled harsher realities. Men and women who are deeply divided and ready to fight for control of their community do not simply stop one day and allow another party to govern. Significantly, the Ormée did not collapse at grape-harvest time, the usual rhythmic pattern in Guienne. In the spring of 1653, and certainly by mid-June, what Filhot calls *la jeunesse*—that is, the younger generation—began to join the Ormiste militiamen doing guard duty. Filhot, whose anti-Ormiste plotting we have already encountered, neverthe-less can be trusted when he describes the coherence, planning, and force of the city's youth as it opposed the Ormée. If twenty Ormiste militiamen were on duty, forty "youths" stood nearby. Scuffling and minor skirmishes may have occurred in back streets between the two groups; but by mid-July, the Ormiste militia-men began to realize that whatever they did collectively and wherever they went as a body, a group of *jeunes* roughly twice as numerous as they would be there, watching them. As a result of this generational attack, the Ormée's control over the militia was gradually diluted. Dureteste no longer really dared order his men to take a forceful step. Whether they were participat-ing in a festival or in defense, the young had relations that cut across status and occupational lines. They therefore constituted a social and political force that was no doubt more popular, in the sense that it represented the "majority," than the Ormée was during its death throes.

At the regional level, one of Épernon's sons, the Duke de Candale, commanded the royal troops and rallied towns and nobles against the Condé party and the Ormée controlling Bor-deaux. The *politesses* that Candale exchanged with Conti cre-ated room for negotiations, and for face-saving. In due course, specific terms were agreed upon that permitted Conti, Madame de Longueville, Lenet, the Princess de Condé, and her little son Enghien to leave Bordeaux with all their retainers. Anti-Conti placards began to be glued to façades throughout the city. Having accused Conti and Madame de Longueville of tyranny, one particularly vehement placard continued:

I do not despair for the *Salut Public* [Public Safety], knowing as I do that the slaves of the Ormée, pensioners of the [Prince of Condé] . . . and of his humpbacked highness [Conti was indeed humpbacked], this dregs of Bordelais blood, the empowered beggars, the milords of the terrace, men metamorphosed into trees by the revolt [an allusion to the elms and the terrace where they grew], these senators of the marketplace . . . finally, that riff-raff of the marketplace, have contributed to this glorious situation under the orders of the public executioner [an allusion to Dureteste]. . . . We will not cease to propagandize; we will put a flyer on the nose and the hump of Conti, and in the bed of his prostitute of a sister [Madame de Longueville].

On 20 July 1653, at two in the afternoon, "deputies from all the corporations and the youth" assembled at the archepiscopal palace, in the presence of Conti, Madame de Longueville, the Princess de Condé, and little Enghien, to approve four proposals: (1) the Ormée was forbidden to meet; (2) all the captains of the militia would be changed; (3) all troops would leave the city; and (4) an immediate effort would be made to reach a peace agreement. On the door of the Exchange, one of Bordeaux's more public places, appeared a portrait of the king in a garland of laurel leaves. When someone tried to post a picture of Condé there, he was nearly beaten to death as his assailants shouted, "Get the Ormiste!" Dureteste and his immediate followers found the door of the Hôtel de Ville locked, and no one was willing to open it for them. Subsequently caught while attempting to escape from Bordeaux under a pile of hay, Dureteste was tried and executed by being broken on a wheel among the elms of the Ormée terrace.

What, in the end, were the Ormée's most revolutionary actions? They certainly were neither primarily economic nor social; rather, they were largely political and judicial. Their revolutionary action lay in exerting a gradually increasing pressure to exile the parlementaires and their other enemies, regardless of occupation, a pressure that appeared early in the Ormée's rise to power and that continued to shape its debates and proceedings. Their revolutionary action also lay in their attempt to attain social harmony. The equitable settling of debts, without resort to expensive royal legal procedures, was very probably consistent with a vision of Bordeaux's uniqueness as a privileged free city in the realm. And the assertion that all (male) Bordelais had a right to meet and to debate issues had made the Ormistes a powerful political force that challenged parlementaire claims to represent the city and to decide which strategy best assured its liberties.

NINE

The Princely Fronde

T HE Fronde in Bordeaux and its culmination in the Ormée
revolution of 1652–53 did not take place independently
of the general military and political duels for supreme
power in the realm. On one level, the leaders of the princely
Fronde both in and out of prison (the princes were arrested on
18 January 1650) and their generals and supporters made every
attempt to link the revolutionary activity in Bordeaux to rebel
military power in northeast France, thereby increasing pressure upon Mazarin and against his authority in the Council of
State. As the imprisoned Condé read history and watered his
flowers in the tall keep of Vincennes castle, he had plenty of
time to think over an already well-established Europe-wide mil-
itary-political strategy that brought together the Spanish, the
Ormistes in Bordeaux, Turenne and the rebel army in the
Northeast, and his own supporters in Paris, notably in the
Parlement.

Not all the Ormistes were entirely absorbed in the intense
duel for control over the city, especially in 1650; but the analysis of the Bordeaux revolution in the preceding chapter accurately presents what happened in Guienne and Bordeaux, or at
least how the participants understood the events they lived. The
outbursts of loyalty they expressed for the imprisoned prince
and his wife and son, especially after the latter two arrived in
Bordeaux, were certainly sincere; but they showed no precise
understanding of the pincers-like strategies involved in the duel
for the control of the realm in which Condé and Mazarin were
engaged. In 1650, awareness of the commercial and political
dynamics at work on Bordeaux's fate certainly remained strong
among the Parlementaires and the wholesale merchants at the
Hôtel de Ville. But in the subsequent Ormiste revolution of

1652–53, awareness changed about the European and French theaters of war in which they were playing a part, to the point that at least part of the Ormiste elite seems to have taken seriously the half-baked plans for securing support from the English. Desperation and illusion, built shakily upon primarily regional and neighborhood concerns, veiled perceptions of the strategies fixed by Mazarin and Condé.

In the preceding two chapters, the Fronde in Bordeaux appears as an almost localized, even autonomous revolutionary phenomenon. From the journals kept by militiamen and from the legislation passed by the Ormée, it is evident that the civic-minded revolutionary leaders in that city perceived their experience in this quite specifically delineated way. Allusions to historical-structural conflicts with the monarchy, such as the rebellion in Bordeaux of 1548, appeared and were evoked over and over again, but strategic coordination between revolutionary Bordeaux and Turenne's army, or Retz's attempt to build a party in Paris to overthrow Mazarin and release the princes, remained out of their purview. Lenet, Condé's highly intelligent manager of funds and patronage in Bordeaux, was not privy to his patron's political-military strategy. He received orders telling him to favor the strongest party in rebellion in Bordeaux at all times, no matter what it was. Nor was Conti, the prince's brother, privy to the overall strategic issues. Only the Duke de Bouillon, an experienced plotter and armchair strategist on how to create both political and military confrontations that would force the crown to change its policies, probably had a fair idea of the specific aims and timing that Condé had in mind. The Fronde of the Princes is strategically complex, a duel between Condé and Mazarin that involved ultimate political-military control of the realm. Generally speaking, the rest of the population, Frondeurs and anti-Frondeurs alike, were pawns in the game of attempting to capture specific military sites and to capitalize on the effects victory had on public opinion.

This is not to say that the Bordeaux Frondeurs' immediate aims to defend their city by building a new fort at St. George were strategically naive or unimportant. This was certainly not the case. Still, in the strategic planning for ultimate control of the realm worked out in the king's name by his prime minister, these new defenses in Bordeaux were not very important. The Bordelais had a way of rebelling and building fortresses in the spring and of then wanting to suspend these activities in order to go out and bring in the grape harvest come fall, a fact known both to Condé and to Mazarin.

The arrest of the princes in January 1650 had been a *coup d'autorité,* an act designed to prevent further rebellion by intimidation. Anne and Mazarin could easily foresee an intense outburst of hostility for the government as a result of this decision. In point of fact, however, it was either arrest the princes or totally capitulate to Condé and give him control of the Council of State and the power to appoint governors.

The outburst of hostility toward Anne, Gaston, and Mazarin prompted by the princes' arrest strained the deepest threads in the social fabric, particularly among the nobility. Condé was not particularly loved by his clients and householders, but he was respected for his royal blood, high rank, and military courage. The prince had inherited literally hundreds of *fidèles,* or clients, who lived on his estates, manned garrisons, or held church benefices or judicial offices in virtually every province. Condé's rebellion forced them to make a hard choice between himself and the king in ways that inevitably focused attention on Mazarin as the source of the conflict. The king was too young to be at fault, the regent too controlled by her ministers. Hostility to Mazarin therefore became a way out of the dilemma of having to choose between Condé and the crown. Did Condé so well understand the dynamics of opinion formation that he realized that his own arrest would coalesce opinions in his favor?

The headstrong Count de Coligny, who remained in the prince's service for most of his life, observed that he had only two masters: the Prince de Condé and the king. Bitter but stoical, Coligny portrayed Condé as a punctilious egomaniac who could not bear to be beholden to anyone for the smallest service and who took no pleasure in rendering service to others. Some aspects of this assessment of the prince's character are suspect, but it nonetheless sheds light on why Condé's arrest turned a quite minor rebellious situation into a full-scale civil war. Coligny observed: ". . . Being bound to his fortune, I believed that honor and magnanimity obliged me not to abandon him in his [time of] adversity." The psychological-social links between the prince and this reluctantly dependent army officer indicate how the self-esteem and sense of upright conduct of an entire class or estate could be tested by Condé's arrest. Coligny needed his own sphere of autonomy, that is, independence from the state based on his noble rank and his respect for upright rules of conduct. If someone of Condé's rank could be arbitrarily arrested, what could happen to men of Coligny's rank? Coligny believed that on one level the Prince de Condé was qualitatively the same man that he was, that is, a man of honor. On a deeper level, the men were different because the prince possessed more of this shared noble quality owing to his family name and to the personal courage he had shown while serving the king. The decision to arrest Condé, his brother, and his brother-in-law and to put his mother, sister, and wife under effective house arrest violated the principle that the state was guarantor of the civil-monarchical order. This was a kind of revolution from above that, by attacking the prince, attacked a social estate. Or so it seemed to the prince's householders and officers. Coligny was put in the position of having to defend a patron whom he did not love and who he knew did not love him. Still, for thirteen years Coligny risked life and limb in the prince's service, as a *fidèle* who went over to the Spanish army after the end of the Fronde, in order to carry on the fight against Mazarin. The very typicality of Coligny's loyalty to the prince and of his treason against his king, even though the king had personally treated him well, elucidates how the princely Fronde became a civil war against the state.

For Mazarin, Anne, and young Louis XIV, the year of the arrests was also a year of "going to the country" to stimulate support for the government from persons at all ranks in the society. It was predicted that the outburst of anger, shock, and protest over the princes' arrests would subside into attempts to create alliances between various rival bodies and groups in the realm, in order to force Mazarin into disgrace and obtain the princes' release. As a result of the arrest, Mazarin became the issue over which alliances and enmities were created. His alleged betrayals, bribing, cheating, and sexual-social passions became the object of powerful publicity campaigns based on ethnic vilification. For the xenophobic French of the seventeenth century, being Italian meant being untrustworthy, over-sexed, infected with venereal disease, or homosexual.

To counteract this movement, Mazarin turned to an old technique that had succeeded before: displaying the young king to his subjects during a series of carefully staged trips across the realm. Previous queen mothers—Catherine de Medici and Marie de Medici—had done the same thing during their troubled regencies, usually just before the king reached the age of majority. Clothes encrusted with gold and jewels, beautiful horses and coaches, and including local dignitaries, religious orders, city fathers and guildsmen in processions, receptions, dinners, greetings and leavetakings, functioned on one level to enhance the authority of both the king and his Council of State. Below this spectatorial level were the everpresent Mazarin and the other members of the Council of State hearing petitions, settling disputes, distributing patronage, and arranging marriages. The resolution of local disputes, which often included the release of persons who had been in prison for months or years, worked like magic on the local level. This type of direct, activist government-by-council in the royal presence confirmed not just elite but also popular conceptions of how the monarchy should function.

As noted in Chapter 7, 1650 would be a year of royal progresses, first to Normandy, then to Burgundy, and finally down through the Southwest to Guienne and Bordeaux. Louis XIV always played his role well. The boy sat his horse with dignity, greeted persons of every rank with just the right salutation, and reassured everyone by his presence. The sequence of the trips to the provinces is revealing of the overall strategy directed at building support for the government. They began by visits to those provinces that were relatively favorable not only to Louis (all across France, everyone was personally favorable to *him*) but also to the government; and they ended with a journey to the province whose capital was in open rebellion.

The royal travels need not be analyzed in a general essay on the Fronde, but it is important to note four points that shed light on the specific political-military strategy that Mazarin had decided to follow. During the trip into Burgundy, the royal party split up so that Mazarin could take the young king off to Bellegarde to encourage the troops who were besieging this great but barely modernized medieval fortress on the Saône River, between Châlons-sur-Marne and Verdun. Bellegarde's strength hung like a strategic knife above the rich and populous Burgundian *pays* to the south. And that knife was controlled by the Frondeur Tavannes, commander of Bellegarde. Would Turenne and the rebel princely army to the north drive hard into

Burgundy? What was especially feared was joint Spanish-Fron-
deur military operations. And so as Mazarin and Louis XIV
pushed forward, the royal cause was well received.

At Bellegarde the boy king experienced one of the first in
a long succession of intoxicating moments. As he appeared in
the distance, plume-hatted and in splendid clothes, and moved
across the hillocks and redoubts of *his* besieging army, shouts
of *Vive le roi!* became verbal salvoes of such intensity that both
the besiegers and the beseiged manning the walls of Bellegarde
responded in kind. The two armies soon joined in a shouting
match, to see which side would best acclaim their king.

Mazarin quietly negotiated with the Frondeurs and worked
out a settlement based on an amnesty for the rebels holding
Bellegarde. Over the next few months it would be his strategy
to follow up with a royal declaration that "forgot the past" and
unleashed a dynamic of pardoning that excluded only the highest ranking or most radical Frondeurs. This strategy slowly
brought the Bordelais to turn ever so little away from Condé
and to lean instead toward the government.

The second point to note is that after the Burgundian trip
Mazarin hurried to Compiègne to supervise the placement of
military forces against the Spanish spring offensive. Small French
fortified towns were besieged and taken by the Spanish, notably
Le Catelet and Guise; but the Spanish had in effect shot their
bolt for the year, and a joint operation involving the Spanish
and Turenne's army failed to materialize.

The trip south and west with the boy king went amazingly
well in July and August, at least until the Richon affair broke
the dynamic of displaying the king and offering amnesty. The
royal army had gained control of Vayres, a small castle near
Bordeaux, when the soldiers holding it rallied to the king and
left its Frondeur commander, Richon, to be captured. Acting
in a way that was typical and deemed necessary, Anne of Austria ordered Richon hanged in a marketplace, an exemplary
punishment appropriate for a royal officer who had held a fortress against the king.

When the news of this sentence reached Bordeaux, a wild
and frenzied popular outburst took both Frondeur and non-
Frondeur leaders by surprise. A negotiated settlement on the
basis of amnesty had become the predictable pattern for settling these disputes, and there was every expectation that a set-

tlement of this sort would also be worked out with the Bordelais Frondeurs. But then the news of Richon's hanging arrived. The Princess de Condé, the Prince de Conti, La Rochefoucauld, and Bouillon hastily met, conferred with Frondeurs from Bordeaux, and decided that one of the soldiers they had captured would be hanged in retaliation. Lots were drawn and a young nobleman was hastily executed. The Frondeurs held the city very firmly, for people questioned whether a royal declaration of amnesty could in fact be trusted, in view of Richon's execution.

The royal army, which was not all that strong, then besieged the city. Thus the policy of displaying Louis XIV and declaring amnesty had to be abandoned for Frondeur Bordeaux. Seen from within the Frondeur city, these were heroic days in which the citizens stood up to a menacing army at the service of an Italian tyrant who had the boy king and his mother under his spell. We shall see that the news of the siege electrified Paris, for it seemed that nothing could stop Cardinal Mazarin. Success prompted jealous enemies in the Parlement and the city government to unite once again beneath the banner of freedom for Condé and Conti.

In point of fact, the approaching wine harvest in the Bordelais region, more than military success against the city, created the impetus required for opening negotiations. Amnesty was granted to all Frondeurs, with the exception of the Princess de Condé, La Rochefoucauld, and Bouillon. The only condition was that the king be allowed to enter the city in what amounted to a triumphal procession. The reception of Louis XIV and his mother on 5 October 1650 was indeed very solemn and joyous, but the animosities that had been so fierce only a few days before were barely papered over by outbursts of ceremonial affection for the king. No one was duped.

I. The Battles around Rethel

The Frondeurs in Paris, especially Coadjutor Retz, were perfectly aware of the fact that the campaign to rally the realm behind the queen regent and her minister Mazarin had been successful, at least up to the final phase of negotiations with the Frondeurs in Bordeaux. For Mazarin, it was apparent that if he could defeat Turenne's army in the Northeast and hold Paris, the shaky settlement in Bordeaux would hold and deepen into peace.

As the court moved north, Mazarin became aware of the mounting pressure on Gaston d'Orléans to favor Condé and Conti's release. Surrounded by persons such as Retz, who were either loyal to Condé or motivated by ambitions to wield supreme powers themselves, Gaston clung to his position in favor of the arrest, though he no longer really believed that it would promote peace. Should Gaston be attended to and firmed up against the advice he was hearing? Mazarin left that task to the queen regent and started northeast to put himself in a position to direct the king's army, which was seeking to drive the Spaniards from the realm. Would the Spanish coordinate their attack with the Frondeurs?

At the head of the Frondeur army was none other than Marshal Turenne, who had recently attempted to coordinate the pressures against Mazarin in the Southwest through his brother Bouillon, the principal military strategist in Frondeur Bordeaux. As Mazarin approached, the general commanding the royal army, who was a Mazarin *fidèle,* decided to besiege Frondeur-held Rethel, in the Ardennes mountains. Another of the many fortified towns of the Northeast that served as a gate through which rebellious nobles and their troops joined up with enemy Spanish troops, Rethel fell on 14 December 1650. Though the victory was certainly important for the royal army and Mazarin, Turenne and his Frondeur army were still in the field. Camped on high ground about twenty miles from Rethel, Turenne made the mistake of seeking a battle when he could have avoided it. He, his princely troops, and his Spanish allies suffered a really serious military defeat. The outcome of this battle made it seem that if Paris and Bordeaux would stay within the royal obedience.

II. The Slingshot Dynamic

Cardinal Mazarin was careful not to take the credit he deserved for consolidating the Council of State's power in 1650 and for coordinating the victories in and around Rethel that successfully prevented the Spanish from invading the realm from the

Spanish Netherlands. But this made no difference. His very success made detaining Condé and Conti in prison seem incongruous and "cruel." On 30 December 1650, Councillor Deslandes-Payen, perpetual Frondeur and ally of Retz, solemnly asked the Parlement to make formal remonstrances to the queen regent for the release of the princes. President Nesmond and other prominent Condé supporters then quickly mounted a test in the Parlement. As long as Mazarin's and the Council's prestige and military force remained steadfast, the princely party could not muster the votes for such strong action on behalf of Condé and Conti. Now, none other than First President Molé covertly switched sides and came out in favor of the princes' release.

In January the party favoring the princes' release built up quickly, not only in the Parlement but also among churchmen and in the streets. The Assembly of the Clergy, where Retz guided his supporters with his usual fine hand, protested that it was illegal to hold Conti in prison, for he was a man of the church—a legalism, it might seem, but one with medieval origins and with popular appeal among the rank and file of parish priests, vicars, and Sorbonne doctors eager to preserve the privileges of the First Estate. This protest marked an important step by the church toward rebellion.

Throughout the fall of 1650, Gaston d'Orléans, at Retz's instigation, had curried support among militia officers and other prominent bourgeois in the capital. While Mazarin was away in the Northeast, Gaston effectively assumed the role of commander-in-chief of the militia, which enabled him to create a crisis atmosphere in the capital whenever he wished. Anti-Condé judges in the Parlement were jeered and jostled by paid "*gens de main,*" or henchmen, who crowded into the halls and galleries of the Palais de Justice, just outside the Great Chamber. Rumors raced through the halls that the queen regent would soon be relieved of her duties and that Gaston would assume the title of regent for an indefinite period.

A putsch-like atmosphere developed in the capital. The transfer of the princes from Vincennes to remote Le Havre, in Normandy, had increased sympathies for them, sympathies carefully nourished by Condé clients in Paris. On 20 January 1651, President Molé spoke before Anne in favor of releasing the princes. A few days later Anne made a haughty reply through her chancellor, saying that she was accountable for her actions to God alone and that this arrest was none of the Parlement's business. In point of fact, at the time of the arrest Anne, Mazarin, and Gaston had been careful to explain their reasons to the Parlement. Yet anti-Mazarin pamphlets flowed out across the capital at a very high rate, much as they had in early 1649. Rumors circulated to the effect that the king was about to be captured and confined to a rural monastery. Tensions increased to the point where Anne and Louis dared not leave the Palais Royal for fear they would be captured by a crowd in Condé's pay or simply taken into custody by a militia company seeking to "protect" them. Retz, the author of *The Conspiracy of Fiesque*, felt that he had the city entirely under his control. The crucial alliance between the Parlement and the *peuple* was once again possible, and the campaign to vilify Cardinal Mazarin was heating up. The rallying cry went from the Parlement to the streets and echoed back again through influential members of the clergy. How could princes of the blood, especially a defender of the realm who had defeated the Spanish at Rocroy, be detained in prison while an ambitious, foreign, and lascivious leech retained his power as prime minister?

III. *Mazarin's Exile*

In this atmosphere, memories of the Saint Bartholomew's night massacre of 1572 and of the barricades erected in 1588 and 1648 prompted collective fears and wishes to secure the city. Gaston refused to attend meetings of the Council of State or come to the Palais Royal; he ordered the militia guards posted at the city gates. Columns of sober citizens (and sometimes not so sober ones) assumed posts outside the Palais Royal, to "keep order." On 7 February 1651, at eleven in the evening, Mazarin—wearing boots and dressed in gray with red trimmings—walked out of the city at the head of an armed guard. Rumors to the effect that similarly dressed men had appeared at several city gates and that no one knew which was the real Mazarin stimulated imaginings that the cardinal was a duplicitous wizard. Carrying with him a royal order to release the prisoners, Mazarin drove in haste through the night to the princes' prison at Le Havre.

The next day, Anne was forced to capitulate by Gaston, Retz, and the recently appointed Keeper of the Seals Molé and signed a second order for the princes' release, to be carried out by the Frondeurs. The cardinal won the race to Le Havre and thus earned the symbolic credit in the public eye for releasing the illustrious prisoners. By arriving first, he managed to keep alive a bare, thin, brittle concept of royal authority—and his own power in the government as well. Could anyone have been duped? When Gaston and Molé went over to the other side, Mazarin lost his margin for maneuver in the Council of State, owing to the threat of another bloodbath in Paris. Had Gaston made the vaguest allusion to murder, it is possible that either militia guards or Retz's gentlemen friends would have assassinated the cardinal, Le Tellier, Lionne, Ondedei, and others known to be attached to his party.

Once Mazarin, a prince of the church, had made the required low bow before the newly released prisoners, he tried to make some sort of settlement with Condé, his one-time intimate friend. The cardinal could offer pardons for all Condé's followers, plus a huge monetary payment and a seat on the Council of State for the prince himself. The meal the prince and the cardinal ate together that night was a terrible duel of poses and innuendos. Neither said nor dared say what he thought of the other. The cardinal may have tried to bargain with the prince, but he also probably had no illusions about the possibilities of an accommodation. Condé then took his leave and headed straight for Paris, where he knew a triumphal entry was being staged for him. The cardinal negotiated with local aristocrats in an attempt to maintain some control over the falling dominoes of council authority over Normandy. He had no real army at this point, for his troops in the Northeast were outnumbered and could be outfought by the prince's army. Condé had not only an army but a smoldering rebellion in Bordeaux and a strong party in Paris. Gaston and hundreds of his followers, the city fathers, the militia captains, and hundreds of other retainers and well-wishers went out of the city to meet the princes and conduct them into the capital in triumph.

Bonfires of celebration burned late into the night, and wine flowed freely among the well-wishers. How much of the popular celebration was staged by Retz and his followers? While this question is impossible to answer empirically, it is important to note that in the seventeenth century, participating in a fête that honored a prince signified genuine affection or respect. On one level the royal blood in Condé's veins and his reputation as a general sufficed for him to be honored and well-received in the capital; but on another level, it is far from evident that the militia captains and the wholesale merchants of the capital forgot that this was the same Condé who, at the head of a royal army, had besieged the city in 1649 and defeated its troops at Charenton. There is some evidence that only a few months earlier bonfires had likewise been lighted in his honor—but to celebrate his arrest. Learned observers like to note the "fickleness" of the *peuple*, who sang the praises of someone one week and forced him to leave town the next. In early-modern Europe, the links among politics, fêtes, and ceremony were so complex that historians living in another era dare not attempt unidimensional interpretations of crowd behavior along the lines of political notions such as "support for . . ." or "opposition to . . ." This point will become still more evident as we watch the relations between the Parisian populace and the prince deteriorate during the summer of 1652.

At the level of the Council of State, Condé's return meant a strong push to appoint his clients to key positions in the government and to collect as much cash as possible from the royal treasurers for unpaid pensions and army payments. The prince enjoyed such prestige that the administrative machinery—which required specific signatures on payment orders, letters patent, or letters of appointment, to mention only three examples— was put to a severe test. How could a minor royal official refuse a haughty intendant from the princely household who dared obfuscate on a matter of administrative detail? There is evidence that these minor officials tried to preserve the routine concerning payment regulations and that in doing so they imperiled their careers and, to an extent, their family's prosperity. Condé's men were not only haughty but intimidating and vindictive. In fundamentally egalitarian societies, the bureaucrat does not put himself at risk when he insists on respect for established administrative procedures. This was certainly not the case in a society that joined prestige, rank, potential violence, and enormous wealth. The Prince de Condé's signature carried the day and, as a councillor of state, rivaled the signatures of Anne and Gaston.

Over the previous decades the rivalry between Gaston and the Condé's, first father and then son, had been one of the constants in the power struggles going on in the upper reaches of the government. Retz's ambition and his advice to Gaston had led to an alliance of the two parties. The result was, of course, Mazarin's forced departure. Of the two men now in control of Paris, Condé, not Gaston, had the ideas and the clients to place, though Gaston played high politics by attempting to arrange a series of marriage alliances between the major rival aristocratic houses. The strategy of assuring domestic peace and enhanced social dignity through illustrious marriage alliances was one of the principal continuities of the aristocracy that dated from the High Middle Ages. A marriage project that joined Condé, Chevreuse, and perhaps Gaston d'Orléans through their children would enhance political stability, it was thought. At this level of society, private princely self-interest and interest of state were one.

The call for an Estates-General coming from both the assembled clergy and an informal assembly of nobles in the capital quickly led to a quarrel over the proposed date. Jockeying for some type of control over a meeting of the estates led to acrimony between Anne and Condé, with Gaston, withdrawn as always, too unsure of himself to seize the initiative. The removal of Anne as regent was also discussed, as was the establishment of a reformed Council of State consisting of twenty-one members, including the king, Condé, Gaston, and six representatives from each of the three orders. This project probably never had Condé's approval and may not even have been shown to him. Princes of Condé's rank had dozens of advisers and speechwriters at their disposal. These men often came up with quite utopian proposals for governmental reform, but the princes themselves usually sifted through these proposals, killing the undesired ones in their infancy. Thanks to their patronage powers, the princes had tremendous co-optive power in ancien régime political culture.

While Condé and Gaston continued to protest loyalty and affection for each other in Paris, Mazarin moved from army post to army post along the northern border. The detachments of royal troops that were beginning to prepare for the spring campaign against the Spanish were commanded by officers appointed by Mazarin and Le Tellier. The governors of the key fortresses also expressed loyalty not only to the king but to the cardinal as well. Condé perceived what was up and recognized that just because Mazarin had been forced to leave Paris, he had not given up the military duel for control of the realm. Direct communication between Anne and Mazarin was not always frequent, but in his private coded correspondence with her the cardinal laid out guiding principles to follow. In the uneasy atmosphere at the Palais Royal during March 1651, Anne was advised to conform to Condé's advice on all matters, but not to Gaston's, and of course to temporize. The guiding principle in both Mazarin's and Condé's strategic considerations was to favor the initiatives of the stronger party in any duel for ultimate control of the state. Condé advised this over and over again in his correspondence with Lenet, his agent in revolutionary Bordeaux. Mazarin gave the same advice to Anne and probably knew that sooner or later the little decisions made in accordance with this advice would lead to an explosion between her and Gaston, a new split among the Frondeurs and a chance for the cardinal to intervene on one side or the other.

Condé and Gaston controlled the Parlement with a heavy hand during the spring of 1651 and encouraged the Frondeur members to make incessant demands that a price be put on Mazarin's head and that Le Tellier and Lionne be replaced on the Council because they were Mazarin's "creatures." The Parlement also began to wake up to the dangers of having an Estates-General actually meet, because it would claim to be a representative corps in the realm. All the old arguments were trotted out, leading to abusive exchanges between the nobles and Molé. None of this was either revolutionary or surprising; the structural conflicts between the Parlement and the Estates-General went back at least a century. These conflicts over the time and place for a meeting of the Estates-General did not cause Anne or Condé to worry about disorder, nor did they offer Mazarin an opportunity to break the unity of the Frondeurs. Only a split at the highest level of government could alter the situation.

Perhaps it was with Condé's full approval, or perhaps somewhat on her own but guided by Mazarin's advice, that Anne invited the Count de Chavigny to return and resume his position as minister in the Council of State. A second-rate but decidedly not an incompetent practitioner of high-council politics and also Mazarin's former rival for dominance within the Council and for the prime ministership as well, Chavigny had long since become Condé's client in the battles for control of the government at the highest level. Nominally at least, Anne had the power to appoint and dismiss councillors during the regency, but this time she did not bother to consult with Gaston d'Orléans. Chavigny's reappointment meant, of course, an increase in Condé's control over the government. Gaston took immediate offense. And if this was not enough, Keeper of the Seals Châteauneuf, who had joined Retz and the arch intriguer the Duchess de Chevreuse, was thanked for his services and replaced by First President Molé of the Parlement.

This dramatic shift in the membership of the Council of State was important for two reasons: first, it signaled the end of the unified aristocratic party headed by Gaston and Condé that had driven Mazarin into exile; and second, it revealed the almost structural necessity encountered by high-ranking aristocratic party leaders to reward their powerful supporters with increased power. On the one hand, Condé needed more votes on the Council; on the other, he had raised expectations for advancement among his supporters that needed to be recognized. By bringing Chavigny and Molé into the Council, Anne and Condé threatened Gaston's position; but at the same time they did not bring in anyone who was so strong and independent that he could not be sacked later on.

During this duel for control of the Council, Molé held the seals for a mere two weeks, a period of intense in-fighting between not only Condé and Gaston but also Molé and the clients of disgraced Séguier and Châteauneuf, in the Chancery. As Mazarin made his way to Brühl, a short distance from Cologne, the wheel of fortune kept turning in Condé's favor—so much so that he dared to reject the projected marriage alliance with the Chevreuse family that would have transformed his brother from an ecclesiastic weighed down with enormous sums of church revenue into the Duchess de Chevreuse's son-in-law. Marriage into the Bourbon house would have been a great *coup de prestige* for Chevreuse, so Condé's refusal constituted an affront for anyone of the Chevreuse rank and pretentions, and was doubly painful because the news had been made public. The affront that the perceptive and powerful duchess (and through her, Retz) suffered at the hands of Condé left her no other alternative but to seek a rapprochement with the disgraced prime minister in far-off Brühl.

During the months of April, May, and June 1651, Condé's virtual control over the royal signature enabled him to reward several dozen of his key followers with governorships, lieutenancies, and captaincies of fortresses and regiments here and there throughout the realm. Without giving up Guienne, he took back for himself the governments of Burgundy and Berry, and claimed that of Champagne for his servile brother, Conti. This gave him a pincers-like military potential in both North and South. With Champagne and Burgundy under his control, how could Mazarin move his army from the Northeast to cut off the prince's links to Montrond, in the Center, and to Bordeaux?

Gaston was powerless to do anything about Condé's increased power: he had been outwitted. So he withdrew to recover and to make certain that the Parisian militia companies and his *fidèles* in the Parlement had remained loyal to him. Retz had not only a firm control over a claque in the Great Chamber and among the clergy, but the author of the *Conspiracy of Fiesque* had acquired experience in mobilizing bourgeois guards in the capital to create a climate of fear and panic. Beneath Gaston's benign gaze, Retz had done this to Mazarin in February 1651. Why not do the same to Condé?

In the middle of the night of 5–6 July 1651, Condé jumped out of bed, dressed rapidly, and with only a few retainers left Paris and headed for his small château at Saint-Maur, just east of the city. Real conspiracies had certainly been hatched to kill Condé on the street or capture him in some small room, but this one was probably a product of the prince's imagination. Plots of this sort are much more Fiesque-like than the ones worked out by anxious regents or by the insecure Henry III, all of which centered on capture or murder in the room where the council of state met. During the weeks that followed Condé's hasty departure, an intense duel for control of the Council of State ended in the rotation and disgrace of several ministers. From Saint-Maur, Condé pressed for the disgrace of the men in control of foreign affairs and war: Servien, Lionne, and Le Tellier. They were all sacked. Chavigny thought he could take advantage of the situation, but Anne sent him packing as well. In reality, the competitors for power and patronage had been

eliminated from the Council. And while Condé may have interpreted these moves as a gain for him, in fact the divisions between
the prince and Gaston had become so intense that the Parisian
populace would again play a major role. Condé returned to his
great residence near the Luxembourg, outwardly serene but
uncertain about how to bring sufficient pressure to bear on Anne
to be granted control over the Council of State. The queen regent
had no intention of doing so and by now could withstand such
pressures.

In early August 1651, Anne struck a bargain with Retz. In
return for standing up to Condé and convincing him either to
be satisfied with his current offices and pensions or to leave the
city, Anne promised Retz that he would receive the next French
nomination to a cardinalcy. Only partly motivated by ambitions
for a cardinal's hat, Retz took on the task and became a member
of the Council of State. That is, he became the effective leader
of Gaston's and his own supporters. This was, he recognized,
his big opportunity. Always desperate for power, Retz had hoped
and plotted, trying simultaneously to remain in Anne's good
graces at all times and to drive his rival, Mazarin, into definitive
exile. Certainly aware that Mazarin was still advising the queen
through secret emissaries, Retz hoped that his success in a confrontation with Condé would consolidate his seat on the Council and that he would become prime minister.

With Condé back in the capital and still demanding to be
the one to make all government decisions, Anne took Retz's
advice and went on the offensive. She invited all prominent
persons with political influence to meet at the Palais Royal on
17 August 1651 to hear a royal declaration of charges against
Condé. Princes mingled with the provost of merchants and the
échevins, with marshals of France and with high-ranking judges
from the sovereign courts, who all assembled to hear Condé
accused of ingratitude and dissatisfaction and of carrying on
preparations for a civil war. The fortifications under his command were being improved, the Declaration noted, and the
prince had maintained his ties with foreign powers. This frontal attack on Condé prompted debates and confrontations in
the capital—a sign of Retz-style politics, which contrasted sharply
with those of Mazarin. The cardinal habitually temporized and
relied on both patronage and private discussions; he did not
attempt to mobilize public opinion. To be fair to Retz, one must

remember that he was using the only weapons that he had against Condé. He and Gaston had learned to orchestrate putsch-like incidents to force first Mazarin and then Condé to leave the city, for fear of assassination. But Condé had returned. And he was totally fearless as he went about Paris, much like the Duke de Guise in 1588. Condé nonetheless lacked Guise's popular support.

The prince appeared in the Great Chamber of the Parlement on 18 August and, with Retz present, denied the charges made against him in the royal declaration. The coadjutor supported Anne's declaration, but a showdown was avoided by the lateness of the hour. The next session of Parlement, both parties realized, would bring a dramatic and potentially violent showdown. Would factional fighting lead to shooting in the streets of Paris, as it had in Bordeaux?

The Parlement had become the scene of a battle over control of the Council of State. No one quite knew whether its legislative and moral authority would be sufficient to resolve the conflict. Gaston and Retz had a strong party in the Great Chamber, and so did Condé. Over the next several days, judges were counted and lobbied, since no one knew whether a vote would take place or which party would carry the day. For this brief period the Council and the Parlement became politically one, as parties seeking to control the state squared off in a political duel.

At the meeting of the Parlement of Paris on 21 August 1651, the leader of each party arrived at the head of hundreds of armed retainers and friends. Anne had supplied Retz with troops from her light-horse regiment. By eight in the morning, the Palais de Justice was filled with two barely divided armies. A misfire or an accidental detonation could have triggered a bloodbath. Seeing the danger, and wanting to make a gesture that would keep the peace, Condé sent La Rochefoucauld to evacuate his armed supporters. The wily Retz went in person to do the same. In the ensuing mêlée, La Rochefoucauld managed to corner Retz and squeeze him between the heavy double doors of the Great Chamber. He was freed only a few moments later. Retz's possible death was less important than the fact that this incident gave the coadjutor a pretext to appear before the assembled court as the endangered and offended ecclesiastic. Incidents of this sort crop up like signatures wherever Retz steps onto the stage of the Fronde. The author of the *Conspiracy of Fiesque* knew how to stage political scenarios that occasionally gave him the high ground. In this case, the way in which his life had been threatened confirmed the accuracy of the declaration charging Condé with ingratitude, discourtesy, and intimidation.

The Parisian militia columns usually were called upon to evacuate riotous crowds from the Palais de Justice, but this time they either were not summoned or failed in their duty to keep order. Yet it is significant to note that it was Champlâtreux, the colonel of the quarter in which the Palais was located, who extricated Retz from between the double doors and from the threat of death. A firm supporter of Condé, yet also a recently promoted judge in the Parlement and the son of First President Molé, Champlâtreux preferred debate, no matter how divisive, to blood spilled on the floor of the Palais de Justice.

Though each party had prepared for a showdown vote in the Parlement, and though there is evidence that judges' wives mobilized their friends to exert pressure in favor of Retz, Molé, who had resumed his office as first president after his fortnight excursion into the Council as keeper of seals, steered the debate and the voting in such a complex, almost contradictory direction that there was neither a winner nor a loser by the end of the session. Always seeking hierarchy and harmony of authorities within the state, Molé effectively formed a series of issues that could be addressed to Anne—a way of gaining time and of maintaining at least the appearances of parlementary loyalty to the crown *and* respect for all the members of the Council, even Condé and Retz. Had Molé definitively gone over to the prince in order to remain on good terms with his Condéist son? It is doubtful, as he did not use the powers of his office of first president to favor Condé on this occasion. Molé did not wish to enhance the powers of his court on matters affecting the powers of the various institutions that constituted the state. Like so many earlier confrontations, the carefully staged duel between Retz and Condé and their followers resolved nothing; but in the minds of the Parisian elites, it left memories of attempts to resolve conflicts in the state.

What had made Condé press so hard to win at this time? He knew that he probably did not have all that much time to gain control of the Council. Louis XIV was rapidly approaching the age of majority, which by custom was fixed at thirteen years. Had Condé managed to capture control of the Council, and with it the royal seals, and had he appointed a keeper who would do his bidding, it is highly likely that he would have compelled Louis to issue a decree in the name of Condé and the Council, postponing his majority until his seventeenth or eighteenth birthday. The Council of State had become something of a nonentity, owing to the disgrace of everyone but the reappointed but uninfluential Chancellor Séguier, Superintendant of Finances Maisons, and Retz. Gaston wavered in and out, more or less the way Retz wanted him to. The king's uncle was aware that Mazarin still had to be definitively beaten or exiled and that to achieve this he needed Condé's support. Yet being allied with Condé meant that Gaston lost on every front of patronage and military influence. And this too was intolerable.

IV. The Rentier Rebellion

Safe investments for monies saved up, either by institutions such as hospitals or by private individuals, were scarce in the seventeenth century. This accounts for the success, and the popularity, of the *rentes* or bonds on the Hôtel de Ville. They paid a fairly high interest rate for the period (8 percent) and no taxes were levied on the income from this quite secure investment.

The investor merely presented himself before a syndic or his representative, bearing his capital in cash or, occasionally, as a letter of credit. He then loaned the money to the Hôtel de Ville in return for regular quarterly interest payments. In fact, the *rente* officials played only a supervisory role over the capital they received from investors. The capital was quickly turned over to the royal treasury to be spent on war matériel, expenses of the royal household, and pensions for officials. The prestige of the Hôtel de Ville gave the *rentes* they issued an image of security and of probity in capital management that did not in fact exist. Since the beginning of the war with Spain, interest payments were irregular at best and by the mid-1640s were so long overdue that the capital value of the more recently purchased *rentes* had declined precipitously. On the eve of the Fronde, investors feared an arbitrary cancellation of some *rentes,* which could be done by a royal order from the Council of State invalidating certain issues of *rentes* owing to "irregularities" that had developed. As the interest payments became irregular, speculators bought up the *rentes* (the capital) at very low prices and trusted that in the future their political connections would see that they were reimbursed at par value.

Arrears in payments for leases on land, reduced toll income, and arrears in *taille* payments reduced the ready cash available to royal treasurers for interest payments on the *rentes*. Certain favored revenues such as the *gabelle*, the salt tax, were supposed to be assigned to paying the interest on the *rentes;* but as the financial crisis deepened because of the war, these revenues were diverted to that effort. In fact, just like the interest payments on the *rentes*, the *gages*—that is, the payments due royal officials holding venal offices (and this included the judges in the various parlements)—were supposed to come from secure high-revenue sources. If revenue flowed in at all, it was to be allocated, in theory at least, to *gages* and *rentes*.

No study of the owners of *rentes* has been made by historians, so it is impossible to say just how far down into the artisanal and laboring classes this form of investment reached. In the protesting cries and pamphlets that arose over the delays in interest payments, hapless widows and hospitals were always mentioned. There is no doubt that investment in *rentes* was one of the vertical features of urban society, linking the very rich to the most modest shopkeeper or artisan who wanted to invest his or her savings. Small shares in the *rentes* amounting to only 50 *livres* are cited in the inventories after death of persons of very modest means. In the inventories of such wealthier Parisians as wholesale merchants or parlementaires, *rentes* could total as much as 200,000 *livres*. Seen from the distance of the twentieth century, it is surprising that the protests over delayed interest payments did not surface earlier and more virulently, in 1648.

The judges who solemnly favored the creation of a defensive army in the winter of 1649 must have known that this would have the effect of reducing still further the possibility that interest would be paid on the *rentes*. More likely, they saw their only recourse as one of defense: they would break the government in order to alter fundamentally the war policy that had impoverished *rentiers*, royal judges, and taxpayers alike. Thus delayed interest payments on the *rentes*, like higher taxes and the creation of new offices such as the masters of requests, were all part of a policy that resulted from the war effort. The nearly complete cessation of *taille* payments by the peasants in the spring of 1648 unleashed bitterness and mobilized the *rentiers* in the capital.

The social verticality of *rente* ownership meant that the neighborhood assemblies of protesters included the rich and the almost poor, as well as representatives of hospitals, parishes, and monastic communities. In fact, neighborhood protest meetings quickly became a new political force with which the other participants in the Fronde had to reckon. The committees that the *rentiers* quickly set up prompted scrutiny by the Parlement. This prestigious court disliked any and all political bodies, committees, or movements that could dilute its prestige and power as lawful "spokesman" for all Parisians, indeed all Frenchmen.

A *Mazarinade* printed in 1649 that took the form of a *factum* or legal brief makes the point that the royal councillors should not take offense if the *rentiers* meet at the Hôtel de Ville. "It is because some wish to pass off tears as criminal [activity] by accusing those who assemble of sedition and revolt in order to stifle their voice by this strategy." To the contrary, all they have done is to join together to look for the means of avoiding their joint ruin. And the anonymous author adds: "People of all ages, all social *conditions*, should assemble—women and children included—everyone who has an interest has a right to enter and give advice." One after the other, the officials charged with getting to the bottom of why interest was not being paid were accused of impropriety. The reason is simple for the author of this factum: "The whole fortune of the state is today locked up in the single person of the tax farmer." What is the point of attempting to prosecute these men as long as the provost of merchants refuses to enter their houses and seize their account books and property? "Prison is a *délice* for them." In conclusion the author appeals to the Parlement to intervene in the matter. It would be interesting to attempt to discern whether the author took up his pen again to protest the very elitist results of the Parlement's intervention in the contestation over the *rentes*.

The protest movement of the *rentiers* became so strong that it created an institutional expression. Indeed, on 29 November 1649 the Parlement granted a charter for an institution through

which the protest should be expressed. Its first clause authorized an assembly in the Hôtel de Ville to be composed of the
provost of merchants and the *échevins,* deputies from the Parlement, the Chamber of Accounts and the Court of Excises, the
town councillors, officials from the various quarters of the city,
and "four notable bourgeois" from each quarter. Gathered for
a special ceremonial meeting, they would elect "eighteen deputies who will take care of the six types of rentes, that is, three
for the *gabelles,* three for the clergy, three for the excise taxes
(aides), three for general receipts, three for customs, and three
for the *rentes* on the Cinq Grosses Fermes."

The second clause of the "charter" established that the four
bourgeois from each quarter would be selected by thirty bourgeois from that quarter of the city, all of whom held *rentes* total-
ing at least 500 *livres* and who had no ties whatever with tax
contractors or royal loans. The third clause stated that the general assembly created by the first clause would meet every six
months.

This attempt to channel a protest movement into a co-optive,
oligarchic, and wealthy assembly is very revealing of the mech-
anisms at work in seventeenth-century French society. On the
one hand, the protest movement over *rentes* was impeded from
developing its own autonomy under the direction of the provost of merchants and the *échevins,* as a result of the presence
in the assembly of the ex officio delegates from the three great
superior courts. On the other hand, the qualification of owning
at least 500 *livres* in *rentes* excluded the angry small investor.
Clearly the Parlement feared a new power in the capital, one
consisting of the *rente* protesters at the Hôtel de Ville, who could
turn either "Mazarinist" or more radically Frondeur, as the
Ormistes would later do in Bordeaux.

The Parlement's "charter" would not be the last word on
the *rentier* protest movement. Indeed, the next several years saw
more meetings, protests, and challenges to the fact that some
delegates were indeed corrupt and in collusion with the totally
discredited syndic officials. To complicate matters further,
decrees from the royal council annulled decrees issued by the
Parlement and attempted to establish alternative procedures for
channeling interest payments on the *rentes.* Competing protest
meetings, both Frondeur and anti-Frondeur, appeared as early
as 1650.

The contestation over interest payments turned nasty when protesters demanded, through legal redress, the seizure of the account books, furniture, personal effects, and houses of the tax contractors who had defaulted on their payment to the Hôtel de Ville. Protests increased during the spring of 1651, when demands were made that "syndics and the said tax collectors, their wives, and their children should be arrested and put in the Conciergerie prison." Rumors floated about to the effect that Mazarin had taken the *rentes* interest when he precipitously left the city for Le Havre to release the princes. More evident still was Gaston's factually established seizure of monies destined for interest payments, when he was raising an army in the spring of 1651. It had long since become obvious to the more observant Parisians that protests neither by assembled *rentiers* nor by the provost of merchants nor even by the Parlement would be any more successful than the royal government had been at extracting money from the tax collectors, who had solemnly agreed to pay certain sums by certain dates. Claiming later that they were bankrupt and that the tax revenues they had a legal right to collect were not being paid, the tax farmers either refused to pay or were unable to do so.

Agitation over the *rentes* continued for years after the Fronde, because interest payments were not regularly paid until the early 1660s, when the "reforms" legislated by Controller General Jean-Baptiste Colbert brought the fraud to a halt. The special citizen watchdog committees that arose out of the *rentier* protest and that constituted a popular-leaning Frondeur movement had been carefully channeled into elitist political protest by the Parlement. Distrust of these committees persisted, however, on the part of both the Parlement and the city fathers, who felt threatened or diminished in their power by the rise of any new institution or neighborhood organization. Political power in seventeenth-century France always had a territorial-jurisdictional foundation. The jealousies and resentments between old, established institutions easily became ferocious outbursts aimed at quashing any new quasi-institutional force. This was true not only for the *rentier* watchdog committees but also for the assemblies of nobles held in Paris at about the same time. In a revolutionary moment, new groups and institutions rise out of the masses of protesters in the streets.

As we have seen, the descent of the Parlement into angry

recrimination and division over charges of corruption eliminated it as a powerful force in the Fronde. The witch-hunt
atmosphere, with its legalese, its self-criticism, and its demands
that judges disqualify themselves, did not respond to the broader,
more powerful issues that had brought the realm from foreign
war to civil war. But the explosive and divisive debates over
corruption did respond to the crescendo of *rentier* protests. The
Parlement's "charter" offering an institutional structure for the
protesters contained specific clauses to the effect that representatives selected to investigate accounts must have no personal
or family links to the tax farmers. This stipulation certainly
responded to the angry mood of the *rentiers,* who had received
no interest payments, but it also went straight to the heart of
what the moral probity of a judge in the Parlement *ought* to be.
And in the meetings held in each quarter of the city to select
the delegates who would investigate the accounts for the *rentes,*
parlementaires and their clients found themselves scrutinized
by their neighbors—and perhaps disqualified precisely because
the candidate had been involved with a tax farmer in a marriage, a loan, or a real estate transaction.

During the Fronde of 1648–49, the Parlement had carried
on its own attempt to alter its power relations with the Council.
Yet it also worked effectively to channel popular forces into
calmer, more sober committees of *rentiers* and nobles that would
be less threatening to the social-political order, by reason of the
deference paid to well-to-do *gens de bien* who had power to effect
the payment of the *rentes.* The tough social ligatures connecting
wealth, rank, and political power held firm in the Fronde.

V. *The Assemblies of Nobles*

As they had done during the Regency crisis of 1612 and 1613,
various members of the political elite made an urgent appeal
for an Estates-General. The Estates-General of 1614 had temporarily cleared the air of aristocratic plots and consolidated
the regent's power to govern. The idea was discussed frequently in the royal council in 1651 and 1652 and, as was the
case with everything else, the Estates became a source of intense
rivalry among the principal factions that were competing for
control of the government. A meeting of the Estates would be

a test of strength for the factions. In 1614, the Grand Condé's father had hoped to garner enough votes to impose his will on Marie de Médicis and her councillors, but this did not work out. In the selection-election of deputies across the realm, Marie and her Council did well, and the Condéist threat to use the Estates collapsed.

Would holding an Estates-General in 1651 do the same for Anne of Austria? As royal decrees went out ordering the selection-election of deputies, the old question of a site for the meeting served as the focal point in the duel for control of the realm that was going on between Anne and Condé. For the prince now had Gaston's support. Anne, no doubt advised by Mazarin and others, wanted the meeting to be held in the Loire Valley, that is, away from Paris. In 1650–51, Mazarin clearly perceived that a political shift was taking place within the realm, toward stability and support for the regent. From his exile he frequently wrote Anne that as long as she and the young king remained in Paris they were virtually powerless, if not prisoners of the Fronde; but in the open country and in other cities, they would have a great deal of power. Condé and Gaston continually pressed to have the Estates meet in Paris, a very important clue to understanding where they believed the locus of their Frondeur power to be.

Mazarin remained sanguine about the prospect of an Estates-General, perhaps more so than the parlementaires. For the Cardinal the proposal prompted a review of preparations. He knew that abundant *grâces*—that is, bribes, gifts and minor offices—would have to be distributed to assure a favorable outcome of the process of selecting-electing deputies. At no point does he seem to have perceived the holding of an Estates-General as a threatening action that would undermine the absolutist state founded by Cardinal Richelieu. As a thinker about these questions, Mazarin remained pragmatic. He fully understood constitutionalist-absolutist visions of French political and social institutions, but he was not an ideologue who insisted on fighting openly on every issue so that the absolutist vision would prevail over a government with power diffused in a variety of institutions. Instead, Mazarin took the position that if there was going to be an Estates, then it would have to be planned for. If there was something Mazarin feared, it was lack of foresight in government.

As in so many other battles of the Fronde, the struggle over the meeting place of the Estates boiled down to who would control the royal signature. Such a meeting could not be called without the royal signature, and this was something Anne knew full well. So she demanded and received absolute obedience on this question from the chancellor-keeper of the seals. As we have seen, a series of very significant rotations in the offices of chancellor-keeper of the seals took place, as the Condéist faction intimidated Anne with ever more intensity. The Parlement viewed with hostility the proposal to convoke an Estates-General. Its claim to represent the realm sufficiently without an Estates-General always weakened when political debates centered on holding this assembly as the "sole manner" to resolve the duels for power at the highest level of the government.

So many rumors, orders, and counterorders were issued about the meeting places and times for the Estates-General that the king's subjects realized that their solemn expressions of loyalty and willingness to serve the king would have little weight in the balance of forces that divided the realm into warring camps.

Finally, in November 1652, orders went out to select-elect deputies for an Estates to be held at Sens. Through their clients, Condé and Gaston had continued to press for a transfer of the meeting to Paris. In fact, the Estates never really met, for Anne successfully resisted the pressure to transfer the meeting to Paris. After that, Condé's and Gaston's interest in this assembly waned, perhaps because they realized that they would be unable to use the Estates to intimidate Anne.

What is important, however, is the perception of the realm as a wellspring not only of royalism but also of deep loyalty to the regent and her son. Marie de Medici and her minor son, Louis XIII, had certainly enjoyed this genuine realmwide support. Had an Estates-General met in 1651, it is practically certain that Anne of Austria and Louis XIV would have received a similar expression of loyalty, especially if Mazarin had remained in exile. No other explanation holds for Gaston's and Condé's intense hostility to the meeting planned for Angers, Tours, or Sens.

Concurrent with the struggle over the Estates-General there arose, not quite spontaneously, an assembly of nobles in Paris. Royal councillors and parlementaires alike challenged the legality of this assembly, but in point of fact some of Gaston's and Condé's *fidèles,* the Perigourdin Montrésor being a prominent example, carefully cultivated an assembly of nobles. There is no doubt that a considerable number of these nobles joined out of a solemn desire to serve their monarch in whatever way he or his mother deemed appropriate. Certainly not all of the nobles were princely clients, though the spokesmen and managers of the body were certainly Condé-Gaston managers. But it is one thing to assure one's patron of control over a body of noblemen and quite another to be able actually to deliver either their swords or their votes.

The nobles continued to meet yet received no specific orders about what they were supposed to do or the sort of advice they were to give. They soon began to recriminate against the Council, the Parlement, and the realm in general, and more specifically against attacks on the privileges due them as nobles. It was not long before they started to bicker among themselves over derogations, pretensions, and failed marks of respect within the ranks of the Second Estate itself. Little in these recriminations addressed the more general, realm-wide issues of governance, the cost of the war, or fiscal policies. This point is important because it sheds light on how French politics and society in the seventeenth century were constituted of really quite separate *grand corps,* and this became powerfully apparent when political crises occurred. In their recriminations about noble privileges, the assembly looked every bit as self-interested as the parlementaires had in their criticisms of mushrooming sales of judicial offices and of the crown's failure to pay the *gages* due them.

As the political stalemate over power within the royal council continued, the number of nobles attending the assembly slowly but steadily dwindled. A stay in or near the capital was expensive, because each nobleman was obliged to dress and entertain in a manner appropriate to his rank. The parlementaires manifested their hostility to this assembly quite explicitly, largely on the grounds that the meetings had not been called and were therefore illegal.

The judges' efforts to monopolize political power prompted attacks on the *rentier* assembly, co-optive legislation regulating the *rentier* protest, hostility to the calling of an Estates-General, and finally charges that the assembly of nobles was illegal. If the Fronde never became a revolution in the sense of a mass realm-wide movement aimed at overthrowing constituted authority, it was largely because the cleavages between different segments of the society were so strong, and the pretensions of the Parlement over other "representative bodies" were so powerfully manifested. It is doubtful that hostility from the Parlement had very much effect on the assembled nobles. They understood the pretensions of that body and would have acted, despite these admonitions, had the regent given them a specific task. But Anne did not even ask for their advice; she did not thank them for attending her and expressing their willingness to render service. Gaston's ineffectualness and Retz's all-too-apparent machinations to become prime minister may also have disgusted the nobles. And so they returned to their country estates. Their meeting had not changed the duel for power in the princely Fronde.

In the autumn of 1651, the sense of frustration and disgust that Mazarin had observed to be only barely noticeable a year earlier now grew increasingly strong in various segments of the body politic. Criticism ran high, and passionate demands for a solution, any solution, echoed in the speeches that provincial deputies gave before councillors, Condé, Gaston, and even the Parlement. The *Mazarinades* echoed the change of tone, though they still vituperated against the cardinal. The rise of frustration over a stalemated political crisis is a phenomenon that historians of revolution have often noted but have never really analyzed. In the princely Fronde it was something quite distinct from what in other times and societies is called counterrevolution. In Paris, city fathers, guild officers, and clergy lamented theft, rape, and the destruction of buildings and crops, and prayed for an end to the Fronde, without specifying what end.

In mid-December 1651, Cardinal Mazarin moved southward toward Sedan, at the head of an tiny army of 3,000 cavalry, 600 dragoons, 900 infantrymen, and two cannons. Attempts to reach a compromise with Condé, Gaston, and their clients would soon end. Condé was clearly losing the duel for the upper hand in public opinion. Since his clients in the Parlement lacked a majority, that body could do little but wring its collective hands on the sidelines. In fact, the judges had sought cover under Gaston's aegis; they remained quite eager to do anything he asked, and this included producing still more funds to pay an army. But with all their pretensions and serious commitments to determine the course of action, the judges had come down heavily in favor of Gaston and Condé, without making any difference at all in the outcome of the Fronde. The end to the revolution that was the Fronde would be determined by another, larger civil war.

VI. The Lit de Justice Declaring Louis XIV's Majority

Louis XIV had been born on 5 September 1638. Thus a solemn ceremony that took the form of a *lit de justice* was held at the Palais de Justice on 7 September 1651, during which the king received *hommage* and oaths of fidelity from all his most powerful subjects, his mother and the Parlement of Paris included. The young king played his role superbly. Condé chose not to attend the *lit* and remained in the country, a grave political error in view of the expressions of genuine support and affection for the monarchy and for young Louis XIV voiced on that occasion. But given Condé's intelligence, it is also possible to interpret this decision as founded on the realization that his attempt to win by a showdown had failed.

Though only thirteen, Louis XIV simply ignored a letter from Condé that arrived the next day informing the monarch that the prince's return to Paris would be possible if the king delayed appointing new councillors. The game was up. The regency was over. Condé had evolved from loyalty and youth to rebellion and overbearing maturity. But it was one thing to be demanding and rude to Mazarin, Gaston, Anne, and even Retz, and quite another to behave in an intimidating way toward the king. Centuries of custom, manners, and courtesies in a deeply monarchical culture spelled defeat for Condé. And if it is difficult to understand how the French could bear the often haughty conduct of the Sun King at Versailles over the next fifty years, the answer lies in an unstated respect for, a tolerance of, and a psychological empathy for the young monarch who had refused to be intimidated by the Prince de Condé.

The intense negotiations that took place over a meeting place for the Estates-General also consolidated the new Council's strength. As might be expected, Gaston and Retz wanted the meeting held in Paris, where their chances for putting pressure on the delegates were far greater than they would be at

Tours or Pontoise. In fact, delegates were loyally turning up in Tours, where they awaited the king's orders. On 17 November 1651, the Parisian delegates left for that city, a signal to Gaston that he could not be certain of his power in the capital. Throughout the fall, the Parlement spent most of its time fulminating against Mazarin and eventually passed a resolution that whoever assassinated the cardinal would be rewarded by 150,000 *livres* of the sums obtained from the sale of his library.

Just a few days later, Louis XIV appointed several new councillors. Molé became keeper of the seals for the second time that year. Châteauneuf and La Vieuville also joined the Council. To be fair to Retz at this point, it is evident that he was trying to establish a third party that would be beholden neither to Gaston nor to Condé. In fact, both princes were furious. Gaston sulked. Condé headed for his great fortified castle of Montrond. Could the new government stand up to Condé and his allies, who commanded armies in the East and Southwest?

Retz, with the cardinal's rank newly bestowed upon him, must be given credit for recognizing the military-strategic realities. But what chance did a third party have without troops to back it up? The fate of the princely Fronde hung in the balance. In point of fact, Retz lacked a client network of loyal generals placed in strategic places across the realm, preferably in the North. It was one thing to mount putsches in Paris, and to mobilize opinion—be it popular or parlementaire—and bring it to bear on the struggles within the royal council for supreme power in the realm. It was quite another thing to put together the military forces needed to stand against Condé in the field. Like his great teacher Richelieu, Mazarin was at his best when it came to selecting military nobility that would not only be faithful but would succeed in military confrontations with rebellious towns and princes. Retz suddenly found that the burdens of his ecclesiastic office were requiring much of his time. And Anne was no longer really listening to him.

By contrast, Gaston and his advisers and clients became quite energetic about attempting to raise still another army. As soon as the king and his mother left for the Southwest, they forced the Parisians to "volunteer" contributions and to make "loans" for troops. Would it be possible to pull together an effective anti-Mazarin force in the capital? The Parlement spent hours, days, weeks, even months, vituperating against Mazarin.

The majority of the judges settled down, waiting for Gaston or Retz to tell them what to do. And Condé had a strong party in the court that allied with Gaston's supporters, finally under the aegis of the eminent First President Molé. For the second time, the Parlement dealt itself out of the Fronde.

TEN

The End of the Fronde

THE Fronde began as a tax revolt provoked by the monarchy's desperate need for funds to continue the war against Spain. The intricate and seemingly interminable negotiations to end the European war involved all parties, including France and her ally Sweden, and finally culminated in a peace signed in October 1648 at Münster, in Westphalia. France had intervened in this war, first with many subsidies to foreign powers and then with troops, to impede the transformation of Hapsburg imperial powers into a more centralized and powerful German state. The most recent campaigns had wreaked destruction and death on the German population as nothing had done before in history. The troops on both sides lacked supplies and money; pillage, extortion, and rape became a way of life for thousands of soldiers. A fiscal explanation has usually been proposed for this terrible scourge on the civilian population: when officers lacked funds to pay their troops, discipline disintegrated and pillage became the rule. While this explanation is certainly true, it is also important to note how pillage, and the burning of entire peasant villages, became a strategic factor. Newspapers and woodcut pictures quickly informed not only all Germans but Europeans in general of the atrocities in Germany, and an escalation of atrocities by one side quickly prompted equal destruction by the other.

In the military campaigns of 1649, but more particularly those of 1650 and 1652 in civil-war–ridden France, not only individual officers and soldiers but entire regiments and small "armies" that had become accustomed to committing atrocities in Germany maneuvered and fought in the French countryside. This extension of the most cruel and barbaric aspect of the Thirty Years' War into a France divided by civil war has often been noted; but it rarely has been linked to the rise of anger, pain, and a peace-at-any-price mood in 1652. When historians ask, "Why did the Frondeurs not fight on to defend their revolutionary challenge to absolute monarchical power?" their principal answer is military maneuvers, that scourge on the rural population.

The end of the war in Germany enabled Mazarin and the French army to concentrate on the war with the other Hapsburgs, that is, the Spanish. But with what forces? The lack of funds to pay troops and buy supplies ruled out a dramatic knockout drive by the French deep into the Spanish Netherlands, into Spanish territory in Italy, or into Spain itself, from the Catalonian bridgehead. Moreover, boundary complexities in the Rhineland, and in the west of it as well, affected the war aims on both sides. Should the principal towns and fortresses be besieged? Or should mobile strategies be used to defeat enemy armies? Neither the French nor the Spanish could quite decide, so both strategies were tried. As noted before, several of the heads of leading aristocratic houses in France and in the Spanish Netherlands claimed virtual sovereignty over various towns, forts, duchies, and principalities in the region; and these claims, like the Spanish claims to various towns and duchies more or less controlled by the French, created fluid, still-feudal, and chaotic legal conditions in the region. Indeed, it remained quite unclear where the boundaries of the Holy Roman Empire lay.

Men of the stamp of Condé, Fuensaldagne, Hocquincourt, and Turenne saw no particular reason why the yearly seasonal military campaigns should ever stop. There was glory to be gained and money, land, and army commissions for younger brothers and clients to be had in these annual campaigns. A "warlord" society and culture made its presence felt throughout Europe in the mid-seventeenth century, and neither governments nor social critics and moralists knew what to do about it. As a result of centuries of stated and restated chivalric ideals, the courage of these men who rode their horses into a blaze of bullets commanded enormous respect. And in their train came the companion-in-arms of the aristocratic captain: the often brutal soldier-bandit.

During the Fronde, generals active in the civil war lamented the terrible suffering experienced by the civilian population, but a war-is-war attitude had settled in, as a result of year after

year of military campaigns. If Condéist officers such as Balthazar and Hocquincourt were warlords, their regiments were often
little more than assemblages of savage males over whom the
warlords had minimal discipline. Only the increased power and
administration that marked the reign of Louis XIV would rid
French society of this scourge. Consensus in French society lay
here, if anywhere: the realm must be rid of marauding soldiers.
Indeed, as a cultural and social force, the military blurred to
extinction the boundary between civil and international war.
Condé had signed an agreement with the Spanish, and he would
sign several more such agreements in return for money and
eventually a military command in the Spanish army. The effect
was to assert that his rank as first prince of the blood prevailed
over any legal formalities and any courts of law, which required
every French person to seek the king's permission before negotiating with the head of a foreign state. The lofty rank of Condé
(and the less lofty rank of city fathers like those in Bordeaux),
the rank of other princes such as the Duke de Bouillon and the
Viscount de Turenne on the "civic" side, and the princely rank
of cardinals Mazarin and Retz on the "spiritual" side were like
so many breaches in the walls of the French constitution. The
princely Fronde was a civil war fought over these ranks and
over claims to being independent from the authority of the king
and his Council. Not all these extra-French alliances redounded
to the side of the Fronde: Turenne eventually negotiated a special arrangement with Oliver Cromwell that brought English
troops into the war against the Spanish. True, he did the negotiating with Mazarin's and the king's approval, but he nonetheless did it largely in his own name, as the head of the Protestant
house of La Tour d'Auvergne.

When Condé began to negotiate a firm alliance with Gaston d'Orléans during the fall of 1651, the latter was chary of
the way the princely Frondeur had embraced Spain. The problem lay in finding sufficient force to drive Mazarin not only
from the realm but also from Anne's and Louis XIV's minds.
Gaston had inspired many plots before, or had at least been
their focal point; but late in 1651, when he virtually controlled
the Parlement of Paris and the militia forces of the capital, he
had somehow to avoid an alliance with Condé that included
embracing Spain. The laws, customs, and habits of the French
monarchy could be flouted time after time, as Gaston well knew;

but they remained sufficiently strong to create a powerful shockwave were the king's uncle to ally openly with the Spanish. Anti-Spanish sentiment, indeed the law of treason or lese majesty remained an institutional foundation not only in magisterial circles but also in Parisian artisan communities and in peasant villages of northern France. Capital punishment for treason, meted out to make an example, had made its mark on the Parisians since the Wars of Religion, and the royal decrees charging Condé with that crime had been widely distributed during the princely Fronde.

More powerful than this awareness of Condé's error in allying with the Spanish, however, was the strident collective resolve that Mazarin must be disgraced, and that any action, alliance with a foreign power, murder, or capture and trial was justifiable to achieve this end. Condé had a party of faithful clients in the Parlement, so the possibility of his being brought to trial and condemned for treason was remote. In any event, Condé, by rank, claimed to be a law unto himself and maintained that he could only be tried by a court of his peers. Bearing the title "first prince of the blood," his only equals or superiors were Gaston d'Orléans, Gaston's infant son, the king's brother Philippe, and Louis XIV himself.

At least some of the judges of the Parlement of Paris behaved as if vituperating against Mazarin relieved them of their sense of duty and permitted them to avoid considering the treason charges lodged against Condé. Prominent judges such as President de Mêmes, Advocate General Omer Talon, and First President and sometime Keeper of the Seals Mathieu Molé spoke in favor of Mazarin's elimination from the government once and for all.

Interestingly enough, over the final months of 1651 Condé kept open the channels of negotiation with Mazarin while Gaston began to view the Cardinal as some sort of monster. Put more analytically, Gaston continued to be swayed, and to sway with the deeper, more fundamental themes in the French political-cultural consciousness at the midpoint of the seventeenth century. Though he had blinked in order to avoid an overt alliance with Spain, and though he perceived Mazarin as duplicitous and base-born, in the end the duke's anti-Spanish and anti-Mazarin fears and fantasies were part of the xenophobic and patriotic anti-Italian consciousness. On the surface, this synthesis seems illogical, since Mazarin was leading the effort to defeat Spain and had been accused of using delaying tactics to prevent a peace. On a deeper level, however, hatred of the Spanish and of Mazarin had similar xenophobic foundations—that is, a hatred of all foreigners—and this xenophobia was fanned by Condé's, Gaston's, and Retz's systematic use of the press against Mazarin in 1651–52. The outburst of *Mazarinades* during the princely Fronde was very largely of Condé's and Retz's making. The need to mobilize opinions and create putsch-like dynamics in the capital ended in crude and brutal xenophobic journalism. Ethnic self-hatred? Gaston at one point remarked, "Do you not know that I am from Florentine stock?" And Gondi de Retz, whose ancestors had come from Italy less than a century before, must have felt that he was killing off his own repulsive self as he successfully passed as a Frenchman while publicly reviling Mazarin for being an Italian. A psycho-xenophobic interpretation of Gaston and Retz's systematic campaign to raise fears in 1652 would be about as valid as any other interpretation in accounting for the aberrant, indeed wild behavior of the leading Parisian Frondeurs and of the judges in the Parlement and in the other sovereign courts, as they vilified Mazarin. It is not all that evident that the Parisian lower classes were as given to Italian-baiting as the authors of the *Mazarinades* who sought to fan this hatred supposed.

Alternatively, the attempt to focus all complaints, protests, and rage on the head of one individual may have been little more than a technique for mobilizing public opinion. How could one reestablish the alliance between the *peuple* and the judges that had come into being as early as 1649, only to fall apart? Through their pamphleteers, Retz and Condé may have been simply playing gutter politics. If such was the case, they failed. The point is important only insofar as it may shed light on the extent of xenophobic fears among the *peuple* who went about the streets of Paris protesting against Mazarin. Despite vilification by symbols, pamphlets, and seizure of his property, once heads had cooled Mazarin returned to live among the Parisians.

But there was more to it than the xenophobic element. Among the men with some political engagement—and this certainly included royal officials, merchants, wealthier artisans, and Parisian *curés*—the power to exclude Mazarin from the government became the test, par excellence, of political power as such.

That Mazarin survived in office, despite the crescendo of opposition to him, prompted various groups and institutions to join ranks behind a common aim: his disgrace. The Parlement of Paris had confiscated his property, defiled his residence by letting anyone who wished to wander through it, and declared him a public enemy. A price of 50,000 *livres* had been put on his head, dead or alive. Coming from an august body of judges, these incredibly harsh and fanatical measures merit some scrutiny.

One either has power to effect change in government or one has not; in the Paris of 1651, being powerful came to mean, collectively, the ability to effect the disgrace, exile, and/or death of Mazarin. It was at precisely this point, when power had been defined as what it took to remove Mazarin, that the character of the French state became succinctly evident: the state was an absolutist political force that was increasing its power over all elements within itself and outside it. The power to choose royal councillors and to appoint ministers of state or retire others, like the use of the royal signature and seals, constituted that thin, apparently brittle, almost solely symbolic veneer of state power. Yet these were the symbolic monarchical powers that Anne, Louis XIV, and Mazarin fought resolutely to keep. And they won. True, Mazarin never entirely lost control over the army, but at several points he was blackmailed by its officers, to the point that his (and Le Tellier's) power to determine strategy and appoint officers within the ranks was severely curtailed.

Thus, in joining the anti-Mazarinist ranks, the politically engaged persons and institutions in the realm—from the highest-ranking individuals led by Condé and Gaston to the lowliest of the artisans and cabaret keepers—were combatting absolutism as it is typically defined by historians. Civic power came to be defined as the power needed to rid the realm of the queen regent's principal minister.

During the princely Fronde, Mazarin went into exile not just once, but twice. As political actions, both exiles were of enormous significance. The first occurred in the putsch climate created in February 1651 by Gaston's control of the Parlement and the princes, and by Retz's mobilization of the clergy. As the cardinal moved across northern France, from fort to fort and from army camp to army camp, it became evident that his "flight" to release the princes in Le Havre and his eventual residence in

Brühl, near Cologne, constituted some sort of symbolic victory for the Parisian Frondeurs. A victory over absolutism? The more "Tacitean"—that is, not only the more suspicious but also the more observant courtiers and judges in Paris—and even the Condéist authors of *Mazarinades* knew full well that Anne continued to receive advice from the cardinal. Still, other experienced councillors now assumed greater power, and it seemed for a while that a government made up of Anne, Gaston, Châteauneuf, La Vieuville, Chavigny—and Retz, of course—would be able to establish itself as an effective ruling agent. But this did not happen. Anne so effectively used her power to rotate councillors that suspicions were aroused between Condé and Gaston and also among the protesting *rentiers,* tax farmers, and parlementaires. The unity that had been achieved over the need to disgrace Mazarin could scarcely be turned into a positive force that would bring Condé to accept peace in Bordeaux and, with it, some limits on his greed for offices in the state.

A second Mazarin exile in 1652 was decided more as a result of powerful symbolic initiatives than of coercion forged by his enemies. This exile created a feeling that authority was absent at the highest levels of the state. This sense of the absence of authority resulted, of course, from the military preparations and maneuvers that were taking place. The divided Parlement sank into powerlessness, Gaston into indolence, and Condé and Mazarin into preparations for civil war.

In the fall of 1651, the princely Fronde turned entirely on Condé, with his control of Bordeaux and environs, his army at Stenay in the North, and his fortress of Montrond in the Center. Gaston held Paris through the Parlement and the militia, so negotiations to unite the two princes against the exiled Mazarin had to succeed, with or without Gaston's agreement to accept Spanish support. As the arrangements were struck to create an alliance for a princely Fronde, it was becoming evident to Retz that forcing Mazarin into exile had brought him no closer to complete control of the government. To Condé, Retz was and always would be a mere conspiring prelate. After all, the first prince of the blood had strongly suggested to Gaston that Retz be excluded from his circle in the Luxembourg Palace!

This would not be the first or the last time that the Frondeurs came around full circle. Condé remained resolutely opposed to Retz's ambitions, and vice versa. And Retz had only a stable of writers and *curés* at his disposal, no troops. As he clung to his influence over Gaston, the wily prelate may have realized he could never effectively bar Mazarin's or Condé's return to the Council, and that no matter which of the two men carried the realm on the battlefield, *he* would be the loser.

I. From Revolution and Civil War to Civil War

When revolutions descend into civil wars—and it is always possible analytically to distinguish one from the other—the historian must perforce suspend analysis and turn to informed narrative. The very outcome of the revolution-civil war lies in the events themselves. The reader who bears in mind what has been built up before by way of analysis and description of structures and powers can, like the participant in the Fronde, experience the outcome. It is commonplace to note the structural repetitions occurring in societies shaken by revolution, but what often goes unnoticed is the failure of attempts to repeat over and over again the same disestablishing shocks to the socio-political order within a relatively short interval of time. For example, the intensity and activism that seized the Parisians in 1649 would not be repeated again in 1652, though both military and strategic conditions lent themselves to such a state of mind and though political leaders attempted to arouse the same fever-pitch activity. The increasing and ineluctable awareness that every strategy and every power maneuver had been tried by virtually all parties, and that it would be fruitless to try them over again, counted heavily toward revived political stability after 1650.

If such a thing as a collective political consciousness existed in the Parisian population during the Fronde, and this historian believes strongly that it did, there may also have been a sense that the king's armies with Mazarin at their head constituted nowhere near the threat to lives and property that Condé's army had posed in 1649. More important still, the king's army kept some distance away from the capital. And no matter how often and how sincerely the parlementaires expressed their respect for Gaston, those same parlementaires, and the rest of the Parisians, had doubts about the affection for Paris felt by the duke's new-found ally in the Fronde, Condé. To be sure, the prince had his householders and his clients and would be able to generate a popular party directed by his activist client Pénis, a minor royal official from Tulle who had launched a vigilante type of civic defense force in the streets of Paris. Pénis quickly set about extorting money and food supplies from his followers, but the Parisians remained suspicious of, if not hostile to, Condé.

In evaluating Condé's military leadership, an awareness that the prince would burn and kill in order to win may have been an integral part of cabaret banter. If such was the case, each major move during the final military maneuvers around the capital falls into place and can be understood. Put another way, the capital remained, as always, hostile to marauding armies and troop-quartering in or near the city, and the one army the Parisians feared most was Condé's. Though the armies commanded by Nemours, Beaufort, or Lorraine aroused considerable apprehension, they lacked sufficient force to blockade or besiege the capital, should alliances shift again. None of these armies was powerful enough to blockade such a large population or to take the city gates by assault, but they disrupted economic activity and were a scourge on the rural population. The Parisians constructed a consistent political vision of the military factors of civil war that rested profoundly on civic, human, economic, and social factors, and to a far lesser degree on Frondeur and anti-Frondeur loyalties. And so, though Condé was allied with Gaston in 1651–52 and the capital was quite firmly under Gaston's control, it was still Condé's army the Parisians feared most.

The end of the Fronde came as a result of four distinct but related factors: (1) the successful distribution of military commands by Mazarin to ensure that his generals would remain loyal and would be willing to face Condé on a battlefield; (2) the rise of disgust and anger over the civil war among the more politically engaged and the wealthier elements of the urban populations of Paris and Bordeaux; (3) the shift of enough high-ranking aristocrats to the side of the crown, which impeded Condé-Gaston putsches in Provence, Languedoc, and Normandy; and (4) the defeat of the Condé-Beaufort forces by troops loyal to the crown. The Fronde ended after the declaration of Louis XIV's majority in September 1651, when royal authority increased step by step at the expense of loyalty and support for

Gaston and Condé. Before developing each of these factors in an informed narrative of the events that took place, it is essential to explore more deeply the role played by the king's uncle, Gaston d'Orléans. A structural role in the history of the French monarchy can be discerned in the ambiguity, ambition, and rebellious tendencies of the Orléanist princes of the ruling Bourbon family.

The younger brother of Louis XIII had entered the regency government with a heritage of plotting against the state and betraying those supporters who had followed his lead. The blood of several men beheaded for treason stained Gaston's hands by 1643. Louis XIII and Richelieu had pursued very authoritarian principles and policies in the period 1624–43, and Gaston's stature might have increased had he died in one of the plots perpetrated against Richelieu. The prince's immunity from prosecution rested on the fact that he was the heir to the throne until 1638, when the future Louis XIV was born. The king could not prosecute his heir for treason. Gaston's stature in the monarchy prompted sympathy but also derision for his failures to save the lives of the men who had plotted with him.

During the regency and the first phases of the Fronde, Gaston stuck resolutely by Anne of Austria and her sons; but as early as the summer of 1648 and the negotiations over the creation of the St. Louis Chamber, the prince had invited the contesting parties to his residence, the Luxembourg Palace, to seek a compromise. In so doing, he became a focal point for a third force that strengthened the impulse toward revolution in the Parlement. During the regency period, that is, 1643–51, Gaston developed a habit of supporting Anne publicly by being present at her side during important negotiations and then offering privately, or semi-officially, a compromise position that was both Frondeur and anti-Frondeur. In a political showdown where every major institution and person in the realm had to take a stand on a certain number of issues, Gaston's ambiguity no doubt weakened the crown as Louis XIII and Richelieu had defined it and as Anne and Mazarin were trying to maintain it.

On the other hand, by offering a locus for negotiations and "third party" sentiment, Gaston may also have kept the Fronde from becoming a much deeper social revolution. He often made statements upholding royal *dignitas* in the Parlement, and his support for the arrest of Condé and Conti and their sister,

Madame de Longueville, in January 1650 indicates that Gaston could at times share the arch, authoritarian concept of the state that his brother and Richelieu had done so much to make a reality. Rivalries had been going on for decades between the legitimate members of the Bourbon family—that is, kings Henry IV and Louis XIII and their cousins the Condés and the bastard Bourbons of Vendôme (the offspring of a natural son of Henry IV). Gaston was jealous of Condé's great military reputation; and he was unforgiving of the fact that Condé's father had made his peace with Richelieu and had become one of the most loyal servants of the authoritarian state. But under Retz's influence and in a fit of pique after Anne selected councillors who momentarily increased Condé's influence in the government, Gaston turned violently anti-Mazarin.

The princely Fronde would have evaporated into a regional rebellion and a military skirmish near Stenay had it not been for the Condé-Gaston alliance struck in the spring of 1652. Mazarin tried to head off this development, but Gaston had come to enjoy controlling the capital. With the Parlement also in his pocket (the Condé clients supported him) and the capital more or less ready to do his bidding as a result of his influence over the militia captains and Retz's influence over the *curés,* Gaston became a major player in the game of French politics for the first time in his life.

If we assess Retz by his own criteria for inspiring and leading factions, his success in moving Gaston over to an alliance with Condé can be seen as his greatest achievement—and the source of his downfall. Very slowly Retz came to realize the consequences of a Condé-Gaston alliance: rivalry between the two went so deep that as long as this double leadership remained so deeply divided, it would be impossible to form a solid party for political action. In fact, Gaston and Condé only managed to ally when they wanted to stop Mazarin or halt the distribution of patronage to people who were not their clients. Neither prince had a deep sense of how to govern the realm. The two men never trusted one another, but they continued to cooperate in order to turn the princely Fronde into a civil war. One held Bordeaux, the other Paris. Languedoc would support its governor, Gaston; Guienne would stand for Condé. Other towns and regions weighed in the balance. All eyes turned to the armies maneuvering in the northeastern corner of France, and people wondered which way the important towns along the Loire would go, among them Angers and Orléans.

Condé always tried to keep opinion in his favor, so he sponsored pamphlet writers to do just that in 1651 to 1653. But in the end he always counted on military force to sway, or if necessary to intimidate. Like Richelieu, he believed that it was better for a sovereign to be loved than respected; but respect, even if it required cohesion and violence, could suffice for governing. Condé was more of an *étatiste* than Gaston was. Had he changed places with his cousin Louis XIV, he might have learned to avail himself of the services of such men as Colbert, and by 1715 the trajectory of French state-building might have been almost the same as it was under the Sun King.

As enigmatic as Gaston, but by no means as irresolute or as tainted by past failures, was the Viscount de Turenne, the principal commander of the largest force loyal to the king. His tergiversations during the early years of the Fronde need not be summed up here, but it is important to recall that Mazarin succeeded in striking a bargain with Turenne's older brother, the Duke de Bouillon, to settle the principal grievances of the La Tour d'Auvergne family. Huguenot origins and links to the house of Orange-Nassau gave this family pretensions to a rank among the top four or five aristocratic families of the realm. Turenne was always courteous to Condé and protested his utmost respect for his former commander, but he also cast a wary eye toward the enormous patronage power that the Condé family had acquired. Would anything be left for the La Tour d'Auvergnes? Cautious and taciturn, yet utterly fearless and profoundly familiar with all the military and governing elites of northern France, the Rhineland, and the Netherlands, Turenne decided to cast his lot with Mazarin in the fall of 1651. His older brother, Bouillon, did the same. Never really a creature or a client of the cardinal's, although the latter liked to believe he was, Turenne perceived rather clearly the impact that Louis XIV's majority was having on the realm. Thus he bonded to his young sovereign somewhat abstractly, but nonetheless deeply.

Here again were structural shifts. When Condé had been Mazarin's principal general and had blockaded Paris in 1649, Turenne had followed his brother into rebellion. The political loyalties alternated back and forth between the leading commanders, their families, their clients, their regiments. Indeed, at one point, when Turenne tried to bring his army over to rebellion, his troops had refused to follow him. Just how influential this incident was can never be established, but it is evident that Turenne's upbringing, experience, and temperament helped him to understand that there were forces in the French monarchy that transcended personalities and patronage. As the princely Fronde became more and more a test of two military capabilities, and less and less a question of parlementary power or popular insurrection, Turenne found it possible, while on campaign deep into Germany, to coordinate military strategy with Michel Le Tellier, the secretary of state for war, and therefore with Mazarin himself. Turenne learned to feel comfortable with the power of the state.

The argument that Turenne knew he would always be second in command if he joined Gaston and Condé, but first in command under Mazarin, attracts by its simplicity. This type of thinking—the overwhelming drive to be recognized as number one in rank—was a very strong social phenomenon in seventeenth-century French society, and among the military aristocracy in particular. However, Turenne possessed both a great deal of self-confidence and an elusive but discernible magnanimity about such matters. Be he under the command of Condé, his former "instructor" in the art of war, or commander in his own right, Turenne exuded assurance that his reputation would be preserved. The fact that Turenne let Mazarin believe that he, Turenne, was more a creature of the cardinal than he actually was, must be recognized as but one of the facets of this supreme self-confidence. By contrast, Condé had great difficulty coping with anyone to whom he felt the least bit beholden.

Of a very different order of rank and wealth was the Vendôme branch of the Bourbon family. César de Vendôme, Henry IV's natural son by the beautiful Gabrielle d'Estrées, was Gaston's illegitimate half-brother and failed to cast off the taint of bastardy despite the numerous decrees the Parlement had promulgated in favor of his legitimacy. His litigious frame of mind about his bastardy (and about its direct effect, little wealth and little land) prompted Vendôme to plot and do virtually everything short of murder to enhance the Vendôme rank in the hierarchy of dukes and peers.

Vendôme's older son, the flamboyant Duke de Beaufort, became a genuinely popular figure during the Parisian Fronde.

He played to the boisterous crowd, used scatalogical language about Mazarin in public, and took pride in his ability to disperse angry and threatening mobs. At other times, he would plunge into bouts of religious fervor that must have alienated the *bien pensant* and sober merchants of the capital. Retz and Beaufort both worked the parish finance committees and confraternities to build political support for their parties, but these maneuvers had become so obvious by 1652 that they no longer produced genuine political support.

Beaufort's younger brother, the Duke de Mercoeur, developed a strong animosity toward Beaufort, to the point that he became willing to support Mazarin, for a price. César de Vendôme carefully counseled his sons, as one became a leading Frondeur in Paris and the other went secretly to Brühl, Mazarin's residence on the Rhine near Cologne, to marry one of the cardinal's nieces. Through this marriage contract César de Vendôme finally captured the very prestigious and lucrative office of admiral of France, held in right of survival for his son Mercoeur, and a huge dowry, most of it paid directly out of the royal treasury.

Gaston and Condé loathed these marriage arrangements. They perceived the Vendôme pretensions to higher rank as inevitably lowering their own rank and were deeply offended by Mazarin's willingness to promote the Vendômes to high royal office. For years Condé had wanted the admiralty for himself or for one of his relatives; and now it had not only escaped him, it would be used to enhance Mazarin's power in the Council of State, for admirals were *ex officio* members of this highest governing body in the realm. Vendôme quickly assumed his duty as commander-in-chief of the royal fleet and, joined by ships that Mazarin himself had purchased, began to blockade Bordeaux, not only keeping the Spanish from entering the port but also preventing the entry of merchant vessels seeking to buy wine, cognac, and prunes in the Gironde River area.

In turn, Mercoeur was assigned the really quite delicate task of dispelling Frondeur sympathies in Provence, chiefly by distributing patronage in ways that reestablished hierarchies of rank and power among rival local families.

To the west, the crucial province of Normandy slowly turned Mazarinist, largely because the governor, Longueville, was noting stronger and stronger anti-Frondeur sympathies in the province. His estrangement from his young and vivacious Frondeur wife (Condé's sister, who was helping to direct the Fronde in Bordeaux) also contributed to Longueville's willingness to ally with Mazarin. At two or three crucial moments in the civil war of 1651 and 1652, the bags of gold that Longueville supplied from Norman tax revenues permitted the Council of State and Mazarin to keep the initiative in the fighting. Thus, seen from a narrowly dynastic perspective, the legitimate Bourbons eventually stood allied with their bastard cousins, the Vendômes and the Longuevilles, against their close and legitimate cousins, Condé, Conti, and Madame de Longueville—two brothers and a sister—and their supporters, Rohan-Chabot, La Rochefoucauld, La Trémouille, and their *fidèles* in the Southwest.

II. *Mazarin's Army Invades France*

While in Brühl, Mazarin had collected—with the help of Le Tellier, Isaac Fabert, the governor of Sedan, and the courageous and indefatigable Abbé Foucquet—the funds needed to hire a small army of mercenaries that would be his alone. The end of the war in Germany had idled experienced and hardened fighters. Since the near certainty of a Spanish invasion from the north during an annual spring campaign prevented Mazarin from withdrawing all the troops from the northern fortresses, he was forced to create this new force of his own. Further complicating things was Condé's army in Stenay, which always had to be watched.

As Mazarin moved quickly southwest with his little army in January 1652, he announced through published broadsides that the many benefits he had received from Louis XIV obliged him to do his utmost to serve the king. This certainly was the cardinal himself speaking: his political philosophy rested on a belief that stability among humankind could be achieved through a distribution of benefits and through the bonds of gratitude that these benefits created, rather than through some strictly defined sense of public welfare, as Richelieu had proclaimed. By binding commanders to him, Mazarin quite deliberately distributed promotions and pensions in return for loyalty and effectiveness on the battlefield. In this he was entirely typical not only of

French royal ministers (Richelieu had hired Bernard of Saxe-Weimar) but of sovereigns and their ministers throughout Europe. The power to promote men to the office of marshal of France rested with Anne and Mazarin, and they used this power extensively to promote faithful officers. On a still deeper level, in order to bind the very greedy Hocquincourt to the royal cause, Mazarin not only promoted this member of the solid Picard nobility, he pensioned him and bestowed on his brother the very rich abbey of Corbie, with its 35,000 *livres* in annual revenues. This is an interesting example of international, anti-Frondeur, and familial policy all pulled together into one coherent action. In an eventual campaign against the Spanish, Hocquincourt could presumably be counted on to move more vigorously than before, as a result of his brother's control of this strategically located abbey, located along the route through Picardy that the Spanish often took to invade France.

Mazarin's other commanders, La Ferté-Senneterre and Palluau, also received enormous favors in return for their willingness to fight Condé. This prompted a new and harsh tide of criticism against the cardinal, but as the war tension mounted during the fall of 1651, it was the cardinal who bested the Frondeurs in the number of army offices and pensions distributed. Condé and Gaston lacked the power of the royal signature, and while they might promise to favor someone's promotion as marshal of France, Anne and Mazarin were in a position to deliver the letters patent and the brevets bearing the appropriate seals, signatures, and secretarial countersignatures. In this rush to gain adherents and military commanders, where was loyalty to the king? Through their pamphleteers, Gaston and Condé had powerfully articulated an already established argument, namely that the king was a virtual prisoner in a household dominated by his mother, who was under Mazarin's spell. Accordingly, Frondeur commanders and anti-Frondeur commanders alike protested deep personal loyalty to their young king. When Mazarin's 5,000-man army, under Hocquincourt's command, reached the court at Poitiers in late January 1652, the young king went some distance to meet the army, greet the cardinal, and conduct him into the city. Indeed, by numerous public actions of this sort in 1651 and 1652, the king made it increasingly difficult to believe that he was in fact a prisoner. Moreover, there was a coherence to his actions, and they were all anti-Frondeur, down to the slightest nod of his head or expression of thanks.

Just where Mazarin procured the funds to raise the little army that invaded France early in 1652 remains something of a mystery. Rumors circulated to the effect that Châteauneuf and La Vieuville had secretly shipped him the revenues collected to pay interest on the *rentes*. It is certain that funds from the royal treasury were reaching him, but the money for his war chest was obtained through the cardinal's ability to borrow and, unbeknownst to the lenders, use the same collateral for several different loans.

Why were lenders willing to take such a great risk? In his letters to Anne, Mazarin asserted time and time again that the whole realm was turning in the direction of the young king, his mother, and his councillors. Revenues were voted by the Estates of Languedoc and Brittany, tax contracts on the fiscal district of central France known as the Cinq Grosses Fermes were being awarded to the highest bidders, and Mazarin found lenders. His financial agent in Paris, Jean-Baptiste Colbert, carried on a valiant fight to keep at bay the creditors and prosecutors who were moving in for the kill. The prominent Huguenot financier, Hervart, lent large sums. The cardinal did most of his borrowing on the European-wide financial market and more or less abandoned the smaller credit-fiscal nexus located in Lyon and Paris. In response to this, the Parlement of Paris, under Broussel's guidance, spent a great deal of time deliberating about how to draw the maximum sums from the sale of Mazarin's library and other personal properties, and how to block him legally from collecting revenues from his benefices. The Fronde in Paris had begun over the crown's efforts to create new venal offices; it was to end in a fanatical outburst against a cardinal who managed to fund an army despite the Fronde's attempts to kill him and confiscate his fortune.

On the side of the princely Frondeurs, Condé's financial position remains unclear. The flow of Spanish funds was never substantial. In Bordeaux, the prince's intendant, Lenet, reported careful harboring of funds and borrowing, both privately and from the city itself; but by the late spring of 1652 the financial situation had become desperate. Troops were unpaid and Conti was having trouble reassuring commanders that their interests were being remembered. Just how much of his own income, capital, and credit Condé put into the balance during the campaign of 1652 remains unclear. There are vague indications that he was trying to keep his private fortune somewhat separate from the war effort.

In Paris, Gaston made numerous public moves to tax the Parisians in all the old forced-loan ways, but little money was forthcoming. His allies, Beaufort and Nemours, were not rich and had little capacity to borrow. In announcing a war chest of over 1,000,000 *livres*, Gaston may have been playing to opinion—and trying to consolidate it on his side. He certainly used his own credit to borrow, however. The Grande Mademoiselle, his daughter, loaned her father 50,000 *livres*, but it is possible that the little circle of tax farmers who lived in Gaston's shadow, and who managed his household, dragged their feet at this crucial moment of fund-raising for the war effort. As Gaston posted his military forces east of Paris, between Meaux and Melun, to meet Mazarin's little army as it moved south, funds to pay the Frondeur troops were certainly scarce.

The Frondeur judges in the Parlement solemnly deputized two of their colleagues to go out and confront the Mazarinist army and to read it an *arrêt* about the laws of the realm regarding the presence of troops near the capital and the price that had been put on Mazarin's head. The scene must have been rather tragi-comical, for the troops captured the black-robed judges and turned them over to the cardinal's personal guard. One of the judges, Bitaut, was obliged to travel with the Mazarinist army for some time afterward, which enraged the Frondeurs in Paris. The incident, however, indicates the shift from the power of words to military force. From the beginning, Frondeur judicial radicalism had exaggerated the power of words, and of the Parlement, despite the paramilitary impulses of some of its members.

This time the cardinal moved south toward the Loire, carefully avoiding any engagement with the Frondeur troops. His reason may have been the weakness of his army, but it is possible to suggest that he also realized the danger of further radicalizing the capital by approaching it with an army and by engaging its troops. Indeed, had Mazarin moved toward Paris, it is almost certain that Gaston and the Frondeurs would have received more funds and more support. Once in the Loire valley, the cardinal asked to enter Gien with his troops and was admitted.

It was quickly publicized that Mazarin and his little army had been received by a town without first threatening military violence, but there is no evidence that this isolated event had an immediate domino-like impact on opinions in other towns. Local rivalries and traditions and the client networks of powerful aristocratic families still determined the stand a town would take during the princely Fronde. On the Frondeur side, Angers, situated on the Maine River to the west, opted for the princes, owing to a large extent to the influence of its governor, the Duke de Rohan-Chabot, and his *fidèles,* who fortified the city. Mazarin realized that he must lay siege to Angers, and that the success or failure of his entire campaign hung in the balance.

Orléans, to take another example of a Loire-valley town, was the "capital" of Gaston's duchy and *appanage* and as such could be expected to remain loyal to him and shut its gates to Mazarin's troops. But Gaston's changes of party and his general inactivity had caused him to lose his traditional supporters not only in Orléans but also far to the south, in the province of Languedoc, where he was governor. Accompanied by her ladies-in-waiting, his daughter, the Grande Mademoiselle, gained admittance to Orléans and, temporarily at least, brought the city over to the princely Fronde. The effect was negligible, however, since only the defeat of one or the other of the military forces in the realm would determine the Fronde's course.

Mazarin was careful not to lose the initiative that he had gained by his quick and almost violence-free entry into the center of the realm. But what to do next? Anne's councillors in Poitiers were divided over the strategy to follow. Some, led by Châteauneuf, advised a march to the southwest, to attack Condé and his allies in the region where they were strongest. This would have meant leaving Paris in Gaston's hands and the North subject to further marauding by the Condé regiments stationed in Stenay.

In fact, Condé was already in trouble in the Southwest. The troops loyal to the king under Harcourt's command had beaten the prince's troops and driven him back to seek cover in the town of Agen. Mazarin, his experienced eye on the general strategic factors, argued that the center of the realm could be lost if the king's troops charged south toward Bordeaux. The Frondeur army commanded by Beaufort and Nemours was already south of Paris, in the Hurepoix, and Condé could supply a small army with the munitions stored in his great fortress of Montrond. A serious debate over strategy took place, so serious that it came to be defined as a duel for power in the Council between Châteauneuf and Mazarin.

The cardinal's plan to keep the principal army in the Loire Valley eventually prevailed, but this led to Châteauneuf's resignation from office. Anne promptly accepted not only his departure but those of the men faithful to him. Like Retz, Chavigny, Condé, and Mazarin himself, Châteauneuf had sought to gain supreme power over the realm by controlling the Council. His decision to resign indicated that he had the intelligence to analyze the situation correctly. Mazarin held the loyalties of the military commanders on the northern frontier, of Harcourt in the Southwest, and of Hocquincourt and Turenne in the Center. The cardinal's strategic plans proved to be sound. Until his death in 1661, he henceforth completely dominated general and day-to-day policy decisions in the French monarchy. But it is important to recall that between 1643 and 1652 he was challenged for supreme power in the Council by several very experienced former councillors, such as Chavigny and Châteauneuf, and by a number of highly intelligent, ambitious, and inexperienced councillors—for example, Potier, the bishop of Beauvais, in 1643 and Retz, the coadjutor of Paris, in 1651. By the time the crisis over military strategy loomed, the decisions were no longer Anne's to make; the young king's presence on the Council was already making that old conspirator Châteauneuf uncomfortable. Mazarin had given Louis XIV an excellent early political education centered on the principles of loyalty and gratitude. The highest confidence in the government shifted slowly from the link Anne-and-Mazarin to Mazarin-and-Louis XIV.

From Poitiers the court moved north with a military force that combined Mazarin's own army and a portion of the royal army that had been fighting in the South. They went first to Amboise and then to Blois. It was mid-March 1652, and many months of good weather for military operations lay ahead. At exactly what point did Condé realize that the army Mazarin had put together and that was circulating in the Loire Valley was not going to descend into Guienne after him? Aware that his own officers could hold their own and that a military action in the Southwest to decide the civil war was probably impossible, Condé rode north at breakneck speed, with just a few servants, and took charge of military operations. The prince must also have been impatient with Gaston and Retz's mobilization efforts in Paris. He may have sensed that he was losing the war of opinion and that a *coup* was necessary.

During the tireless ride north, Condé drew near the Frondeur army commanded by Beaufort and Nemours. Learning that the king's army (by now divided into two camps) was nearby, he whipped his horse, took command of the Frondeur army, and led it in an attack upon the unprepared, dispersed, and confused royal troops at a place called Bléneau. The other segment of the royal army, commanded by Turenne, quickly moved in to support Hocquincourt's routed troops. Observing the devastated troops and the burning villages, Turenne uttered his famous remark: "Monsieur le Prince has arrived." The point is much more than anecdotal. Neither Beaufort nor Nemours had the experience or the fortitude to carry on military operations of the scope, destructiveness, and brutality that Condé had just perpetrated. This is not to suggest that Beaufort and Nemours were personally lacking in courage. Quite the contrary. But those veterans of the northern campaigns fought against hardened Spanish troops; those soldiers who had marched deep into Germany or had held Catalonia were of different mettle. The civil-war dimensions of the Fronde were a two-faceted experience. The more terrible facet resulted from state-of-the-art, international techniques of violence, that is to say troop movements and artillery; the other facet was inexperienced, idyllic, and even poetic in its violence. Only a few weeks later, after a quarrel over rank and the command of the army, Nemours challenged Beaufort to a duel. Seeing no alternative to save his honor, Beaufort accepted and shot Nemours dead.

Turenne's army prevented Condé from advancing farther after the rout of Hocquincourt's troops at Bléneau. But instead of settling down to fight to the finish, Condé rode straight to Paris. Like Mazarin, the prince was fully cognizant of the capital's military and political importance. The army that held the capital, one way or the other, would win the civil war.

The prince's reception in the capital was mixed at best, and hostile in crucial sectors. When he attended the various sovereign courts in Gaston's company, the prince was accorded the respect due his rank; but he was also subjected to explicit criticism for having prompted a civil war. One judge pointedly remarked that "His Highness had French bloodstains on his hands, while sitting on the tapestried lilies of France," an allusion to the ideals of justice and peace to which the members of the sovereign courts were devoted.

In rejoinder, Condé's and Gaston's clients unleashed an intensified anti-Mazarinist pamphlet campaign. Under Broussel's leadership, the Parlement once more warmed to the task of hating and baiting the cardinal; but neither major sources of new revenue nor troops were forthcoming from the Parisians. Some militia companies expressed eagerness to go out and defend the capital against "Mazarinist" troops. Since some 4,000 bourgeois formally expressed their willingness to serve in Condé's army, the princely Fronde certainly had popular support in the capital.

The arrival of the Duke of Lorraine at the head of some eight or ten thousand troops, which camped just east of the capital in May 1652, did not help Condé and Gaston win Parisian opinion over to the princely Fronde. Gaston's wife, who was Lorraine's sister, had negotiated the arrival of this new military scourge in the countryside. Champagne had literally been pillaged and robbed by these hardened veterans of the German campaigns; peasant delegations came into Paris seeking help and asking to speak to the Parlement. What could the judges reply?

Lorraine left his army encamped outside the capital and entered the city, ostensibly to see his sister and attend various entertainments but really to wring further concessions from Gaston. Never inattentive to financial proposals, Mazarin's agents agreed to pay the duke more money if he would leave than Gaston could give him for staying and fighting on the side of the princely Fronde. As a result, Lorraine's army broke camp and departed, without every really engaging either the pro-Gaston and pro-Condé Frondeur army, or Mazarin's anti-Frondeur army. This was a major Mazarinist success.

Declining the services of the troops from Lorraine, after having first bribed their commander, strengthened Mazarin's hand. Had he attempted to join Lorraine with Turenne, Hocquincourt, and his other commanders, the cardinal would have found himself Lorraine's virtual political prisoner, owing to the duke's high rank, his family connections to Gaston, and his claims on the basis of rank to command all the royal troops. Managing to avoid pitfalls not only on the strategic front but also in his relationships with the high aristocracy was a sign of Mazarin's both superior political intelligence and firm understanding of the socio-political forces within the realm.

Gaston's agreements with the Duke of Lorraine, and the duke's subsequent arrival in Paris, had had a chilling effect on opinion in Paris. In June 1652, the city's governing elite—the heads of the principal guilds, the provost of merchants, and the *échevins*—quickly became hostile to Condé and grudgingly silent about Gaston. The protesters who were demanding that interest be paid on their *rentes* maintained their pressure on the city fathers and the sovereign courts and insisted that something be done to restore order. At first this shift in elite opinion was more covert than overt: it came to be couched in terms that stressed the need to protect the capital from violence and to assure adequate bread supplies. Anti-Mazarin opinions still held sway in the Parlement; and in the streets and in cabarets, strong support for killing the cardinal persisted. Gaston made several dramatic attempts to change the officers of the militia companies, with the undoubted aim of consolidating his control over them. Just how effective he was remains unclear. He already had strong support. Frondeur sympathies remained fervent enough to prompt occasional calls for a general uprising and for adoption of the Ormée program in Paris. News from Bordeaux probably consolidated opinion in the capital, both Frondeur and anti-Frondeur. But what is important, indeed anti-revolutionary, was that people perceived that a morally regenerated society was possible.

Though anti-Frondeur and pro-Frondeur sympathies—and in some sense parties—continued to exist and even became stronger as a result of the *Mazarinades* and of Pénis's activities, this polarization was mitigated by a consensus founded on hostility to all military maneuvers around the capital. Thus Gaston was forced to attempt a mobilization of his forces, ostensibly to protect the capital from the king's troops commanded by Turenne and Hocquincourt. But in point of fact, the Frondeur armies and Lorraine's troops were perceived as just as great a threat to the capital's well-being. Condé left Paris in order to join the troops that he had ordered south from Stenay and Brussels.

In the spring and early summer months of 1652, the Frondeur and anti-Frondeur armies maneuvered southwest of Paris, in and around Étampes, each trying to catch the other. Finally it became evident that Beaufort and Nemours would not come out of that city to stand and fight a pitched battle. A brief attempt was made to besiege Étampes, but then Mazarin, Turenne, and Hocquincourt agreed to divide their troops, with Hocquincourt staying near Étampes with sufficient forces to keep the Frondeur army cooped up in that city and Turenne ranging freely to pursue Condé and the troops he had pulled together from the capital and the North. Anne, the king, the Council, and Mazarin followed in Turenne's train as they moved west and north, eventually stopping at Saint-Germain-en-Laye, the important old royal castle that could make the Parisians feel the king was present, even though he was not actually in the capital. This close proximity unleashed debates in the Parlement in favor of resolutions that the king be invited to Paris. An amendment was immediately proposed by the Frondeur judges: "without Cardinal Mazarin."

The Parlement remained stalemated. Few resolutions passed, and when they did they had little effect on events. A sense of urgency that the king should be in *his* capital grew stronger in late June. The presence of the court would also mean increased work for thousands of Parisian artisans. The ceremonies carried out for the royal majority in September 1651 had been particularly successful in consolidating simple, uncomplicated feelings of loyalty to the young king, certainly among elite elements in the population and perhaps among militia as well. Already so dignified, elegant, well-mannered, and courteous to anyone he addressed, Louis XIV was, at fourteen, a political force to be reckoned with. As Gaston and Retz stormed about, trying to raise funds for troops, the invisible presence of the king partly undermined their efforts. Fears of armies in general did the rest.

Turenne maneuvered to trap Condé and force him into battle. Each commander knew the terrain of the Ile de France perfectly, and each was confident of victory. Dramatic river crossings on pontoon bridges, forced marches at night across the countryside and through gardens, and careful attention to the possible intervention of such "external factors" as the arrival of another army or a sortie from Paris were all taken into account by the two commanders. Finally, largely as a result of Gaston's reluctance to let Condé march through his beloved Luxembourg gardens, the Prince de Condé and his army became trapped in a confined space just outside the city gate at the Bastille, in the Faubourg Saint-Antoine. Turenne was forced to move so quickly that his artillery had not yet arrived when it became apparent that he must attack Condé. Turenne should perhaps have waited for his artillery to make the outcome of the battle certain from the beginning, but the political situation was explosive. The provost of merchants and the *échevins* had solemnly ordered the Saint-Antoine gate to the city closed, which meant that Condé and his troops could not count upon a retreat into the capital should their attempt to break through Turenne's lines fail. Divided and sitting on its hands, the Parlement had lost the control it had exercised over the Hôtel de Ville since the Day of the Barricades. Gaston had retired to his palace, "indisposed." But given the speedy shifts of opinion in the capital, and the ability of thousands of Parisians to mobilize almost instantly, delay was very dangerous for Turenne.

At seven in the morning, on 2 July 1652, the two armies confronted one another, ready to do battle at opposite ends of the streets that led out from the Bastille like spokes. All morning, Turenne sent cavalry charge upon cavalry charge down these streets, and Condé, at the head of his troops, repulsed them. Both sides suffered heavy casualities. No one misinterpreted a midday lull as signaling the end of the engagement. Then, quite early in the afternoon, Turenne's artillery arrived. Now he could fight the type of battle he had mastered in the Rhineland. He would draw Condé and his cavalry down one street, while moving quietly down another to place his cannon in a position that would prevent the prince from returning to the bulk of his army. This tactic almost worked; but just in time Condé saw what was happening and was able to fight his way back to the little square in front of the city gate. Historians have noted the comic-opera aspects of military encounters during the princely Fronde, but the trap Turenne set for Condé certainly must not be counted as one of them. Turenne did everything in his power to win the battle.

At this point, despite Condé's successful return to the square, it was only a matter of time before the prince would be forced to surrender or die in combat. With his artillery in place, Turenne could simply wear down his adversary, move the cannon forward, and eventually rake the little square (actually a half-circle) in which Condé was trapped.

Inside the city gates the militiamen held firm to the orders given by the provost of merchants. There was a consensus in the capital that no army should be allowed entry. As she had done at Orléans, the Grande Mademoiselle suddenly seized the initiative, went to her "ailing" father, and cajoled him to order the city gates opened and the guns of the Bastille trained on Turenne's attacking army. Since Gaston held the office of lieutenant-general of the realm, his authority over the militia exceeded that of the provost of merchants. When the latter saw the hastily signed order to open the Saint-Antoine gates, he had little choice but to send a runner bearing the order to the captain in charge of the gate. Some contemporary observers concluded that the breakdown of a militia captain with Frondeur sympathies accounted for the subsequent dramatic turn of events; but such was not the case. Copies of the written orders survived the fighting and clearly indicate complete military discipline within the militia.

After the Day of the Barricades, Broussel had been appointed governor of the Bastille, a crucially important post that he had soon transferred to his son, with the approval of the Parlement. Thus on 2 July 1652, it was none other than the son of this old leader of the Fronde who received the messenger's orders to turn the cannons in the direction of Turenne's attacking army. Condé's troops beat a quick retreat into the capital through the open gates, under the cover of the cannons of the Bastille.

Contemporaries reported that as many as 3,000 to 4,000 Parisian militiamen fought on the prince's side in the battle of the Faubourg Saint-Antoine. This should come as no surprise. Condé had a large household in Paris and stray *fidèle* loyalties in families belonging to virtually every group and institution in Parisian society. Bourgeois militiamen from Pénis's forces, and from other militia companies as well, may well have joined the princely army.

The militia columns in the Faubourg Saint-Germain, where

the Hôtel de Condé stood, did not go over to the prince. De Sève, its colonel, had expressed overt anti-Condé views prior to the battle. At the same time, it is possible that he would have blanched in anger had someone in the street called him a Mazarinist. A vague, unspoken party that above all wanted to protect the city from troops had stiffened the Hôtel de Ville's determination to take the strong stand it did, until Gaston issued his counter-orders.

The strategy employed by Condé and his *fidèles* to consolidate power in the capital strongly resembles that used by various governors in hostile provincial capitals, notably by Alais at Aix and Épernon at Bordeaux. In the forty-eight-hour interval between the nearly disastrous defeat at the Saint-Antoine gates and the general meeting called at the Hôtel de Ville for the afternoon of 4 July 1652, a carefully planned and highly coercive political fraternity-like rush came over the capital, obliging all Parisians to stick a nosegay of straw into their hats or belts. Rowdy companies of soldiers went through the streets, insisting that everyone wear one of these straw cockades, regardless of rank. Even monks were forced to wear them, and there is some evidence that women were likewise obliged to do so. The point is interesting because it indicates some definition of civil status, vague though it was. If someone declined to wear a bit of straw, he or she was at first gently persuaded to cooperate; but if persuasion proved insufficient, those refusing to wear straw were driven indoors.

What did this enforced wearing of straw signify? Historians have yet to study the patterns of symbol-wearing by Parisian political and religious parties over the centuries. During the Wars of Religion, several brief campaigns had been made to force persons in the street to wear a sign showing support for one or the other of the religious parties. In the campaign conducted by Condé's supporters in July 1652, the straw meant "Union" between the capital and the prince—a deliberate attempt to alter the Hôtel de Ville's anti-Condé stance by demonstrating massive popular support for him. Children, beggars, and even horses and donkeys were soon festooned with straw, in a mock festive air.

Gaston and Condé announced that they would like to come to the Hôtel de Ville on 4 July to discuss "plans." The precise record showing the names of all those who attended that day

reveals that every major corporation in the capital was represented, including guilds and monastic communities. Precedents
for such general, quite democratic assemblies usually dated from
times of civil war, food shortages, or threats of plague. There
was an air of emergency about these meetings, but it was difficult to predict what their results would be. In attendance were
the governor of Paris, the provost of merchants and the *échevins,* the city councillors, an ecclesiastical delegation headed by
the archbishop, and deputies from the principal chapters and
monastic communities. Then followed the *quarteniers* for the
sixteen quarters into which the city was divided, each accompanied by ten or fifteen sober citizens; and the deputies from
the six major guilds: drapers, grocers, mercers, *freniers,* hatters,
and silversmiths. Judges delegated by the Parlement, the Court
of Excises, the Chamber of Accounts, the masters of requests,
the *avocats,* and the *procureurs* were also present, as were the
militia colonels. The *curés* from each parish also attended this
meeting of some 300 of the most powerful and highly respected
notables of Paris.

The assembly opened in a typically legalistic fashion, that
is, with a reading of the parlementary *arrêt* that had convoked
it. A lengthy speech about the miseries of civil war followed, its
only real recommendation being an invitation to the king to
return to Paris. Hours went by as the delegates waited for Gaston and Condé. Finally, at six in the evening, when everyone
was about to leave, the princes arrived by carriage, accompanied by Beaufort, Guémené and Sully, and "other persons of
condition," all with straw in their hats or hands. His Royal
Highness Gaston was no exception. Recounting his sincere efforts
to bring relief to the capital and to impede the arrival of Mazarinist soldiers, he concluded by saying that his aim was to oppose
Mazarin until it pleased the king to drive him from the realm.

Condé opened his speech by saying that he had nothing to
add to Gaston's statement and that everything he had done had
been for the "preservation and security" of Paris. There followed expressions of thanks from the governor and the provost
of merchants. As Condé and Gaston rose to leave, they waved
their straw cockades in a menacing way.

During the hours of waiting, Condé's troops, with straw
tucked into their hats, had carefully blocked all the streets around
the Hôtel de Ville and had infiltrated the noisy crowd in the

square in front of it. When it became clear that no formal expression of "Union" with the princes would be acclaimed or voted, shooting broke out and fires were kindled at the doors of the Hôtel de Ville. It was a hot day and the windows were open. Bullets began to rain in on the assemblymen. Panic broke out when they realized that the exits were blocked. Trapped, they exchanged clothes with their servants, hid in closets and cellars, or lay flat on the floor to avoid the gunfire.

The militia column posted in front of the Hôtel de Ville may have been Condéist. Some of the shots seemed to have come from their ranks, and the men did little to impede the fires set in front of the doors. A white flag soon was displayed at one of the windows as a sign of surrender, and slips marked "Union" were thrown out into the crowd that packed the square. But the gunfire and the flames continued. For a time, the governor of Paris and his guards kept the invaders from going up the stairs leading to the great assembly hall, but he finally gave up and sneaked out, with a servant's help. The *curé* of the nearby church of Saint-Jean-en-Grève arrived with the sacred host of the Eucharist in an attempt to intervene and stop the gunfire; but he and his attendants were brutally knocked to the ground. In one more desperate attempt to stop the firing, the governor, the provost of merchants, and other notables attending the meeting hastily drew up a document expressing "Union" with the princes. But as Miron du Tremblay, Frondeur and member of a prominent family, came out the door to deliver the paper, he was shot down. The gunfire and flames continued for some six hours.

The attack on the Hôtel de Ville by Condé's followers and troops on 4 July 1652 has been frequently narrated but rarely interpreted. The campaign requiring everyone to wear straw clearly set in motion a general movement aimed at intimidating the governing elite into expressing their support for Gaston and Condé; and this movement culminated in a highly coercive showdown at the Hôtel de Ville. Confronted by an entire population bedecked with straw, the city fathers and other notables were supposed to vote an expression of support for the princes. But they did not. By standing firm and merely listening to a speech in favor of the king's return, the assemblymen continued the deliberately established policy that had led to closing the gates to Condé and his troops prior to the battle of 2 July.

The calling of so general, indeed so democratic, an assembly also aimed to influence the provost of merchants and the *échevins* to change their tune and become more favorable to the princely Fronde. But it did not work. In fact, despite the campaign to wear straw, the assembled body clearly supported the resolution to keep military forces out of the capital. Gaston's speech failed to bring the assembled company around, for at the critical moment no motion for union with the princes came from the floor. Not that Gaston and Condé totally lacked support in the assembly. If we go through the roster of people attending this meeting of the Parlement, it is evident that sympathizers for Gaston and Condé were among them. Sensing perhaps hostility toward Condé within the group, they dared not make the motion in favor of "Union." More likely, Condé simply was relying on the persuasive powers of rowdyism and of coercing people to wear straw in the streets and had not really worked out a political maneuver that would produce a majority in his favor at the meeting. As the firing began, shouts were heard in the crowd to the effect that the city fathers were all Mazarinists. At least a hundred people, ranging from prominent parlementaires down to an iron merchant and a grocer, were killed in the attack. As the shooting drew to an end, Beaufort rode in, found some wine that had been stored in the Hôtel de Ville, broke it open and left the attackers to get drunk. In fact, almost the entire Hôtel de Ville was pillaged, and the records of court proceedings were spilled about and valuables carried off.

The attack on the Hôtel de Ville of 4 July left the city fathers no choice but to resign their offices. A veritable *coup* took place as Broussel became provost of merchants and, in Gaston's presence, took an oath to fulfill the duties of the office. Beaufort became governor of the Bastille, thereby assuring that the fortress and the military supplies it housed would be available to the princes. Still another purge of the militia colonels occurred, with Gaston attempting to consolidate his control over every quarter of the city. Accompanying the increased control over the Hôtel de Ville was the appointment of a special council to advise the king's uncle. This was a clear attempt to give more weight to his office of lieutenant-general of the realm by adding well-known and influential government officials to his circle of advisers. Chancellor Séguier accepted membership on Gaston's council, as did Nesmond and Maisons, two presidents in the Parlement who were Condé's clients, and as did other prominent judges, among them Viole and Broussel, and the Duke de Beaufort and Chavigny. What is important about this move is that it marked an emphatic effort to continue the civil war by strengthening the princely political base among the governing elite of the capital. So often described as indecisive, Gaston remained active this time and showed no signs of giving up.

The political and social climate in Paris after the 4 July attack on the Hôtel de Ville remained tense and sullen. Force had been used to alter the city government. Many of the senior and wealthier judges ceased attending sessions of Parlement. And so, according to their seniority, younger and younger judges were forced to preside over a rump parlement made up of some seventy to eighty judges who remained loyal to Gaston and Condé. Deputies headed by President Nesmond shuttled back and forth between Saint-Germain-en-Laye, the Luxembourg Palace, and the Great Chamber of the Parlement, in a kind of metaphorical negotiation that focused on asking the king to return to Paris, once he had sent Mazarin away. One of the most important cases taken up by the court at this time was the negotiation of the royal letters patent making Rohan-Chabot a duke and peer. This move was a clear payoff to the duke for having attempted to hold Angers for the princes. In what must have been an unusually illogical, indeed incoherent speech, Broussel proposed to his colleagues that Gaston be declared regent of France! This proposal would have required a dramatic undoing not only of the parlementary declaration making Anne of Austria regent but also of the Parlement's solemn declaration of the king's majority in September 1651. Broussel probably was thinking of the office of lieutenant-general that Gaston would shortly assume. The old Frondeur, now provost of merchants thanks to Condé's gunners, lost the authority he had once had among non-Frondeur factions. During this time of military buildup in the countryside and Condé *coups* in Paris, Broussel had remained obsessively preoccupied with selling Mazarin's books and furniture. Had he become senile? Could he not perceive military realities beyond his Tacitean obsession with corruption?

By mid-July, some 3,000 Spanish troops approached Noyon, in Picardy. To confront the Spanish threat, Turenne shifted from his surveillance of Paris and of the Condé army stationed partly within the city and partly outside it. Throughout these weeks of war and phony war, Condé stormed about trying to raise funds for his troops. He eventually learned that it was one thing to intimidate and undermine a city government and quite another to extract money from the citizenry, by borrowing or by force. In early August, news arrived that the Condé stronghold of Montrond had fallen to the royal army. The impact on opinions was not lost. The prince had been unable to gain control over the entire countryside around Bordeaux; now he had failed to impede the fall of this fortress, which was not only militarily powerful but also of great symbolic importance. Palluau, who had conducted the siege for the crown, immediately hired several thousand peasants to pillage the chateau and tear down the fortifications. Within weeks, Montrond had been demolished, not simply because victorious soldiers made it a habit to pillage, but by royal order.

If we can judge by the lamentable decline in number and battle-readiness of the princely army, encamped on the Left Bank just beyond the great Saint Victor's abbey, it is evident that Condé did not throw his personal fortune into the war effort. Barely 1,500 sick and acrimonious soldiers, commanded by disputing officers, remained when the time came to establish winter quarters. Turenne certainly was also short of supplies, and there were disputes over command between him and the prickly La Ferté-Senneterre, but it is evident that the king's army remained more effective than Condé's.

All through the summer, the political climate in the capital remained morose. The families of leading actors in the Fronde suffered illnesses and deep personal losses that seemed the sign of divine retribution for opposing the king's will. Gaston's infant son, the Duke de Valois, died of dysentery. From Bordeaux came the news that the Princess of Condé was dangerously ill. The archbishop of Paris, who was Retz's uncle, fell gravely ill, and so did Omer Talon, the eminent advocate general in the Parlement. These deaths and illnesses hung like a pall over the population. The fatal duel between Nemours and Beaufort was followed by others, prompted in part by disputes over the seating in Gaston's new council and the order in which the various nobles and other dignitaries could enter the council chamber. When Chancellor Séguier quietly began to indicate that he wished to leave Paris and in effect abandon the princely Fronde, Gaston refused him a passport, a painful humiliation for so eminent a royal official. Séguier eventually found his way out of the capital, in monk's garb. Other prominent officials disguised themselves as bourgeois and left the city in public coaches.

III. *Mazarin's Second Exile*

At the court—first at Saint-Denis, then at Pontoise and Compiègne—the Council of State, effectively headed by Mathieu Molé, again keeper of the seals, busily issued royal decrees anulling every bit of legislation promulgated by Gaston, the Parlement of Paris, and the provost of merchants. Never for a minute did the Council cease to thunder opposition to the Frondeurs. And gradually, somewhat mysteriously, a quickly publicized dialogue developed between the king and his Council and the Frondeurs of Paris. A decree ordering the Parlement to take up its duties at Pontoise could not, in itself, have produced a powerful effect. The Frondeur judges could simply ignore it, and they did. But accompanying this decree were some loose, vague, but terribly significant exchanges about the conditions under which it might please the king to send away Mazarin.

Like great ideological-emotional blocks, an edifice of terms fell into place in which the newly summoned Pontoise Parlement demanded that Mazarin go once again into exile and that the princes lay down their arms. Louis XIV refused to attend the very first meeting of the Parlement of Pontoise, because one judge was not garbed in a red robe. But then it subsequently became apparent that under Molé's leadership, this parlement—which at first had only thirteen members—would really require Mazarin's exile. On his own, the cardinal had negotiated an exchange of benefices that enabled him to become bishop of Metz. Why? The three sees of Metz, Verdun, and Toul had legal-political links with the French monarchy, but they also possessed foreign, indeed Holy-Roman Imperial, affiliations as well. And so, by becoming the bishop of Metz, Mazarin moved toward an image of foreignness. But for Molé, eager to consolidate royal authority in the Parlement of Pontoise, the Metz caper would not suffice. A parlementary decree announcing

Mazarin's exile was accepted by Louis XIV. It had the effect of informing the Frondeur judges and the Parisians that the Parlement of Pontoise was more powerful than the Frondeur Parlement: it could make Mazarin leave.

Observers were suspicious. Was this just another ploy? Mazarin perhaps thought so himself. But Molé, the other royal councillors, and perhaps Louis and Anne signified that the cardinal really must leave France. The king announced that it was with great regret that he was losing such a faithful and effective minister, and he went so far as to suggest that Mazarin had stated his express desire to leave. To everyone's surprise, except perhaps Molé's, Mazarin discovered that he must make a journey to Lorraine and complete some negotiations. Accompanied by a guard of some 500 men, the cardinal not only went to Metz, he continued on to Sedan and began to raise more troops.

In Paris, Gaston tried to prevent all the printers in the capital from publishing the *arrêts* issued at Pontoise, a sure sign of the importance of opinions in the capital. He and Condé also quickly insisted that Mazarin must remain beyond French borders; otherwise they would not cashier their troops. But for a population weary of the miseries of war, this condition carried little weight. Additional prominent judges made their way out of the capital. The Parlement of Pontoise was gaining in prestige and numbers. Accompanied by a huge retinue of clerics and prelates riding in thirty carriages, Retz dramatically left the city and joined the court at Compiègne. Anne and Louis received him with smiles and bestowed the cardinal's hat upon him in the official ceremony of royal nomination to the cardinalcy. To the contemporary observer it now seemed that Anne's powers were subsiding and that a new era had begun, with Louis increasing his power by following the advice of his councillors and of the Parlement of Pontoise. The cordiality with which the king received such dignitaries as Séguier and Retz was feigned; he wanted to win the duel for favorable opinion that the king, his mother, and Molé were waging with the Frondeurs and thus sap the princes' control over Paris.

The *arrêt* issued by the Parlement of Pontoise that contained articles about Mazarin's exile included an article about excusing Parisian property owners from paying the taxes on their *portes-cochères* that had been levied by Gaston. This move was clearly designed to appeal to property owners in the capital, who were the very elements of the population that had organized a strong movement to force the payment of interest on the *rentes*. Occasional supporters of Gaston and Condé would go through the streets and try to raise the taxes created by the Frondeurs; but they soon began to fear for their lives and property. Some lenders loaned Gaston 40,000 *livres,* which he promptly sent to the munitioneers, to supply the army; but the financial situation of the Frondeurs had in fact become desperate. For the Parisians realized that Turenne's army would neither blockade nor attack the city. But, like all armies, it would pillage. Though the Frondeurs called attention to horrible pillaging committed by troops loyal to the king, this did not produce increased revenue or loans to Gaston. And, as had been the case throughout the Fronde, the private property of the leaders of the various parties came in for systematic devastation. Turenne's army pillaged around Gonesse and burned President Nesmond's estate. This was the price the eminent judge had to pay for his fidelity to the house of Condé.

In August 1652, a slight groundswell in favor of inviting the king back to Paris could be sensed among the elite guild communities, but disputes persisted over whether this invitation should permit Mazarin's return. Condé and Gaston had guards and regiments. Over the population lay the threat of coercive force by princely houliganism and of pillaging by the *gens sans aveu,* that is, the rough crowd that assembled around the city gates and in the Palais de Justice.

Condé's brutal seizure of power at the Hôtel de Ville, which had made Broussel the provost of merchants, was challenged in mid-August, when elections were scheduled for the principal city officials. On 12 August 1652, an order went out to the officials of every quarter of the city, requesting them to call meetings of all:

cinquantainiers and *dizainiers* [volunteer subordinate neighborhood officials], with eight of the most visible residents in each quarter, whether they be royal officers, bourgeois nobles [sic], or notable merchants not engaged in handcrafts, [to assemble] on pain of being stripped of their privileges as bourgeois, franchises and liberties according to the king's lists [of the names of bourgeois], and they are to swear in the hands of the most notable of the said eight, to elect four of the eight men, and those four should stay in their houses next

Friday, the sixteenth of this month, until ten in the morning, and we will inform them to come to the Hôtel de Ville in order to proceed to the election of a provost of merchants.

Things seemed to be progressing according to form until a royal order arrived on 12 August, forbidding the election and maintaining in office those who had been forced to resign in July! The assembled Condéist city fathers decided to ignore the royal order and proceed with the election.

The political maneuvers were not over. At a meeting of the city fathers held on 15 August, the eve of the election, a letter from Gaston was delivered. He asked the city fathers to continue Broussel in office. The king's uncle, that princely Frondeur, made the case for this choice by emphasizing the perilous times and Broussel's reputation and his opposition to Mazarin. Gaston added:

I would receive a very particular satisfaction, not only because of the esteem in which I hold his [Broussel's] merit, but because of the true affection I have for you, Sirs, your very good friend.

GASTON

Broussel expressed surprise when he heard the letter read; he then recounted how he had been "swept up" into the office he occupied in Luxembourg Palace, where he had received assurances that his predecessor had resigned. Broussel ended by commenting that he lacked the strength to continue in office.

The next day, election day, the assembled officials and electors from all over the city heard mass, proceeded to draw up lists of electors for each quarter, and listened to the reading of various letters, including Gaston's. Ballot counters were selected, one a royal official, another a town councillor, another from the *quarteniers,* and still another from the bourgeois. The voters deposited their ballots. Later in the day, the Duke de Beaufort drove up to the Hôtel de Ville, called the four ballot counters to his coach, and drove them to the Luxembourg Palace, where they reported the results of the vote to the bedridden Gaston. Broussel had literally been swept back into office, this time, it seemed, with a solid mandate behind him. Gaston and Condé did not really control Broussel, but by putting him into office and seeing to his reelection, the princes were assured that the Hôtel de Ville would not become a platform for a Mazarinist political countermove against the control that the princes now exerted over the city.

The *quarteniers* had selected their eight fellow residents carefully, no doubt excluding "Mazarinists." But more than that, the Parisians simply could not vote against Broussel, the venerable judge who had so often inveighed against the corruption of the fiscal administration and of Mazarin. Did he not realize that he was being used to legitimate Gaston's political control of the capital? By hinting that Broussel was senile, historians have missed an opportunity to clarify what politics had been and always would be for the eminent judges of the Long Robe. Broussel was a believer in the power of words, in the power of the Parlement. He lacked a real perspective on the strategic military and aristocratic dynamics of the princely Fronde. It is doubtful that he was able to perceive the derision in which Condé held the Parlement. Certainly Broussel did not realize that the prince was every bit as absolutist about royal authority as Mazarin was. Broussel's failures were not the result of age, any more than Gaston's were the result of "indecisiveness." Instead, these really quite worthy and well-intentioned political figures had no clear idea of the havoc and violence that Condé (and Mazarin) were willing to wreak in order to win the civil war. It was not the last time that French political culture would turn to aged leaders of enormous prestige but incapable of perceiving the stakes in a duel for power that put the very survival of that political culture in doubt.

Despite the apparent solidarity of mid-August, the princely party in Paris was on the verge of collapse one month later. Reports of bourgeois assembling here and there, notably in the arcades surrounding the cemetery of the Holy Innocents, contributed to a mood of civic activism. An anonymous sheet circulated, requesting a meeting of the bourgeois in the Palais Royal: this produced an assembly of some 300 or 400 people that conveyed to Broussel the message that he should resign. Those who attended this meeting had removed the straw cockades from their hats and had replaced them with bits of paper, a certain sign of hostility to Condé. Broussel expressed his readiness to resign, which certainly must have shaken Gaston, now aware of the fragility of his hold over the Hôtel de Ville. Additional guards were posted around the Palais Royal to prevent further meetings. With the Hôtel de Ville under Condéist control, the Parisians now had nowhere to meet.

The militia columns were the heart of increasing political activity. Young men were being pulled into the columns and trained by marching drill on the Pré aux Clercs, another sign of rising civic-military consciousness among merchants, artisans, royal officials, and the men who were their commanders as militia colonels. The news that the self-same militia colonels were talking about going out to see the king and to respectfully ask him to return to Paris must have spread quietly from cabaret to cabaret for some weeks before the decision to take this step was actually made in mid-October. Rumor also floated about to the effect that some of the city fathers—men not put into office by Condé and Gaston—were requesting passports to visit the court at Saint-Germain-en-Laye.

The royal councillors, and Molé was first among them, were careful to answer every feeler, meet every expression of concern with a reply. A vague, non-partisan "little language" developed in speeches and decrees and enabled opposing sides to talk without alluding to the issues that could continue to divide them. The word "movements" took on the special meaning: it referred to all the Frondeur activities of the preceding three years. "Present occurrences" was a phrase that allowed a non-partisan evocation of the divisions. Talk of amnesty, especially of the need for a general amnesty—properly registered in the Parlement of Paris, as Gaston put it—was accompanied by talks about a ceasefire in early October. In the Hôtel de Ville, the Condéists quietly melted away, and an overt shift of opinion led to a resolution favoring the recall of the men who had been forced to resign in July.

The Duke de Beaufort argued and stampeded an attempt to keep the Frondeurs in place, but to no avail. When the terms of a ceasefire became final, Gaston accepted them, as did Beaufort. But not Condé. As the princely army started to move away from Paris, the colonels and the other officers of the militia, some 250 strong, made their way out to Saint-Germain-en-Laye and invited the king to return to Paris. A magnificent reception was offered to the militiamen, who returned to the city in excellent humor and convinced that peace was certain. In fact, they had waited until Condé's troops had gone as far as Caumartin, and even beyond, before making their move. The Parisians feared what the prince might do, and could do, at the head of his approximately 1,500 troops, no matter how few, how sickly, how poorly equipped they might be. As the militiamen returned to the capital on 20 October, it was learned that Broussel's son had been relieved of his office of governor of the Bastille and replaced by a certain Monsieur Drouet, captain of the royal guards. The former governor of Paris, L'Hôpital, had been returned to office, while Beaufort had stood up in the Great Chamber and solemnly sworn that his every act had been done in the royal service.

The fall of 1652 was a time of rapidly consolidating authority by the Council of State. Condé and his troops joined the Spanish army; Turenne pursued these combined forces and drove them back, eventually obliging them to leave the realm. Still believing in the power of his own rank and in his abilities as a negotiator, Gaston discovered that the political atmosphere had changed. He could not really negotiate an accommodation; and only a few days after the dramatic return of the militia and the restoration of the old city administration, he was quietly forced to leave the capital. On 18 October, the Grande Mademoiselle received a letter from Louis XIV requesting her to move out of the Tuileries Palace. The Louvre was also ordered vacated and the exiled king and queen of England shifted to the Palais Royal. The king and his court reached Paris at about seven in the evening and in the glare of torches moved on horseback through the Saint-Honoré gate. On all sides an enormous crowd shouted, *"Vive le roi!"*

Conclusion

THE Fronde began as a work-stoppage by government tax officers who refused to carry out their duties. Attempts to coerce these officials to return to work by threatening their self-esteem and property backfired. Indeed, as the Council of State tried to intimidate its own officials, virtually the entire royal administration rallied to their striking colleagues or at least reserved judgment about the Council's abusive power.

The use of physical force in the form of arbitrary arrest and the blockade of Paris left the striking officials no alternative but to admit defeat or meet "force with force," in the words of President de Mêmes. Employing against the Parisians the military forces customarily used against foreigners had the effect of mobilizing larger and larger segments of the population to support the striking judges and tax officials.

When the striking officials resorted to using their administrative powers to cancel tax legislation and negotiate ever-lower taxes, the Fronde moved from a strike to a revolutionary action. Negotiations about the rights of striking officials to assemble when they wished, discuss any subject they wished, and, most important of all, vote tax relief for all the king's subjects ended in a colossal defeat for those royal councillors who had decided that arrest and military force would make the striking judges, the Parisians, and the rebellious provincials submit to coercive techniques of governance.

Despite claims to the contrary by the Frondeur leadership, their revolution remained a narrowly elitist phenomenon. As private and familial preoccupations gave way before civic concern in the minds of tens of thousands of Parisians, Aixois, Toulousains, Bordelais, and Rouennais, the leadership of the Fronde revolution remained firmly in the hands of some of the leading judges and princes of the realm. Despite this elitism, the mobilization of opinions by the Frondeurs, the defense efforts made by the population, and the debates and writings they prompted extended political life and engagement, if only temporarily, to a broader segment of the population. Sporadic rebellions and peasant anger prompted the judges to act on the peasants' behalf. When thousands of Parisians marched behind the Parlement on the Day of the Barricades, the queen regent and her ministers peered into the abyss of a bloodbath, and they flinched. That Anne of Austria courted Parisian opinion by thanking the militia captains was a testimonial to the political force that could be wielded by the population of the capital.

The philosophers and historians of antiquity who were so influential in the seventeenth century all stated that the political actions of the "people"—that is, large civic populations such as that of ancient Rome—were fickle and totally unpredictable. This was certainly not the case in the Paris of the Fronde. Inchoate like some twentieth-century urban populations, and lacking channels and representatives other than the militia, the Parisians nonetheless strove to defend themselves against life-threatening blockades. They also supported the striking judges, especially the venerable Broussel, by transforming the capital into an gigantic armed camp. The elite leadership of the Fronde often vacillated in its aims, but the *peuple* did not.

What of the Prince de Condé? Historians, like his contemporaries, reproach him for not accepting parlementaire and popular support in his duel with Mazarin. Those same historians (and those same contemporaries) express awe at the hubris of this man who gave quarter to no one. Had he been questioned about his attitude toward the Parlement and the *peuple,* Monsieur le Prince might well have uttered the phrase often attributed to his royal cousin: *"L'Etat, c'est moi."* Long months of reading and meditation in prison transformed Condé from a hypersensitive general into a party leader who used his clients and the press to force Mazarin from the realm. These vitriolic attacks against the cardinal did not, however, win the Parisians over to the prince. Unable to rally the capital politically, Condé had no choice but to slink away with his ragged little army. For the Parisians forgot neither Monsieur le Prince's brutal attack upon Charenton nor his bloody siege of the Hôtel de Ville. Lacking the firepower to stand and fight the prince, they defeated him by declining to give him their hearts, as Henry IV might have put it.

Many of the gains made by the striking officials would not be permanent. The expected shift in the powers of the state toward a more diffuse ultimate authority—the Council of State *and* the Parlement—did not occur. Did this make the Fronde any less revolutionary? The failure or success of revolution ought not to be measured by the criterion of permanent change. The fact that millions of peasants and city-dwellers paid substantially lower taxes, or no taxes at all for two or three years, must be considered an important revolutionary accomplishment.

Did the Council of State learn anything from the terrible confrontation with its striking officials and their supporters in the cities? Later in the century, violent coercion during tax collection would occur briefly and sporadically in some areas, but after the Fronde large-scale armed force would never again be employed. The state would learn that *douceur* could be more effective than force for increasing tax revenues. By the end of the seventeenth century, royal revenues would be approximately twice what they were at the time of the Fronde, and this despite bad weather and crop failures. And the dialectical relation between fiscal policies and the use or non-use of force became a permanent feature of French political culture after the Fronde, as Louis XVI's ministers were to discover in 1789.

The terrain to be occupied by the newer state power was, of course, the military. Cardinal Mazarin knew that it would be extremely difficult to find capable military leaders who would remain loyal to him (and to the boy king) *after* they had won a victory. A defeated general rarely posed a threat to royal authority in the still very militarist and masculinist society of the seventeenth century. On the other hand, a single victorious general, especially if royal blood ran in his veins, was a far greater menace to state power than several hundred striking royal officials. In the end—and here he followed and even outdid Richelieu—Mazarin selected obscure military figures who would remain faithful to him and the king, even in victory. By contrast, the generals who fought for a price—veritable *condottiere* like Hocquincourt and Harcourt—rode off into the sunset as Michel Le Tellier and Mazarin shaped "obscure" nobles into a hierarchically rewarded and stable military force. Condé's relations with his subordinate officers were never particularly good, and in the end he was defeated because Mazarin knew how to select effective generals who would fight for the king. The army too was a sphere for civic action where loyalty to the king would prevail.

The Fronde also brought an end to the use of *gens d'armes,* those hastily raised regiments of nobles that repressed rebellion or intimidated any city or province unwilling to pay taxes. The rise of a standing army composed of hardened and well-trained soldiers who were quite willing to shoot into a crowd or annihilate a column of militiamen definitively altered the terms of the relationship between "strong society" and "weak state" in the France of the later seventeenth century. This was the principal result of the Frondeurs' defeat. When Louis XIV approached a rebellious Marseilles at the head of his troops in 1660, the city fathers quickly learned that the Fronde as a way of military life was over. Six thousand troops occupied the city. The rebels were quickly brought to justice, and symbolic as well as real repression was rapidly meted out.

As the routine of annual military campaigns against Spain continued, and as duties, occupations, and family concerns once again came to the fore, the events of the Fronde ceased to preoccupy the governing elites. There were harsh and theatrical moments of political repression. The Bordelais Dureteste was tried and executed by being broken on the wheel before his former supporters. So were other Frondeurs, usually men of modest social origins. The great Frondeurs—Broussel, Pithou, Blancmesnil, Retz, Gaston d'Orléans, Conti, Viole, and Condé, to mention only a few—died in their beds. So did the anti-Frondeurs. The prisons of the realm were not filled with political opponents, as they had been during Richelieu's administration. The Fronde was less bloody and less destructive of crops than the great religious upheaval of the sixteenth century, which had dragged in its wake such atrocities as the St. Bartholomew's Night Massacre, the Guise assassinations, and the regicides of Henry III and Henry IV.

The more eloquent participants in the Fronde turned to writing their memoirs. In French political culture, writing about political action *is* political action, even if it is only about oneself and about what one has said or done, be it in a tower study, on the field of battle, or in the Parlement. The variety, the richness, indeed the complexity, ambiguity, honesty, and at the same time self-servingness of these memoirs written by both men and women have encouraged civic activism since the early eighteenth century.

The participants in the Fronde, and Saint-Simon after them, were fond of noting that Louis XIV remembered the humiliations his mother and Mazarin had suffered at the hands of the Frondeurs. Was this in fact true? The Sun King had a prodigious memory for slights against his family and his royal person. When Condé negotiated and eventually obtained a royal pardon, Louis XIV may well have forgiven him for his rebellion. This is not to say, however, that the king forgot what had taken place or ever really trusted the prince again. Similarly, the mental space between Versailles, the Parlement, and the Parisians proved far greater than the geographic distance that separated the state administration from the Hôtel de Ville of Paris. Throughout his long reign, the Sun King slighted the ex-Frondeurs in a very telling way: save for a few brief visits to the capital, he denied them the honor of his royal presence.

Bibliographic Essay

THIS book was written as an introductory essay on the Fronde, a pendant to my *Paris in the Age of Absolutism* (New York, 1968). For that reason it has no notes. Specialists whose works I have drawn on so heavily will have little trouble recognizing my indebtedness to them. My profound expression of thanks for their help. Nonspecialists may find the following brief characterizations of some of these works helpful for interpreting the historiography of the Fronde.

Adolphe Chéruel's *Histoire de France pendant la Minorité de Louis XIV* (Paris, 1879), 4 vols., ranks among the very best and most important works ever written in French history. My indebtedness to Chéruel lies not only in facts and interpretation, but still more in his skeptical, mordant, occasionally Tacitean view of politics and human nature. Chéruel's historiographical *parcours*, not unlike that of some contemporary French historians, became more conservative as he lived through the changing political regimes of the nineteenth century and studied Mazarin. Chéruel's vision is focused on applied individual political intelligence. Never an out-and-out admirer of Mazarin, he nonetheless traces and assesses the cardinal's ability to survive and prevail in the framework of competing political intelligences. Mazarin defeated Retz, Condé, and a host of lesser antagonists because of his understanding of human nature and the revolutionary moment in French political culture in the mid-seventeenth century.

Ernst Kossman's *La Fronde* (Leiden, 1954) is an erudite reconstruction of the revolution, essentially from a Robe and constitutionalist perspective. Because Robe eloquence was so powerfully articulated, morally coherent, and grounded in a sense of French history, it attracts historians to fundamentally constitutionalist perspectives. The evidence of high investment in tax farms by Robe officials, as discerned by Daniel Dessert, does not undermine the value of the constitutionalist perspective. For Mazarin and Chéruel, this disparity between lofty declarations of principle and personal financial interest was obvious, a "normative" feature of political life. A charge of corruption was a political weapon, like many other weapons, nothing more and nothing less; but when Mazarin offered an abbey in return for a vote, his candor pierced the veil that separated public discourse from private action, and this infuriated the judges.

A. L. Moote's *Revolt of the Judges* (Princeton, 1971) is an extension and refinement of Kossman's work, with considerable evidence added about the Robe's action that was inconsistent with its rhetoric. Moote's argument that, had the judges not revolted to curb the increase of kingly powers, the Ludovician state would in the end have tipped even more heavily than it did toward state despotism justifies the judicial Fronde in terms consistent with Robe constitutionalist thought. What impressed Chéruel was the deadlocked, impotent Parlement of the princely Fronde. The rise of Napoleon III and the willingness of the Parisians to accept a strong, paternalist state could only derive, again, from a deadlocked political body. Moote's argument is not refuted by Chéruel's perspective; the political culture of the 1650s will require more research to elucidate the crucial relations between the population in the capital and the rest of the realm.

Roland Mousnier's *La Vénalité des offices* (Rouen, 1945; reprinted Paris, 1971), while not specifically about the Fronde, probes deeply into the social, ontological, and institutional foundations of Robe political power. What gave the Parlementaires their strength? Mousnier's very influential articles, notably on the Sully-Bellièvre debate over the moral, professional, and political consequences of inheritable venal office (see below), confirm the historian's aspirations that history is not just a series of events or accidents, but that there is a deeper relation between state policy, social change, and power relations not unlike what Montesquieu and Tocqueville discerned. Did venality as inheritable property consolidate the king's power over the sovereign courts, or did it provide a fulcrum of autonomy with which the judges could challenge the course of state revolution in 1648?

These fundamental questions will always lie at the substructural level of any study of the Fronde; there are similar momentous questions in the study of every other revolution. I provide only oblique answers to these questions, preferring a middle course, offering Chéruelian emphasis on individual human intelligence as the most deeply historical dimension of the Fronde, but the fundamental questions are always there. No answers can be found to them, however, in Mazarin's speeches or letters; all the answers, in remarkable contradiction, can be found in Retz's *Mémoires*.

In alphabetical order, the following works have been particularly useful in supplying general critical interpretations of salient features of the Fronde. Françoise Bayard's *Le Monde des Financiers au XVIIe siècle* (Paris, 1988) is an awesomely erudite study of the "*partisans.*" Her work provides all the evidence needed for understanding why the Robe wanted both to reject and to be a part of the most rapidly growing part of the state, the tax-farming milieu. Paul Bénichou's brilliant *Morales du Grand Siècle* (Paris, 1948) reveals the theatrical backdrop of the Fronde, the aristocratic radical individualism, and the belief that the *peuple* could become, or always were, a "distant ally," an important first step toward eighteenth-century imaginations about the "public." Yves-Marie Bercé's *Histoire des Croquants* (Geneva, 1974), 2 vols., elucidates in beautiful prose the social and political dynamics of southwestern communities when threatened by "outside" forces, including the royal tax collector. Hubert Carrier's *Les Mazarinades* (Geneva, 1992), 2 vols., presents all the efforts through print to participate in and extend the force of public life and to co-opt adherents or weaken opponents made by Robe, princely, councillor, and ecclesiastical patrons and their stables of writers. The people who read the *Mazarinades* as they came off the presses began to apply literary-critical criteria for judging them—a distinctly dangerous mode of perceiving politics from the radical Frondeur perspective. Writers and writing, with their inevitable emphasis on the personal, seem to be small-fry in the Grande Fronde hierarchy of *grandes âmes*. A public there certainly was in France during the Fronde. It was certainly not the public that would appear in the 1760s, but it is not unimportant to note the reappearance of the word Fronde in the late eighteenth century, indicating that those older civic-minded historians of the nineteenth century were at least partially right in elucidating a historicist, constitutionalist tradition in Paris dating not only from the Fronde but from the days of Etienne Marcel.

Yves Castan's *Honnêtetés et relations sociales en Languedoc au XVIIIe siècle* (Paris, 1974) encouraged me to accept as really socially true, and not "just" rhetorical, the questions of self-esteem, slander, and lawbreaking in the Fronde. Perhaps Mazarin could not answer his slanderers because, in a sense, the only reply to a slanderous attack is a challenge to a duel or seeking redress in a court of law. Jean-Paul Charmeil's *Les Trésoriers de France pendant la Fronde* (Paris, 1964) demonstrates completely how corporatism and the *Etat de droit* infused the monarchy in the seventeenth century. The notes contain archival treasures and often report gossip, as gossip, from the sources. Natalie Zemon Davis's "The Rites of Violence" in *Society and Culture in Early Modern France* (Stanford, 1975) is a major landmark in understanding popular protest. Her insights hold true for all crowd behavior in the Fronde, be it led by a nobleman, a peasant woman, or a paid "agitator." Seeing the morally upright aims of rioters also helps clarify what has often been described as Retz's "complicity" with the populace. Robert Descimon's research on the militias, finances, and parlementary prosopography (see below) is fundamental to understanding the Fronde; it confirms my belief in the existence of a civic consciousness in early-modern French cities, perhaps not as developed as historical sociology once posited, nor as republican as the Florentine in the time of Machiavelli, but all the same present and focused on defense and on some degree of participatory politics.

Georges Dethan's Ecole des Chartes thesis on Gaston d'Orléans (1947) and his books on that intelligent but unauthoritarian prince, and on Mazarin (see below) helped me at every point to understand how contradictory expectations about the roles that Gaston was supposed to play account for the duration and complexity of the Fronde. Dethan, the grand-nephew of Chéruel, discerns with sympathy the two men who perhaps loathed each other the most by 1652, Gaston and Mazarin. (From Mazarin's point of view, the alternative candidate to loathe would be Retz.) It is a measure of Mazarin's greatness as a statesman that he tried to keep Gaston from humiliating himself still further in defeat, for after all the cardinal owed loyalty, respect, and support to this prince, as a prince.

Sarah Hanley's *The Lit de Justice* (Princeton, 1983) deeply enriches the constitutionalist and absolutist perspectives on ancien regime power relations by discerning mythical elements in the history of the *lit de justice* as both parties dueled over using the ceremony for their own ends in the Fronde. Jean Jacquart's "La Fronde des Princes . . . ," in the *Revue d'Histoire moderne et contemporaine*, 7 (1960): 257–90, remains absolutely fundamental to any study of the civil war that was the Fronde. Christian Jouhaud's *La Fronde des Mots* (Paris, 1985) is a landmark in the rediscovery of the power of words by a "community" of historians for whom social structural history had made the study of words, phrases, pamphlets, and ideologies all but superfluous, because there was no power in discourse.

Sharon Kettering's *Judicial Politics and Urban Revolt in Seventeenth-Century France* (Princeton, 1978) and her *Patrons, Brokers and Clients in Seventeenth-Century France* (New York, 1986) offer a backdrop to every aspect of this essay. The Fronde was not the English Revolution. The Robe view of the Council's increased power never extended so deeply into Parisian politics, and the "country" remained largely unaware of it. Clientage therefore played a far greater role in the Fronde than it did in the English Revolution. While I am sure that the Parlement of Aix was not typical of the provincial sovereign courts, it nonetheless has tended to be perceived as such in my essay, with the result that I have largely ignored what happened in the non-Parisian sovereign courts during the Fronde. Bordeaux and Paris, and their Parlements, were the strategic focal points of the Fronde, be it for Mazarin, for Retz, for Condé, for Bouillon; all the other parlements would fall into step as a result of what occurred in these two. It would seem harsh to say that what happened in Aix, in Rouen, in Toulouse, and so on did not really count, for it violates the historian's sense that everything counts; but the Fronde was a revolution that, along with a civil war, left much of the realm on the sidelines. It is always astonishing to observe how such forcefully popular phenomena as revolutions come to be directed by a handful of individuals. Kettering's work on the brokers will be confirmed by future studies of other provinces and of their relations with the royal councillors. Not all disorder and contestation during the Fronde was revolutionary, with the result that while Mazarin was in exile most of his brokers held the realm for him in a tight grip.

René Pillorget's *Les Mouvements insurrectionnels de Provence entre 1596 et 1715* (Paris, 1975) provides a prefect-like perspective on disorder, and once again it becomes evident that men of state, be they prefects or historians, can analyze empirically every type of group social relation. The statistics that he provides for Provence reveal that with the exception of a single terrible outburst of violence against Moslem immigrants in Marseilles, Provence was really a socially and politically stable society, albeit one that contemporaries perceived to be fraught with "disorder." To be sure, exchanges of shots in the streets of Aix between leading city fathers and their clients were disturbing, but casualties were low and there was almost no outburst of social protest. Aix was not Bordeaux; violence and gang warfare are not revolution.

Sal Westrich's *The Ormée of Bordeaux* (Baltimore, 1972) may not have convinced this reader of the class-grounded character of the *Ormée*, but it provides solid evidence for the genuinely activist popular revolutionary movement that could come forth when city fathers, parlementaires, and princes permitted the Bordelais to become a threat to the established order.

Manuscript Sources

D'Argenson, René Voyer, *Procès verbal, séjour à Bordeaux, avril, 1649*, BN (Bibliothèque National), Ms. fr. 18752 (Séguier papers).
Broussel, *Papiers,* BN, Coll. Baluze, 29.
Chains, Streets of Paris, BN, Ms. fr. 21699 (Delamare papers).
Commissaire des Pauvres, St. Etienne du Mont, St. Nicolas du Chardonnet, and St. Hilaire, *Comptes,* 1649–1650, BN, Coll. Morel de Thoisy, 152.
Conseil secret du Parlement de Paris, AN, U 1042.
Estat des Gages, 1642, Herzog August Bibliothek, Wolfenbüttel, Cod. Grieef 31.75.
Extraits, Registres du Bureau de l'Hôtel de Ville de Paris, BN, Coll. Moreau, 1070.
Joly, Claude, *Mémoires,* Bibliothèque de l'Institut, Ms. 4454.
Journal des Débats du Parlement de Paris, 14 dec. 1650–8 aug. 1651, Herzog August Bibliothek, Wolfenbüttel, Cod Guelf 3.1.72.2.
Le Boindre?, *Journal des Débats du Parlement de Paris . . . ,* AN, U 336. An edition of text will be published by Orest and Patricia Ranum in 1993.

Lenet, Pierre, *Papiers, Comptes* . . . , BN, Mss. fr. 6703, 6704, 6727, 6725, 6729, 6731.

Le Tellier, Michel, *Correspondance,* BN, Ms. fr. 4179.

Mazarin, Jules, *Comptes, 1641–1648; Traités parmi différents princes; promesse de Mazarin donnée au prince de Condé deux jours devant sa prison,* BN, Coll. Dupuy, 775.

Newsletters of the Fronde, BN, Mss. fr. 25025, 25026. This source is now completely transcribed on computer and will be published in a small edition when funding permits.

Municipal elections, Paris, 1630's, Chantilly, Cabinet des livres H / 3.

Oath of the princes, 25 mars 1649, BN, Ms. fr. 3854.

Portraits de Messieurs les ministres des requêtes, BN, Coll. Cinq Cent Colbert, 214.

Registre du Parlement, 1649–1651, AN, U 334.

Registre secret de la cour des Aydes, BN, Ms. fr. 11091.

Remarques journalières et véritables . . . 1648, BN, Ms. fr. 10273.

Répertoire des registres . . . saisies réelles, 1633–51, AN, ZZ² 764.

Rolle des colonels, BN, Cinq Cent Colbert, 484.

Rolle des Taxes . . . 1649, AN, U 185.

Séguier, Pierre, *Correspondance,* BN, Ms. fr. 17335, on rentes and *chambres de justice;* registre du conseil secret, BN, Ms. fr. 16430.

Tronson, Louis, *Mémoires de quantités d'actions particulières qui se sont passées pendant les troubles de Paris, 1649,* British Library, Ms. Egerton 1676. An edition of this unique text written by a militia officer will be forthcoming.

Vineuil, Louis Ardier de, *Guerre de Paris,* Chantilly, Cabinet des livres 99ᴰ8.

Works

Books

Aumale, Henri duc de. *Histoire des princes de Condé.* 8 vols. Paris: Calmann-Lévy, 1863–1896.

Aya, Rod. *Rethinking Revolutions and Collective Violence.* Amsterdam: Spinhuis, 1990.

Babelon, Jean-Pierre. *Le Palais de Justice.* Paris: Editions du Temps, 1966.

Barante, A. *Le Parlement et la Fronde.* Paris: Didier, 1859.

Bayard, Françoise. *Le monde des Financiers au XVIIᵉ siècle.* Paris: Flammarion, 1988.

Bénichou, Paul. *Les morales du Grand Siècle.* Paris: Gallimard, 1948. English version, *Man and Ethics.* Translated by Elizabeth Hughes. New York: Doubleday, 1971.

Béranger, J. *Turenne*. Paris: Fayard, 1987.

Bercé, Yves-Marie. *Histoire des Croquants: étude des soulèvements populaires au XVIIe siècle dans le Sud-Ouest de la France*. 2 vols. Geneva: Droz, 1947.

Bertière, André. *Le Cardinal de Retz*. Paris: Klincksieck, 1977.

Birnstiel, E. *Die Fronde in Bordeaux, 1648–53*. Frankfurt-am-Main: P. Lang, 1985.

Blet, Pierre. *Le clergé de France et la monarchie, 1615–1666*. 2 vols. Rome: Gregorian University Press, 1959.

Boas, George. *Vox populi: Essays in the History of an Idea*. Baltimore: The Johns Hopkins University Press, 1969.

Bonney, Richard. *The King's Debts, Finance and Politics in France, 1589–1661*. Oxford: Clarendon, 1981.

Bonney, Richard. *Political Change in France under Richelieu and Mazarin, 1624–1661*. Oxford: Oxford University Press, 1978.

Bouyer, Christian. *Michel Particelli d'Hemery*. Paris: M.U. / AuDIR, Hachette, 1975.

Carrier, Hubert. *La Fronde, contestation démocratique et misère paysanne*. 2 vols. Paris: Edhis, 1981.

Carrier, Hubert. *La Presse et la Fronde (1648–1653)*. 2 vols. Geneva: Droz, 1989–91.

Charmeil, J.-P. *Les trésoriers de France à l'époque de la Fronde*. Paris: Picard, 1964.

Chéruel, Adolphe. *Histoire de France pendant la Minorité de Louis XIV*. 4 vols. Paris: Hachette, 1878–1880.

Collins, James. *Fiscal Limits of Absolutism*. Berkeley: University of California Press, 1988.

Communay, Arnaud. *L'Ormée à Bordeaux d'après le journal inédit de Jacques Filhot*. Bordeaux: n. p., 1887.

Courteault, Henri. *La Fronde à Paris*. Paris: Firmin-Didot, 1930.

Cousin, Victor. *Madame de Longueville*. Paris: Didier, 1859.

Cremieux, Adolph. *Marseille et la royauté pendant la minorité de Louis XIV (1643–1660)*. 2 vols. Paris and Marseille: Hachette, 1917.

Debidour, Antonin. *La Fronde angevine*. Paris: Thorin, 1877.

Dent, Julian. *Crisis in Finance: Crown, Financiers and Society in Seventeenth-Century France*. Newton Abbot: David and Charles, 1973.

Desmaze, C. *Le Parlement de Paris*. Paris: Imprimerie de la jurisprudence, 1860.

Dethan, Georges. *Gaston d'Orléans et la Fronde*. Thesis, Ecole des Chartes, 1947.

Dethan, Georges. *Gaston d'Orléans, conspirateur et prince charmant*. Paris: Fayard, 1959.

Dethan, Georges. *La Vie de Gaston d'Orléans*. Paris: Fallois, 1992.

Dethan, Georges. *Mazarin et ses amis*. Paris: Berger-Levrault, 1968.

Dethan, Georges. *Mazarin, un homme de paix à l'âge baroque*. Paris: Imprimerie nationale, 1981.

Dinges, Martin. *Stadtarmut in Bordeaux (1525–1675)*. Bonn: Bouvier, 1988.

Doolin, P. R. *The Fronde*. Cambridge, Mass: Harvard University Press, 1935.

Duchêne, Roger, and Pierre Ronzeaud, eds. *La Fronde en questions: Actes du Centre méridonal de rencontres sur le XVIIe siècle*. Aix-en-Provence: Publications de l'Université de Provence, 1988.

Dulong, Claude. *La fortune de Mazarin*. Paris: Perrin, 1990.

Feillet, Alphonse. *La misère au temps de la Fronde*. Paris: Didier, 1862.

Féron, Alexandre. *Vie et oeuvres de Charles Maignart de Bernières*. Rouen: Wolf, 1930.

Fessenden, Nicholas Buck. "Épernon and Guyenne: Provincial Politics under Louis XIII." Ph. D. diss., Columbia University, 1972.

Fogel, Michele. *Les cérémonies de l'information*. Paris: Fayard, 1989.

Foisil, Madeleine. *La révolte des Nu-pieds et les révoltes normandes de 1639*. Paris: Presses Universitaires de France, 1970.

Golden, Richard. *The Godly Rebellion: Parisian Curés and the Religious Fronde, 1652–1662*. Chapel Hill: University of North Carolina Press, 1981.

Gordon, George Stuart. *The Fronde*. Oxford: Clarendon Press, 1905.

Grand-Mesnil, Marie-Noële. *Mazarin, la Fronde et la presse, 1647–1649*. Paris: Colin, 1967.

Hamscher, Albert N. *The Parlement of Paris after the Fronde*. Pittsburgh: University of Pittsburg Press, 1976.

Hanley, Sarah. *The 'Lit de Justice' of the Kings of France: Constitutional Ideology in Legend, Ritual and Discourse*. Princeton: Princeton University Press, 1983.

Holt, Mack, ed. *Society and Institutions in Early-Modern France*. Athens: University of Georgia Press, 1991.

Jacquart, Jean. *La crise rurale en Ile-de-France*. Paris: Colin, 1974.

Jouanna, Arlette. *Le devoir de révolte: la noblesse française et la gestation de l'Etat moderne (1559–1661)*. Paris: Wolf, 1989.

Jouhaud, Christian. *Mazarinades: la Fronde des mots*. Paris: Aubier, 1985.

Jullian, Camille. *Histoire de Bordeaux*. Bordeaux: Feret, 1895.

Kerviler, Pierre. *Le Chancelier Séguier*. 2d ed. Paris: Didier, 1875.

Kettering, Sharon. *Judicial Politics and Urban Revolt in Seventeenth-Century France*. Princeton: Princeton University Press, 1978.

Kettering, Sharon. *Patrons, Brokers and Clients in Seventeenth-Century France*. New York: Oxford University Press, 1986.

Kleinman, Ruth. *Anne of Austria*. Columbus: Ohio State University Press, 1985.

Koetting, H. *Die Ormée (1651–1652): Gestaltende Kräfte und Personen-*

verdindungen des Bordelaiser Fronde. Munster: Aschendorff, 1983.

Kossmann, Ernst H. *La Fronde.* Leiden: Universitaire Pers, 1954.

Labatut, Jean-Pierre. *Les ducs et pairs de France au XVIIe siècle.* Paris: Presses Universitaires de France, 1972.

La Roche-flavin, Bernard de. *Treize livres des parlements de France.* Geneva: Berjon, 1621.

Lassaigne, Jean-Dominique. *Les assemblées de noblesse de France aux XVIIe et XVIIIe siècles.* Paris: Cujas, 1965.

Laurin-Portemer, Madeleine. *Etudes mazarines.* Paris: Boccard, 1981.

Lecestre, Léon. *La bourgeoisie parisienne au temps de la Fronde.* Paris: Plon-Nourrit, 1913.

Logié, P. *La Fronde en Normandie.* 3 vols. Amiens: n.p., 1951–52.

Lorris, Pierre-Georges. *La Fronde.* Paris: A. Michel, 1961.

Merrimian, Roger B. *Six Contemporaneous Revolutions.* Oxford: Clarendon Press, 1938.

Méthivier, Hubert. *La Fronde.* Paris: Presses Universitaires de France, 1984.

Michelet, Jules. *Histoire de France aux dix-septième siècle [Richelieu et la Fronde].* n.p., n.d.

Moote, Lloyd. *The Revolt of the Judges: the Parlement of Paris and the Fronde, 1643–52.* Princeton: Princeton University Press, 1971.

Moreau, Célestin, ed. *Choix des mazarinades.* 2 vols. Paris: Société de l'Histoire de France, 1853.

Mousnier, Roland. *Le conseil du roi de Louis XII à la Révolution.* Paris: Presses Universitaires de France, 1970.

Mousnier, Roland. *La plume, la faucille et le marteau.* Paris: Presses Universitaires de France, 1970.

Normand, Charles. *La Bourgeoisie française au XVIIe siècle.* Paris: Alcan, 1908.

Salmon, J. H. M. *Cardinal Retz.* London: Macmillan, 1969.

Ségur, Pierre de. *La jeunesse du Maréchal de Luxembourg.* Paris: Calmann-Levy, 1900.

Skinner, Q. ed. *The Return of Grand Theory in the Human Sciences.* Cambridge: Cambridge University Press, 1985.

Stein, Henri. *Le Palais de Justice et la Sainte-Chapelle du Palais.* Paris: Longuet, 1927.

Subtelny, Orest. *Domination of Eastern Europe, Native Nobilities and Foreign Absolutism, 1500–1715.* York: York University Press, 1986.

Tilly, Charles. *La France contestée de 1600 à nos jours.* Paris: Fayard, 1986.

Tilly, Louise, and Charles Tilly. *Class Conflict and Collective Action.* London: Sage, 1981.

Venard, Marc. *Bourgeois et paysans au XVIIe siècle.* Paris: S.E.V.P.E.N., 1957.

Watts, Derek. *Cardinal de Retz*. Oxford: Oxford University Press, 1980.
Wolf, John B. *Louis XIV*. New York: Norton, 1968.

Articles

Adams, Elizabeth C. "The Projected Estates General of 1649." Unpublished. Duquesne History Forum, 1977.
Barbiche, Bernard. "La hiérarchie des dignités et des charges." *XVIIe Siècle* 157 (1987): 359–70.
Barthélemy, Edouard de. "Etude sur Omer Talon." *Annales, Société académique de Saint-Quentin* 12 (1875).
Bayard, Françoise. "Du rôle exact de l'argent dans le déclanchement de la Fronde." In *La Fronde en questions*, edited by Roger Duchêne and Pierre Ronzeaud, 73–84. Aix-en-Provence: Publications de l'Université de Provence, 1988.
Bayard, Françoise. "Les financiers et la Fronde." *XVIIe Siècle* 145 (1984): 355–62.
Beik, William. "Urban Factions and the Social Order during the Minority of Louis XIV." *French Historical Studies* 15 (1987): 36–67.
Bercé, Yves-Marie. "La bourgeoisie bordelaise et le fisc sous Louis XIII." *Revue historique de Bordeaux et du département de la Gironde* 13 (1964): 41–66.
Bonney, Richard. "The French Civil War, 1649–53." *European Studies Review* 8 (1978): 71–100.
Bonney, Richard. "Cardinal Mazarin and the Great Nobility during the Fronde." *English Historical Review* 96 (1981): 818–33.
Bonney, Richard. "La Fronde des officiers." *XVIIe Siècle* 145 (1984): 323–39.
Bosher, John, "Chambres de Justice in the French Monarchy." In *French Government and Society, 1500–1850*, edited by John Bosher. London: Athlone, 1973: 19–40.
Carrier, Hubert. "Mécénat et politique: l'action de Mazarin jugée par les pamphletaires de la Fronde." In *L'âge d'or du mécénat*, pp. 247–61. Edited by Roland Mousnier and Jean Mesnard. Paris: C.N.R.S., 1985.
Certeau, Michel de. "Politique et mystique: René d'Argenson (1596–1651)." *Revue d'ascètique et de mystique* 39 (1963): 45–82.
Collins, James. "Sur l'histoire fiscale du XVIIe siècle." *Annales, Economies, Sociétés, Civilisations* 34 (1979): 325–47.
Constant, Jean-Marie. "La troisième Fronde: les gentilhommes et les libertés nobiliaires." *XVIIe Siècle* 145 (1984): 341–54.

Constant, Jean-Marie. "L'assemblée de noblesse de 1651: une autre conception de la Monarchie française." In *La Fronde en questions*, pp. 277–86. Edited by Roger Duchêne and Pierre Ronzeaud. Aix-en-Provence: Publications de l'Université de Provence, 1988.

Cornette, J. "Fiction et réalité de l'Etat baroque." In *L'Etat baroque*, edited by H. Méchoulan, 9–87. Paris: Vrin, 1985.

Corvisier, André. "Le pouvoir militaire et les villes." In *Pouvoir, ville et société en Europe, 1650–1750*, edited by Georges Livet and Bernard Vogler, 11–20 Paris: Editions Ophrys, 1983.

Cubells, Monique. "Le Parlement de Paris pendant la Fronde." *XVIIe Siècle* 35 (1957): 170–98.

Descimon, Robert. "Le financement frondeur de la Guerre de Paris." In *La France d'Ancien Régime. Etudes réunies en l'honneur de Pierre Goubert*, 195–206. Toulouse: Alain Croix, Privat, 1984.

Descimon, Robert. "Les barricades frondeuses." In *La Fronde en questions*, 245–61. Edited by Roger Duchêne and Pierre Ronzeaud. Aix-en-Provence: Publications de l'Université de Provence, 1988.

Descimon, Robert. "Solidarité communautaire et sociabilité armée: les compagnies de la milice bourgeoise à Paris (XVI–XVIIe siècles)." In *Sociabilité, pouvoirs et société*, Actes du colloque de Rouen (Nov. 1983), edited by Françoise Thélamon. Rouen: Publications de l'Université de Rouen, 1987, 599–620.

Descimon, Robert, and Christian Jouhaud. "La Fronde en mouvement." *XVIIe Siècle* 145 (1984): 305–22.

Descimon, Robert, and J. Nagle. "Les quartiers de Paris du Moyen Age au XVIIIe siècle." *Annales, Economies, Sociétés, Civilisations* 34 (1979): 956–74.

Descimon, Robert. "Les barricades de la Fronde parisienne." *Annales, Economies, Sociétés, Civilisations* 45 (1990): 397–422.

Descimon, Robert, and Christian Jouhaud. "De Paris à Bordeaux: pour qui court le peuple pendant la Fronde?" In *Mouvements populaires et conscience sociale, XVIe–XIXe siècles*, edited by Jean Nicolas, 31–42. Paris: Maloine, 1985.

Dessert, Daniel. "Finances et société au XVIIe siècle: à propos de la chambre de justice de 1661." *Annales, Economies, Sociétés, Civilisations* 29 (1974) 847–84.

Dessert, Daniel. "Pouvoir et finance au XVIIe siècle: la fortune de Mazarin." *Revue d'Histoire moderne et contemporaine* 23 (1976): 161–81.

Dethan, Georges. "Retz, juge de Mazarin." In *Il Cardinale Mazzarino in Francia; atti dei convegni Lincei*, pp. 77–85. Rome, 1977.

Deyon, Pierre. "A propos des rapports entre la noblesse française et la monarchie absolue." *Revue historique* 227 (1962): 33–66.

Emmanuelli, F.-X. "Pouvoir royal et représentation provençale du XVIIe au XVIIIe siècles." *Parliament, Estates, and Representation* 4 (1984): 45–50.

Farge, Arlette, and André Zysberg. "Les théâtres de la violence à Paris au XVIIIe siècle." *Annales, économies, sociétés, civilisations* 34 (1979): 894–1015.

Feillet, Alphonse. "La journée des barricades." *Revue des sociétés savantes des départements* (4th series) 5 (1865): 324–37.

Foisil, Madeleine. "Le système des valeurs dans les mémoires de Bigot de Monville." In *Les valeurs chez les mémorialistes français*, colloque de Strasbourg et de Metz, edited by Noémie Hepp, 237–46. Paris: Klincksiek, 1979.

Gelelin, F. "Récit de la Fronde bordelaise." *Revue historique de Bordeaux et du département de la Gironde* 7 (1914): 5–17.

Golden, Richard. "The Mentality of Opposition; the Jansenism of the Parisian Curés during the Religious Fronde." *Catholic Historical Review* 64 (1978): 565–80.

Hamscher, Albert. "Ouvrages sur la Fronde parus en anglais depuis 1970." *XVIIe Siècle* 145 (1984): 380–83.

Holt, Mack. "The King in Parlement: The Problem of the Lit de Justice in Sixteenth-Century France." *The Historical Journal* 31 (1988): 507–23.

Jacquart, Jean. "La Fronde de princes dans la région parisienne et ses conséquences matérielles." *Revue d'Histoire moderne et contemporaine* 7 (1960): 257–90.

Jennings, R. M., and A. P. Trout. "Internal Control: Public Finance in Seventeenth-Century France." *Journal of European Economic History* 1 (1972): 647–60.

Jones, Colin. "The Organization of Conspiracy and Revolt in the *Mémoires* of the Cardinal de Retz." *European Studies Review* 11 (1981): 125–50.

Jouanna, Arlette. "Le pouvoir royal et les barons des Etats de Languedoc." *Parliaments, Estates, and Representation* 4 (1984): 37–43.

Jouhaud, Christian. "Geoffry Gay: une lecture de la Fronde bordelaise." *Annales du Midi* 91 (1979): 273–95.

Jouhaud, Christian. "Ecriture et action du XVIIe siècle: sur un corpus de Mazarinades." *Annales, Economies, Sociétés, Civilisations* 38 (1983): 42–64.

Kettering, Sharon. "Forum: Fidelity and Clientage: Patronage and Politics during the Fronde." *French Historical Studies* 14 (1986): 409–41.

Kettering, Sharon. "The Decline of Great Noble Clientage during the Reign of Louis XIV." *Canadian Journal of History* 24 (1989): 157–77.

Knecht, R. J. "The Fronde." In *Historical Association, Appreciations in History, V.* (London, 1975).

Koetting, H. "L'Ormée (1651–1653); Dynamique sociale dans la Fronde bordelaise." *XVIIᵉ Siècle* 145 (1984): 377–79.

Labatut, J.-P. "Situation sociale du quartier du Marais pendant la Fronde." *XVIIᵉ Siècle* 38 (1958): 56–81.

Lefebvre, P. "Aspects de la 'fidelité' en France au XVIIᵉ siècle." *Revue Historique* 201 (1973): 59–106.

Malettke, Klaus. "Vénalité des offices et mobilité sociale: problèmes et questions de recherches comparées." In *Diritto e Potere: Nella Storia Europea*, in honor of B. Paradisi, pp. 685–716. Florence: Olschki, 1982.

Malettke, K. "Wirtschafliche, soziale und politische Aspekte der Fronde." In *Soziale und Politische Konflikte in Frankreich des Ancien Regime*, 24–65. Berlin: KNO, 1982. (ISBN: 3-7678-0527-8.)

Masson, G. "Ordres des miliciens à Paris pendant la Fronde." *Le Cabinet historique* 20: 106–14. (BN, Lᵉ73.)

McTighe, Sheila. "Nicolas Poussin's Representations of Storms and Libertinage." *Word and Image* 5 (1989): 333–61.

Mears, John A. "The Early-Modern Origins of the Concept of Political Revolution." In *The Consortium on Revolutionary Europe, Proceedings*, pp. 9–20. Athens: University of Georgia Press, 1986.

Meuvret, Jean. "Comment les Français du XVIIᵉ siècle voyaient l'impôt." *XVIIᵉ Siècle*, 25–26 (1955): 59–82.

Moote, Lloyd. "The French Crown versus its Judicial and Financial Officials." *Journal of Modern History* 34 (1962): 146–60.

Moote, Lloyd. "The Parlementary Fronde and Seventeenth-Century Robe Solidarity." *French Historical Studies* 2 (1962): 330–55.

Mousnier, Roland. "Sully et le Conseil d'Etat et des Finances: la lutte entre Bellièvre et Sully." *Revue Historique* 192 (1941): 68–86.

Mousnier, Roland. "Quelques raisons de la Fronde: les causes des journées révolutionaires parisiennes de 1648." *XVIIᵉ Siècle* 2 (1949): 33–78.

Mousnier, Roland. "Comment les Français du XVIIᵉ siècle voyaient la constitution." *XVIIᵉ Siècle* 25–26 (1955): 9–36.

Mousnier, Roland. "Recherches sur les syndicats d'officiers pendant la Fronde." *XVIIᵉ Siècle* 42–43 (1959): 76–117.

Ozanam, D. "Etat moderne et Croquants." *Bibliothèque de l'Ecole des Chartes* 134 (1976): 406–17.

Ranum, Orest. "L'argent du roi: pillage populaire et recherche parlementaire pendant la Fronde parisienne." In *La Fronde en questions*, edited by Roger Duchêne et Pierre Ronzeaud, 287–96. Aix-en-Provence: Publications de l'Université de Provence, 1989.

Ranum, Orest. "La 'Colonne' de miliciens bourgeois du faubourg Saint-

Germain pendant le blocus de 1649." In *La France d'Ancien Régime, Etudes réunies en l'honneur de Pierre Goubert*, 615–22. Toulouse: Privat, 1984.

Sawyer, Jeffry. "Judicial Corruption and Legal Reform in Early Seventeenth-Century France." *Law and History Review* 6 (1988): 95–117.

Stocker, Christopher. "Party, Clientage and Lineage in the Fifteenth-Century Parlement of Paris." *Proceedings of the Western Society for French History* 13 (1986): 10–20.

Vance, S. "Retz's Narration of the Monstrous Body of History." In *Biblio 17, Papers on Seventeenth-Century French Literature*, edited by C. G. S. Williams, 245–57. Paris, Seattle, Tubingen, 1990.

Vernes, S. "Un Frondeur, le Président Viole." *Revue d'histoire diplomatique* 65 (1951): 16–38.

Vicherd, Christine. "Des Raisons idéologiques de l'échec du Parlement de Paris." *La Fronde en questions,* edited by Roger Duchêne and Pierre Ronzeaud, 319–28. Aix-en-Provence: Publications de l'Université de Provence, 1989.

Index

Act of Union (1648), 106–14
  precedents for, 109–10
  Council of State's rejection of,
    112–13
  Council of State's acceptance of,
    118, 119, 121
Agen:
  court of excises at, 226
  in princely Fronde, 321
aides, see excise taxes; wine taxes
Aix-en-Provence, Parlement of, 34,
    176, 233
Aix-en-Provence and Provence, 12,
    34, 35, 36, 54, 176–77, 223,
    239, 240, 311, 316, 329, 354
Alais, Governor, 176, 223, 233, 239,
    329
Angers:
  as proposed Estates-General site,
    297
  Frondeur princes supported by,
    321
Anjou, Philip, Duke of, 82, 247
Anne of Austria, Queen Regent of
    France, 5, 22
  regency powers of, 18, 19, 46–49,
    95–96, 226, 333
  Mazarin's relationship with, 20,
    118, 119, 309
  Louis XIV's relationship with, 20–
    21
  personality of, 20–21
  Louis XIII's relationship with, 46,
    47
  observers of, 53
  Talon and, 54, 78, 89

addressed by the "people," 54–55
and Parlement's link to the "peo-
    ple," 57
alleged gift to Retz from, 79
and tax proposals of 1648, 84,
    91–92, 93
and troop deployment of 1648, 90
in lit de justice of 14 January 1648,
    91–92
masters of requests confronted by,
    93
and legal status of lit de justice, 96–
    97
courts' union and, 104, 106, 109,
    110, 112–13, 121
Parlement of Paris summoned by,
    112–13
and compromise efforts after Act
    of Union, 115–24, 133, 139,
    141, 142
on St. John's Day of 1648, 120–21
D'Hemery removed by, 126
in lit de justice of 31 July 1648, 141
and judges' debates after lit de jus-
    tice, 145, 150
in Te Deum of 26 August 1648,
    152
and Day of the Barricades, 157–
    59, 160–62, 164, 165, 167, 344
and judges' continued debates
    after Broussel's release, 170
and military move on Paris, 180
Fronde-controlled Paris and, 182–
    83, 184, 186, 187, 195
in negotiations to open Paris, 208,
    209

Anne of Austria (*continued*)
  return of, to Paris (1649), 213–14
  Bordeaux Fronde and, 240, 277
  and arrest of the princes, 242,
    273, 277, 279–81
  on provincial visits, 243, 247, 274,
    277
  Princess de Condé exiled by, 245
  and power struggles after Condé's
    release, 255, 283–88
  Richon's execution ordered by,
    276
  rumored removal of, 279
  and debate on Estates-General,
    296, 297
  assembly of nobles ignored by,
    299
  Paris left by, 301
  Retz's declining influence with,
    301
  princely Fronde and, 301, 305,
    308, 309, 313, 321, 326, 336
  and princes' efforts against Maza-
    rin, 305
  and symbols of royal authority,
    308
  Gaston's early support of, 312
  and power to create marshals, 318
  Mazarin's exile and, 336
  Retz's return accepted by, 336
  Fronde's effect on, 347
annual fees (*droits annuels; Paulette*):
  explanation of, 86–87
  controversy over renewal of, 104,
    106–7, 108, 110, 140, 141
  origin of, 134
"appeal," uses of term, 69–70
Argenson, René Voyer d', 230, 231,
    232, 239
Aristotle, 46
arrest of the princes, 242, 243, 246,
    271–74, 277, 278–81, 312–13
Arsenal of Paris, 186–87, 195, 211
Articles of Union (1652), 259–62
assembly of nobles, 13, 297–99

Bachaumont, Judge, 183
Bailleul, President, 161
Balthazar, Jean, 305

Barillon, President, 73, 99
  popularity of, 79–80
Bastille:
  control of, 183, 186, 211
  fighting near, 326–29
Bayard, Françoise, 351
Beaufort, Duke de, 13
  in Parisian Fronde, 193, 198, 211,
    212, 239–40, 315–16
  and parlementary factionalism of
    late 1649, 241
  in princely Fronde, 311, 320, 322,
    323, 326, 330, 332, 333, 338,
    340, 341
  Nemours killed in duel with, 323,
    334
beggars and *marginaux*, 33–34, 58
Bellegarde, royal visit to, 275–76
Bénichou, Paul, 351
Bercé, Yves-Marie, 351
Bernac, Judge, 263–64
Berry, Condé as governor of, 286
bibliographic essay, 349–63
Bitaut, Judge, 320
Blancmesnil, President, 346
  and courts' Act of Union, 109,
    110, 112
  and parlementaires linked to
    king's debt, 131
  arrest of, 153, 161, 169
Bléneau, battle of, 323
Blois, ordonnance of, 137
bonds, *see rentes*
Bordeaux and Guienne, 329
  crop failures in, 11
  Fronde in, 14, 34, 36, 215–16, 226–
    41, 244–47, 272–74, 276–77
  military threat against, 176–77,
    226–33, 243
  risk of revolution in, 176–78
  description of, 215–21
  taxes in, 216, 218–20, 222–27,
    248, 250–51, 267
  riots and pillaging in, 216, 224–
    25, 232, 238
  food supplies in, 216–17, 227,
    238, 267
  popular participation in Fronde
    in, 216–17, 228–35, 244–47

elites in, 218
merchants in, 218, 221, 222
unrest in, before Fronde, 221–25
Condé as governor of, 224, 249, 255, 260, 286
Fronde in Paris vs., 232, 238
blockade of, 233–40
taxes for defense of, 236–38, 239
Épernon's 1649 negotiations with, 238, 239
amnesty in, 242
royal visit to, 243, 275
renewed civil war in, 244, 245–47
Council of State's enemies welcomed into, 245–47
in peace settlement of 1650, 247
Condé's control of, 309, 313
princely Fronde in, 309, 313
weariness with Fronde in, 311
see also jurade; Ormée, Ormistes; Parlement of Bordeaux
Bordeaux military forces, 238
Bordeaux militia companies, 223, 232
buildup of, 228–30
during blockade, 233, 234–38
renewed civil war and, 246
Ormée and, 251, 253, 254, 255, 257–58, 267–68
Bouillon, Duke de, 245, 247, 256, 272, 277, 278, 305, 314
Bouillon family, 23
Boullanger, Judge, 132
Bourbon family, rivalry within, 191
bourgeois:
Parisian, 56, 86, 90–91, 155, 159, 324, 337–38, 339; *see also* Parisian militia companies
rentes and, 212, 293
in Bordeaux, 249, 258, 259, 266; *see also* Bordeaux militia companies
see also merchant guilds, merchant class
Bourse of Bordeaux, 233, 234, 237
Bouthillier, Claude, 48–49
bread supplies, in Paris blockade, 197–203
Brittany, Estates of, 238, 319

Brittany, Parlement of, 127
Broussel, Governor (Pierre's son), 105, 186, 328, 341
Broussel, Pierre, 324, 346
papers of, 52
leadership and authority of, 80, 101
and debate on status of *lit de justice,* 95
excise tax debate and, 98–99, 100
description of, 101
Council of State's pressure on, 105
in Act of Union debate, 106–9
intendants attacked by, 123
at Luxembourg Conferences, 128
in debates after *lit de justice* of 31 July 1648, 142–45, 149
arrest and release of, 152–69, 211
popularity of, 169, 344
tax increases opposed by, 169–71
and Parlement of Paris's army mobilization, 180, 183
as governor of the Bastille, 186, 328
and parlementary factionalism of late 1649, 241, 242
as provost of merchants, 332, 337, 338
on Gaston's special council, 333
political perspective lacked by, 339
Bullion, Claude, 75, 77, 79
Burgundy:
royal visit to, 243, 275–76
Condé as governor of, 286

Cadau (merchant), 57
Cadillac, castle of, 227, 238
Candale, Duke de, 268
Carrier, Hubert, 351–52
Castan, Yves, 352
Catelan, François, 149
Catherine de Medici, 275
Catholic Church, Catholicism:
limited Fronde role of, 13
and Parlement of Paris, 16, 59, 63–67
interest payment denounced by, 40
thanksgiving services in, 42, 66, 150, 152–54

Catholic Church (*continued*)
  royal authority and, 84
  Protestant rights and, 109
  in Bordeaux, 217, 259–62, 267,
    268
  and arrest of the princes, 279
  and Hôtel de Ville assembly of
    4 July 1652, 330
Cayrac, Pierre, 228–30, 232
Chamber of Accounts, 7, 15, 18, 93,
    101–3, 106, 107, 142, 208, 293,
    330
Chamber of the Edict, 62–63, 108–9
chambre de justice, 38–39
Chambreret, Benjamin, 234
Champagne, 34, 286
Champlâtreux, Colonel, 155, 289
Charenton, Condé's attack on, 206,
    207, 344
Charles I, King of England, 83, 341
Charmeil, Jean-Paul, 352
Charton, President, 153
Châteauneuf, Marquis de, 285, 301,
    309, 319
  strategy of, in princely Fronde,
    321, 322
  resignation of, 322
Chavigny, Léon Bouthillier, Count
    de, 21, 22, 48
  Richelieu and, 46
  repression of judges advocated by,
    151–52
  return of, to Council of State,
    284–85, 286–87, 309
  Mazarin challenged by, 322
  on Gaston's special council, 333
Chéruel, Adolphe, 349
Chevreuse, Duchess de, 283, 285–86
city councillors of Paris (Hôtel de
    Ville):
  and troop deployment of 1648, 90
  in Fronde-controlled Paris, 185–
    87, 190, 205, 208, 238
  rentes administration and, 190,
    290, 294
  Parlement of Paris's control over,
    238, 327
  during princely Fronde, 327, 329,
    330, 332, 337–39

  elections of 1652 for, 337–39
civil rights, 136–39, 171
civil war, revolution vs., 310
Clanleu, Bertrand de, 207
class and social status, 9, 148–49
Colbert, Jean-Baptiste, 294, 319
Coligny, Count de, 273–74
Colombel, Sieur, 74–76
Compiègne:
  in war with Spain, 276
  court at, 335
compoix, 26, 29
Concini, Concino, 78, 114
Condé, Charlotte de Montmorency,
    Princess de (Grand Condé's
    mother), 244–45, 274
Condé, Claire-Clémence de Maillé-
    Brézé, Princess de (Grand
    Condé's wife), 244–45, 246–47,
    256, 268, 269, 271, 277
  house arrest of, 274
  illness of, 334
Condé, Henri II de Bourbon, Prince
    de (Grand Condé's father), 19,
    22, 179, 244, 283, 313
  Louis XIII's last will and, 46
  Anne's full powers accepted by, 47
  new judgeships advocated by, 74–
    76
  in Estates-General of 1614, 296
Condé, Louis II de Bourbon, Prince
    de (Grand Condé), 13, 17, 19,
    192, 196, 346
  reasons for revolt of, 22
  Mazarin and, 22, 113, 134, 179,
    241, 255, 271, 272, 306, 307
  and tax proposals of 1648, 85, 87
  with army in North, 85, 177, 179,
    203–4, 210
  and compromise efforts after Act
    of Union, 118
  Lens victory of, 146, 150, 152–53
  and threat of Paris blockade, 150–
    51, 176, 180
  political stature of, 179
  Paris blockaded by, 197–211, 314
  Charenton captured by, 206, 207,
    334
  in negotiations to open Paris, 210

and end of Paris blockade, 210,
    213
as Guienne governor, 224, 249,
    255, 260, 286
Louis XIII's death and, 226
sovereignty in Southwest sought
    by, 240, 242
Bordeaux Fronde and, 240, 242,
    244, 273, 276
and parlementary factionalism in
    late 1649, 241
arrest of, 242, 243, 246, 271–74,
    277, 278–81, 312–13
rebel supporters of, 245
Ormée and, 249, 252, 253, 255–
    58, 260, 266, 267, 269
Spanish alliance of, 255, 256–57,
    305, 306, 319, 341
character of, 273, 311, 315, 323,
    344, 345–46
princely Fronde and, 273–90,
    296–340
release of, 281
in power struggles after his
    release, 282–90
conspiracies feared by, 286
governorships of Burgundy and
    Berry acquired by, 286
royal charges against, 287, 306
and debate on Estates-General,
    296, 297
assembly of nobles cultivated by,
    297
final efforts at compromise with,
    299–300
Louis XIV's majority *lit de justice*
    avoided by, 300
Parisians' fear of, 310–11
on force and public opinion, 314
Mazarin's army and, 317, 318,
    322–23
financial situation of, 319–20, 334
at battle of Bléneau, 323
in fighting near Paris, 323–29
at battle of Faubourg Saint-
    Antoine, 326–29
and Hôtel de Ville assembly of
    4 July 1652, 329–32
assessment of, 344–45

officers' relationship with, 345–46
pardon of, 347
Condé family, 23, 188, 224, 244
Conspiracy of Fiesque (Retz), 175
Contarini (Mazarin's banker), 195
Conti, Prince de, 141, 272, 317, 319,
    346
    Parisian Fronde forces com-
        manded by, 189–90, 192–93,
        196, 198–99, 206, 207, 209,
        210
    arrested with Condé and Longue-
        ville, 242, 243, 246, 271–74,
        277, 278–81, 312–13
    Ormée supported by, 252, 253,
        255, 256, 265, 267, 268–69
    Bordeaux Fronde and, 277
convoy, 219, 222, 236
Corbeil, Frondeurs' aborted march
    on, 198, 206, 207
Corbeville, Judge, 97–98
Cosnac, Daniel de, 265–66
Council of State, 7, 16–17
    master of requests' administrative
        link to, 15
    membership of, 18–22, 118, 232
    tax amounts fixed by, 28–29, 35,
        70
    wartime tax collection and, 38
    Louis XIII's last will on powers of,
        46–47
    power struggles on, after Louis
        XIII's death, 48–49
    as advisor to king, 67
    appeals to, 68
    and contracts for royal offices, 72,
        87
    parlementaires exiled by (1635),
        74
    Gaston's marriage annulled by, 75
    enrichment of members of, 82
    courts' growing solidarity against,
        82–114
    and tax proposals of 1648, 83–85,
        87, 91
    and troop deployment of 1648,
        89–91
    and debate on status of *lit de jus-
        tice*, 95, 96–97

Council of State (*continued*)
 Chamber of Accounts in conflict
  with, 101–3
 annual fees and, 106, 108, 110
 and courts' Act of Union, 106–
  14
 and compromise efforts after Act
  of Union, 115–21
 on royal authority, 119
 Parlement of Paris's measures
  curbing power of, 121–40
 D'Hemery's disgrace and, 127–28
 judges' debate of remonstrance to,
  142–46
 and Parlement of Paris's debates
  after *lit de justice* of 31 July
  1648, 142–51
 Spain policy of, 150–51
 repression of judges by, 151–63,
  165, 168
 and Day of the Barricades, 164,
  165
 and judges' continued debates
  after Broussel's release, 169–70
 provincial challenges to, 176
 Parlement of Paris ordered to
  leave Paris by, 187
 and Fronde control of Paris, 196,
  198, 203, 207, 208–9
 Bordeaux and, 222, 230, 240, 242,
  260
 provinces loyal to, 238–39
 increasing authority of, 244
 Condé's conflict with, 255
 Ormée and, 260
 and provincial trips, 275
 consolidation of power of, 278
 power struggles on, after Condé's
  release, 281–90
 proposed reform of, 283
 rentier protests and, 290–91
 and debate on Estates-General,
  300
 princely Fronde and, 321, 322,
  326, 331, 332, 341
 Fronde's effect on, 345
Courrier Bordelois, 254, 262
Court of Excises of Agen, 226

Court of Excises of Libourne, 226
Court of Excises of Paris, 7, 15, 18,
 106, 107, 142, 208
 arrest of judges of, 137
 rentier protests and, 293
 at Hôtel de Ville assembly of
  4 July 1652, 330
courts:
 combined meetings of, *see* St.
  Louis Chamber meetings
 move to union among, 15–18,
  82–114
 cancellation of *gages* of, 106–10,
  112, 122, 147, 291
 prerogatives of, 107
 measures to reduce Council of
  State's power debated in, 121–
  40
 legal and civil rights debated in,
  136–39
 lit de justice sanctioning reforms of,
  140–42
 in debates after *lit de justice* of
  31 July 1648, 142–51, 169
 Council of State's repression of,
  151–63
 in debates after Broussel's release,
  170–71
 see also specific courts
Cromwell, Oliver, 258, 267, 305
Cudos, château of, burning of, 264

dancing, 26
Davis, Natalie Zemon, 352
Day of the Barricades (1588), 89–90
Day of the Barricades (1648), 148,
 151, 153–71, 344
 return of property stolen on, 160,
  166
 looting feared in, 164–68
 explanations of, 164–69
Day of the Dupes, 247
Declaration of 24 October 1648,
 169–71, 211
Descimon, Robert, 352
Deslandes-Payen, Councillor, 180–
 81, 183, 206, 279
Desroches, Colonel, 155

Dessert, Daniel, 350
Dethan, Georges, 352
Dijon, royal visit to, 243, 244
droits annuels, see annual fees
Drouet, Governor, 341
Dureteste, Christophe, 250, 261, 262, 263, 265, 268, 269, 346
Dutch Protestants, 39

Eaubonne, Judge, 73
échevins, 182, 186, 190
    rentier protests and, 293
    during princely Fronde, 325, 327, 330, 332
Elbeuf, Duke d', 188–89, 192–93, 196, 204, 206
Enghien, Duke d' (Grand Condé's son), 244, 246, 247, 256, 268, 269, 271
England:
    civil war in, 83
    Ormée appeal to, 258, 267, 272
    French alliance with, 305
Épernon, Bernard de Nogaret, Duke d', 176, 223–24, 252, 329
    military buildup of, 226–33
    Bordeaux blockaded by, 233–40
    dismissal of, 242, 246, 255
    renewed pressure on Bordeaux by, 243, 245, 248
Épernon, Jean-Louis de Nogaret, Duke d', 223–24, 228
Erlach, Sigismond d', 157, 180
Estates-General, call for, 13, 107, 283, 284, 295–97, 300–301
Estates-General of 1614, 68, 295–96
Estrées, Gabrielle d', 315
Étampes, brief siege of, 326
excise taxes *(aides)*, 27, 293
    system of, 36–38, 41
    proposed increases in, 86
    debated in Parlement of Paris, 98–100
    rentes paid from, 140, 212
    and Declaration of 24 October 1648, 170
    in Bordeaux, 218
exemplary punishment, 31

Fabert, Isaac, 317
Faubourg Saint-Antoine, battle of, 326–29
Festival of the Three Kings (1649), 182–83
festivals, 25–26, 120–21, 182–83
Filhot, Jacques, 264, 265–66
floods (1648–1649), 41, 83, 198
Fonteneil, Jacques, 230–31, 235, 237, 239
foodstuffs tax, *see* excise taxes
food supplies:
    in Paris, 58, 197–203
    in Bordeaux, 216–17, 227, 238, 267
Foucault, Judge, 73
Foucquet, Abbé, 317
franc alleu, 86
Francis I, King of France, 250
French political culture, 242, 346
Fronde:
    in Bordeaux, *see* Bordeaux and Guienne; Ormée, Ormistes
    in Paris, *see* Paris; Parlement of Paris
    of Princes, *see* princely Fronde
    meaning of word, 5, 52
    actors participating in, 9–23
    centers of, 34–36, 176
    historical imagination and, 49–50
    beginning point of, 121
    reasons for end of, 304
    assessment of, 343–47
    bibliographic essay on, 349–63
Fronde, La (Kossman), 349–50
Fronde des Mots, La (Jouhaud), 353
"Fronde des Princes . . . , La" (Jacquart), 353

gabelle (salt tax), 27, 170, 218, 291, 293
gages, cancellation of, 106–10, 112, 122, 147, 291
Gaston, Duke d'Orléans, 17, 19, 22, 112, 346
    and assembly of nobles, 13, 298, 299

Gaston, Duke d'Orléans (*continued*)
    in plots against Louis XIII, 19, 46,
        48, 85, 312
    Louis XIII's death and, 46, 48,
        226
    Anne's full powers accepted by, 47
    addressed by the "people," 54–55
    annulment of marriage of, 75, 79
    Le Coigneux's relationship with,
        78, 95, 131, 143, 144, 183
    Louis XIV's smallpox and, 82
    and tax proposals of 1648, 84–86,
        87, 92
    as political intermediary, 85–86
    in *lit de justice* of 14 January 1648,
        91
    at Chamber of Accounts, 102, 103
    Mazarin's relationship with, 113
    Luxembourg Conferences orga-
        nized by, 115, 116–20, 124–26,
        128–30, 133, 135, 139, 170,
        312
    compromise efforts of, after Act
        of Union, 115, 116–20, 124–30,
        133–36, 139–41, 312
    Parlement of Paris's *taille* debate
        and, 130
    betrayal by judges seen by, 133–
        34
    and special court for tax farmers,
        135–36
    lettres de cachet defended by, 137
    curbs on arbitrary arrests accepted
        by, 139
    and debates after *lit de justice* of
        31 July 1648, 143, 145, 146
    Broussel's release and, 161
    and Louis XIV's flight, 184
    and Fronde control of Paris, 187,
        196
    in negotiations to open Paris, 208,
        209
    and parlementary factionalism of
        late 1649, 241
    Bordeaux Fronde and, 242
    and arrest of the princes, 242,
        273, 278, 280, 281, 312–13
    Anne's rumored removal and,
        279

    and support from militia, 279,
        280, 286, 305, 309, 325, 332
    and power struggles after Condé's
        release, 281, 283, 284, 286, 287,
        288, 290
    seizure of *rentes* interest by, 294
    and debate on Estates-General,
        296, 297, 300, 301
    princely Fronde and, 299–340
    new army raised by, 301
    in continuing power struggles,
        302
    Mazarin demonized by, 306–7
    assessment of role of, 312–13
    Lorraine brought to Paris by, 325
    Saint-Antoine gates ordered open
        by, 328, 329
    and Hôtel de Ville assembly of
        4 July 1652, 329–32
    special council of, 332–33, 334
    Séguier's flight hindered by, 335
    and city elections of 1652, 338
    Dethan on, 352
Gay, Father, 231
Germany, war in, 82–83, 303, 304,
        315
grain trade, 211–12
    in Bordeaux, 216–17
Grande Mademoiselle, *see* Montpen-
        sier, Anne-Marie-Louise
        d'Orléans, 320, 321, 328, 341
Great Chamber, *see* Parlement of
        Paris
Great Council, 7, 15, 106, 107
Grenoble, 36
Guienne, *see* Bordeaux and
        Guienne; Parlement of Bor-
        deaux

Hâ, Château du, 228, 255
Hanley, Sarah, 352–53
Hapsburgs, 82–83, 85, 303
Hapsburg-Valois wars, 222
Harcourt, Count d', 164, 321, 322,
        345
Hemery, Particelli d', 19–20, 22
    fund-raising proposals of, 19–20,
        43–44

disgrace of, 20, 21, 22, 126–27
appointed to Council of State, 49
financial dealings of, 49, 55, 132–33
mob's threats against house of, 57, 90
and contracts for royal offices, 72
and tax proposals of 1648, 83–88, 104–6
and troop deployment of 1648, 90
and *lit de justice* of 14 January 1648, 93
Parlement of Paris pressured by, 104–6
annual fees granted by, 106
and courts' move to union, 107, 108, 109, 112
and compromise efforts after Act of Union, 117, 118
Henrietta Maria, Queen of England, 161, 341
Henry III, King of France, 89, 286
Henry IV, King of France, 23, 62, 110, 134, 247, 313, 315
and venality of office, 71–72
Hervart, Barthélemy, 319
Histoire de France pendant la Minorité de Louis XIV (Chéruel), 349
Histoire des Croquants (Bercé), 351
historical imaginations, 49–50
History of the Revolution in France, The (Priorato), 9
Hocquincourt, Charles de Monchy d', 304, 318, 322, 324–25, 345
at Bléneau, 323
Hodic, Judge, 143
Honnêtetés et relations sociales en Languedoc au XVIIIe siècle (Castan), 352
Hôtel de Ville of Bordeaux:
Épernon's defeat at, 235
Ormée and control of, 249, 254, 264, 269
see also jurade
Hôtel de Ville of Paris:
assembly at (4 July 1652), 330–33
attack on, 331–33, 344
see also city councillors of Paris
House of Commons, 67

Inquests subchamber of Parlement of Paris, 59, 61, 73, 78, 104, 105, 130, 181, 202
intendants of justice and finance, 30–32
Parlement of Paris and status of, 31, 35, 99, 122, 123, 125, 130, 133, 135, 140, 227, 228
in Bordeaux region, 222
Italians, French xenophobia about, 21, 132–33, 274, 306–7
Italy:
political analysis in, 9
war with, 29

Jacquart, Jean, 353
Jews, 261
Joseph, Father, 186
Jouhaud, Christian, 353
judges, *see* courts; Robe families
Judicial Politics and Urban Revolt in Seventeenth-Century France (Kettering), 353
jurade, 248
before Fronde, 218, 219–20, 222–23
selection of, 219–20, 222–23
in escalating conflict with Épernon, 228–31
in blockade of Bordeaux, 234–39
revenue raising by, 236
collapse of authority of, 244
Ormée and, 254, 259, 265

Kettering, Sharon, 353
Kossman, Ernst, 349–50

La Brède, château of, burning of, 264
La Ferté-Senneterre, Duke de, 318, 334
Laffemas, Isaac de, 31, 88
Lainé (or Laisné), Judge, 73, 108, 143
La Meilleraie, Marshal de, 127, 128, 129
on Day of the Barricades, 157–58, 160
Bordeaux attacked by, 245–46

Lamoignon, Colonel, 199, 200, 201
landownership, taxation and, 26–27, 29, 86
Languedoc, 311, 313, 321, 352
Languedoc, Estates of, 238, 319
la Roche, Judge de, 254
La Rochefoucauld, Duke de, 245, 247, 256, 277, 288, 317
La Rochefoucauld family, 12
La Tour d'Auvergne family, 314
La Trémouille, Duke de, 317
La Trémouille family, 12
La Vieuville, Duke de, 301, 308, 319
Lavye, Advocate General, 232
Le Coigneux, President:
  Gaston's relationship with, 78, 95, 131, 143, 144, 183
  tax-farmer ties of, 80, 131
  and debate on status of *lit de justice*, 95, 97, 98
  in debate after *lit de justice* of 31 July 1648, 143–44
  on Day of the Barricades, 162
  in Fronde-controlled Paris, 183–84, 198, 208
Le Febvre, Judge, 73
Le Havre, princes' detention in, 279, 280–81
Le Jay, President, 61
Le Meunier, Judge, 98
Lenet, Pierre, 253, 255, 258, 262, 265–68, 272, 284, 391
Lens, French victory at, 146, 150, 152–53
Le Tellier, Michel:
  D'Hemery's disgrace and, 126
  military affairs and, 177–78, 203, 283, 308, 315, 317, 345
  as Retz's ally, 281
  removed from Council of State, 284, 286
  lettres de cachet, 136–37, 138, 152, 171
  parlementaires' arrest ordered in, 73
  acceptance of new judges ordered in, 75
L'Hôpital, Governor, 341

Libourne, court of excises at, 226
Libourne, fortifications at, 227, 228, 231, 234, 239
  Bordeaux troops' attack on, 234, 235
Limousin, 11
Lionne, Hugues de, 281, 284
Lit de Justice, The (Hanley), 352–53
lits de justice, 59, 60, 66
  traditional limited use of, 17
  Anne accorded regency powers in (15 May 1643), 47
  new judgeships in Parlement of Paris created by (10 December 1635), 72–73
  and tax proposals of 1648, 88, 91–92
  evolving nature of, 91, 94
  tax measures imposed in (14 January 1648), 91–92
  debate on status of, 92–101
  Parlement of Paris's reforms accepted in (31 July 1648), 133, 136, 139, 140–42, 169, 211
  judges' debates on, 145–46, 169
  agreed to, in accords of Saint-Germain-en-Laye, 210
  Louis XIV's majority marked in (7 September 1651), 300
Loire Valley:
  as proposed site of Estates-General, 296
  Mazarin's army in, 320, 322
Longueil, Judge, 208
Longueville, Anne-Geneviève, Duchess de, 192, 195–96, 240, 317
  Ormée supported by, 252, 256, 266, 268, 269
  house arrest of, 274, 312–13
  estranged from husband, 317
Longueville, Duke de, 189, 192, 240, 316–17
  arrested with Condé and Conti, 242, 243, 246, 271–74, 278–81, 312–13
  estranged from wife, 317

Longueville family, 23
Lorraine, Duke de, 311, 324–26
Louis XIII, King of France:
  death of, 8, 47, 55, 225
  reliance of, on Richelieu, 19
  Gaston's conspiracies against, 19,
    46, 48, 85, 312
  Anne's relationship with, 19–20,
    46, 47
  Mazarin's relationship with, 20,
    48
  tax increases under, 30
  and war with Spain, 44
  last will of, 46–47, 70, 96, 138,
    225–26
  and increased royal authority, 46–
    48, 51, 63, 70, 312, 313
  rumored poisoning of, 55
  new judgeships in Parlement of
    Paris created by, 60, 72–78
  dueling commissions created by,
    64
  Concini "executed" by, 78
  Barillon exiled by, 80
  lit de justice and, 94
  trials brought before Parlement of
    Paris by, 116
  royal ordonnances violated by,
    137
  Parlement of Paris's promises
    questioned by, 138
  Bordeaux and, 221, 225
  early reign of, 244, 297
Louis XIV, King of France, 5, 16–
    17, 18
  accession of, 19
  Mazarin's relationship with, 20
  personality of, 20
  Anne's relationship with, 20–21
  smallpox of, 82
  in *lit de justice* of 14 January 1648,
    91
  and courts' Act of Union, 113
  on St. John's Day of 1648, 120
  in *lit de justice* of 31 July 1648, 141
  in *Te Deum* of 26 August 1648,
    152
  judges' loyalty to, 181

and Fronde-controlled Paris, 182–
    83, 184, 187, 188, 195
  return of, to Paris (1649), 213–14
  Bordeaux and, 221, 277
  on provincial visits, 243, 244, 247,
    274–76, 277
  Ormée and, 260
  and arrest of the princes, 273
  security concerns for, 280, 296
  majority of, 289–90, 300–302,
    311–12, 314, 333
  and debate on Estates-General,
    297
  in *lit de justice* of 7 September
    1651, 300
  new councillors appointed by, 301
  in Southwest, 301
  military discipline improved by,
    305
  and princes' efforts against Maza-
    rin, 305
  symbols of royal authority
    defended by, 308
  and Mazarin's army, 317, 318–19
  growing authority of, 322, 326,
    336
  Mazarin's exile accepted by, 335–
    36
  Retz's return accepted by, 336
  return of, to Paris (1652), 340,
    341
  Fronde's effect on, 346, 347
Luxembourg Conferences (1648),
    115, 116–20, 124–26, 128–30,
    133, 135, 139, 170, 312
Lyon, Fronde absent in, 14, 36

Maisons, President, 212, 290, 333
Manifeste des Bourdelais, 240, 250–52,
    259, 265
Marchin, Count de, 253, 256
marginaux and beggars, 33–34, 58
Marie de Medici, 78, 180, 244, 275,
    296, 297
Marillac, Chancellor, 222
marriage alliances, 283, 285, 316
Marseilles, rebellion in, 346

masters of requests:
responsibilities of, 15
work stoppage of, 15, 35, 93
proposed increase in number of,
17, 86–89, 93, 100, 104, 140,
193–94, 227, 292
law on inheritance of offices of,
72
Parlement of Paris in solidarity
with, 87–88, 103
Council of State's tactics against,
96–97, 109
and Hôtel de Ville assembly of
4 July 1652, 330
Mazarin, Jules Cardinal, 22, 57, 212,
224
background and personality of,
20
Louis XIV's relationship with, 20
Richelieu and, 20, 46
Louis XIII's relationship with, 20,
48
Anne's relationship with, 20, 118,
119, 309
anti-Italian sentiment directed
against, 21, 274, 306–7
Condé and, 22, 113, 134, 179,
241, 255, 271, 272, 306
and war with Spain, 22, 134, 150,
177, 192, 208–9, 304, 305, 307
D'Hemery's support of, 49
physical appearance of, 51
damage to stables of, 51, 52
public opinion and, 52–53, 201,
214, 273
Talon courted by, 78, 113–14
and tax proposals of 1648, 85, 87,
88, 92, 105
in *lit de justice* of 14 January 1648,
91
Talon's speech criticized by, 92
and debate on status of *lit de justice,* 96
and courts' Act of Union, 109
death threats against, 114
and compromise efforts after Act
of Union, 118, 119
visible role eschewed by, 127
money allegedly sent to Italy by,
132
and Parlement of Paris's reform
efforts, 133
in *lit de justice* of 31 July 1648,
141
and judges' debates after *lit de justice,* 145
challenges to power of, 151–52
Broussel's release and, 161
and Day of the Barricades, 164
Parlement of Paris efforts against,
170, 184–85, 193, 195, 210,
211, 284, 301–2, 306, 307, 308,
319, 320, 324, 325
revolution viewed as unlikely by,
176
and negotiations with Spain, 177,
192, 208–9
and provincial parlements' revolt,
177
and blockade of Paris, 180, 201,
203, 207, 208, 314
Elbeuf and, 188
parlementary supporters of, 193–
94
in negotiations to open Paris, 202,
209, 210
and non-payment of *rentes,* 212
return of, to Paris, 213–14
Bordeaux Fronde and, 239, 240,
242, 273, 277
and parlementary factionalism of
late 1649, 241, 242
and arrest of the princes, 242,
246, 272–74, 278, 279, 280–81
on provincial visits, 243, 274–
76
Princess de Condé exiled by, 245
Ormée and, 255, 259
Cromwell and, 259
Bordeaux supporters of, 263–64,
267, 268
princely Fronde and, 271, 276–
79, 281, 283–86, 290, 299, 304–
11, 317–26, 335–36, 339
Bellegarde surrender negotiated
by, 276

and military response to princely
Fronde, 278, 318–26
departure of, from Paris, 280
rumored seizure of *rentes* interest
by, 294, 319
and debate on Estates-General,
296, 297
Gaston's hostility toward, 305, 313
attempted disgrace of, 306–8, 313
exiles of, 308–9
troops raised by, 317–19, 336
and power to create marshals, 318
Lorraine paid off by, 324–25
political acumen of, 325, 345
second exile of, 335–36
Chéruel on, 349
Dethan on, 352
Mazarinades, 175–76, 201–2, 243,
262, 263, 280, 292, 307, 324,
325
Mazarinades, Les (Carrier), 351–52
Mêmes, President de, 141, 343
and debate on status of *lit de justice*, 94–95, 97
courts' union favored by, 109
and parlementaires linked to
king's debt, 131
Broussel's release and, 161, 162
in Fronde-controlled Paris, 185,
193
Mazarin's removal advocated by,
306
Mémoires (Retz), 101, 351
memoirs, of Fronde participants,
346–47
Merchant Committee, 239
merchant guilds, merchant class,
163, 170–71
in appeal against forced loans, 55
tax proposals of 1648 opposed by,
86
and troop deployment of 1648,
90–91
Anne's courting of, 121
and Day of the Barricades, 148–
49
in Fronde-controlled Paris, 199
and *rentes*, 212

king's return requested by, 213
in Bordeaux, 218, 221, 222, 233,
234, 237
in Ormée, 266, 267
in princely Fronde, 282, 325
and Hôtel de Ville assembly of
4 July 1652, 330
see also provost of merchants
Mercoeur, Duke de, 316
Metz, 335–36
militia, *see* Bordeaux militia companies; Parisian militia companies
Molé, Mathieu, 127, 141, 155
description of, 61–62
as Keeper of the Seals, 77, 285,
301, 335, 336, 340
during Marie de Medici's regency,
78
masters of requests' cause
accepted by, 88
and debate on status of *lit de justice*, 94, 97
as spokesman of Parlement of
Paris, 102
and courts' move to union, 102,
104–5
Nicolaï and, 103
general assemblies avoided by,
104–5
and compromise efforts after Act
of Union, 117
and parlementaires linked to
king's debt, 131–32
in *lit de justice* of 31 July 1648, 136,
140
in debates after *lit de justice*, 143,
146
Broussel's release and, 160–64,
165–66
in Fronde-controlled Paris, 183,
185, 189–91, 194, 197, 198,
208
and parlementary factionalism of
late 1649, 241, 242
and arrest of the princes, 279–80,
281
and power struggles after Condé's
release, 284, 285, 289, 302

Molé, Mathieu (*continued*)
  Mazarin's removal advocated by,
    306
monarchy, power of, *see* royal
  authority
monasteries:
  in Fronde-controlled Paris, 203
  in Bordeaux, 217, 267
*Monde des Financiers au XVIIe siècle,
  Le* (Bayard), 351
Montargis, Parlement of Paris
  ordered to, 187, 196
Montbazon, Governor, 55, 184
Montesquieu, Judge, 263–64
Montpensier, Anne-Marie-Louise
  d'Orléans, 320, 321, 328, 341
Montrésor, Count de, 298
Montrond, fortification at, 255, 301,
    309, 322
  fall of, 334
Moote, A. L., 350
Morales du Grand Siècle (Bénichou),
    351
Motteville, Madame de, 80
Moulins, ordonnance of, 137
Mousnier, Roland, 350–51
*Mouvements insurrectionnels de Pro-
  vence entre 1596 et 1715, Les*
  (Pillorget), 354

Nemours, Duke de, 311, 320, 322,
    326
  killed in duel with Beaufort, 323,
    334
Nesmond, President de, 198, 208,
    279, 333, 337
Netherlands, 82, 304
Nicolaï, President, 101–3
nobles:
  in rural areas, 11–13
  daily life of, 26
  and Parlement of Paris, 64–65
  political activities of, 209–10
Normandy, 11, 35
  "Nu-pieds" Revolt in, 13, 44, 45,
    225
  royal visit to, 243, 275
  princely Fronde and, 311, 316–17

Novion, President, 99, 100, 129
"Nu-pieds" (Normandy) Revolt, 13,
    44, 45, 225

offices, sale of, *see* sale of offices
Ondedei (Mazarin's ally), 281
"130," 230, 231, 232–33, 236
Orange-Nassau house, 314
Orléans, Duchess d', 324
Orléans, Frondeur loyalties in, 321
Orléans, Gaston, Duke d', *see* Gaston, Duke d'Orléans
Orléans, ordonnance of, 137
Ormée, Ormistes, 225, 229, 230,
    232, 244, 248–70, 284, 325
  manifesto of, 240, 250–51, 259,
    265
  placards and pamphlets in, 240,
    250–51, 265, 269
  iconography of, 251
  reformist program of, 252, 259–
    62, 266–67, 269–70
  English support sought by, 258–
    59
  social composition of, 263, 266
  demise of, 268–70
  limited perspective of participants
    in, 271–72
Ormée of Bordeaux, The, 354

Palais de Justice, 58–60
  storming of, 57–58
  royal guards repulsed from, 154,
    159, 165
  see also Parlement of Paris; St.
    Louis Chamber meetings
Palluau, Count de, 318, 334
pamphlets, 52–53, 54, 76–77
  Richelieu's use of, 51
  Mazarinades, 175–76, 201–2, 243,
    262, 263, 280, 292, 307, 324,
    325
  in Bordeaux, 217, 240, 250–51,
    262, 263, 265, 269
  in princely Fronde, 280, 307, 314,
    318, 324, 325
  in *rentier* protests, 291, 292

frustration over prolonged crisis
expressed in, 299
Paris:
seventeenth-century drawings of,
32–33
looting prevented in, 34, 57, 160,
164–68, 199
beggars in, 34, 58
flooding in, 41, 83, 198
rumors in, 41–42, 54
fear of Spanish blockade in, 43
before Fronde, 53–85
food supplies in, 58, 197–203
blockade of, 58, 197–211, 213
location of Palais de Justice in, 58
troops deployed in (1648), 89–91
threat of blockade of, 90–91, 176,
179, 180, 182
Parlement control of, 182–211
flight of rich from, 185
Parlement's negotiations for surrender of, 207–11
Louis XIV's return to (1649), 213
Fronde in Bordeaux vs., 232, 238
frustration over prolonged crisis
expressed in, 299
as proposed Estates-General site,
300
military feared in, 310
weariness with Fronde in, 311
Beaufort and Fronde in, 315–16
military encounters and maneuvers near, 320, 323–29, 340–41
straw cockades worn in, 329, 331–
32, 339
elections in, 337–39
Louis XIV's return to (1652), 341
see also city councillors of Paris;
Day of the Barricades; Parlement of Paris; "people," "poor
people"
Parisian military forces, 204–7
Parlement of Paris and mobilization of, 44, 176, 180–81, 183,
185, 190, 191–92, 193, 196–98,
205, 211, 291
command of, 188–92
payment of, 204

Parisian militia companies:
looting prevented by, 34, 57, 160,
164–68, 199
structure of, 56, 155
in Day of the Barricades, 153–69
judges in, 181
in Fronde-controlled Paris, 182–
83, 184, 193, 200, 204–5, 230
Gaston and support from, 279,
280, 286, 305, 309, 325, 332
during princely Fronde, 280, 282,
286, 305, 309, 325, 328–29,
332, 340
and riots at Palais de Justice in
August 1651, 289
purges of, 325, 332
and Hôtel de Ville assembly of
4 July 1652, 330
Parlement of Aix, 34, 176, 233
Parlement of Bordeaux, 271
troops raised by, 176, 228, 236,
239, 240
before Fronde, 217, 219–22, 224–
25, 226
jurat selection and, 291–20, 222–
23
new judgeships opposed by, 220–
21
in escalating conflict with Épernon, 226–33
during blockade, 234–40
collapse of authority of, 244
Princess de Condé and, 245
noble allies of, 245–47
and renewed civil war, 245–47,
248
Ormée conflicts with, 249, 253,
254, 262–64, 265, 269–70
Parlement of Brittany, 127
Parlement of Paris:
judicial work suspended by, 7–8
membership of, 16, 59–61
and growing solidarity against
Council of State, 16–18, 82–114
Anne granted regency powers by,
19, 47–48, 96, 226, 333
source of authority of, 19
and D'Hemery's tax proposals, 20

Parlement of Paris (*continued*)
   fiscal issues and, 20, 38–39, 54,
      57, 67–68, 98–100, 116–18,
      128–29, 169–71, 292–93, 295
   and status of intendants, 31, 35,
      99, 122, 123, 125, 130, 133,
      135, 140, 227, 228
   tax-collection fraud investigated
      by, 38–39
   troop-raising efforts of, 44, 176,
      180–81, 183, 185, 190–93,
      196–98, 205, 211, 291
   Louis XIII's last will and, 47, 96,
      225–26
   and defense of the "people," 54,
      68, 69–70, 77, 80, 97, 112, 129,
      131, 132, 147, 168, 169, 185,
      280
   militia colonels in, 56
   Palais de Justice as seat of, 57, 58–
      60
   mob's storming of, 57–58
   before Fronde, 58–81
   Catholic Church and, 59, 63–67
   structure and traditions of, 59–61,
      66–68, 104
   Louis XIII's creation of new
      judgeships in, 60, 72–78
   president's role in, 62
   prestige of, 62
   nobles and, 64–65
   dress code of, 66
   pressures and bribes in, 66, 78–
      79, 105, 113–14, 131
   exile of judges of (1635), 73–76
   leadership of, 78–81
   tax farmer links of members of,
      80, 108, 131–32
   and appeals against tax proposals
      of 1648, 85–86
   as political intermediary, 85–86
   renewal of judgeships in, 87
   masters of requests' growing soli-
      darity with, 87–88, 103
   and troop deployment of 1648, 89
   strategies of opposition in, 92–98
   lit de justice promulgations debated
      by, 98–100

   tax farmers as viewed in, 99, 100,
      117, 122, 131, 135, 141, 149–
      50, 169–71
   and Act of Union, 106–14
   summoned before Anne, 112–13
   and compromise efforts with
      Council of State, 115–21
   measures to reduce Council of
      State's power debated in, 121–
      40
   taille and, 122, 129, 130, 134, 140,
      146
   revolutionary nature of, 122–23
   divisions in, 130, 155, 241
   and links to king's debt, 131
   legal and civil rights debated in,
      136–39, 171
   lit de justice of 31 July 1648 sanc-
      tioning reforms of, 140–42
   and agreements for end to St.
      Louis Chamber meetings, 140,
      162–63, 167
   in debates after *lit de justice*, 142–
      51
   tax farmers investigated by, 149–
      50
   Spain policy and, 150–51
   Broussel's arrest and, 152–64,
      165, 168
   continued debates of, after Brous-
      sel's release, 169–71
   Mazarin as viewed in, 170, 184–
      85, 193, 210, 211, 284, 301–2,
      306, 307, 308, 319, 320, 324,
      325
   and threatened blockade of Paris,
      179
   and Winter Wars of 1649, 179–
      211
   in Fronde-controlled Paris, 182–
      211
   fortifications seized by, 184
   royal edicts against, 184
   ordered to leave Paris by Council
      of State, 187
   fund raising by, 193–94, 195, 197
   in negotiations to relinquish Paris,
      202, 207–11

effect of, on Bordeaux, 227
factional disputes in (December 1649), 241–43
princely Fronde and, 271, 280, 284, 286, 288, 289, 299–300, 305–6, 310, 312, 327, 335, 340
rentier protests and, 292–93, 294–95
charter for tax institution established by, 292–93, 295
and debate on Estates-General, 297
assembly of nobles criticized by, 298, 299
Vendôme's legitimacy decreed by, 315
Mazarin's army confronted by, 320
and Hôtel de Ville assembly of 4 July 1652, 330
after attack on Hôtel de Ville, 333
Parlement of Pontoise, 335–37
Parlement of Rouen, 13
parlements, 18, 124, 247
    royal authority and, 84
partisans, see tax farmers
Patrons, Brokers and Clients in Seventeenth-Century France (Kettering), 353
Paulette, see annual fees
peasants, 9, 344
    taxes resisted by, 6–7, 10–11, 27–28, 35
    daily life of, 25–28
    protests mounted in Paris by, 124
    around Bordeaux, 233
Pénis (Condé's client), 311, 325, 328
"people," "poor people":
    as actor in Fronde, 8, 9, 13–14, 52–58, 344
    hatred of tax farmers among, 40–41
    historical imaginations of, 49–50
    use of term, 52–53, 56
    in provinces, 54
    composition of, 57–58
    Parlement of Paris in defense of, 68, 69–70, 77, 80, 97, 112, 129,

131, 132, 147, 168, 169, 185, 280
    uprising feared from, 120
    and Day of the Barricades, 151
    and victory in Spain, 151
    attempted mobilization of, 175–76
    Conti's appointment hailed by, 191
    in Bordeaux, 216–17, 228–35, 244–47, 266
    in princely Fronde, 282
    and power struggles after Condé's release, 282, 287, 288
    political consciousness of, 310
Périgord, 11, 44
Philip, Duke of Anjou, 82, 247
physicians and surgeons, 65
Pillorget, René, 354
Pithou, Judge, 123–24, 132, 346
    intendants as viewed by, 133
Politics (Aristotle), 46
Pontavert, Spanish capture of, 210
Pont de l'Arche, fortress of, 241
Pontoise, as proposed Estates-General site, 301
Pontoise, Parlement of, 335–37
"poor people," *see* "people," "poor people"
Portuguese, in France, 261
Potier, Bishop, 322
Prade, Father, 265
princely Fronde, 271–90, 295–341
    fighting in Burgundy, 275–76
    in Northeast, 277–78, 281, 313–14
    and power struggles after Condé's release, 282–90
    and debate on Estates-General, 295–97
    atrocities against civilians in, 303–5
    end of, 303–41
    factors in end of, 311–12
    assessment of actors in, 312–17, 344–47
Priorato, Count Gualdo, 8–9
professional corporations, 65–66

Protestants, 62–63, 267
  courts for, 39, 109, 226
Provence and Aix-en-Provence, 12,
    34, 35, 36, 54, 176–77, 223,
    239, 240, 311, 316, 329, 354
provincial courts, 176
provost of merchants, 164, 182, 186,
    187–88, 190, 206
  and troop deployment of 1648, 90
  rentier protests and, 293, 294
  during princely Fronde, 325, 327,
    328, 330, 332, 335

religion:
  Ormée and, 251, 259–62
  see also Catholic Church, Catholi-
    cism; Protestants
rentes (government bonds), 291, 292,
    319
  tax farmers' speculation in, 39
  excise taxes and, 140, 212
  non-payment of, 212–13, 290–95,
    337
  renewed payment of, 214
rentier watchdog committees, 294–95
rents, 266–67
Requests subchamber of Parlement
    of Paris, 59, 61, 73, 78, 104
Rethel, royal capture of, 278
Retz, Paul de Gondi, Cardinal, 13–
    14, 346
  renewed civil wars foreseen by,
    50
  on revolution and property-
    owning, 54
  Molé described by, 61
  Anne's alleged gift to, 79
  Broussel described by, 101
  repression advocated by, 151
  in *Te Deum* of 26 August 1648,
    152
  on Day of the Barricades, 157–59,
    168
  and mobilization of populace, 175,
    211, 212, 272, 289, 307
  in Fronde-controlled Paris, 189,
    190, 191, 196, 200–201, 206,
    209

  on crowd's welcome of Louis XIV,
    213
  on parlementary factionalism of
    late 1649, 241, 242
  and royal provincial visits, 277
  Deslandes-Payen and, 279
  support from militia sought by,
    279
  and power struggles before
    Condé's release, 280
  and power struggles after Condé's
    release, 281, 283, 285, 286,
    287–89
  assembly of nobles disgusted by,
    299
  and debate on Estates-General,
    300
  independence from Condé and
    Gaston sought by, 301
  princely Fronde and, 305, 307,
    309–10, 313, 316, 323, 326
  Mazarin attacked by, 307, 322
  Mazarin's exile and, 308, 309
  court at Compiègne joined by, 336
Revolt of 1548 (Bordeaux), 221–22
Revolt of the Judges (Moote), 350
revolution:
  definition of, 5
  modern nature of, 77
  breakdowns in group boundaries
    in, 86
  historical study of, 147–48
  civil war vs., 310
Richelieu, Cardinal, 8, 13, 127, 186,
    211, 247, 314, 318
  plots against, 12, 85, 312
  on dignity of officeholders, 18
  Louis XIII's reliance on, 19
  death of, 20
  Mazarin aided by, 20, 46
  Norman revolt repressed by, 32
  and war with Spain, 44–45
  increased royal authority and, 45,
    46–49, 51, 70, 312, 313
  Louis XIII's last will and, 46
  Bouthillier's closeness to, 46, 49
  feigned financial ignorance of, 49
  opinion mobilized by, 51–52

rumored poisoning of Louis XIII
by, 55
new judgeships supported by, 75
Bullion's departure and, 77
Le Coigneux's relationship with,
78
and annulment of Gaston's marriage, 79
Gaston's conspiracies against, 85,
312
Séguier's ties to, 112
Parlement of Paris's relations with,
117
Bordeaux and, 222, 225
political philosophy of, 317
Richon (Frondeur commander),
276–77
Robe, the, *see* courts
Robe families, 103–4
intendants from, 31
and Parlement of Paris, 61, 80
Rocroy, French victory at, 45
Rohan-Chabot, Duke de, 317, 321,
333
Rouen, 34, 35, 36, 176, 225, 240
royal visit to, 243, 244
Rouen, Parlement of, 13
Rouergue, uprising in, 44
royal authority, 16–17
tax legislation and, 28
Louis XIII and Richelieu in
increase of, 45, 46–49, 51, 63,
70, 312, 313
regency and, 46–49
and redress of grievances, 68
and venality of office, 71
and Louis XIII's creation of new
judgeships in Parlement of
Paris, 72–79
lettres de cachet and, 75, 136–37
corporate challenges to, 84
lit de justice and, 91, 94–95, 145–
46
strategies of opposition to, 92–98
two-bodies theory of, 95–96, 97
and Chamber of Accounts, 101–3
and word of king, 108
courts as true defenders of, 112

Anne's defense of, 119, 133
and right to repudiate agreements, 119, 137–38
provincial trips and, 275
absolutism and, 308
symbols of, 308
and Louis XIV's majority, 311–12
royal guards, 157, 165
repulsed from Palais de Justice,
154, 159, 165
Fronde joined by, 196
royal officials:
"lack of zeal" of, 5–8
public debate repressed by, 33
inheritance of offices of, 71–72
see also courts; sale of offices; tax
officials
rural areas:
social and economic conditions in,
11, 25–28
military occupation of, 34–35
calm in, 35
suffering in, 54

St. Eustache Church, procession at,
213–14
St. George, proposed fort at, 272
Saint-Germain-en-Laye, accords of
(1649), 175, 176, 209–11
Saint-Germain-en-Laye, château of,
196, 198, 213, 326, 333
St. John's Day (1648), 120–21
St. Louis Chamber meetings, 115,
169, 312
curbs on Council of State's power
debated in, 121–25, 129, 132,
133, 135
agreements for termination of,
140, 162–63, 167
after *lit de justice* of 31 July 1648,
144
Council of State's military action
against, 154
Saint-Simon, Duke de, 347
sale of offices, 71–79, 214
of new masterships of requests,
17, 86–89, 93, 100, 104, 140,
193–94, 227, 292

sale of offices (*continued*)
  in Parlement of Paris, 60–61
  declining values in, 194
  in Bordeaux, 219–21, 248, 265
  in Agen, 226
  Mousnier on, 350–51
Salomon, Judge, 263–64
salt tax (*gabelle*), 27, 170, 218, 291,
  293
Sauvebeouf, Marquis de, 232, 239–
  40
Saxe-Weimar, Bernard of, 318
Séguier, Pierre, 17, 31, 32, 48, 127,
  158, 336
  powers accorded to, 19
  Richelieu and, 46, 112
  addressed by the "people," 55
  new judgeships defended by, 72–
  73
  and Louis XIII's exile of parlementaires, 74
  and tax proposals of 1648, 84, 87
  in *lit de justice* of 14 January 1648,
  91, 92
  and debate on status of *lit de justice*, 96
  and courts' Act of Union, 109,
  110, 112, 118
  in *lit de justice* of 31 July 1648, 140,
  141
  crowd's assault on, 159–60, 166
  Broussel's release and, 161
  Norman revolt and, 225
  disgrace of, 285
  reappointment of, to Council of
  State, 290
  on Gaston's special council, 332–
  33
  Paris fled by, 333–34
Sens, as proposed Estates-General
  site, 297
Servien, Abel, 286
Sève, Colonel de, 329
Sevin, Judge, 73
social and economic conditions:
  in rural areas, 25–28
  in towns and cities, 33–37
social rank, tax exemption based on,
  28

*Society and Culture in Early Modern
  France* (Davis), 352
Sourdis, Archbishop, 224
Spain:
  Frondeur alliance with, 255, 256–
  57, 276, 278, 305, 306, 319, 341
  Ormée and, 267
Spain, war with, 13, 42–45, 121,
  192, 210
  peace negotiations in, 22, 43, 83,
  150, 177, 192, 208–10
  Mazarin's involvement in, 22, 134,
  150, 177, 192, 208–9, 304, 305,
  307
  thanksgiving services in, 42
  taxes and, 42–45, 83, 149, 151,
  219, 222, 291
  new judgeships in financing of,
  72–73
  Lens victory in, 146, 150, 152–53
  Northern front in, 179, 278–79,
  283–84, 333–34
  and Fronde control of Paris, 203–
  4, 209, 211
  and non-payment of *rentes*, 212,
  290
  Bordeaux Fronde and, 233, 239,
  247, 248
  in Compiègne, 276
  atrocities against civilians in, 303–
  4
  strategies in, 303–4
  English alliance in, 305
  Gaston's loyalties and, 306
  after Fronde, 346
Spanish, in France, 261
straw cockades, 329, 331–32, 339
Sully, Duke de, 71–72
Sweden, 82, 303
Swiss Protestants, 39

taille:
  in North vs. South, 27, 29
  permanent status acquired by,
  28–29
  amount of revenue from, 29–30
  collection of, 111
  Parlement of Paris's measures on,
  122, 129, 130, 134, 140, 146

exemptions from, 218
arrears in, 291, 292
Talon, Omer, 126, 127
renewed civil wars foreseen by, 50
rural suffering described by, 54
on Parlement of Paris's refusal of
new judgeships, 77
Anne and Mazarin's courting of,
78
negotiaton efforts of, 88–89
and legal status of *lit de justice*, 91–
92, 94, 95, 96
on parlementary sovereignty,
100–101
and courts' Act of Union, 110,
112–13
Mazarin's courting of, 113–14
on avoiding ties to royal finances,
131
Mazarin's removal advocated by,
306
illness of, 334
Tambonneau, Judge, 108
Tavannes, Count de, 275–76
taxes, *see* excise taxes; *gabelle; taille*
tax farmers *(partisans)*, 35, 36–41
contracts and bidding of, 21, 37,
38, 41
attitudes toward, 21, 39–41, 55,
61
taille and, 29
loans obtained by, 37–38
fines against, 39
D'Hemery's connections with, 49
Parlement of Paris judges' links
with, 80, 108, 131–32
Parlement of Paris's measures and
sentiment against, 99, 100, 117,
122, 131, 135, 141, 149–50,
169–71
loans to king refused by, 106, 150
Council of State's links with, 112
property confiscation proposed
against, 117
La Meilleraie's negotiations with,
129
special court for prosecution of,
135–36, 142–43, 146, 149,
168

Parlement of Paris's investigation
of, 149–50
and Fronde control of Paris, 201
attacks on, 212
in Bordeaux region, 222
Ormée and, 252–53
rentier protests and, 292, 295
Gaston's fund-raising efforts ham-
pered by, 320
Bayard on, 351
tax officials:
peasants' tax avoidance and, 6–7
attacks on, 11, 212
assessments by, 27
strike of, 149
in Fronde-controlled Paris, 195,
204
in Bordeaux region, 227
rentier protests against, 294
see also intendants of justice and
finance; tax farmers
tax proposals of 1648, 83–106
mobilization against, 84–89
Te Deum (26 August 1648), 150,
152–54
Te Deum services, 42
parlementaires in, 66
Theles, Councillor, 98
Thoré, President, 57, 89, 90, 126–
27
Toulouse, 34, 35, 36, 176, 240
Tours, as proposed Estates-General
site, 297, 301
towns and cities:
social and economic conditions in,
32–36
marginaux in, 33–34
treasurers of France, 72, 108, 140
work stoppage by, 14–15, 35
arrests of, 110–11, 114, 137,
151
Tremblay, Governor, 186, 331
*Trésoriers de France pendant la Fronde,
Les* (Charmeil), 352
Trompette, Château, 228, 234, 235,
250
capture of, 236, 239, 254
Tronson, Louis, 228, 230
Tubeuf, Jacques, 128

Turenne, Viscount de, 210, 271,
    272, 275–76, 305
  during princely Fronde, 278,
    314–15, 322–28, 334, 337, 341
  assessment of, 314–15
  at Bléneau, 323
  in battle of Faubourg Saint-
    Antoine, 326–28
  in war with Spain, 333–34, 341

universities, 65
University of Paris, in solidarity with
    Fronde, 194

Vallier, Jean, 164, 167
Valois, Duke de, 334
Vayres, castle of, 276–77
Vénalité des offices, La (Mousnier),
    350–51
venality of office, *see* sale of offices
Vendôme, César de, 315, 316
Vendôme family, 23
Verthamont, François de, 222

Villars, Pierre, 249, 253
Vincennes castle, princes' detention
    at, 243, 271, 279
Viole, President, 181, 208, 333, 346

warfare, wartime:
  tax level linked to, 29, 38–39,
    42–45, 83, 149, 151, 219, 222,
    291
  taxes in, 38–39
  thanksgiving services in, 42
  attraction of, 304
  see also Spain, war with
Watteville, Jean de, 253, 257
Westphalia, peace talks of, 82–83,
    303
Westrich, Sal, 354
wine taxes, 27, 37, 86, 170
  in Bordeaux, 216, 219, 227
  convoy, 219, 222, 236
wine trade, in Bordeaux, 215–16
winter of 1648, 41, 83
Winter Wars of 1649, 179–211